PRE-COURSE ASSESSMENT

This self-assessment will help you and your instructor see how you develop your college success skills during this course. Be honest and take your time. This is not a test! For each question, rate yourself according to the following scale:

1	2	3	4	5
Definitely Like Me	Somewhat Like Me	Not Sure	Somewhat Unlike Me	Not At All Like Me

Please circle the number which best represents your answer:

1. I am interested in this course because it will help me improve skills I need to succeed in college. 1 2 3 4 5

2. I can find academic, health, and financial help on campus easily. 1 2 3 4 5

3. I feel connected to students and faculty on campus. 1 2 3 4 5

4. I know the responsibilities I need to handle to succeed in college. 1 2 3 4 5

5. I know exactly what my goals are for college. 1 2 3 4 5

6. I am effective at planning and managing my schedule. 1 2 3 4 5

7. I am effective at managing stress (i.e., academic, time, $, health). 1 2 3 4 5

8. I am fully aware of my learning styles and preferences. 1 2 3 4 5

9. I am comfortable with students who are different from me. 1 2 3 4 5

10. I communicate well with peers, faculty, and administrators. 1 2 3 4 5

11. I handle conflict effectively. 1 2 3 4 5

12. I use critical-thinking skills to make important decisions. 1 2 3 4 5

13. I feel prepared to handle the reading in my college courses. 1 2 3 4 5

14. I am an excellent note taker. 1 2 3 4 5

15. I have strong memory and recall abilities. 1 2 3 4 5

16. I am prepared for math and science course work. 1 2 3 4 5

17. I am prepared to write college-level research papers. 1 2 3 4 5

18. I have excellent test-taking skills for college courses. 1 2 3 4 5

19. I manage test anxiety well. 1 2 3 4 5

20. I know how to explore my career options. 1 2 3 4 5

21. I manage my finances and budget well. 1 2 3 4 5

22. I am confident that I will succeed in college. 1 2 3 4 5

POST-COURSE ASSESSMENT

This self-assessment will help you and your instructor see how you developed skills during this course. Please be honest, take your time, and answer each question in terms of your experience in the course. For each question, rate yourself according to the following scale:

1	2	3	4	5
Definitely Like Me	Somewhat Like Me	Not Sure	Somewhat Unlike Me	Not At All Like Me

1. This course helped me improve the study skills I need to succeed in college.　　1　2　3　4　5

2. I can find academic, health, and financial help on campus easily.　　1　2　3　4　5

3. I feel connected to students and faculty on campus.　　1　2　3　4　5

4. I know the responsibilities I need to handle to succeed in college.　　1　2　3　4　5

5. I know exactly what my goals are for college.　　1　2　3　4　5

6. I am effective at planning and managing my schedule.　　1　2　3　4　5

7. I am effective at managing stress (i.e., academic, time, $, health).　　1　2　3　4　5

8. I am fully aware of my learning styles and preferences.　　1　2　3　4　5

9. I am comfortable with students who are different from me.　　1　2　3　4　5

10. I communicate well with peers, faculty, and administrators.　　1　2　3　4　5

11. I handle conflict effectively.　　1　2　3　4　5

12. I use critical-thinking skills to make important decisions.　　1　2　3　4　5

13. I feel prepared to handle the reading in my college courses.　　1　2　3　4　5

14. I am an excellent note taker.　　1　2　3　4　5

15. I have strong memory and recall abilities.　　1　2　3　4　5

16. I am prepared for math and science course work.　　1　2　3　4　5

17. I feel prepared to write college-level research papers.　　1　2　3　4　5

18. I have excellent test-taking skills for college courses.　　1　2　3　4　5

19. I manage test anxiety well.　　1　2　3　4　5

20. I know how to explore my career options.　　1　2　3　4　5

21. I manage my finances and budget well.　　1　2　3　4　5

22. I am confident that I will succeed in college.　　1　2　3　4　5

Keys to Effective Learning

DEVELOPING POWERFUL HABITS OF MIND

FIFTH EDITION

Carol Carter

Joyce Bishop

Sarah Lyman Kravits

PEARSON

Prentice Hall

Upper Saddle River, New Jersey

Columbus, Ohio

Library of Congress Cataloging-in-Publication Data

Carter, Carol.
    Keys to effective learning : developing powerful habits of mind / Carol Carter,
Joyce Bishop, Sarah Lyman Kravits. — 5th ed.
        p. cm.
Includes bibliographical references and index.
ISBN 0-13-229540-7 (pbk.)
    1. Study skills.   2. Learning.   3. Cognitive styles.   4. Note-taking.   5. Test-taking skills.
I. Bishop, Joyce (Joyce L.).   II. Kravits, Sarah Lyman.   III. Title.
    LB2395.C27 2008
    378.1'70281—dc22

                                                                        2006027232

Vice President and Executive Publisher: Jeffery W. Johnston
Executive Editor: Sande Johnson
Development Editor: Charlotte Morrissey
Editorial Assistant: Lynda Cramer
Production Editor: Alexandrina Benedicto Wolf
Production Coordination: Thistle Hill Publishing Services, LLC
Design Coordinator: Diane C. Lorenzo
Text Designer: Aerocraft Charter Art Services
Cover Designer: Jeff Vanik
Cover Image: Super Stock
Production Manager: Pamela D. Bennett
Director of Marketing: David Gesell
Senior Marketing Manager: Amy Judd
Marketing Coordinator: Brian Mounts

This book was set in Sabon by Integra Software Services. It was printed and bound by R.R. Donnelley & Sons Company. The cover
was printed by Phoenix Color Corp.

Habits of Mind excerpts: From *Developing Minds: A Resource Book for Teaching Thinking*, 3rd ed., edited by Arthur L. Costa.
Copyright © 2001 by Association for Supervision and Curriculum Development (www.ascd.org). Reprinted with permission from
ASCD. All rights reserved.

Pearson Education LTD.
Pearson Education Singapore, Pte. Ltd
Pearson Education, Canada, Ltd
Pearson Education–Japan

Pearson Education Australia Pty. Limited
Pearson Education North Asia Ltd
Pearson Educación de Mexico, S.A. de C.V.
Pearson Education Malaysia, Pte. Ltd.

10 9 8 7 6 5 4 3 2 1
ISBN-13: 978-0-13-229540-6
ISBN-10: 0-13-229540-7

Mission Statement

Our mission is to give students the resources, perspective, and encouragement to understand the opportunities and challenges in today's global world so that they can thrive in it and achieve their personal and professional goals. We are committed to supporting students so that the contributions they make today will secure a bright future for themselves and the generations to come.

Brief Contents

Each chapter in this text focuses on a specific habit of mind that will help you reach your potential in school, at work, and in your personal life. A preview of the habits that you will build as you progress through the chapters appears below. Each habit is listed in green underneath the title of the chapter where it is featured.

Contents

Chapter 3

DIVERSITY MATTERS: LEARNING STYLES AND COMMUNICATION   68

Habit of Mind—Gather Data Through All Senses   69

Chapter 4

CRITICAL AND CREATIVE THINKING: SOLVING PROBLEMS AND MAKING DECISIONS   104

Habit of Mind—Question and Pose Problems   105

Chapter 8

TEST TAKING: SHOWING WHAT YOU KNOW   242

Habit of Mind—Take Responsible Risks   243

HOW CAN PREPARATION IMPROVE TEST PERFORMANCE?   244

GET PREPARED: TAKE ACTION—*Organize for Test Success*   247

HOW CAN YOU WORK THROUGH TEST ANXIETY?   249

WHAT GENERAL STRATEGIES CAN HELP YOU SUCCEED ON TESTS?   252

HOW CAN YOU MASTER DIFFERENT TYPES OF TEST QUESTIONS?   255

GET PREPARED: TAKE ACTION—*Develop Strategies for Test Success*   262

HOW CAN YOU LEARN FROM TEST MISTAKES?   266

MULTIPLE INTELLIGENCE STRATEGIES FOR OBJECTIVE AND ESSAY EXAMS   267

GET PREPARED: TAKE ACTION—*Learn from Your Mistakes*   269

Chapter 9

QUANTITATIVE LEARNING: BECOMING COMFORTABLE WITH MATH AND SCIENCE   276

Habit of Mind—Strive for Precision and Accuracy   277

HOW ARE MATH AND SCIENCE PART OF YOUR DAILY LIFE?   278

HOW CAN YOU MASTER MATH AND SCIENCE BASICS?   279

Chapter 10

EFFECTIVE WRITING: COMMUNICATING YOUR MESSAGE   308

Habit of Mind—Communicate with Clarity and Precision   309

Chapter 11

CREATING YOUR LIFE: BUILDING A SUCCESSFUL FUTURE   338

Habit of Mind—Stay Open to Continuous Learning   339

NOTE: *Every effort has been made to provide accurate and current Internet information in this book. However, the Internet and information posted on it are constantly changing, so it is inevitable that some of the Internet addresses listed in this textbook will change.*

Foreword

College is a time of transition and growth. You will depend on yourself in new ways, challenge the way you see the world, learn information and skills that may change your life, and make important decisions that influence your future. *Keys to Effective Learning* is here to help you as you begin this exciting journey.

Whether you graduated from high school a few months or a few years ago, you will see that college asks more of you. How you approach your coursework in the first few months of school will set the stage for your academic success in college. The study skills discussed in *Keys to Effective Learning* will help you establish habits that will carry you through academic challenges. Take the time in *this* course to find strategies that will work for you in *all* your courses. These strategies will take you far.

Of course, success in college involves more than study skills. This textbook covers other important topics that influence what you get out of the experience.

Time management. With the spread-out feeling of a college schedule, it may seem like there is a lot of time to finish large projects. But those deadlines creep up quickly and, before you know it, you're scrambling to get the work done any way you can. When you're under pressure, both the results and your learning are less than ideal. To minimize mad dashes at deadline time, study for exams well in advance and start on papers and projects as soon as they're assigned.

College resources. College is a gold mine of support and advice. From the school's library and career center to your instructors and advisors, you can probably find answers to most (if not all) of your questions. Take advantage of organizations and offices that support students, and visit your professors and other faculty during office hours. Seek out a mentor—a positive and vital role model who knows the ropes at your school and can cheer you on, help you when you're stuck, and show you all the benefits of college. *Never hesitate to ask for help.*

Learn from others. Through study groups or other activities, get to know other students, and be open to learning from them. Seek to connect with students from different backgrounds, cultures, and perspectives. As you work together and interact, you will learn about yourself and the world, building communication and teamwork skills that will stay with you for the rest of your life.

Nina Dunn

Caleb Fields

Brittany Henning

Kathryn Moberg

Dan Morrissey

Preparing for a career. College is the place to explore your career interests by taking related courses and talking to people who are further along the career road about their experiences. Take advantage of winter break and other vacations to apply for and work at internships or jobs in your area of interest.

Striking a balance. Maintain a healthy balance between work and play. It's tough to accomplish anything if you're too stressed. Take breaks. Get involved in organizations or activities on campus that interest you. Try not to dwell on failures. Know that every experience is important as long as you learn from it and move on.

Set the stage for lifelong learning. Be open-minded and curious about everything. Challenge yourself in your coursework by taking new classes that expand your knowledge and perspective. One of the best things about college is that it disciplines you to think and puts you in the routine of learning. Life offers endless opportunities to those who devote themselves to continual learning.

It's up to you to determine where you want your education to take you and then to get yourself there. With *Keys to Effective Learning* to help you get a great start, you will be on a strong and steady course toward success in college and in your future career. We wish you all the best!

Sincerely,

Nina Dunn

Caleb Fields

Brittany Henning

Kathryn Moberg

Dan Morrissey

Preface

Welcome to the fifth edition of *Keys to Effective Learning*, a more comprehensive opportunity to build powerful habits of mind. As we work with instructors and students around the country, we hear echoes of one particular challenge facing students and instructors—*being prepared*. **Students need to prepare themselves to handle the personal, academic, and social challenges in college and career. Instructors need prepared students so that learning sinks in, takes root, and flourishes.**

This fifth edition of *Keys to Effective Learning*—with its enhanced **Habits of Mind** theme—will help students and instructors meet the challenges of preparing for college success.

Habits of Mind Prepare You to Solve Problems and Meet Challenges

Developed by educator Arthur Costa, who was intrigued by how successful students work through problems, the *habits of mind** are problem-solving skills that can transfer to school, work, and life. Important research indicates that developing these habits can improve college academic performance. The text and accompanying supplemental resources, working together, help you understand and practice the habits and assess your progress. Each of the 11 chapters in *Keys to Effective Learning* features a different habit that will help you become a more aware, competent learner. In-text exercises and case studies on the Companion Website help you apply the habit. Online quizzes and tests assess your understanding of each habit.

To enhance the habits of mind presentation, Chapter 1 provides an even stronger introduction to the habits, demonstrating how they aid student success. In addition to text discussion, two applied activities and one exercise per chapter help you acquire and develop each habit. Look for the habits of mind icon for ways to increase your habit mastery.

Features and Exercises Personalize and Activate Knowledge

It can be easy to learn information in the moment—and then, after the test or course is over, to forget it all. The best learning is learning that stays with you. The features and exercises in this edition will help build a permanent storehouse of learning by encouraging you to apply techniques to your own situations and needs.

---

*Source: From *Developing Minds: A Resource Book for Teaching Thinking*, 3rd ed., edited by Arthur L. Costa. Copyright © 2001 by Association for Supervision and Curriculum Development (www.ascd.org). Reprinted with permission from ASCD. All rights reserved.

Learning Styles Integration. More than any other text on the market, this text goes beyond just helping students determine their learning styles; it gives them tools to apply those learning styles in a practical way. Among these tools is the Multiple Intelligence Grid, which appears in Chapters 5–11. Each grid offers strategies, related to a chapter topic, geared toward each of the eight intelligences.

Get Prepared: Take Action. Updated for this edition, these in-chapter exercises—two to four per chapter—encourage you to put what you just learned to immediate use.

Reflect & Respond. Twice in each chapter you are given the chance to think about, and then write about, a quote or comment that relates to the chapter material.

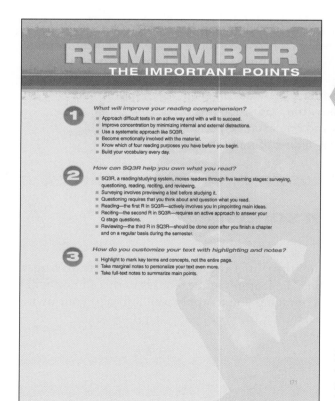

Remember the Important Points. This end-of-chapter summary has been set in easy-to-grasp outline form so that you can quickly and effectively review the main ideas of each chapter.

Building Skills for Successful Learning. This end-of-chapter exercise set has three exercises that help you apply chapter material to your own life. One applies critical thinking to chapter topics; one engages chapter topics in a group setting, building teamwork skills in the process; one gives you the opportunity to practice the habit of mind as you work to improve a chapter-related skill.

Becoming a Better Test Taker. This end-of-part feature gives you tools to synthesize what you have learned. You will revisit all of the *Activate the Habit of Mind* exercises to check on your habit-building progress.

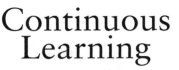

Continuous Learning

Oseola McCarty was able to save $250,000 over a lifetime while working as a cleaning lady with no formal education.

Wanting to help college students get the education she never had, she left the bulk of her money to the University of Southern Mississippi in a scholarship trust. "I just want it to go to someone who will *appreciate it and learn,*" she said.

343

Topic Coverage Prepares You to Succeed Academically and Personally

Solid study skills and life skills are the basis for college success. The fifth edition of *Keys to Effective Learning* covers these vital topics more effectively than ever before. Here are the highlights.

Study skills, the heart of the text, have undergone significant updates, including:

- Expanded coverage of SQ3R, with new material on text notes and highlighting
- Revised coverage of memory, with an expanded section on mnemonic devices
- New material on combining text and class notes
- More detailed discussion of test taking, with new material on approaching test questions
- Streamlined writing chapter, featuring a new writing sample throughout the discussion

The most important practical material for getting students on track at the beginning of the term—including a more significant treatment of academic integrity—has been inserted into Chapter 1.

Learning styles, diversity, and communication have been combined in Chapter 2. Placing diversity in this broader context shows the many ways individuals differ—how they learn, what they value, and how they relate to others—instead of focusing solely on issues such as race and ethnicity. The chapter also provides a skills-based approach to adjusting to and appreciating all types of diversity.

The critical and creative thinking chapter (Chapter 4) has been thoroughly revised and strengthened, with a focus on the practical application of thinking skills.

Library and Internet research material is now in an appendix for handy reference.

Pre-course and post-course assessments. New to this edition! Here is an opportunity to gauge your success. At the beginning of the course, the pre-course assessment gives you a chance to take stock of where you are when you start. At the end, the post-course assessment enables you to evaluate what you have learned, how you have grown, and what you will take from this course into college, career, and life.

Keys to Effective Learning Prepares You to Succeed in All Your Courses

Keys to Effective Learning is not an ordinary college textbook. Whereas other books give you tools to succeed in specific academic areas, this text gives you tools to succeed in *all* areas as it helps you adjust to the personal challenges of college life. As you begin your course work, continually come back to what you learned here, particularly to the eleven habits of mind. It will make all the difference in your life and learning.

Students and instructors: Many of our best suggestions come from you. Send your questions, comments, and ideas about *Keys to Effective Learning* to Carol Carter at **caroljcarter@lifebound. com.** We look forward to hearing from you, and we are grateful for the opportunity to work with you.

Supplemental Resources

INSTRUCTOR SUPPORT

Resources to simplify your life and engage your students.

Book-Specific

Instructor's Manual with Test Bank and PowerPoints	ISBN 0-13-229779-5
PowerPoint Acetates	ISBN 0-13-229780-9

Technology

*"Easy access to online, book-specific **teaching support** is now just a click away!"*

Instructor Resource Center   Register. Redeem. Login. Three easy steps that open the door to a variety of print and media resources in downloadable, digital format, available to instructors exclusively through the Prentice Hall IRC.
www.prenhall.com/

Instructor Resource Center

Register today at www.prenhall.com to access instructor resources digitally.

*"Teaching an online course, offering a hybrid class, or simply introducing your students to **technology** just got a whole lot easier!"*

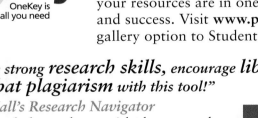

OneKey is all you need

OneKey Course Management   All you and your students need to succeed. OneKey is Prentice Hall's exclusive new resource for instructors and students providing access to the best online teaching and learning tools—24 hours a day, 7 days a week. OneKey means all your resources are in one place for maximum convenience, simplicity and success. Visit **www.prenhall.com/onekey** and scroll through the gallery option to Student Success for additional information.

*"Reinforce strong **research skills**, encourage **library use**, and **combat plagiarism** with this tool!"*

Prentice Hall's Research Navigator

Designed to help students with the research process, from identifying a topic to editing the final draft. It also demonstrates how to make time at the campus library more productive. RN includes four databases of credible and reliable source material to get your research process started: The

Research Navigator.com

RESOURCES FOR COLLEGE RESEARCH ASSIGNMENTS

EBSCO/Content Select, *The New York Times*, Link Library, and *The Financial Times*. Visit **www.researchnavigator.com** for additional information.

"Choose from a wide range of video resources for the classroom!"

Prentice Hall Reference Library: Life Skills Pack ISBN 0-13-127079-6 contains all 4 videos, or they may be requested individually as follows:

- Learning Styles and Self-Awareness, ISBN 0-13-028502-1
- Critical and Creative Thinking, ISBN 0-13-028504-8
- Relating to Others, ISBN 0-13-028511-0
- Personal Wellness, ISBN 0-13-028514-5

Prentice Hall Reference Library: Study Skills Pack ISBN 0-13-127080-X contains all 6 videos, or they may be requested individually as follows:

- Reading Effectively, ISBN 0-13-028505-6
- Listening and Memory, ISBN 0-13-028506-4
- Note Taking and Research, ISBN 0-13-028508-0
- Writing Effectively, ISBN 0-13-028509-9
- Effective Test Taking, ISBN 0-13-028500-5
- Goal Setting and Time Management, ISBN 0-13-028503-X

Prentice Hall Reference Library: Career Skills Pack ISBN 0-13-118529-2 contains all 3 videos, or they may be requested individually as follows:

- Skills for the 21st Century – Technology, ISBN 0-13-028512-9
- Skills for the 21st Century – Math and Science, ISBN 0-13-028513-7
- Managing Career and Money, ISBN 0-13-028516-1

Faculty Video Resources

- Teacher Training Video 1: Critical Thinking, ISBN 0-13-099432-4
- Teacher Training Video 2: Stress Management & Communication, ISBN 0-13-099578-9
- Teacher Training Video 3: Classroom Tips, ISBN 0-13-917205-X
- Student Advice Video, ISBN 0-13-233206-X
- Study Skills Video, ISBN 0-13-096095-0
- Building on Your Best Video, ISBN 0-20-526277-5

Current Issues Videos

- ABC News Video Series: Student Success, ISBN 0-13-031901-5
- ABC News Video Series: Student Success, 3e, ISBN 0-13-152865-3

Faculty Development Series Workshops

- Carter: Faculty Development Workshop DVD, *Top Ten Reasons Why Students Struggle or Drop Out*, ISBN 0-13-199047-0

"Through partnership opportunities, we offer a variety of assessment options!"

LASSI   The LASSI is a 10-scale, 80-item assessment of students' awareness about and use of learning and study strategies. Addressing skill, will, and self-regulation, the focus is on both covert and overt thoughts, behaviors, attitudes, and beliefs that relate to successful learning and that can be altered through educational interventions. Available in two formats: Paper ISBN 0-13-172315-4 or Online ISBN 0-13-172316-2 (Access Card).

Noel Levitz/RMS   This retention tool measures Academic Motivation, General Coping Ability, Receptivity to Support Services, plus Social Motivation. It helps identify at-risk students, the areas with which they struggle, and their receptiveness to support. Available in paper or online formats, as well as short and long versions. Paper Long Form A: ISBN 0-13-072258-8; Paper Short Form B: ISBN 0-13-079193-8; Online Forms A&B: ISBN 0-13-098158-3.

Robbins Self Assessment Library   This compilation teaches students to create a portfolio of skills. S.A.L. is a self-contained, interactive library of 49 behavioral questionnaires that help students discover new ideas about themselves, their attitudes, and their personal strengths and weaknesses. Available in paper, ISBN 0-13-173861-5; CD-ROM, ISBN 0-13-221793-7; and online, ISBN 0-13-243165-3 (Access Card) formats.

Readiness for Education at a Distance Indicator (READI)   READI is a Web-based tool that assesses the overall likelihood for online learning success. READI generates an immediate score and a diagnostic interpretation of results, including recommendations for successful participation in online courses and potential remediation sources. Please visit **www.readi.info** for additional information. ISBN 0-13-188967-2.

"Teaching tolerance and discussing diversity with your students can be challenging!"
Responding to Hate at School   Published by the Southern Poverty Law Center, this handbook is a step-by-step, easy-to-use guide designed to help administrators, counselors, and teachers react promptly and efficiently whenever hate, bias, and prejudice strike. ISBN 0-13-028458-0.

"For a terrific one-stop shop resource, use our Student Success Supersite!"
Supersite   **www.prenhall.com/success**   Students and professors alike may use the Supersite for activities, success stories, links, and more. To access PowerPoint slides, sample syllabi, articles and newsletters, supplemental information and more, instructors should visit the Faculty Lounge. Contact your local Prentice Hall representative for ID and password information.

"For a truly tailored solution that fosters campus connections and increases retention, talk with us about Custom Publishing."
Pearson Custom Publishing   We are the largest custom provider for print and media shaped to your course's needs. Please visit us at **www.pearsoncustom.com** to learn more.

STUDENT SUPPORT

Tools to help make the grade now, and excel in school later.

"We offer an online study aid to help students fully understand each chapter's content, assess their knowledge, and apply what they've learned."
Companion Website   The site includes an online glossary of key terms, practice quizzes of objective and subjective questions, e-journaling activities, Habits of Mind exercises, and case studies. Please visit the site at **www.prenhall.com/carter.**

"We recognize students may want a choice of how their text is delivered."
SafariX eTextbooks Online   This joint venture between the industry's leading technical publishers, O'Reilly Media, Inc. and The Pearson Technology Group, provides an alternative to the traditional print version of the text. The entire book can be purchased in an online format for 50% off the cost. Now students have a choice! Contact your local Prentice Hall representative for details.

Where the Web meets textbooks for STUDENT SAVINGS.

Hear it. Get it.

*Because students are **pressed for time**, we offer an alternative for studying on the go.*

VangoNotes   Students are busy–we get it. With VangoNotes, students can study "in between" all the other things they have to do to succeed in the classroom. These notes are flexible; just download and go. They're efficient; study in the car, at the gym, or walking to class. Visit **www.prenhall.com/vangonotes** for additional information.

"Time management is the #1 challenge students face. We can help."

Prentice Hall Planner   A basic planner that includes a monthly and daily calendar, plus other materials to facilitate organization. 8.5" × 11".

Franklin Covey Planner   This specially designed, annual 4-color collegiate planner includes an academic planning/resources section, monthly planning section (2 pages/month), and weekly planning section (48 weeks; July start date), which facilitate short-term as well as long-term planning. Spiral bound, 6" × 9".

"Journaling activities promote self-discovery and self-awareness."

Student Reflection Journal   Through this vehicle, students are encouraged to track their progress and share their insights, thoughts, and concerns. 8½" × 11" 90 pages.

*"Our **Student Success Supersite** is a one-stop shop for students to learn about career paths, peer stories, and more!"*

Supersite   **www.prenhall.com/success**   Students will benefit from sections on Majors Exploration, Academic Skills, Career Path, Student Union, and more.

*"Learning to adapt to the **diverse** college community is essential to students' success."*

10 Ways to Fight Hate   Produced by the Southern Poverty Law Center, the leading hate-crime and crime-watch organization in the United States, this guide walks students through 10 steps that they can take on their own campus or in their own neighborhood to fight hate every day. ISBN 0-13-028146-8.

*"The **Student Orientation Series** includes short booklets on specialized topics that facilitate greater student understanding."*

S.O.S. Guides   Connolly, *Learning Communities*, ISBN 0-13-232243-9 and Watts, *Service Learning*, ISBN 0-13-232201-3. These booklets help students understand what these opportunities are, how to take advantage of them, and how to learn from their peers while doing so.

Acknowledgments

This significant revision has been produced through the efforts of an extraordinary team. Many thanks to:

- Our reviewers, for their responsiveness and invaluable input: Shirley Flor, San Diego Mesa College; Ken Jones, Metro Community College, Omaha; Christine Laursen, Westwood College; Polly Livingston, Portland State University; Jeanine Long, Southwest Georgia Tech; Maria Parnell, Brevard County Community College; Karla Thompson, New Mexico State University, Carlsbad; Helen Woodman, Ferris State University in Michigan; Barbara Jenista, Cedarville University; Carolyn Kirby, Bluefield State College; and Dessie Williams, Louisiana State University–Alexandria.

- Previous edition reviewers: Erskine P. Ausbrooks III, Dyersburg State Community College; Glenda Belote, Florida International University; John Bennett, Jr., University of Connecticut; Ann Bingham-Newman, California State University–Los Angeles; Mary Bixby, University of Missouri–Columbia; Linda Blair, Pellissippi State Technical Community College; Barbara Blandford, Education Enhancement Center at Lawrenceville, NJ; Jerry Bouchie, St. Cloud State University; Rhonda Carroll, Pulaski Technical College; Mona Casady, Missouri State University; Janet Cutshall, Sussex County Community College; MarieDavisHeim, Mississippi Gulf Coast Community College; Valerie DeAngelis, Miami-Dade Community College; Rita Delude, New Hampshire Community Technical College; Judy Elsley, Weber State University in Utah; Katherine Erdman, South Dakota State University; Jo Ella Fields, Oklahoma State University, Oklahoma City; Carlesa Ramere Finney, Anne Arundel Community College; Sue Halter, Delgado Community College in Louisiana; Vesna Hampel, University of Minnesota, Twin Cities; Suzy Hampton, University of Montana; Maureen Hurley, University of Missouri–Kansas City; Karen Iversen, Heald Colleges; Gary G. John, Richland College; Kathryn K. Kelly, St. Cloud State University; Deborah Kimbrough-Lowe, Nassau Community College; Heidi Koring, Lynchburg College; Nancy Kosmicke, Mesa State College in Colorado; Frank T. Lyman Jr., University of Maryland; Jo McEwan, Fayetteville Technical Community College; Barnette Miller Moore, Indian River Community College in Florida; Kathie Morris, Edison Community College; Rebecca Munro, Gonzaga University in Washington; Virginia Phares, DeVry of Atlanta; Brenda Prinzavalli, Beloit College in Wisconsin; Linda Qualia, Colin County Community College; Laura Reynolds, Fayetteville Technical Community College; Mary Rider, Grossmont College; Tina Royal, Fayetteville Technical Community College; Maria D. Salinas, Del Mar College; Jacqueline Simon, Education Enhancement Center at Lawrenceville, New Jersey; Carolyn Smith, University of Southern Indiana; Joan Stottlemyer, Carroll College in Montana; Thomas Tyson, SUNY Stony Brook; Lisa Taylor-Galizia, Carteret Community College; Karen N. Valencia, South Texas Community College; Mary Walz-Chojnacki, University of Wisconsin at Milwaukee; Peggy Walton,

Howard Community College; Rose Wassman, DeAnza College in California; Michelle G. Wolf, Florida Southern College; Patricia Wright, Lenoir Community College; and Leesa Young, Asheville Buncombe Technical Community College.

■ Art Costa, for his insights that led to the development of the *Habits of Mind* features and for his generosity in permitting us to use the habits as a framework for this text. Also Art's editor Nancy Modrak at ASCD for her endorsement of this collaboration.

■ Debbie Maness, for her collaborative work with the authors on the instructor's manual, and Karla Thompson, for her work on the Companion Website.

■ Carol Howard, Karyn Schulz, and Cheri Tillman—special thanks for their worthwhile feedback and enthusiastic support of this and other *Keys* books.

■ The professors who provided insight and perspective on the development of this manuscript. For this, our gratitude goes to Shirley Flor, San Diego Mesa College; Barbara Jenista, Cedarville University; Carolyn Kirby, Bluefield State College; and Dessie Williams, LSU Alexandria.

■ Our student editors, Nina Dunn, Caleb Fields, Brittany Henning, Kathryn Moberg, and Dan Morrissey, for their insightful comments and hard work.

■ Our editor, Sande Johnson, developmental editor Jennifer Gessner, and editorial assistant Lynda Cramer for their dedication, vision, and efforts.

■ Charlotte Morrissey, for her keen perspectives and assistance on both the editorial and marketing aspects of the text.

■ Our production team for their patience, flexibility, and attention to detail, especially Angela Urquhart and the team at Thistle Hill Publishing Services, John Wincek, JoEllen Gohr, Alex Wolf, Pam Bennett, and typesetters Integra Software Services.

■ Our marketing gurus—especially Amy Judd, our marketing manager, David Gesell, director of marketing, and our student success sales directors Joe Hale, Matt Christopherson, Connie James, Deb Weir, and Patty Ford.

■ Publisher Jeff Johnston, President of Education, Career, and Technology Robin Baliszewski, and Prentice Hall President Tim Bozik, for their interest, commitment, and leadership with the Student Success list.

■ The Prentice Hall representatives and the management team led by national sales manager Brian Kibby.

■ Our families and friends, who have encouraged us and put up with our commitments.

■ A very special thanks to Judy Block, whose research, writing, and editing work was essential and invaluable.

Finally, for their ideas, opinions, and stories, we would like to thank all of the students and professors with whom we work. Joyce in particular would like to thank the thousands of students who have allowed her, as their professor, the privilege of sharing part of their journey through college. We appreciate that, through reading this book, you give us the opportunity to learn and discover with you—in your classroom, in your home, on the bus, and wherever else learning takes place.

PART I
GETTING READY TO LEARN

Welcome to College
OPENING DOORS

Values, Goals, Time, and Stress
MANAGING YOURSELF

Diversity Matters
LEARNING STYLES
AND COMMUNICATION

Critical and Creative Thinking
SOLVING PROBLEMS
AND MAKING DECISIONS

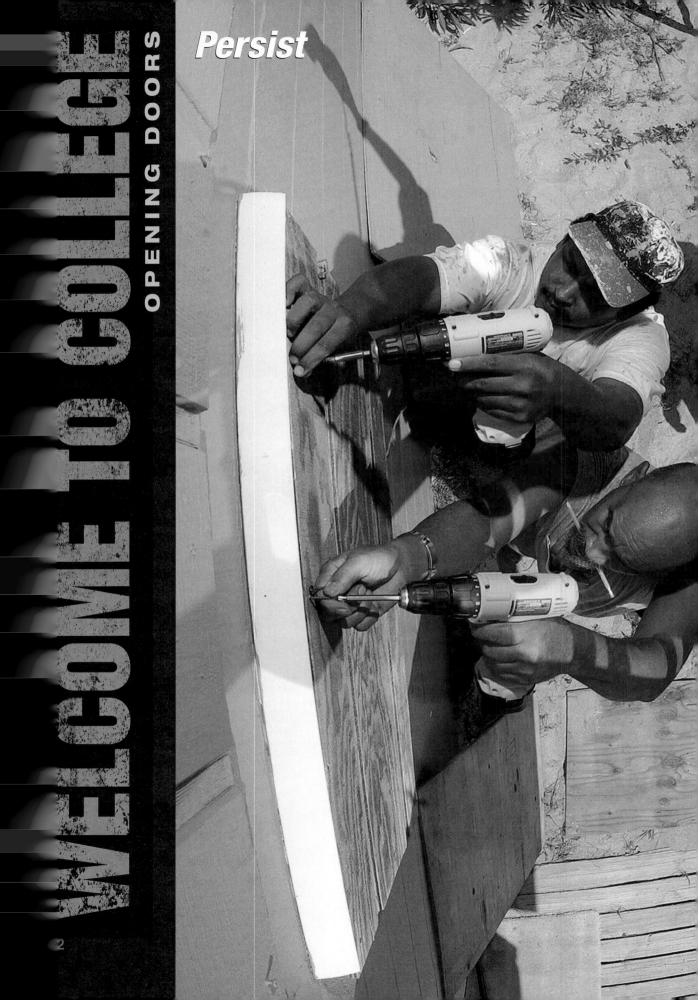

WELCOME TO COLLEGE

OPENING DOORS

2

HABITS OF MIND

7

"Effective problem solvers stick to a task until it is completed. They don't give up easily. They are able to analyze a problem and develop a system, structure, or strategy to attack it."

ART COSTA

PERSIST

Persisting will keep you moving toward goals through the highs and lows of your college experience. If you persist through the obstacles, you will open doors to school and life success.

n the aftermath of hurricanes like Katrina, Isabel, and others that seasonally hit our coasts, persistence is the name of the game for local residents like these men. Whether rebuilding a city or boarding up a home to prevent further damage, persistent follow-through creates results.

Such persistence is an essential tool for you as you face the cycles of hard work and challenge that are part of the college experience and life in general. With dedication and drive, you will be able to explore the world of ideas, acquire information, and develop lifelong skills, achieving success and making a difference in a world dominated by technology and global communication.

This book, and the course for which you are reading it, will prepare you to learn successfully, graduate, and reap the personal and professional rewards of your education. With the tools that you acquire, you will be well equipped to face the challenges of college and the global marketplace and to create the future of your dreams.

In this chapter, you explore answers to the following questions:

- Why is attending college the right decision?
- What basic actions will prepare you for college success?
- What does your college expect of you?
- Why does your success depend on academic integrity?
- Who at school can help you make the most of your education?
- How can habits of mind fuel your success?

Why is attending college the right decision?

Start by congratulating yourself, because accomplishments and *persistence* have brought you to this point. You completed high school or its equivalent. You may have built life skills from experience as a partner or parent. You may have been employed in one or more jobs or completed a tour of duty in the armed forces. You have enrolled in college, found a way to pay for it, signed up for courses, and shown up for class. And, in deciding to pursue a degree, you chose to believe you can accomplish important goals. You have earned this opportunity to be a college student!

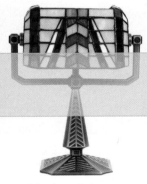

© Craig Foster—Fotolia

> I know the price of success: dedication, hard work, and an unremitting devotion to the things you want to see happen.

FRANK LLOYD WRIGHT, ARCHITECT

To make the most of this opportunity, first understand its value. College is the ideal training ground for acquiring skills that will serve you in the new global marketplace, where workers in the United States are on a level playing field with workers in other parts of the world. Thomas Friedman, author of *The World Is Flat,* explains how the digital revolution has transformed the working environment you will enter after college:

> It is now possible for more people than ever to collaborate and compete in real time with more other people on more different kinds of work from more different corners of the planet and on a more equal footing than in any previous time in the history of the world—using computers, e-mail, networks, teleconferencing, and dynamic new software.[1]

This means that you may be competing for "knowledge work" with highly trained and motivated people from around the globe who may be driven to succeed by a desire to put difficult conditions and times behind them. In order to achieve your goals in this new "flat" world, you will need to acquire solid study skills, commit to lifelong learning and job training, persevere despite obstacles, perform high-quality work on a consistent basis, and embrace change as a way of life. Achieving your personal best has never been more crucial to your success—and if you gather and hone your tools in college, you will be up to the task.

You are responsible for your future, and college can help you achieve the "life success goals" that will get you where you want to go:

- ■ *Life Success Goal: Increased employability and earning potential.* Getting a degree greatly increases your chances of finding and keeping a highly skilled, well-paying job. College graduates earn, on average, around $20,000 more per year than those with only a high school diploma (see Key 1.1). Furthermore, the unemployment rate for college graduates is less than half that of high school graduates (see Key 1.2).

More education is likely to mean more income.   KEY   1.1

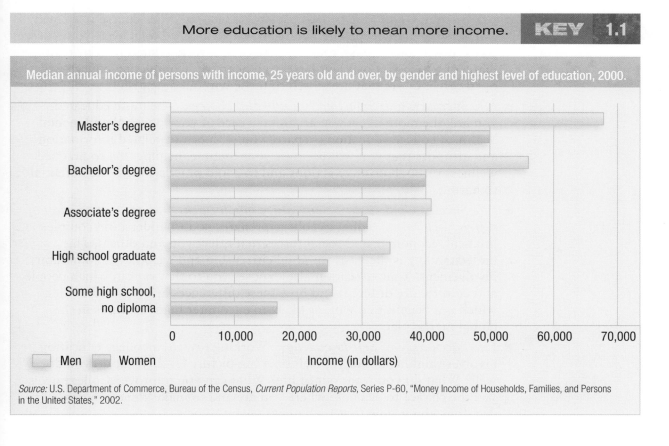

Median annual income of persons with income, 25 years old and over, by gender and highest level of education, 2000.

Source: U.S. Department of Commerce, Bureau of the Census, Current Population Reports, Series P-60, "Money Income of Households, Families, and Persons in the United States," 2002.

More education is likely to mean more consistent employment.   KEY   1.2

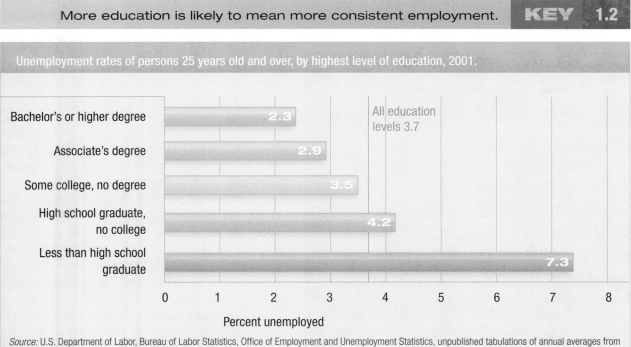

Unemployment rates of persons 25 years old and over, by highest level of education, 2001.

Source: U.S. Department of Labor, Bureau of Labor Statistics, Office of Employment and Unemployment Statistics, unpublished tabulations of annual averages from the Current Population Survey, 2002.

■ *Life Success Goal: Preparation for career success.* Your course work will give you the knowledge and hands-on skills you need to achieve your career goals. It will also expose you to a variety of careers related to your major, many of which you may not have even heard of. Completing college will open career doors that are closed to those without a degree.

■ *Life Success Goal: Smart personal health choices.* The more educated you are, the more likely you are to take care of your physical and mental health. A college education prepares you with health-related information and attitudes that you will use over your lifetime, helping you to practice wellness through positive actions and to avoid practices with the potential to harm.

■ *Life Success Goal: Active community involvement and an appreciation of different cultures.* Going to college prepares you to understand complex political, economic, and social forces that affect you and others. This understanding is the basis for good citizenship and encourages community involvement. Your education also exposes you to the ways in which people and cultures are different and how these differences affect world affairs, which is a benefit to a worker likely to encounter many cultures in the global marketplace.

■ *Life Success Goal: Self-knowledge.* Working toward a college education involves thinking about yourself on a big-picture level. What do you do well? What do you want out of life? What can you improve? College gives you the chance to evaluate where you are and to make some concrete decisions about how to get where you want to be.

This course and this textbook provide an ideal opportunity to kick off this exploration. Throughout the term, the topics you cover will lead you to a deeper understanding of who you are and what you want out of life. Part I, "Getting Ready to Learn," encourages you to examine your preparedness for success in college and beyond, your learning styles, diversity and communication, your values and goals, how you manage time, and how you think creatively and critically. Part II, "Targeting Success in School and Life," promotes exploration of what you do well and what you can improve in your *study skills*—reading, studying, listening, remembering, note taking, test taking, math and science learning, and writing—as well as in *life skills*—personal wellness, financial management, and career goals.

From time to time through this course, think about how you can connect with the topic at hand. Ask yourself, "How is this important to me? How will it help me achieve my goals?" The more you see how material will help you, the greater your ability to *persist.*

Now that you've laid out the big picture, it's time to focus on the nuts-and-bolts basics that will prepare you to *persist*—and ultimately succeed—in college.

REFLECT

People attend college for technical training, for the sake of learning, for increased earning power, and for many other reasons. Think about your own reasons. Why are you here? How do you feel about your reasons for being here? Consider the habit of mind that opened this chapter: Out of all the reasons you are in college, which seem most likely to encourage you to *persist* in your journey, and why?

RESPOND

Persistence

Lance Armstrong, seven-time winner of the grueling
our de France bicycle race, beat the odds against testicular cancer.

With an unshakeable belief in his ability
to prevail, the support of family and friends,
and a dose of good luck, he *persisted
and inspired the rest of us.*

LIVE IT!

What basic actions will prepare you for college success?

Adjusting to college can be a challenge that requires the self-confidence to move forward and the courage to face your fears. It also requires that you take on the responsibilities of being a student. The following information is designed to help you feel more prepared and in control so that you can focus your energy on learning.

Be Responsible

You are in control of your life. In college, this means that you are your own manager, in charge of meeting your obligations and making decisions that move you toward your goals. Your primary responsibility as a student is to pursue academic excellence—to do your very best in every course. You can accomplish this through a series of small but important actions which, although they may sound mundane, are the building blocks of successful student life:

- Read assigned material before it is discussed in class.
- Attend class on time and with a positive attitude.
- Complete assignments on schedule.
- Listen attentively, take notes, and participate in discussions.
- Study for exams, either on your own or with others.
- Communicate with instructors and students, and seek help from them if you need it.

© Jason Stitt—Fotolia

One important responsibility is to thoroughly read your syllabus for every course you are taking and frequently refer to it throughout the term. (A *syllabus* is a comprehensive guide to your course that your instructors will hand out at the first class meeting.) Consider each syllabus as a "contract" between you and your instructor, outlining what your instructor expects of you, such as readings, assignments, and class participation. Because a contract goes both ways, your syllabus also details what responsibilities you can expect of your instructor, such as being available for consultation and covering particular topics at scheduled times. A course has the best chance to meet everyone's expectations when both sides fulfill the terms of this "contract" successfully.

Your syllabus will answer questions you may have about the focus of the course, required and optional reading, schedule of coverage, dates of exams and due dates for assignments, what components make up your final grade, and more. Key 1.3 shows a portion of an actual syllabus with important items noted. Marking up your syllabus in your own way will help remind you of your responsibilities.

Finally, in all of your daily academic tasks, *persist* until you get what you need and complete what you have been assigned. *Persistence* is the responsible student's master key.

Get Motivated

Success is a process, not a fixed mark. *Motivation*—a force that moves a person to action—is what keeps the process in motion. Successful people find ways to motivate themselves to learn, grow, and work toward what they want.

A syllabus helps you stay on schedule and fulfill responsibilities.   **KEY   1.3**

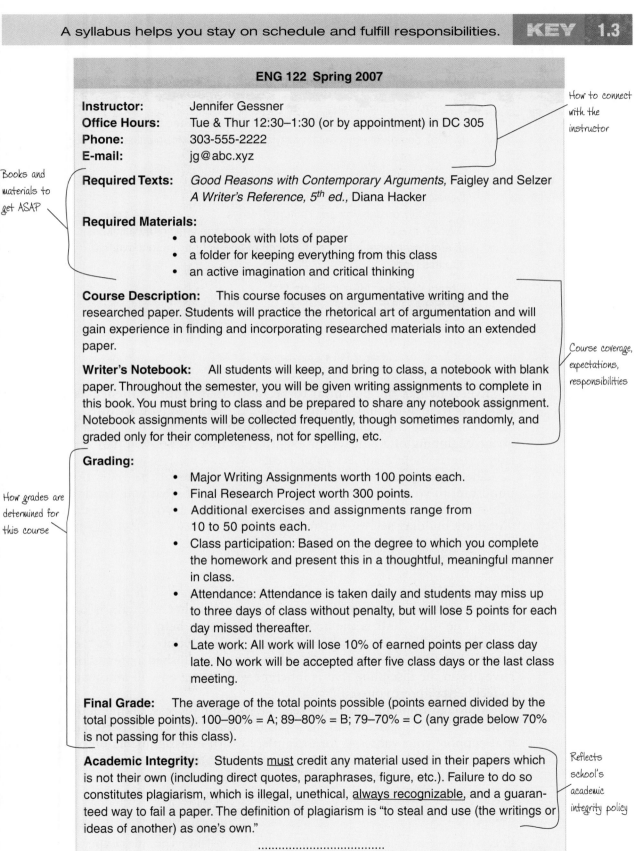

ENG 122 Spring 2007

Instructor: Jennifer Gessner
Office Hours: Tue & Thur 12:30–1:30 (or by appointment) in DC 305
Phone: 303-555-2222
E-mail: jg@abc.xyz

How to connect with the instructor

Required Texts: *Good Reasons with Contemporary Arguments,* Faigley and Selzer
A Writer's Reference, 5th ed., Diana Hacker

Books and materials to get ASAP

Required Materials:
- a notebook with lots of paper
- a folder for keeping everything from this class
- an active imagination and critical thinking

Course Description: This course focuses on argumentative writing and the researched paper. Students will practice the rhetorical art of argumentation and will gain experience in finding and incorporating researched materials into an extended paper.

Writer's Notebook: All students will keep, and bring to class, a notebook with blank paper. Throughout the semester, you will be given writing assignments to complete in this book. You must bring to class and be prepared to share any notebook assignment. Notebook assignments will be collected frequently, though sometimes randomly, and graded only for their completeness, not for spelling, etc.

Course coverage, expectations, responsibilities

Grading:
- Major Writing Assignments worth 100 points each.
- Final Research Project worth 300 points.
- Additional exercises and assignments range from 10 to 50 points each.
- Class participation: Based on the degree to which you complete the homework and present this in a thoughtful, meaningful manner in class.
- Attendance: Attendance is taken daily and students may miss up to three days of class without penalty, but will lose 5 points for each day missed thereafter.
- Late work: All work will lose 10% of earned points per class day late. No work will be accepted after five class days or the last class meeting.

How grades are determined for this course

Final Grade: The average of the total points possible (points earned divided by the total possible points). 100–90% = A; 89–80% = B; 79–70% = C (any grade below 70% is not passing for this class).

Academic Integrity: Students <u>must</u> credit any material used in their papers which is not their own (including direct quotes, paraphrases, figure, etc.). Failure to do so constitutes plagiarism, which is illegal, unethical, <u>always recognizable</u>, and a guaranteed way to fail a paper. The definition of plagiarism is "to steal and use (the writings or ideas of another) as one's own."

Reflects school's academic integrity policy

....

(continued)

(Continued)

Week 4

Topic of that day's class meeting

2/1   The Concise Opinion.
           HW: Complete Paper #1 Rough Draft (5–7 pages double-spaced)

Notice of due date for paper draft

2/3   How Professionals Argue
           HW: Read Jenkins Essay (p 501 of *Good Reasons*) and Rafferty Essay
           (p 525); compare argumentative style, assess and explain efficacy
           of arguments.

Notice of reading assignments to complete

Week 5

2/15   Developing an Argument
           Essay Quiz on Jenkins and Rafferty Essays
           HW: Chap 5 of *Good Reasons;* based on components of a definition
           of argument, write a brief explanation of how your argument might fit
           into this type.

Notice of quiz

2/17   Library Workday: Meet in Room 292
           PAPER #1 DUE

Notice of final due date for paper

Everyone has the potential to be motivated. Your challenge as you begin college is to identify and activate the forces that move you forward. Motivators can change with time and situations. Though grades may be all that interest you at the beginning of a course, for example, as time passes you may feel a motivation to learn about a subject you have grown to love.

The primary key to motivation is to stay aware of the goals that are most important to you and continually remind yourself of what you stand to gain from achieving them. Two other strategies that help to keep you motivated and moving ahead are building self-esteem and facing your fears.

Building Self-Esteem

When people have faith in themselves, their *self-esteem* (belief in one's own value as a person) fuels their motivation to succeed. Belief, though, is only half the game. The other half is the action and effort that help you feel that you have earned your self-esteem—as basketball coach Rick Pitino explains: "Self-esteem is directly linked to deserving success. If you have established a great work ethic and have begun the discipline that is inherent with that, you will automatically begin to feel better about yourself."[2]

Although thinking positively sets the tone for success, taking action gets you there. In order to get moving in a positive direction, create personal guidelines that support your success—for example, "I turn in assignments on or before the deadline." Then, follow up your guideline with the action you've promised to take—in this case, always turning in your assignments on time.

Facing Your Fears

Everyone experiences fear. Anything unknown—new people, experiences, challenges, situations—can be frightening. The challenges you encounter demand a willingness to face your fears and push your limits. The following steps will help you work through fear with courage:

1. *Acknowledge fears.* Naming your fear begins to lessen its hold on you. Be specific.

2. *Examine fears.* Sometimes one fear hides a larger one. Do you fear a test, or the fact that if you pass it you will have to take a tougher class next?

3. *Develop and implement a plan.* Come up with ways to overcome your fear, and put them to work. For example, if reading a play by William Shakespeare intimidates you, you might ask an instructor for advice, attend a performance of a Shakespeare play, or rent a film adaptation of a production.

REFLECT

Writer Betty Bender said, "Anything I've ever done that ultimately was worthwhile . . . initially scared me to death." Describe a fulfilling accomplishment in your life that inspired fear at first. What helped you get past your fear and achieve what you did? Now describe what you fear about college. How might you work through the fear and reach the point of accomplishment?

RESPOND

Learn from Failure and Celebrate Success

Even the most successful people make mistakes and experience failures. In fact, failure is one of the greatest teachers. Failure provides an opportunity to realize what you didn't know so that you can improve. What you learn from a failure will most likely stay with you more intensely and guide you more effectively than many other things you learn.

Learning from Failure

Learning from your failures and mistakes involves careful thinking, as follows:

- *Analyze what happened.* For example, imagine that after a long night of studying for a chemistry test, you forgot to complete an American history paper due the next day. Your focus on the test caused you to overlook other tasks. Now you may face a lower grade on your paper if you turn it in late, or you may be inclined to rush it and turn in a project that isn't as good as it could be.

- *Come up with creative ways to change.* You can make a commitment to note deadlines in a bright color in your planner and to check due dates more often. You can also try arranging your study schedule so that it is more organized and less last-minute.

- *Put your plan into action.* Do what you have decided to do—and keep an eye on how it is working. If you rearrange your study schedule, for example, look carefully at whether it is improving your ability to stay on top of your responsibilities.

Sometimes you can't get motivated to turn things around. Here are some ways to boost your outlook when failure gets you down:

- *Believe you are a capable person.* Focus on your strengths and know you can try again.

■ *Share your disappointment with others.* Blow off steam and exchange creative ideas that can help you learn from what happened.

■ *Look on the bright side.* At worst, you got a lower grade because your paper was late. At best, you learned lessons that will help you avoid the same mistake in the future.

Your value as a human being does not diminish when you make a mistake. People who can manage failure demonstrate to themselves and others that they have the courage to take risks and learn. Employers often value risk takers more than people who always play it safe.

Celebrating Success

Acknowledging your successes, no matter how small, is as important as learning from your mistakes. Earning a B on a paper after you had received a C on the previous one, for example, is worth celebrating. Take a moment to acknowledge

TAKE ACTION

GET PREPARED

Learn from a Mistake

Describe an academic situation—you didn't study enough for a test, you didn't complete an assignment on time, you didn't listen carefully enough to a lecture and missed important information—where you made a mistake. What happened?

_____

_____

What were the consequences of the mistake?

_____

_____

What, if anything, did you learn from your mistake that you will use in similar situations?

_____

_____

What is the advantage of practicing the habit of mind of *persisting* to correct mistakes?

_____

_____

_____

what you have accomplished, whether it is a good grade, a job offer, or any other personal victory. Let your success help you to build your confidence that you can succeed again.

What does your college expect of you?

If you clarify what it means to be a college student before classes start, you will minimize surprises that may be obstacles later on. What is expected of you may be different from anything you encountered in high school or in other educational settings. Because expectations differ from college to college, use the material that follows as general guidelines. For specifics regarding your school, consult your college catalog, student handbook, and school Web site.

Follow Procedures and Fulfill Requirements

Understanding and following your college's directives will smooth your path to success.

Registration

Actual course registration varies from school to school. Registration may take place through your school's computer network, via an automated phone system, or in the school gym or student union. When you register, you may be asked to pay tuition and other fees. Scan the college catalog and Web site and consider these factors as you make your selections:

- Core/general requirements for graduation
- Your major or minor, or courses in departments you are considering
- Electives that sound interesting, even if they are out of your field

In most schools, you can choose to attend a class without earning academic credit by *auditing* the class. The main reason students choose to audit is to explore different areas without worrying about a grade, although tuition charges are generally the same.

Once you decide on courses, but before you register, create a schedule that shows daily class times in order to see if the schedule will work out. Create one or more backup schedules in case classes you want fill up before you register. Meet with your advisor for comments and approval.

Graduation and Curriculum Requirements

Every college has degree requirements stated in the catalog and on the Web site. Make sure you understand those that apply to you. Among the requirements you may encounter are the following:

- Number of credits needed to graduate, including credits in major and minor fields
- Curriculum requirements, including specific course requirements
- Departmental major requirements, including the cumulative average needed for acceptance as a major in the department

School Procedures

Your college has rules and regulations, found in the college handbook and on the Web site, for all students to follow. Among the most common procedures are these:

- *Adding or dropping a class.* This should be done within the first few days of the term if you find that a course is not right for you or that there are better choices. Late-term unexcused withdrawals (almost any withdrawal after a predetermined date, save those approved for special cases) receive a failing grade.

- *Taking an Incomplete.* If you can't finish your work due to circumstances beyond your control—an illness or injury, for example—many colleges allow you to take a grade of Incomplete. The school will require approval from your instructor and you will have to make up the work later.

- *Transferring schools.* If you don't feel your college is the right fit, research the degree requirements of other schools and submit transfer applications. If you are a student at a community college and intend to transfer to a four-year school, be sure to take the courses required for admission to that school. In addition, be sure all your credits are transferable, which means they will be counted toward your degree at the four-year school.

Understand Your School's Grading System

When you receive grades, remember that they reflect your work, not your self-worth. Most schools use grading systems with numerical grades or equivalent letter grades (see Key 1.4). Generally, the highest course grade is an A, or 4.0, and the lowest is an F, or 0.0.

In every course, you earn a certain number of college credits, called *hours*. For example, Accounting 101 may be worth three hours. These numbers generally refer to the number of hours the course meets per week. When you multiply each numerical course grade by the number of hours the course is worth, take the average of all these numbers, and divide by the total number of credit hours you are taking, you obtain your grade point average, or GPA (see Key 1.5).

Learn the minimum GPA needed to remain in good standing and to be accepted and continue in your major. At some schools, for example, courses with grades below 2.0 may not be counted toward your major requirement.

KEY   1.4   Letter grades and equivalent numerical grades per semester hour.

Letter grade	A	A−	B+	B	B−	C+	C	C−	D+	D	F
Numerical grade	4.0	3.7	3.3	3.0	2.7	2.3	2.0	1.7	1.3	1.0	0.0

An example that shows how to calculate your GPA.			KEY 1.5
Course	**Semester hours**	**Grade**	**Grade points**
Chemistry 1	4	C	4 credits × 2 points = 8
Freshman Writing	3	B+	3 credits × 3.3 points = 9.9
Spanish I	3	B−	3 credits × 2.7 points = 8.1
Introduction to Statistics	3	C+	3 credits × 2.3 points = 6.9
Social Justice	2	A−	2 credits × 3.7 points = 7.4

Total semester hours: 15
Total grade points for semester: 40.3

GPA for semester (total grade points divided by semester hours): 40.3 divided by 15 = 2.68
Letter equivalent grade: C+/B−

Make the Most of Your School's Computer System

A large part of the communication and work that you do in college involves the computer. In a given day you might access a syllabus online, e-mail another student, use the Internet to tap into a library database, write a draft of an assignment on a computer, and send a paper draft to an instructor.

In most colleges, it is no longer possible to manage without a computer—your own, one borrowed from school, or one available in computer labs. Most dorm rooms are wired for computers, which gives students access to the campus network—and an increasing number of campuses have wireless networks, which allow students to tap into the Internet from any location. Here are some suggestions for using your computer effectively:

- *Get trained.* Connect to your college network. Then, take training classes to master word processing, data and spreadsheets, and the Internet.
- *Use computers to find information.* If you have specific questions about your school, check the college Web site.
- *Be a cautious user.* To safeguard your work, create regular backups by saving your work periodically onto the hard drive or a diskette, CD, or flash drive. In addition, install an antivirus program and update it regularly.
- *Stay on task.* During study time, try to stay away from Internet surfing and computer games.

If you are required to communicate with your instructor, submit assignments, or take exams via e-mail, use the following suggestions to improve your communication:

- *Use your college's e-mail system.* Register for an e-mail account at your school in order to receive schoolwide e-mails and possibly to access the college library.

Doug Mills/*The New York Times*

Whether a laptop on a wireless connection or a desktop in a college facility, a computer is a tool for both academic work as well as communication with instructors and fellow students.

- *Be clear and complete.* Organize your thoughts. Get to the point in the first paragraph, use short paragraphs, use headings to divide long e-mails into digestible sections, and use lists. Always proofread before hitting "Send."

- *Use proper grammar, spelling, and punctuation.* Write to instructors as though you were writing a letter to send in the regular mail. Save the abbreviations, all-lowercase sentences, and acronyms for when you send IMs and text messages to your friends.

- *Be careful of miscommunication.* Try to be diplomatic, respectful, and pleasant. Because tone can be misread on e-mail, be as straight-forward as possible.

Get Involved

Extracurricular activities give you a chance to meet people who share your interests and to develop teamwork and leadership skills as well as other skills that may be important in your career. In addition, being connected to friends and a supportive network of people is one of the main reasons people stay in school. Studies have shown that students who join organizations tend to *persist* in their educational goals more than those who don't branch out.[3]

Some freshmen take on so many activities that they become overwhelmed. Pace yourself the first year. You can always add activities later.

Know How to Work with Others

Your success at school and at work will depend on your ability to cooperate in a team setting. Students taking the same course may form a group that meets one or more times a week or right before exams. Instructors sometimes initiate student study groups, commonly for math or science courses, known as *peer-assisted study sessions* or *supplemental instruction.*

When you study with one or more people, benefits include the following:

- *Shared and solidified knowledge.* To have students pass on their knowledge to each other in a study group requires less time and energy than for each of those students to learn all of the material alone. Furthermore, when you discuss concepts or teach them to others, you solidify what you know and strengthen your critical thinking.

- *Increased motivation.* Knowing that you are accountable to others and that they will see your level of work and preparation, you may be more motivated to work hard.

- *Increased teamwork ability.* The more you understand the dynamics of working with a group and the more experience you have at it, the more you build your ability to work well with others.

■ *Increased awareness and understanding of diversity.* You will most likely work with students who differ from you in visible ways, in hidden ways such as perspectives and goals, or in both. Teams gain strength from the diversity of their members, because the greater the diversity of a team, the greater the number of choices or solutions when problem solving. Chapter 3 goes into more detail about diversity and communication.

Strategies for Study Group Success

Every study group is unique. The way a group operates may depend on the members' personalities, the subject you study, the location of the group, and the size of the group. But no matter what your particular group's situation, the following general strategies will help:

■ *Set long-term and short-term goals.* At your first meeting, determine what the group wants to accomplish. At the start of each meeting, have one person compile a list of questions to address.

■ *Set a regular schedule.* Determine what your group needs and what the group members' schedules can handle. Try to meet weekly or, at the least, every other week.

■ *Choose a leader for each meeting.* Rotating the leadership among members willing to lead helps all members take ownership of the group.

■ *Share the workload.* The most important factor is a willingness to work, not knowledge level.

■ *Create study materials for one another.* Give each group member the task of finding a piece of information to compile, photocopy, and review for the other group members.

© AlexMax—Fotolia

■ *Help each other learn.* Have group members teach pieces of information, make up quizzes for each other, or go through flash cards together.

■ *Pool your note-taking resources.* Compare notes with group members and fill in any information you don't have. Try different note-taking styles (see chapter 7 for more on note taking).

Study groups and other teams rely on both leaders and participants to accomplish goals. Becoming aware of the roles each plays will increase your effectiveness.[4]

Being an Effective Participant

Some people are most comfortable when participating in a group that someone else leads. Participants, however, are "part owners" of the team process with a responsibility for, and a stake in, the outcome. The following strategies will help you become more effective in this role:

■ *Get involved.* Let people know your views on decisions.

■ *Be organized.* The more focused your ideas, the more people will take them seriously.

■ *Be willing to discuss.* Be respectful and open to the opinions of others.

■ *Keep your word.* Carry out whatever tasks you promise to do.

Being an Effective Leader

Some people prefer to initiate the action, make decisions, and control how things proceed. Leaders often have a broad perspective that allows them to envision how different aspects of a group project will come together. The following strategies help a leader succeed:

- *Define projects.* The leader should define the group's purpose (for example, brainstorming, decision making, or project collaboration) and limit tasks in order to focus efforts.
- *Assign work and set a schedule.* A group functions best when everyone has an assigned task and when deadlines are clear.
- *Set meeting and project agendas.* The leader should, with advice from other group members, establish and communicate goals and define how the work will proceed.
- *Focus and persist.* The leader needs to keep everyone on target and moving ahead.
- *Set the tone.* Be fair, respectful, encouraging, and hardworking.
- *Evaluate results.* The leader should determine whether the team is accomplishing its goals on schedule. If the team is not moving ahead, the leader should make changes.

Understand and Manage Learning Disabilities

Students who have a learning disability face a special challenge to their college success. The National Center for Learning Disabilities (NCLD) defines learning disabilities as follows:[5]

- They are neurological disorders that interfere with one's ability to store, process, and produce information.
- They do *not* include mental retardation, autism, behavioral disorders, impaired vision, hearing loss, or other physical disabilities.
- They do *not* include attention deficit disorder and attention deficit hyperactivity disorder, although these problems may accompany learning disabilities.[6]
- They often run in families and are lifelong, although people who have learning disabilities can use specific strategies to manage and even overcome areas of weakness.
- They must be diagnosed by professionals in order for the person who has a disability to receive federally funded aid.

How can you determine if you should be evaluated for a learning disability? According to the NCLD, persistent problems in any of the following areas may indicate a learning disability:[7]

- Reading or reading comprehension
- Math calculations, understanding language and concepts
- Social skills or interpreting social cues
- Following a schedule, being on time, meeting deadlines
- Reading or following maps

- Balancing a checkbook
- Following directions, especially on multistep tasks
- Writing, sentence structure, spelling, and organizing written work

For an evaluation, contact your school's learning center or student health center for a referral to a licensed professional. If you are diagnosed with a learning disability, the following focused actions will help you manage it and maximize your ability to learn and succeed.

Be informed about your disability. Search the library and the Internet—try the NCLD at **www.ncld.org** or LD Online at **www.ldonline.org** (other Web sites are listed at the end of the chapter). Or call the NCLD at 1-888-575-7373. Make sure you understand your individualized education program (IEP)—the document describing your disability and recommended strategies.

Seek assistance from your school. Speak with your advisor about specific accommodations that will help you learn. Services mandated by law for students who have learning disabilities include extended time on tests, note-taking assistance, assistive technology devices (tape recorders or laptop computers), alternative assessments and test formats, tutoring, and study skills assistance.

Be a dedicated student. Be in class and on time. Read assignments before class. Sit where you can focus. Review notes soon after class. Spend extra time on assignments. Ask for help.

Build a positive attitude. See your accomplishments in light of how far you have come. Rely on people who support you. Know that help will give you the best possible chance to learn and grow.

Why does your success depend on academic integrity?

Having *academic integrity* means following a code of moral values, prizing honesty and fairness in all aspects of academic life—classes, assignments, tests, papers, projects, and relationships with students and faculty. It also means valuing education and learning over grades. Academic integrity promotes learning and ensures a quality education based on *ethics* (your sense of what is right to do) and hard work. Read your school's code of honor, or academic integrity policy, in your student handbook. When you enrolled, you agreed to abide by it.

What Academic Integrity Means

The Center for Academic Integrity, part of the Kenan Institute for Ethics at Duke University, defines *academic integrity* as a commitment to five fundamental values: honesty, trust, fairness, respect, and responsibility.[8] They are the positive actions that define academic integrity.

- *Honesty.* Honesty defines the pursuit of knowledge and implies a search for truth in your classwork, papers and lab reports, and teamwork with other students.

■ *Trust.* Trust means being true to your word. Mutual trust—between instructor and student, as well as among students—makes possible the exchange of ideas that is essential for learning.

■ *Fairness.* Instructors must create a fair academic environment where students are judged against clear standards and in which procedures are well defined.

■ *Respect.* In a respectful academic environment, both students and instructors accept and honor a wide range of opinions, even if the opinions are contrary to core beliefs.

■ *Responsibility.* You are responsible for making choices that will provide you with the best education—choices that reflect fairness and honesty.

Unfortunately, the principles of academic integrity are frequently violated on college campuses. In a recent survey, three out of four college students admitted to cheating at least once during their undergraduate careers.[9] Violations of academic integrity—turning in previously submitted work, using unauthorized devices during an exam, providing unethical aid to another student, or getting unauthorized help with a project—aren't worth the price. Consequences of violations vary from school to school and include participation in academic integrity seminars, grade reduction or course failure, suspension, or expulsion.

Chester Higgins Jr. / *The New York Times*

Maintaining academic integrity at school builds positive habits that enhance relationships with fellow students and coworkers.

How to Avoid Plagiarism

Plagiarism—using an author's words, content, unique approach, or illustrations without crediting the author—is a specific violation of academic integrity and is illegal and unethical. When you incorporate ideas from other sources into your work, you are using other writers' intellectual property. Most instructors consider work to be plagiarized when a student does any of the following:

■ Submits a paper from a Web site that sells or gives away research papers

■ Buys a paper from a non-Internet service

■ Hands in a paper written by a fellow student or faculty member

■ Writes a paper collaboratively with one or more students without instructor approval

■ Copies material directly from a source without quotation marks or source citation

■ Paraphrases material in a paper from a source without proper source citation

The following techniques will help you properly credit sources and avoid plagiarism.

Make source and content notes as you go. Plagiarism often begins accidentally during research; you may intend to cite or paraphrase a source, but forget to do so. To avoid this, write detailed source and content notes during research that indicate direct quotations (see chapter 7).

Know the difference between a quotation and a paraphrase. A *quotation* repeats a source's exact words and is set off by quotation marks. A *paraphrase* is a restatement of the quotation in your own words, requiring that you completely rewrite the idea, not just remove or replace a few words. As Key 1.6 illustrates, a paraphrase may not be acceptable if it is too close to the original.

Use a citation even for an acceptable paraphrase. When you quote from a source, paraphrase it, or use it as evidence, credit the source by writing a footnote or endnote in appropriate format.

Focus on your own ideas and use sources as support. Even if you credit your quote sources, stringing together a series of quotes is not acceptable scholarship. Use small sections of quoted material surrounded by your own explanations, evaluations, and conclusions.

Understand that lifting material off the Internet is plagiarism. Words in electronic form belong to the writer just as words in print form do. If you cut and paste sections from a source document onto your draft, you are committing plagiarism.

Avoid plagiarism by learning how to paraphrase.	KEY 1.6

Quotation

"The most common assumption that is made by persons who are communicating with one another is . . . that the other perceives, judges, thinks, and reasons the way he does. Identical twins communicate with ease. Persons from the same culture but with a different education, age, background, and experience often find communication difficult. American managers communicating with managers from other cultures experience greater difficulties in communication than with managers from their own culture."

Unacceptable Paraphrase

(*The underlined words are taken directly from the quoted source.*)

When we communicate, we assume that the person to whom we are speaking <u>perceives, judges, thinks,</u> and <u>reasons the way</u> we do. This is not always the case. Although <u>identical twins communicate with ease, persons from the same culture but with a different education, age, background, and experience often</u> encounter communication problems. Communication problems are common among American managers as they attempt to <u>communicate with managers from other cultures.</u> They experience greater communication problems than when they communicate <u>with managers from their own culture.</u>

Acceptable Paraphrase

Many people fall into the trap of believing that everyone sees the world exactly as they do and that all people communicate according to the same assumptions. This belief is difficult to support even within our own culture as African-Americans, Hispanic-Americans, Asian-Americans, and others often attempt unsuccessfully to find common ground. When intercultural differences are thrown into the mix, such as when American managers working abroad attempt to communicate with managers from other cultures, clear communication becomes even harder.

Source: Philip R. Harris and Robert T. Moran, *Managing Cultural Differences,* 3rd ed. (Houston, TX: Gulf Publishing Company, 1991), 59.

Why Academic Integrity Is Worth It

Choosing to act with integrity has the following positive effects:

- *Increased self-esteem.* Self-esteem is tied to action. The more you act in respectful and honorable ways, the better you feel about yourself, and the more likely you are to succeed.
- *Acquired knowledge.* If you cheat you might pass a test—and a course—but chances are you won't retain the knowledge and skills you need. Honest work is more likely to result in knowledge that lasts—and that you can use to accomplish career and life goals.
- *Effective behavioral patterns.* When you condition yourself to play fair now, you set a pattern for your behavior at work and with friends and family.
- *Mutual respect.* Respecting the work of others will encourage others to respect your work.

The risk to students who violate standards of integrity is growing because cheating is now easier to discover. Make a commitment to uphold the highest standards of academic integrity.

Who at school can help you make the most of your education?

As you navigate your college experience, instructors, administrators, advisors, and a range of support staff are there to help. Your responsibility is to know what support is available and to take the initiative to seek help when you need it. The individuals and other resources available at your school include instructors and teaching assistants, academic advisors, mentors, tutors, academic centers, administrative staff, other student-centered services, and resources for minority students.

Instructors and Teaching Assistants

The people who teach your courses—instructors and teaching assistants—are your most available human resources at college. You see them from one to five times per week and interact with them more directly than with any other authority on campus. They see your work and, if your class size is small, they hear your ideas and consequently may get to know you quite well. Instructors are potential resources and necessary allies in your education.

What kind of help might you seek from an instructor or teaching assistant?

- Clarification on material presented in class
- Help on homework
- Information about how to prepare for a test
- Consultation on a paper you are working on
- Details about why you received a particular grade on a test or assignment
- Advice about the department—courses, majoring—or related career areas

When you want to speak personally with an instructor for longer than a minute or two, choose your time carefully. Before or after class is usually not the best time for anything more than a quick question. When you need your instructor's full attention, there are three ways to get it: make an appointment during office hours, send e-mail, or leave a voice-mail message.

Office hours. Instructors keep regular office hours during which students can schedule personal conferences. Generally, these appear on your syllabus and are posted on instructors' office doors and on instructors' or departmental Web pages. Always make an appointment for a conference; if you show up unannounced, your instructor may be busy. Face-to-face conferences are ideal for working through ideas and problems (for example, deciding on a term paper topic) or asking for advice (for example, looking for guidance on choosing courses in the department).

E-mail. Use e-mail to clarify assignments and assignment deadlines, to ask questions about lectures or readings, and to clarify what will be covered on a test. Be courteous, and e-mail only when necessary and appropriate. Don't wait until the last minute to ask test-related questions; your instructor may not have time to respond. And don't expect an instructor to respond immediately to a message sent at midnight or to answer your e-mails if you send a dozen after every class. Instructors' e-mail addresses are generally posted on the first day of class and may also appear in your student handbook or syllabus. Links may be available on the college Web site.

Voice mail. If something comes up at the last minute, you can leave a message in your instructor's voice mailbox. Make your message short, but specific ("This is Rick Jones from your 10 o'clock Intro to Psychology class—I'm supposed to present my project today, but I'm sick with a fever"). Avoid calling instructors at home unless they give specific permission to do so.

Teaching assistants. If you are taking a large lecture course, you may have a primary instructor plus a *teaching assistant* (TA) who meets with a small group of students on a regular basis and grades your papers and exams. You may want to approach your TA with course-related questions and problems before approaching the instructor. Because TAs deal with fewer students, they may have more time to devote to specific issues.

Academic Advisors

In most colleges, every student is assigned an advisor who is the student's personal liaison with the college. (At some schools, students receive help at an advising center.) Your advisor will help you choose courses every term, plan your overall academic program, and understand college regulations, including graduation requirements. He or she will point out possible consequences of your decisions ("If you put off taking biology now, you're facing two lab courses next term"), help you shape your educational goals, and monitor your academic progress.

Although you are responsible for fully understanding graduation requirements—including credit requirements—and choosing the courses you need, your advisor is there to help you with these critical decisions. You will most likely be required to

Michelle V. Agins / *The New York Times*

Instructors, advisors, and mentors are invaluable resources. Find out when they are available and take the time to connect with them.

meet with your advisor once each term; however, you can schedule additional meetings if and when you need them.

Mentors

You may find a mentor during college—a trusted counselor or guide who takes a special interest in helping you reach your goals. A mentor can give you a private audience for questions and problems, advice tailored to your needs, support, guidance, and trust. In return, you owe it to your mentor to respectfully take advice into consideration. A mentor might be your advisor, an instructor in your major or minor field, or an academic support person. Some schools have faculty or peer mentoring programs to match students with people who can help them.

Tutors and Academic Centers

Tutors can give you valuable and detailed help on specific academic subjects. Most campuses have private tutoring available, and many schools offer free peer tutoring. If you feel you could benefit from the kind of one-on-one work a tutor can give, ask your instructor or your academic advisor to recommend one. If your school has one or more academic centers, you may be able to find a tutor there. Academic centers—including reading, writing, math, and study skills centers—offer consultations and tutoring to help students improve skills at all levels.

Administrative Staff

The administrative staff enables your college—and the student body—to function. One of the most important administrative offices for students is the Office of the Dean of Student Affairs, which, in many colleges, is the center for student services. Staff members there can answer your questions or direct you to others who can help. You will also encounter administrative offices involved with tuition payments, financial aid, and registration, as follows:

- The *bursar's office* (also called the office of finance, or accounting office) issues bills for tuition and room and board and collects payments from students and financial aid sources.
- The *financial aid office* helps students apply for financial aid and understand the eligibility requirements of different federal, state, and private programs.
- The *registrar's office* handles course registration, sends grade reports, and compiles your official transcript (a comprehensive record of your courses and grades). Graduate school admissions offices require a copy of your transcript, as do many prospective employers.

Student-Centered Services

A host of services helps students succeed in college and deal with problems that arise. Some common services found on most campuses are described here.

Academic computer center. Most schools have computer facilities that are open every day, usually staffed by technicians who can assist with problems. Many facilities also offer training workshops.

Student housing or commuter affairs office. Residential colleges provide on-campus housing for undergraduate students. The housing office handles room and roommate placement and deals with special needs (for example, an allergic student's need for a room air conditioner) and problems. Schools with commuting students may have transportation and parking programs.

Health services. Health services generally include sick care, prescriptions, routine diagnostic tests, vaccinations, and first aid. All clinics are affiliated with nearby hospitals for emergency care. In addition, psychological counseling is sometimes offered through health services, or you may find it at a separate facility. Many colleges require proof of health insurance at the time of registration.

Career services. This office helps students find part-time and full-time jobs, as well as summer jobs and internships. Career offices have reference files on careers and employers; they also help students learn to write résumés and cover letters and search job sites on the Internet; and they hold career fairs and provide space for employers to interview students on campus.

Services for students with disabilities. For students with documented disabilities, federal law requires that assistance be provided in the form of accommodations ranging from interpreters for the hearing impaired to ramps for students in wheelchairs. The office might be called the Disability Resource Center, the Office of Disability Access Services, or some other designation. If you have a disability, visit this office to learn what is offered, and remember that this office is your advocate if you encounter problems.

Veterans' affairs. The Office of Veterans' Affairs provides military veterans with services including academic and personal counseling and current benefit status, which may affect tuition waivers.

Resources for Minority Students

The term *minority* includes students of color, students who are not part of the majority Christian sects, and gay, lesbian, and bisexual students. Along with activities that appeal to the general student population, most colleges have organizations and services that support minority groups, including specialized student associations, cultural centers, arts groups with a minority focus, minority fraternities and sororities, and political action groups.

Many minority students seek a balance, getting involved with members of their group as well as with the college mainstream. For example, a student may join the Latino Students Association as well as organizations for all students, such as the campus newspaper or an athletic team.

TAKE ACTION

Define Yourself as a Student

Colleges design resources to suit the needs of their students. To know how to seek out the resources that will help you succeed in college, you need a solid understanding of how you fit into the current student body. Describe your particular circumstances, opinions, and needs in a short paragraph. Use these questions to inspire thought:

- How would you describe yourself in terms of culture, ethnicity, gender, age, and lifestyle?
- How would you describe your student status—traditional or returning, full- or part-time?
- How long are you planning to be in your current college? Is it likely that you will transfer?
- What family and work obligations do you have?
- What is your current living situation?
- What do you feel are your biggest challenges in college?
- What do you like to study, and why does it interest you?

To make choices as a minority student on campus, ask yourself these questions:

- How do I want to define my ties with my minority group? Will I care if other minority students criticize my choices?
- Do I want to focus my studies on a minority-related field, such as African American studies?
- Do I want to spend part of my time among people who share my background, and part with students from other groups?

As you think about your tools and how you plan to use them to achieve your goals, you may be a bit uneasy about the road ahead and its inevitable stumbling blocks. You can give yourself the best possible chance to succeed if you combine hard work with a set of powerful problem-solving tools called **habits of mind.**

How can habits of mind fuel your success?

Problems—large and small, academic and personal—come up as a part of daily life. Sometimes you know the answer right away. You solve the math problem; you know who to call for emergency child care when your regular sitter cancels and you have to get to class; you have a backup when you don't get the course you want. Often, though, finding the right solution is not so clear-cut. What do you do then?

The answer given by Art Costa, an emeritus professor of education at California State University, Sacramento, and codirector of the Institute for Intelligent Behavior in El Dorado Hills, California, is that you turn to behaviors called the *habits of mind*. "By 'habit of mind,' I mean a disposition toward behaving intelligently when confronted with problems," says Costa. "When we draw upon these resources [the habits], the results are more powerful, of higher quality, and of greater significance."[10]

In situations where you do not know how to respond to a problem right off the bat, your ability to think through and act on the situation in ways that bring about the most favorable results will give you the best chance at success. The essential ingredient of this intelligent problem-solving behavior is "not only having information, but also knowing how to act on it,"[11] reports Costa, who studied how students respond to problems, looking specifically at what they did when working with what they did not yet know. Based on observation and on his evaluation of research, he determined that students tended to solve problems successfully when they demonstrated particular behaviors.

Costa identified 16 different habits of mind that increase the likelihood of goal achievement:

1. Persisting
2. Managing impulsivity
3. Listening to others with understanding and empathy
4. Thinking flexibly
5. Thinking about our thinking (metacognition)
6. Striving for accuracy and precision
7. Questioning and posing problems
8. Applying past knowledge to new situations
9. Thinking and communicating with clarity and precision
10. Gathering data through all senses
11. Creating, imagining, and innovating
12. Responding with wonderment and awe
13. Taking responsible risks
14. Finding humor
15. Thinking interdependently
16. Learning continuously

As you read this book, look for the habit of mind icon. The 11 chapters of *Keys to Effective Learning* build your strength in 11 of these habits in the following ways:

■ Introducing the habit on the chapter-opening pages

- Reinforcing the habit through one "Take Action" exercise and one "Reflect & Respond" exercise
- Closing the chapter with a description of how that habit can help you actively use the chapter material to process your problems and achieve your goals
- Continuing to help you master the habit through the "Activate the Habit of Mind" exercise at the end of the chapter

Ultimately, your goal is to take personal ownership of each habit as you use it regularly to solve problems. Most of the time you will use more than one habit—for example, when brainstorming a problem with a study group, you may think interdependently, listen to others with understanding, and communicate clearly. Let your experience be your guide as you decide what works for you and how to make adjustments to fit your personality and the situation.

The more you make the habits your own, the more effectively and consistently you will approach the problems that inevitably will come your way. The habits of mind are essential tools to keep with you in the quest to maximize your potential in college and beyond.

© Sean Macleay—Fotolia

My motto was always to keep swinging. Whether I was in a slump or feeling badly or having trouble off the field, the only thing to do was keep swinging.

HANK AARON, BASEBALL CHAMPION AND HOLDER OF THE RECORD FOR LIFETIME HOME RUNS

I persist.

Persisting doesn't mean just trying again when the first try doesn't work. Someone using this habit of mind will evaluate a situation to see what might help, stop if one idea isn't working, think about why it didn't work and what might work better, and try something different. You might call this "intelligent trying." Here is an example: When trying to use a key that doesn't fit into a door, you wouldn't keep trying the same key—you would stop, look at the rest of your keys, decide which should work, and then try that one. Another important part of persisting is being able to sustain your focus on a problem long enough to resolve it.

In college and throughout your life, especially in a working world where it is predicted that the country will lose more than 3 million service and professional jobs by 2015,[12] persisting will be essential to your success. It's easy to get pumped up at the beginning—but the road can get long when you hit a tough exam, a subject you feel you just can't master, a drawn-out job hunt, or a workplace with no opportunities for advancement. If you give up entirely or rush to finish tasks because you are tired of how long they are taking, you will miss out on the rewards that come from persisting. Keep going, think as you go, and you will achieve your goals.

REMEMBER
THE IMPORTANT POINTS

1 **Why is attending college the right decision?**

- College prepares you to hold your own in the competitive global marketplace.
- College is a training ground for life success goals: career-related goals; health, community, and culture goals; self-knowledge

2 **What basic actions will prepare you for college success?**

- Be responsible for managing yourself and your actions.
- Use strategies to get and stay motivated.
- Learn from failure and celebrate success.

3 **What does your college expect of you?**

- Follow registration and other procedures and fulfill course and school requirements.
- Understand your school's grading system.
- Know and use your school's computer and electronic communication systems.
- Get involved with organizations and activities.
- Know how to work in a team as a leader or participant.
- Understand and manage learning disabilities.

4 **Why does your success depend on academic integrity?**

- Having academic integrity means being honest and fair in all aspects of academic life.
- Five fundamental values: honesty, trust, fairness, respect, and responsibility.
- Avoid plagiarism by properly crediting authors and sources.
- Academic integrity promotes self-esteem, solidifies knowledge, and builds effective behaviors.

5 **Who at school can help you make the most of your education?**

- Instructors and teaching assistants
- Academic advisors and mentors
- Tutors and academic centers
- Administrative staff
- Student-centered services
- Resources for minority students

6 **How can habits of mind fuel your success?**

- Habits of mind are behaviors that increase the likelihood of goal achievement.
- Art Costa, the educator who performed the research, identified 16 habits.
- Habits are frequently used interdependently.
- Habits of mind are tools to use regularly when solving problems.

CRITICAL THINKING

APPLYING LEARNING TO LIFE

Make your first months count

Campus resources, clubs, student activity groups, and other organizations can enrich your college experience. Put a toe in the water sooner rather than later and you will begin to benefit from what your school has to offer.

Brainstorm Your Ideal Extracurriculars

On a separate piece of paper, write ideas about how you want to spend your time outside of class. To inspire creative ideas, try using one or more of the following questions as a starting point:

- If you had no fear, what horizon-broadening experience would you sign up for?
- When you were in elementary school, what were your favorite activities? Which activities might translate into current interests and pursuits?
- What kinds of organizations, activities, groups, experiences, or people make you think, "Wow, I want to do that"?
- Think about the people who you feel bring out the best in you. What do you like to do with them? What kinds of things are they involved with?
- Who are the people with whom you have little in common? How could you benefit from getting to know them?

Take Steps Toward the Activities You Like

Look back to the "Take Action" feature on page 25. Thinking about how you described yourself in terms of both academics and extracurricular pursuits, look in your student handbook at the resources and organizations your school offers. These may include some or all of the following:

Academic centers (reading, writing, etc.)	*Fraternities/sororities*
Academic organizations	*International student groups*
Adult education center	*Minority student groups*
Arts clubs (music, drama, dance, etc.)	*On-campus work opportunities*

Organizations for students with disabilities   *Sports clubs*

Religious organizations   *Student associations*

School publications   *Student government*

School TV/radio stations   *Volunteer groups*

In the left-hand column on the grid that follows, list the five offices or organizations you most want to check out this term. Then—through school publications and/or a little legwork—fill in the information on the grid, answering the questions shown across the top for each item. Notice that the last column requires action—fill it in when you have made initial contact with each office or organization. Let this exercise be a jumping-off point for real involvement this term.

Office or organization	Location	Hours, or times of meetings	What it offers	Phone number or e-mail	Initial contact—date and what happened
1.					
2.					
3.					
4.					
5.					

TEAM BUILDING

COLLABORATIVE SOLUTIONS

Motivators

Gather in a group of three to five students. Together, brainstorm school motivation blockers—situations or things that most often kill your motivation to succeed in school. When you have as many problems as you have group members, each person should choose one problem and write it at the top of a blank sheet of paper.

Look at the motivation blocker on your page. Under it, write one practical idea about how to overcome it. When everyone is finished, pass the pages one person to the left. Then write an idea about the new blocker at the top of the page you've received. If you can't think of anything, pass the page as is. Continue this way until your original page comes back to you. Then discuss the ideas as a group, analyzing which ideas might work better than others. Add other ideas to the lists if you think of them.

The last step: On your own, keeping in mind your group discussion, list three specific actions that you commit to taking in order to keep motivation high when the going gets rough.

1. _____

2. _____

3. _____

ACTIVATE
THE HABIT OF MIND

*I recognize that my ability to **persist** is essential for me to be able to face challenges and reach my educational and life goals. To encourage my persistence, I will become clear on what I have to accomplish in order to successfully complete a major and graduate. Using the college catalog and Web site, I will explore course and college requirements.*

What general education courses are required in order to graduate?

_____

_____

Here is one major that interests me right now: _____

What courses am I required to take in order to major in that department? List, using a separate page if necessary, the courses in the order they must be taken.

_____

_____

_____

What grade point average do I need to maintain in order to remain in good standing in the college? _____ *To major in my area of interest?* _____

Here are two study-related activities I will start in the next month to help ensure that I will achieve that GPA:

1. _____

2. _____

How am I doing? **Later in the term, be accountable for your progress on page 139.**

SUGGESTED READINGS

Doolin, Mike. *A Guerrilla Manual for the Adult College Student: How to Go to College (Almost) Full Time in Your Spare Time . . . and Still Have Time to Hold Down a Job, Raise a Family, Pay the Bills, and Have Some Fun!* Bangor, ME: Booklocker, 2003.

Light, Richard J. *Making the Most of College: Students Speak Their Minds.* Cambridge, MA: Harvard University Press, 2001.

Malone, Michael S. *The Everything College Survival Book: From Social Life to Study Skills—All You Need to Fit Right In.* Avon, MA: Adams Media, 2005.

Rozakis, Laurie. *The Complete Idiot's Guide to College Survival.* New York: Alpha Books, 2001.

Schindley, Wanda. *Adults in College: A Survival Guide for Nontraditional Students.* Dallas: Dallas Publishing, 2002.

Weinberg, Carol. *The Complete Handbook for College Women: Making the Most of Your College Experience.* New York: New York University Press, 1994.

INTERNET RESOURCES

The Student Center: A Web community for college students, high school students, and teens (**www.student.com**)

Student Now: College Life, Fun, and Resources (**www.studentnow.com**)

Prentice Hall's Student Success Supersite: Student Union (**www.prenhall.com/success/StudentUn/index.html**)

Prentice Hall's Student Success Supersite: Success Stories (**www.prenhall.com/success/Stories/index.html**)

Habits of Mind Web site (**www.habits-of-mind.net**)

ENDNOTES

1. Thomas Friedman, *The World Is Flat,* New York: Farrar, Straus & Giroux, 2005, p. 8.

2. Rick Pitino, *Success Is a Choice,* New York: Broadway Books, 1997, p. 40.

3. Alexander W. Astin, *Preventing Students from Dropping Out,* San Francisco: Jossey-Bass, 1976.

4. Louis E. Boone, David L. Kurtz, and Judy R. Block, *Contemporary Business Communication,* Upper Saddle River, NJ: Prentice Hall, 1994, pp. 489–499.

5. National Center for Learning Disabilities, "LD at a Glance," accessed May 2006 (**www.ncld.org/LDInfoZone/InfoZone_FactSheet_LD.cfm**).

6. National Center for Learning Disabilities, "Talking About LD" (LD Advocate's Guide), accessed May 2006 (**www.ld.org/Advocacy/tutorial_talking_about.cfm**).

7. National Center for Learning Disabilities, "Adult Learning Disabilities: A Learning Disability Isn't Something You Outgrow—It's Something You Learn to Master" (pamphlet), New York: National Center for Learning Disabilities.

8. Center for Academic Integrity, Kenan Institute for Ethics, Duke University, "A Report from the Center for Academic Integrity," October 1999, accessed March 2006 (**www.academicintegrity.org**).

9. Ibid.

10. Arthur L. Costa, "Habits of Mind," in *Developing Minds: A Resource Book for Teaching Thinking,* Arthur L. Costa, ed., Alexandria, VA: Association for Supervision and Curriculum Development, 2001, p. 80. Reprinted by permission. The Association for Supervision and Curriculum Development is a worldwide community of educators advocating sound policies and sharing best practices to achieve the success of each learner. To learn more, visit ASCD at www.ascd.org

11. Ibid.

12. Friedman, *The World Is Flat,* p. 40.

VALUES, GOALS, TIME, & STRESS

MANAGING YOURSELF

Manage impulsivity

MTA METRO-NORTH
TIMETABLES

34

"Effective problem solvers think before they act.

They intentionally form a vision of a product,

a plan of action, a goal, or a destination

before they begin."

ART COSTA

MANAGE IMPULSIVITY

Every time management or goal-setting strategy can be put under the umbrella of "thinking before you act." If you avoid quick and impulsive decisions, you will be able to make the best use of your time and forge the most effective paths toward your goals.

very day, people use clocks and time-telling devices to manage their impulsivity, gauging how much time they need to eat a meal, read a brief for a meeting, or make a phone call before arriving to work or class on time.

Similarly, achieving your most important goals depends on your ability to manage yourself, taking charge of your life much like a CEO heads up a business. This chapter divides self-management into distinct parts: using values to guide goal setting, working through a process to achieve goals, managing time in a way that propels you toward goals, and—throughout the journey—managing the stress that will often arise. It also outlines, as a follow-up to goal setting, the important goal of choosing a major.

School, work, and personal life can create obstacles and produce stress. Everyone has problems; what counts is how you handle them. Your ability to manage yourself and think before you act will help you cope with what you encounter, achieve your goals, and build productive habits.

In this chapter, you explore answers to the following questions:

- Why is it important to know what you value?
- How do you set and achieve goals?
- How can you choose a major?
- How can you effectively manage your time?
- How do you cope with the stress of college life?

Why is it important to know what you value?

You make life choices—what to do, what to believe, what to buy, how to act—based on your personal *values*—principles or qualities that you consider important. Your choice to pursue a degree, for example, reflects that you value the personal and professional growth that come from a college education. Being on time for your classes shows that you value punctuality. Paying bills regularly and on time shows that you value financial stability.

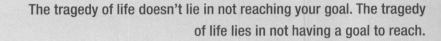

> The tragedy of life doesn't lie in not reaching your goal. The tragedy of life lies in not having a goal to reach.
>
> **MARIAN WRIGHT EDELMAN,** FOUNDER AND PRESIDENT OF THE CHILDREN'S DEFENSE FUND

Values play a key role in your drive to achieve important goals, because they help you to do the following:

- *Understand what you want out of life.* Your most meaningful goals should reflect what you value most.
- *Build "rules for life."* Your values form the foundation for your decisions. You will return repeatedly to them for guidance, especially when you find yourself in unfamiliar territory.
- *Find people who inspire you.* Spending time with people who share similar values will help you clarify how you want to live and find support as you work toward what's important to you.

How do you identify values? Your value system is complex, built piece by piece over time. Begin to think about your values by pondering some general questions: What do you consider important to be, to do, or to have? How would you describe a successful day in your life? At a retirement dinner in your honor, what would you like the speaker to be able to say about who you are and what you have accomplished? If your home caught fire, what five things would you take out? Answers to questions like these will point you toward identifying what is important to you.

Evaluating Values

Look carefully at your values to see if they make sense for you. Many forces affect your values—family, friends, culture, media, school, work, neighborhood, religious beliefs, world events. No matter how powerful these external influences may be, whether a value feels right should be your primary consideration in deciding to adopt it.

Consider something specific that you value. Then, answer the following questions to evaluate whether the value "feels right":

- Where did the value come from?
- What other different values could I consider?

- What might happen as a result of adopting this value?
- Have I made a personal commitment to this choice? Have I told others about it?
- Do my life goals and day-to-day actions reflect this value?

Even the most solid set of values needs a reevaluation from time to time, because life experience and education give you new perspectives that may alter what you consider important. For example, a fun-loving student who overcomes a serious health crisis may place greater value on academics after the crisis than he did before. If you let your values shift to fit you as you grow, you will always have a base on which to build achievable goals and wise decisions.

How Values Affect Your Educational Experience

Values that have positive effects can lead to smart choices while you are in school. As you develop the habit of mind of thinking about your values before you act, they will help you to do the following:

- *Keep going when the going gets tough.* Translate your value of education into specific actions. Remind yourself that actions such as turning in papers on time and attending classes are part of how you will earn lasting benefit from your college course work.

- *Choose your major and a career direction.* If you've always been an environmentalist, then you may choose to major in environmental science. If you feel fulfilled when you help people, then you might consider a career in social work.

- *Choose friends and activities that enrich your life.* Having friends who share your desire to succeed in school will increase your motivation and reduce your stress. Joining organizations whose activities support your values will broaden your educational experience.

- *Choose what you want out of school.* What kinds of skills and knowledge do you wish to build? Do you want to focus on course work that leads to career success? Are you interested in Egyptian archaeology? Do you want to read every novel Toni Morrison wrote? Decide also how hard you are willing to work to achieve your goals. Going above and beyond will build your drive to succeed and will hone work habits—two useful qualities in a competitive job market.

Finally, your values affect your success at school and beyond. As you recall from reading about academic integrity in chapter 1, the more ethical a student you are, the more likely you are to stay in school and to build lasting knowledge and skills.

Writer and activist Gloria Steinem said, "We can tell our values by looking at our checkbook stubs." Think about it: What do your checkbook stubs—or your computer banking program or online debit records—indicate about where the bulk of your time and money goes? What do your checkbook stubs or debit card receipts say about you? Does this conclusion differ from your idea of what your values are or should be?

Values help you to successfully relate to, work with, and understand the people around you in many ways. One of the most important ways is that being open to different values, often linked with different cultures, can enhance your understanding of cultural diversity.

Values and Cultural Diversity

At college, you may meet people who seem different in ways that you may not expect. Many of these differences stem from attitudes and behaviors that are unfamiliar to you. These attitudes and behaviors are rooted in the values that people acquire from their culture, either from the continuing influence of family and community in the United States or from their homeland. *Culture* refers to a set of values, behaviors, tastes, knowledge, attitudes, and habits shared by a group of people.

Cultural misunderstandings can interfere with relationships in college, career, and life. As someone who accepts and appreciates diversity, your goal is to develop what is referred to as *cultural competence*. Cultural competence is defined as the ability to understand and appreciate differences and to respond to people of all cultures in a way that values their worth, respects their beliefs and practices, and builds communication and relationships.[1] Chapter 3 will go into more detail about how to be a culturally competent communicator.

Joyce Dopkeen/ *The New York Times*

Valuing both education and family has led this returning pre-med student to find ways to combine academic life with parenting duties.

As you continue to read *Keys to Effective Learning*, think of the wisdom of cultural diversity consultant Helen Turnbull on turning differences into strengths:

> We must suspend our judgment. We should not judge others negatively because they are indirect, or their accents aren't clear, or their tone of voice is tentative, or they avoid eye contact. We must learn patience and suspend judgment long enough to realize these differences don't make one of us right and the other wrong. They simply mean that we approach communication from a different frame of reference and, many times, a different value system.[2]

Although clarifying your values will help you choose your educational path, goal-setting and goal-achievement skills will help you travel that path to the end. Goals turn values into tools and put them to practical use.

How do you set and achieve goals?

When you identify something that you want, you set a *goal*—an end toward which effort is directed, an aim or intention. Actually *getting* what you want—from college, career, or life—demands working to *achieve* your goals.

Goal achievement is not a product of impulsive action. Achieving goals, whether they are short-term or long-term, involves the careful formulation and execution of a goal-achievement plan. Think of the plan you are about to read as a map; with it helping you to establish each segment of the trip, you will be able to define your route and follow it successfully.

Set Long-Term Goals

Start by establishing the goals that have the largest scope, the *long-term goals* that you aim to attain over a period of six months, a year, or more. As a student, your long-term goals include attending school and earning a degree or certificate. Getting an education is a significant goal that often takes years to reach.

Some long-term goals have an open-ended time frame. For example, if your goal is to become a better musician, you may work at it over a lifetime. These goals also invite more creative thinking; you have more time and freedom to consider all sorts of paths to your goal. Other goals, such as completing all the courses in your major, have a shorter scope, a more definite end, and often fewer options for how to get from A to Z.

The following long-term goal statement, written by Carol Carter, a *Keys to Effective Learning* author, may take extensive forethought and years to complete:

> My goal is to build my own business in which I create opportunities for students to maximize their talents. In this business, I will reach thousands of students and teachers through books, the Internet, teacher seminars, and student-oriented programs.

Carol also has long-term goals that she hopes to accomplish in no more than a year:

> Develop and publish one book. Design three seminars for teachers with accompanying PowerPoints and other materials. Create Internet-based materials that encourage student success and use them in student seminars.

Just as Carol's goals are tailored to her personality, abilities, and values, your goals should reflect your uniqueness. To determine your long-term goals, think now about what you think is important to accomplish while you are in school and after you graduate. Here are some ways that values can be linked to professional goals:

- *Values:* Health and fitness, helping others
  Goal: To become a physical therapist
- *Values:* Independence, financial success
  Goal: To obtain a degree in business and start a company

Basing your long-term goals on values increases your motivation. The more your goals focus on what is most important to you, the greater your drive to reach them.

Set Short-Term Goals

Short-term goals are smaller steps that move you toward a long-term goal. Lasting as short as a few hours or as long as a few months, these goals help you manage your broader aspirations as they narrow your focus and encourage

Impulse Management

Sara Krulwich/*The New York Times*

Whoopi Goldberg faced dyslexia and was illiterate throughout her childhood.

By managing the impulse to avoid hard wor and to give up, Goldberg learned to read when she was an adult. Goldberg *developed a vision of what she wanted to achieve* and worked hard to overcome illiteracy.

progress. If you had a long-term goal of graduating with a degree in nursing, for example, you may set the following short-term goals to accomplish in the next six months:

- I will learn the names, locations, and functions of every human bone and muscle.
- I will work with a study group to understand the musculoskeletal system.

These goals can be broken down into even smaller parts, such as the following one-month goals:

- I will work with onscreen tutorials of the musculoskeletal system until I understand and memorize the material.
- I will spend three hours a week with my study partners.

In addition to monthly goals, you may have short-term goals that extend for a week, a day, or even a couple of hours in a given day. To support your month-long goal of regularly meeting with your study partners, you may wish to set the following short-term goals:

- *By the end of today:* Call study partners to ask them about when they might be able to meet
- *One week from now:* Have scheduled each of our weekly meetings this month
- *Two weeks from now:* Have had our first meeting
- *Three weeks from now:* Type and distribute notes from first meeting; have second meeting

Try to pay special attention to goals that are intermediate in length—for example, one-month or one-term goals on the way to a yearlong goal. Why? Because your motivation is at its peak when you begin to move toward a goal and when you are about to achieve that goal. If you work hard to stay motivated in the middle, you will have a more successful journey and a better result.

As you consider your long- and short-term goals, notice how all of your goals are linked to one another. As Key 2.1 shows, your long-term goals establish a context for the short-term goals. In turn, your short-term goals make the long-term goals seem clearer and more reachable.

At any given time, you will be working toward goals of varying importance. Setting priorities helps you decide where and when to focus your energy and time.

Prioritize Goals

When you *prioritize* (meaning to arrange or deal with things in order of importance), you evaluate everything you are working toward, decide which goals are most important, and plan how you will focus on them. Prioritizing helps you avoid impulsive decisions about how to spend your time. What should you consider as you evaluate?

- *Your values.* Thinking about what you value will help you establish the goals that take top priority—for example, graduating in the top 25 percent of your class or developing a strong network of personal contacts.
- *Your personal situation.* Are you going to school and working part-time? Are you taking three classes or five classes? Are you a parent with young

KEY 2.1   Goals reinforce one another.

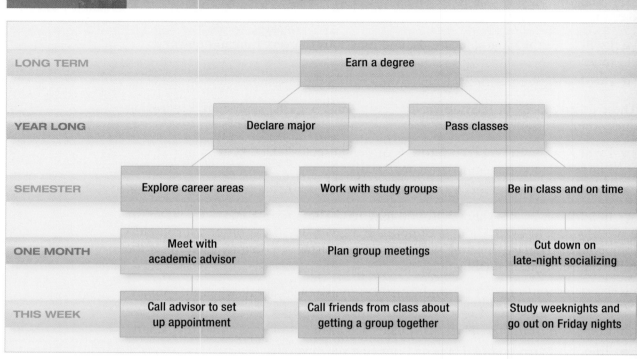

LONG TERM		Earn a degree	
YEAR LONG	Declare major		Pass classes
SEMESTER	Explore career areas	Work with study groups	Be in class and on time
ONE MONTH	Meet with academic advisor	Plan group meetings	Cut down on late-night socializing
THIS WEEK	Call advisor to set up appointment	Call friends from class about getting a group together	Study weeknights and go out on Friday nights

children? Are you an athlete on a sports team? Every individual situation requires unique priorities and scheduling.

■ *Your time commitments.* Hours of your day may already be committed to class, team practices, a part-time job, or sleep. Your challenge is to make sure these commitments reflect what you value and to establish priorities for the remaining hours.

As you will see later in the chapter, setting clear priorities will help you manage your time and accomplish more.

Work to Achieve Goals

When you've done all the work to think through a goal you want to achieve, the following practical steps will help you take action to achieve it. Remember, the more specific your plans, the more likely you are to fulfill them.

■ *Define your goal-setting strategy:* How do you plan to reach your goal? Brainstorm different paths that might get you there. Choose one path; then map out its steps and strategies. Focus on specific behaviors and events that are under your control and that are measurable.

■ *Set a timetable:* When do you want to accomplish your goal? Set a realistic time line that includes specific deadlines for each step and strategy you have defined. Charting your progress will help you stay on track.

■ *Be accountable for your progress:* What safeguards will keep you on track? Define a personal reporting or buddy system that makes accountability a priority.

TAKE ACTION

Map Out a Path to a Personal Goal

Name one important personal goal you have for this year:

_____

Now imagine that you have made it to the end—you already achieved your goal—and an impressed friend asks you to describe how you did it. Write your answer here, in a paragraph, as though you were telling this person about the specific steps you took to achieve your goal:

_____

_____

_____

_____

_____

_____

_____

_____

Finally, examine what you've written. You just created a potential plan! Consider putting it—or a plan similar to it—to work. As you begin, let the image of the success you created in this exercise motivate and inspire you.

■ *Get unstuck:* What will you do if you hit a roadblock? Define two ways to get help with your efforts if you run into trouble. Be ready to pursue more creative ideas if those don't work.

How can you choose a major?

At some point in the next two years, after you complete your general education requirements, you will be asked to declare a *major* (an academic subject area chosen as a field of specialization, requiring a specific course of study). Through this act you largely determine the courses you take, what you learn, and with whom you spend your school time. Your major may also have a significant influence on your future career.

Think of declaring a major as a long-term goal made up of the multiple steps (short-term goals) that follow. You will be wise to start the process now, even though you probably don't need to decide right away—and even if, as is true of many students, you don't yet know what you want to study.

Short-Term Goal #1: Use Learning Styles Assessments to Identify Interests and Talents

Considering what you like and what you do well can lead to a fulfilling area of study. You may have sensed a career direction since you were young, or you may still be figuring out what inspires you. When you identify your interests and talents and choose a major that focuses on them, you are likely to have a positive attitude and perform at your highest level.

To pinpoint the areas that spark your interest, consider the following questions:

- What courses have I enjoyed the most in college and high school? What do these courses have in common?
- What subjects am I drawn to in my personal reading?
- What activities do I look forward to most?
- In what skills or academic areas do I perform best? Am I a "natural" in any area?
- What do people say I do well?
- What are my dominant learning styles? (See chapter 3 for learning styles assessments.)

Short-Term Goal #2: Explore Academic Options

Next, find out about the academic choices available at your school. Plan to achieve the following minigoals in order to reach this short-term goal:

Jim Wilson/ *The New York Times*

If you are aiming for a specific career, explore what majors may support your goals. These software engineers may have majored in information technology or computer science.

Learn what's possible. Consult your college catalog for guidelines on declaring (and changing) your major. Find answers to these questions:

- When do I have to declare a major? (generally at the end of the second year for four-year programs; earlier for associate or certificate programs)
- What are my options in majoring? (double majors, minors, interdisciplinary majors)
- What majors are offered at my school?

If a major looks interesting, explore it further by answering these questions:

- What minimum grade point average (GPA), if any, does the department require before it will accept me as a major?

- What GPA must I maintain in the courses included in the major?
- What preparatory courses (prerequisites) are required?
- What courses will I be required to take and in what sequence? How many credits do I need to graduate in the major?
- Will I have to write a thesis to graduate in this major?

Talk to people who can help. Early on, begin discussing your major with your advisor; he or she can help you evaluate different options. You also may want to ask students who are a year or two ahead of you to describe their experiences with the courses, the workload, and the instructors.

Visit the department. When considering a major, analyze your comfort with the academic department as well as with the material. Some departments are small and close-knit, and others are larger and more wide-ranging. To learn more about the department, ask the department secretary for information. Then sit in on several classes to get a feel for the instructors and the work. Consider asking an instructor for an appointment to discuss the major.

Consider creative options for majoring. Think beyond the traditional majoring path, and investigate the possibilities at your school. One or more of the following may be open to you:

- *Double majors.* If, for example, you want to major in English and philosophy, ask your academic advisor if it is possible to meet the requirements for both departments.
- *Interdisciplinary majors.* If your preferred major isn't in the catalog, consult your advisor. Some schools allow students to design majors with guidance from advisors and instructors.
- *Minors.* A minor involves a concentration of departmental courses but has fewer requirements than a major. Many students choose a minor suited for a career. For example, a sociology major who wants to work in an urban hospital might consider a minor in a language.
- *Majors involving courses outside your school.* Some schools may offer study abroad programs (in which students spend a term or a year at an affiliated college in a different country) or opportunities to take courses at nearby schools. Such courses might apply to a major that interests you.

Short-Term Goal #3: Establish Your Academic Schedule

Look at your time frame. How many years do you plan to study as an undergraduate or graduate student? Do you plan to attend graduate school? If so, do you plan to go there directly after graduation or take time off?

Set timing for short-term goals. Within your time frame, pinpoint when to accomplish the important short-term goals that lead to graduation. What are the deadlines for completing core requirements, declaring a major, writing a thesis? Although you won't need to plan out your entire college course load at the beginning of your first term, drafting a tentative curriculum—both within and outside your major—can help clarify where you are heading. (A *curriculum* is the particular set of courses required for a degree.)

Identify dates connected to your goal fulfillment. Pay attention to academic dates (you will find an academic calendar in each year's college catalog and on the college's Web site). Such dates include registration dates, final date to declare a major, final date to drop a course, and so forth. Plan ahead so you don't miss a deadline.

Be Flexible as You Come to a Decision

As with any serious challenge that involves defining your path, flexibility is essential. Many students change their minds as they consider majors; some declare a major and then change it one or more times before finding a good fit. Just be sure to act on any change right away—once you have considered it carefully—by informing your advisor, completing any required paperwork, and redesigning your schedule to reflect your new choices.

Through this process, you will often be thinking about how well you are using your time. In fact, being able to achieve any significant goal is directly linked to effective time management.

How can you effectively manage your time?

© Norma Cornes—Fotolia

Time is a universal resource; everyone has the same 24 hours in a day, every day. Depending on what's happening in your life, however, your sense of time may change. On some days you feel like you have hours to spare, while on others the clock becomes your worst enemy.

Your challenge is to turn time into a goal-achievement tool. If you think about time before you act, you are more likely to make smart choices about how to use it. Consider each day as a jigsaw puzzle: You have all the pieces in a pile, and your task is to form a picture of how you want your day to look. Successful time management starts with identifying your time-related needs and preferences. This self-knowledge sets the stage for building and managing your schedule, avoiding procrastination, and being flexible in the face of change.

Identify Your Time-Related Needs and Preferences

Body rhythms and habits affect how each person deals with time. Some people are night owls; others are at their best in the morning. Some people are chronically late; others get everything done with time to spare. Individual tendencies become clear as people build up "records" of behavior.

A mismatch between your habits and your schedule causes stress and drains energy. For example, a person who loses steam in the midafternoon may struggle in classes that meet between 3:00 and 5:00 P.M. However, an awareness of your needs and preferences will help you create a schedule that maximizes your strengths and cuts down on stress. If you are a morning person, for example, look for sections of required courses that meet early in the day. If you work best at night, schedule most of your study time at a library that stays open late.

Take the following steps to identify your time-related needs and preferences:

- *Create a personal time "profile."* Ask yourself these questions: At what time of day do I have the most energy? The least energy? Do I tend to be early, on time, or late? Do I focus well for long stretches or need regular breaks? Your answers will help you find the schedule setup that works best for you.

- *Evaluate the effects of your profile.* Which of your time-related habits and preferences will have a positive impact on your success at school? Which are likely to cause problems?

- *Establish what schedule preferences suit your profile best.* Make a list of these preferences—or even map out an ideal schedule as a way of illustrating them. For example, one student's preference list might read: "Classes bunched together on Mondays, Wednesdays, and Fridays. Tuesdays and Thursdays free for studying and research. Study time primarily during the day."

Next, it's time to build the schedule that takes all of this information into account, helping you maximize your strengths and compensate for your weaker time-management areas.

Build a Schedule

You've set up your "goal map," with all of the steps that you need in order to reach your destination. With a schedule you place each step in time and, by doing so, commit to making it happen. Schedules help you gain control of your life in two ways: They provide segments of time for tasks related to the fulfillment of your goals, and they remind you of tasks, events, due dates, responsibilities, and deadlines.

Use a Planner

A planner is the ideal practical tool for managing the time you have scheduled. With it, you can keep track of events and commitments, schedule goal-related tasks, and rank tasks according to priority. Time-management expert Paul Timm says that "rule number one in a thoughtful planning process is: Use some form of a planner where you can write things down."[3]

There are two major types of planners. One is a book or notebook in which to note commitments. If you write detailed daily plans, look for the kind that devotes a page to each day. If you prefer to see more days at a glance, try the kind that shows a week's schedule on a two-page spread. Some planners contain sections for monthly and yearly goals.

The other option is an electronic planner or personal digital assistant (PDA) such as a Palm Pilot, BlackBerry, or Sidekick. Basic PDA functions allow you to schedule days and weeks, note due dates, make to-do lists, perform mathematical calculations, and create and store an address book. You can enter information with an onscreen or attachable keyboard or handwrite with a stylus. You can also transfer information to and from a computer.

Though electronic planners are handy and have a large data capacity, they cost more than the paper versions, and their small size means they can be easy to lose. Analyze your preferences and options, and decide which tool you are most likely to use every day. A dime-store notebook, used conscientiously, may work as well for some people as a top-of-the-line PDA.

© Kevin Mclachlan—Fotolia

Keep Track of Events and Commitments

Your planner is designed to help you schedule and remember events and commitments. A quick look at your notations will remind you when items are approaching. Your syllabus for any class is also a key tool for identifying and noting important dates for when readings and assignments are due and when quizzes and tests will take place (see the sample syllabus on pages 9–10 in chapter 1).

Putting your schedule in writing will help you think ahead to prepare for crunch times. For example, if you see that you have three tests and a presentation coming up all in one week, you may have to rearrange your schedule during the preceding week to create extra study time.

Among the events and commitments worth noting in your planner are these:

- Test and quiz dates, due dates for papers, projects, and presentations
- Details of your academic schedule, including term and holiday breaks
- Club and organizational meetings
- Personal items—medical appointments, due dates for bills, birthdays, social events
- Milestones toward a goal, such as due dates for sections of a project

Although many students don't think to do so, it's important to include class prep time—reading and studying, writing and working on assignments and projects—in the planner. According to one reasonable formula, you should schedule at least two hours of preparation for every hour of class—that is, if you take 15 credits, you should study about 30 hours a week, making your total classroom and preparation time 45 hours.

Surveys have shown, however, that most students study 15 or fewer hours per week, and some study even less—often not enough to master the material. A crucial part of academic success is doing whatever you can to maintain adequate study time. Students who hold jobs or have families, or both, have to fit study time in where they can. These kinds of situations demand creative time management and close attention to following your schedule.

Schedule Tasks and Activities That Support Your Goals

Linking the events in your planner to your goals will give meaning to your efforts and bring order to your schedule. Planning study time for an economics test, for example, will mean more to you if you link the hours you spend to your goal of being accepted into business school. The simple act of relating what you do day to day to what you want in your future has enormous power to move you forward.

Here is how a student might translate her goal of entering business school into action steps over a year's time:

This year:	Complete enough courses to meet curriculum requirements for business school and maintain class standing
This term:	Complete my economics class with a B average or higher
This month:	Set up economics study group schedule to coincide with quizzes and tests

This week: Meet with study group; go over material for Friday's test
Today: Go over chapter 3 in econ text

The student can then arrange her time to move her in the direction of her goal. She schedules activities that support the short-term goal of doing well on the test and writes them in her planner as shown in the example below. Achieving the overarching long-term goal of doing well in a course she needs for business school is the source of her motivation.

Monday	Tuesday	Wednesday	Thursday	Friday	Saturday	Sunday
9 AM: Economics class Talk with study group members to schedule meeting.	3–5 PM: Study econ chapter 3.	9 AM: Economics class Drop by instructor's office hours to ask question about test	6 PM: Go over chapter 3 7–9 PM: Study group meeting.	9 AM: Economics class—Test 3:30 PM: Meet w/advisor to discuss GMAT and other business school requirements	Sleep in— schedule some down time	5 PM: Go over quiz questions with study partner

Before each week begins, remind yourself of your long-term goals and what you can accomplish over the next seven days to move you closer to them. Key 2.2 shows parts of a daily schedule and a weekly schedule.

Indicate Priority Levels

Just as your goals have varying degrees of importance, so too do your daily and weekly tasks. Prioritizing these items boosts scheduling success in two ways. First, it helps you to identify your most important tasks and to focus the bulk of your energy and time on them. Second, it helps you plan when in your day to get things done. Because many top-priority items (classes, work) occur at designated times, prioritizing helps you lock in these activities and schedule less urgent items around them.

Indicate level of importance using three different categories. Identify these categories by using any coding system that makes sense to you. Some people use numbers, some use letters (A, B, C), and some use different-colored pens. The three categories are as follows:

- *Priority 1* items are the most crucial. They may include attending class, completing school assignments, working at a job, picking up a child from day care, and paying bills. Enter Priority 1 items on your planner first, before scheduling anything else.
- *Priority 2* items are important but more flexible parts of your routine. Examples include library study time, completing an assignment for a school club, and working out. Schedule these around Priority 1 items.

KEY 2.2 Note daily and weekly tasks.

Monday, March 14

TIME	TASKS	PRIORITY
6:00 A.M.		
7:00		
8:00	Up at 8am — finish homew	
9:00		
10:00	Business Administration	
11:00	Renew driver's license @ D	
12:00 P.M.		
1:00	Lunch	
2:00	Writing Seminar (peer edit	
3:00	↓	
4:00	check on Ms. Schwartz's o	
5:00	5:30 work out	
6:00	↳ 6:30	
7:00	Dinner	
8:00	Read two chapters for	
9:00	Business Admin.	
10:00	↓	
11:00		
12:00		

Monday, March 28

8		Call: Mike Blair	1
9	BIO 212	Finanical Aid Office	2
10		EMS 262 *Paramedic	3
11	CHEM 203	role-play*	4
12			5
Evening	6pm yoga class		

Tuesday, March 29

8	Finish reading assignment!	Work @ library	1
9			2
10	ENG 112	(study for quiz)	3
11	↓		4
12			5
Evening		↓ until 7pm	

Wednesday, March 30

8		Meet w/advisor	1
9	BIO 212		2
10		EMS 262	3
11	CHEM 203 *Quiz		4
12		Pick up photos	5
Evening	6pm Dinner w/study group		

■ *Priority 3* items are least important—the "it would be nice if I could get to that" items. Examples include phoning a friend, downloading a dozen new songs onto your iPod, and cleaning out a closet. Many people don't enter Priority 3 tasks in their planners until they know they have time for them. Others keep a separate list of these tasks so that when they have free time they can consult it and choose what they want to accomplish.

Use Scheduling Techniques

There are a number of strategies to help you turn your scheduling activities into tools that move you closer to your goals. Five such strategies are discussed here.

Plan regularly. Set aside a regular time each day, and perhaps a longer time at the end of each week, to plan out your schedule. Being methodical about scheduling will help you reduce stress, *manage impulsivity,* and save the hassle

MARCH

SUNDAY	MONDAY	TUESDAY	WEDNESDAY	THURSDAY	FRIDAY	SATURDAY
	1 WORK	2 Turn in English paper topic	3 Dentist 2pm	4 WORK	5	6
7 Frank's birthday	8 Psych Test 9am WORK	9	10 6:30 pm Meeting @ Student Ctr.	11 WORK	12	13 Dinner @ Ryan's
14	15 English paper due WORK	16 Western Civ paper—Library research	17	18 Library 6 p.m. WORK	19 Western Civ makeup class	20
21	22 WORK	23 2 p.m. meeting, psych group project	24 Start running program: 2 miles	25 WORK	26 Run 2 miles	27
28 Run 3 miles	29 WORK	30 Western Civ paper due	30 Run 2 miles			

that might result if you forget something important. However, your planner only helps you when you use it—keep it with you and check it throughout the day.

Make and use to-do lists. Use a to-do list to record the things you want to accomplish on a given day or week. Write your to-do items on a separate piece of paper so you can set priorities. Then transfer the items you plan to accomplish each day to open time periods in your planner. To-do lists are critical time-management tools during exam week and when major projects are due. They will help you rank your responsibilities so that you get things done in order of importance.

Post monthly and yearly calendars at home. Keeping track of your major commitments on a monthly wall calendar will give you the overview you need to focus on responsibilities and upcoming events. Key 2.3 shows a monthly calendar.

TAKE ACTION

GET PREPARED

Make a To-Do List

Manage impulsivity and reduce stress by making a to-do list for what you have to do on your busiest day this week. To build this habit of mind, include all the tasks and events you know about, including attending class and study time, and the activities you would like to do (working out at the gym, watching your favorite TV show) if you have extra time. Then prioritize your list using the coding system of your choice.

Date: _____

1. _____   7. _____
2. _____   8. _____
3. _____   9. _____
4. _____   10. _____
5. _____   11. _____
6. _____   12. _____

After examining this list, record your daily schedule in your planner (if you have a busy day, you may want to list Priority 3 items separately to complete if time permits). At the end of the day, evaluate this system. Did the list help you to manage your time and tasks effectively? If you liked it, use this exercise as a guide for using to-do lists regularly.

If you live with family or friends, create a group calendar to stay aware of each other's plans and avoid scheduling conflicts.

Avoid time traps. Try to stay away from situations that eat up time unnecessarily. Say "no" graciously if you don't have time for a project; curb excess social time that interferes with academics; declare your cell phone off-limits when you study; delegate chores if you find yourself overloaded. Carefully rein in how much time you spend surfing the Internet and instant messaging with friends, because these activities can eat up hours before you know it.

Schedule down time. Leisure time is more than just a nice break—it's essential to your health and success. A little down time will refresh you and actually improve your productivity when you get back on task. Even half an hour a day helps. Fill the time with whatever relaxes you—reading, watching television, chatting online, playing a game or sport, walking, writing, or just doing nothing.

Fight Procrastination

It's human, and common for busy students, to leave difficult or undesirable tasks until later. If taken to the extreme, however, *procrastination*—the act of putting off a task until another time—can develop into a habit that causes serious problems. Being impulsive is often part of procrastinating, as a procrastinator often does not think through the consequences of putting something off.

This excerpt from the Study Skills Library at California Polytechnic State University at San Luis Obispo illustrates how procrastination can quickly turn into a destructive pattern:

> The procrastinator is often remarkably optimistic about his ability to complete a task on a tight deadline. . . . For example, he may estimate that a paper will take only five days to write; he has fifteen days; there is plenty of time, no need to start. Lulled by a false sense of security, time passes. At some point, he crosses over an imaginary starting time and suddenly realizes, "Oh no! I am not in control! There isn't enough time!"
>
> At this point, considerable effort is directed toward completing the task, and work progresses. This sudden spurt of energy is the source of the erroneous feeling that "I work well only under pressure." Actually, at this point you are making progress only because you haven't any choice. . . . Progress is being made, but you have lost your freedom.
>
> Barely completed in time, the paper may actually earn a fairly good grade; whereupon the student experiences mixed feelings: pride of accomplishment (sort of), scorn for the professor who cannot recognize substandard work, and guilt for getting an undeserved grade. But the net result is *reinforcement:* The procrastinator is rewarded positively for his poor behavior ("Look what a decent grade I got after all!"). As a result, the counterproductive behavior is repeated time and time again.[4]

Among the reasons people procrastinate are these:

- *Perfectionism.* According to Jane B. Burka and Lenora M. Yuen, authors of *Procrastination: Why You Do It, What to Do About It,* habitual procrastinators often gauge their self-worth solely by their ability to achieve. In other words, "an outstanding performance means an outstanding person; a mediocre performance means a mediocre person."[5] To the perfectionist procrastinator, not trying at all is better than an attempt that falls short of perfection.

- *Fear of limitations.* Some people procrastinate in order to avoid the truth about what they can achieve. "As long as you procrastinate, you never have to confront the real limits of your ability, whatever those limits are,"[6] say Burka and Yuen. If you procrastinate and fail, you can blame the failure on waiting too long, not on any personal shortcoming.

- *Being unsure of the next step.* If you get stuck and don't know what to do, sometimes it seems easier to procrastinate than to make the leap to the next level of your goal.

- *Facing an overwhelming task.* Some projects are so big that they create immobilizing fear. If a person facing such a task fears failure, she may procrastinate in order to avoid confronting the fear.

Although it can bring relief in the short term, avoiding tasks almost always causes problems, such as a buildup of responsibilities and less time to complete them, work that is not up to par, the disappointment of others who are depending on your work, and stress brought on by the weight of the unfinished tasks. Particular strategies can help you think before you act so that you can avoid procrastination and the problems associated with it.

Analyze the effects of procrastinating. What may happen if you continue to put off a responsibility? You will almost always benefit more in the long run from facing the task head-on.

Set reasonable goals. Unreasonable goals can intimidate and immobilize you. Set manageable goals and allow enough time to complete them.

Break tasks into smaller parts. If you concentrate on achieving one small step at a time, the task may become less burdensome. Setting concrete time limits for each task may help you feel more in control.

Get started whether or not you "feel like it." The motivation techniques from chapter 1 might help you take the first step. Once you start, you may find it easier to continue.

Ask for help. You don't have to go it alone. Once you identify what's holding you up, see who can help you face the task. Another person may come up with an innovative way that you can get moving.

Don't expect perfection. No one is perfect. Most people learn by starting at the beginning, making mistakes, and learning from those mistakes. It's better to try your best than to do nothing at all.

First, reflect on procrastination. What kind of task or situation tends to lead you to procrastinate? When you procrastinate, what are the effects on your work, your feelings, your self-perception, and others around you? Then, think about how the habit of mind of *managing impulsivity* relates to procrastination. What is impulsive about the ways in which you procrastinate? How can managing your impulsivity make you less likely to put off tasks and bring you closer to achieving your goals?

Reward yourself. Find ways to boost your confidence when you accomplish a particular task. Remind yourself—with a break, a movie, some kind of treat—that you are making progress.

Be Flexible

No matter how well you think ahead and plan your time, sudden changes can upend your plans. Any change, whether minor (a room change for a class) or major (a medical emergency), can cause stress. As your stress level rises, your sense of control dwindles.

Although you can't always choose your circumstances, you have some control over how you handle them. Your ability to evaluate situations, come up with creative options, and put practical plans to work will help you manage the changes that you will inevitably encounter. Think of change as part of life, and you will be better prepared to brainstorm solutions when dilemmas arise.

Small changes—the need to work an hour overtime at your after-school job, a meeting that runs late—can result in priority shifts that jumble your schedule. For changes that occur frequently, think through a backup plan ahead of time. For surprises, the best you can do is to keep an open mind about possibilities and rely on your internal and external resources.

When change involves serious problems—your car breaks down and you have no way to get to school, you fail a class and have to consider summer school, a family member develops a medical problem and needs you more at home—use problem-solving skills to help you through. As you will see in chapter 4, problem solving involves identifying and analyzing the problem, brainstorming and exploring possible solutions, and choosing the solution you decide is best. There are resources available at your college to help you throughout this process. Your academic advisor, counselor, dean, financial aid advisor, and instructors may have ideas and assistance.

Change is one of many factors associated with stress. In fact, stress is part of the normal college experience. If you take charge of how you manage stress, then you can keep it from taking charge of you.

How do you cope with the stress of college life?

If you are feeling more stress in your everyday life as a student, you are not alone.[7] Stress levels among college students have increased dramatically, according to an annual survey conducted at the University of California at Los Angeles. More than 30 percent of the freshmen polled at 683 two- and four-year colleges and universities nationwide reported that they frequently felt overwhelmed—almost double the rate in 1985. Stress factors for college students include being in a new environment; facing increased work and difficult decisions; and juggling school, work, and personal responsibilities.

Stress refers to the way in which your mind and body react to pressure. Pressure comes from situations like heavy workloads (final exam week), excitement (being a finalist for the lead in a play), change (new school, new courses), being short on time (working 20 hours a week at a job and finding time to study), or illness (having a head cold that wipes you out for a week).

The Social Readjustment Rating Scale, developed by psychologists T. H. Holmes and R. H. Rahe, measures the intensity of people's reaction to change and the level of stress related to it (see Key 2.4). Holmes and Rahe found that people experience

Stephen Crowley/ *The New York Times*

Activities such as team sports, combining physical activity with camaraderie, can provide stress relief.

KEY   2.4   Use the Holmes-Rahe scale to find your "stress score."

To find your current "stress score," add the values of the events that you experienced in the past year. The higher the number, the greater the stress. Scoring over 300 points puts you at high risk for developing a stress-related health problem. A score between 150 and 299 reduces your risk by 30 percent, and a score under 150 means that you have only a small chance of a problem.

Event	Value	Event	Value
Death of spouse or partner	100	Son or daughter leaving home	29
Divorce	73	Trouble with in-laws	29
Marital separation	65	Outstanding personal achievement	28
Jail term	63	Spouse begins or stops work	26
Personal injury	53	Starting or finishing school	26
Marriage	50	Change in living conditions	25
Fired from work	47	Revision of personal habits	24
Marital reconciliation	45	Trouble with boss	23
Retirement	45	Change in work hours, conditions	20
Changes in family member's health	44	Change in residence	20
Pregnancy	40	Change in schools	20
Sex difficulties	39	Change in recreational habits	19
Addition to family	39	Change in religious activities	19
Business readjustment	39	Change in social activities	18
Change in financial status	38	Mortgage or loan under $10,000	17
Death of a close friend	37	Change in sleeping habits	16
Change to different line of work	36	Change in # of family gatherings	15
Change in # of marital arguments	35	Change in eating habits	15
Mortgage or loan over $10,000	31	Vacation	13
Foreclosure of mortgage or loan	30	Christmas season	12
Change in work responsibilities	29	Minor violation of the law	11

Source: Reprinted from *Journal of Psychosomatic Research, 11*(2), T. H. Holmes and R. H. Rahe, "The Social Readjustment Rating Scale," 1967, with permission from Elsevier.

Stress levels can help or hinder performance. **KEY 2.5**

Source: From *Your Maximum Mind* by Herbert Benson, M.D., copyright © 1987 by Random House, Inc. Used by permission of Time Books, a division of Random House, Inc.

both positive and negative events as stressors. For example, whereas some events like the death of a relative are clearly negative, other stressors, like moving to a new house or even taking a vacation, are generally positive.

At their worst, stress reactions can make you physically ill (chapter 11 will examine stress-related health issues—situations in which stress goes beyond normal levels, causing physical and emotional problems). But stress can also supply the heightened readiness you need to do well on tests, finish assignments on time, prepare for a class presentation, or befriend new people. Your goal is to find a manageable balance. Key 2.5, based on research conducted by Robert M. Yerkes and John E. Dodson, shows that stress can be helpful or harmful, depending on how much you experience.

Successful Time Management and Goal Setting

Dealing with the stress of college life is, and will continue to be, one of your biggest challenges. But here's a piece of good news: Every goal-achievement and time-management strategy you have read in this chapter contributes to your ability to cope with stress. Remember that stress refers to how you react to pressure. When you think ahead and set up effective plans to move toward goals, you reduce pressure. When you set a schedule that works for you and stick to it, you reduce pressure. Less pressure, less stress.

Analyze the relationship between stress and your time-management habits. Often, people create extra stress for themselves without realizing it. For example, say you're a night person with early classes and are consistently stressed about waking up in time for them. Reduce your stress by using scheduling strategies from the time management material earlier in this chapter. If taking later classes isn't a possibility, try to go to bed earlier a few nights a week, nap in the afternoon, or exercise briefly before class to boost energy. Reduce anxiety by thinking before you act.

Stress-Management Strategies

Here are some practical strategies for coping with the day-to-day stress of being a college student:

- *Eat right.* The healthier you are, the stronger you are—and the more able you will be to weather tough situations like all-nighters, illnesses, and challenging academics. Try to maintain a healthy weight, eat a balanced, low-fat diet, and avoid overloading on junk food.
- *Exercise.* Physical exercise will help you manage your stress. Find a type of exercise you like and make it a regular part of your life.
- *Get sleep.* Avoid the systemwide dysfunction that sleep deprivation can create. Figure out how much sleep you need and do your best to get it. When you pull an all-nighter, make sure you play catch-up over the next couple of days.
- *Think positively.* Try to think of all you have to do as challenges, not problems.
- *Seek balance.* A balanced life includes time by yourself—for your thoughts, hopes, and plans—and time for relaxation, in whatever form you choose.
- *Address issues.* Try not to let things lie too long. Analyze stressful situations and use problem-solving strategies (see chapter 4) to decide on a specific plan of action.
- *Set boundaries and learn to say no.* Try to delegate. Review obligations regularly; if you evaluate that something has become a burden, consider dropping it from your list of activities.
- *Surround yourself with people who are good for you.* Focus on friends who listen and support you when things get rough. Friendship and humor go a long way toward reducing stress.

Sometimes you'll be able to pull out the strategies that fit the situation, finding ways to cope with the stress you encounter. Sometimes stress will make you feel frozen, not knowing where to turn to work your way out of it. At those times, remember: *Any step toward a goal is a stress-management strategy because it reduces pressure.* In that sense, this entire book is a stress-management strategy. Every useful tool, from test-taking hints to job-hunting strategies, will help you reduce the pressure and cover the distance toward your dreams.

Even if you're on the right track, you'll get run over if you just sit there.

WILL ROGERS, EARLY 20TH CENTURY HUMORIST

I manage impulsivity.

Student life is, most often, a jumble of responsibilities and events. In the attempt to keep up with everything to do and everywhere to be, students often make impulsive decisions about how to spend their time or try to achieve a challenging goal in a too-short time frame. If you have ever abandoned your studying for a social event or forgotten about an assignment until the night before it was due, you understand how this can happen.

If you can manage your impulsivity—in basic terms, think about the consequences before you make a decision about how to spend your time or achieve a goal—you can boost your success. First of all, mapping out a plan in advance will help you devote an appropriate amount of time to each element, bringing the most ideal results. Second, the act of thinking ahead will help you avoid situations that lead to impulsive decisions. Managing impulsivity means that you give yourself a chance to think—and therefore to succeed.

REMEMBER
THE IMPORTANT POINTS

Why is it important to know what you value?

- Values are principles or qualities that you consider important.
- Values help you to understand what you want out of life, build "rules for life," and find people who inspire you.
- Evaluate values by asking specific questions about their sources and effects.
- In school, values help you to stay committed, choose a major, choose enriching activities, decide what you want out of school, and understand the values of others.

How do you set and achieve goals?

- A goal is an aim or intention—an end toward which you direct your effort.
- Long-term goals have a scope of six months, a year, or may have open-ended time frame.
- Short-term goals are smaller steps, in shorter time frames, toward a long-term goal.
- Prioritizing goals means choosing the most important goals and focusing on them.
- Use a four-step goal-fulfillment strategy to reach your goals.

How can you choose a major?

- Use learning styles assessments to identify interests and talents.
- Explore academic options: see what's possible, get advice from advisors and departments, and explore creative options for majoring.
- Establish your academic schedule.
- Be flexible as you come to a decision.

How can you effectively manage your time?

- Identify your time-related needs and preferences.
- Build a schedule by using a planner, keeping track of events and commitments, scheduling tasks and activities that support your goals, and prioritizing.
- Fight procrastination.
- Be flexible.

How do you cope with the stress of college life?

- Know that stress is common for college students.
- Understand that moderate levels of stress can aid performance.
- Manage your time and set goals effectively.
- Use practical stress-management strategies.

CRITICAL THINKING
APPLYING LEARNING TO LIFE

Use the tables here to record data; answer questions and write additional thoughts on a separate piece of paper or in a journal.

Discover How You Spend Your Time

In the table below, estimate the total time you think you spend per week on each listed activity. Then, add the hours. If your number is over 168 (the number of hours in a week), rethink your estimates and recalculate so that the total is equal to 168.

Activity	Estimated Time Spent	Activity	Estimated Time Spent
Class		Chores and personal business	
Work		Friends and important relationships	
Studying		Telephone time	
Sleeping		Leisure/entertainment	
Eating		Spiritual life	
Family time/child care		Other	
Commuting/travelling		**TOTAL**	

Now, spend a week recording exactly how you spend your time. The chart on pages 62–63 has blocks showing half-hour increments. As you go through the week, write in what you do each hour, indicating when you started and stopped. Don't forget activities that don't feel like "activities," such as sleeping or watching TV. Finally, be sure to record your actual activities instead of how you want to have, or think you should have, spent your time. There are no wrong answers.

After a week, go through the chart and add up how many hours you spent on the activities for which you previously estimated your hours. Tally the hours in the boxes in the table on page 64 using straight tally marks; round off to half hours

Monday		Tuesday		Wednesday		Thursday	
TIME	ACTIVITY	TIME	ACTIVITY	TIME	ACTIVITY	TIME	ACTIVITY
6:00 A.M.		6:00 A.M.		6:00 A.M.		6:00 A.M.	
6:30 A.M.		6:30 A.M.		6:30 A.M.		6:30 A.M.	
7:00 A.M.		7:00 A.M.		7:00 A.M.		7:00 A.M.	
7:30 A.M.		7:30 A.M.		7:30 A.M.		7:30 A.M.	
8:00 A.M.		8:00 A.M.		8:00 A.M.		8:00 A.M.	
8:30 A.M.		8:30 A.M.		8:30 A.M.		8:30 A.M.	
9:00 A.M.		9:00 A.M.		9:00 A.M.		9:00 A.M.	
9:30 A.M.		9:30 A.M.		9:30 A.M.		9:30 A.M.	
10:00 A.M.		10:00 A.M.		10:00 A.M.		10:00 A.M.	
10:30 A.M.		10:30 A.M.		10:30 A.M.		10:30 A.M.	
11:00 A.M.		11:00 A.M.		11:00 A.M.		11:00 A.M.	
11:30 A.M.		11:30 A.M.		11:30 A.M.		11:30 A.M.	
12:00 P.M.		12:00 P.M.		12:00 P.M.		12:00 P.M.	
12:30 P.M.		12:30 P.M.		12:30 P.M.		12:30 P.M.	
1:00 P.M.		1:00 P.M.		1:00 P.M.		1:00 P.M.	
1:30 P.M.		1:30 P.M.		1:30 P.M.		1:30 P.M.	
2:00 P.M.		2:00 P.M.		2:00 P.M.		2:00 P.M.	
2:30 P.M.		2:30 P.M.		2:30 P.M.		2:30 P.M.	
3:00 P.M.		3:00 P.M.		3:00 P.M.		3:00 P.M.	
3:30 P.M.		3:30 P.M.		3:30 P.M.		3:30 P.M.	
4:00 P.M.		4:00 P.M.		4:00 P.M.		4:00 P.M.	
4:30 P.M.		4:30 P.M.		4:30 P.M.		4:30 P.M.	
5:00 P.M.		5:00 P.M.		5:00 P.M.		5:00 P.M.	
5:30 P.M.		5:30 P.M.		5:30 P.M.		5:30 P.M.	
6:00 P.M.		6:00 P.M.		6:00 P.M.		6:00 P.M.	
6:30 P.M.		6:30 P.M.		6:30 P.M.		6:30 P.M.	
7:00 P.M.		7:00 P.M.		7:00 P.M.		7:00 P.M.	
7:30 P.M.		7:30 P.M.		7:30 P.M.		7:30 P.M.	
8:00 P.M.		8:00 P.M.		8:00 P.M.		8:00 P.M.	
8:30 P.M.		8:30 P.M.		8:30 P.M.		8:30 P.M.	
9:00 P.M.		9:00 P.M.		9:00 P.M.		9:00 P.M.	
9:30 P.M.		9:30 P.M.		9:30 P.M.		9:30 P.M.	
10:00 P.M.		10:00 P.M.		10:00 P.M.		10:00 P.M	
10:30 P.M.		10:30 P.M.		10:30 P.M.		10:30 P.M	
11:00 P.M.		11:00 P.M.		11:00 P.M.		11:00 P.M	
11:30 P.M.		11:30 P.M.		11:30 P.M.		11:30 P.M	
12–6 A.M.		12–6 A.M.		12–6 A.M.		12–6 A.M	

| Friday | | Saturday | | Sunday | | Notes |
TIME	ACTIVITY	TIME	ACTIVITY	TIME	ACTIVITY	
6:00 A.M.		6:00 A.M.		6:00 A.M.		
6:30 A.M.		6:30 A.M.		6:30 A.M.		
7:00 A.M.		7:00 A.M.		7:00 A.M.		
7:30 A.M.		7:30 A.M.		7:30 A.M.		
8:00 A.M.		8:00 A.M.		8:00 A.M.		
8:30 A.M.		8:30 A.M.		8:30 A.M.		
9:00 A.M.		9:00 A.M.		9:00 A.M.		
9:30 A.M.		9:30 A.M.		9:30 A.M.		
10:00 A.M.		10:00 A.M.		10:00 A.M.		
10:30 A.M.		10:30 A.M.		10:30 A.M.		
11:00 A.M.		11:00 A.M.		11:00 A.M.		
11:30 A.M.		11:30 A.M.		11:30 A.M.		
12:00 P.M.		12:00 P.M.		12:00 P.M.		
12:30 P.M.		12:30 P.M.		12:30 P.M.		
1:00 P.M.		1:00 P.M.		1:00 P.M.		
1:30 P.M.		1:30 P.M.		1:30 P.M.		
2:00 P.M.		2:00 P.M.		2:00 P.M.		
2:30 P.M.		2:30 P.M.		2:30 P.M.		
3:00 P.M.		3:00 P.M.		3:00 P.M.		
3:30 P.M.		3:30 P.M.		3:30 P.M.		
4:00 P.M.		4:00 P.M.		4:00 P.M.		
4:30 P.M.		4:30 P.M.		4:30 P.M.		
5:00 P.M.		5:00 P.M.		5:00 P.M.		
5:30 P.M.		5:30 P.M.		5:30 P.M.		
6:00 P.M.		6:00 P.M.		6:00 P.M.		
6:30 P.M.		6:30 P.M.		6:30 P.M.		
7:00 P.M.		7:00 P.M.		7:00 P.M.		
7:30 P.M.		7:30 P.M.		7:30 P.M.		
8:00 P.M.		8:00 P.M.		8:00 P.M.		
8:30 P.M.		8:30 P.M.		8:30 P.M.		
9:00 P.M.		9:00 P.M.		9:00 P.M.		
9:30 P.M.		9:30 P.M.		9:30 P.M.		
10:00 P.M.		10:00 P.M.		10:00 P.M.		
10:30 P.M.		10:30 P.M.		10:30 P.M.		
11:00 P.M.		11:00 P.M.		11:00 P.M.		
11:30 P.M.		11:30 P.M.		11:30 P.M.		
12–6 A.M.		12–6 A.M.		12–6 A.M.		

and use a short tally mark for each half hour. In the third column, total the hours for each activity. Leave the "Ideal Time in Hours" column blank for now.

Activity	Time Tallied Over One-Week Period	Total Time in Hours	Ideal Time in Hours
Example: Class	IHI IHI IHI Ii	16.5	
Class			
Work			
Studying			
Sleeping			
Eating			
Family time/child care			
Commuting/traveling			
Chores and personal business			
Friends and important relationships			
Telephone time			
Leisure/entertainment			
Spiritual life			
Other			

Add the totals in the third column to find your grand total. Compare your grand total to your estimated grand total; compare your actual activity hour totals to your estimated activity hour totals. Use a separate sheet of paper to answer the following questions:

■ What matches and what doesn't? Describe the most interesting similarities and differences.

■ Where do you waste the most time? What do you think that is costing you?

Now evaluate what kinds of changes might improve your ability to achieve goals. Analyze what you do daily, weekly, and monthly. Go back to the chart and fill in the "Ideal Time in Hours" column. Consider the difference between actual hours and ideal hours. Ask questions:

■ On what activities do you think you should spend more or less time?

■ What are you willing to do to change, and why?

Finally, write a short paragraph describing two key time-management changes in detail. Describe what goal you are aiming for, and map out how you plan to put the changes into action.

TEAM BUILDING

COLLABORATIVE SOLUTIONS

Multiple Paths to a Goal

In a group of three or four, brainstorm goals that focus on building a life skill—for example, leadership, teamwork, learning a language. Write your ideas on a piece of paper. From that list, pick out one goal to explore together.

Each group member takes two minutes alone to think about this goal in terms of the first goal-achievement step on page 42—defining a strategy. In other words, answer the question "How would I do it?" Each person writes down all of the paths he or she can think of.

The group then gathers and everyone shares their strategies. The group evaluates strategies and chooses one that seems effective. Finally, as a group, brainstorm the rest of the goal-achievement process, based on the chosen strategy or path:

- *Set a timetable.* When do you plan to reach your goal? Discuss different time frames and how each might change the path.

- *Be accountable.* What safeguards will keep you on track? Talk about different ways to make sure you are moving ahead consistently.

- *Get unstuck.* What will you do if you hit a roadblock? Brainstorm the kinds of roadblocks that could get in the way of this goal. For each, come up with ways to overcome the obstacle.

At the end of the process, you should have a wealth of ideas for how to approach one particular goal—and an appreciation for how many paths you could take in order to get there.

I recognize that my ability to **manage impulsivity** and think before I act is essential for successful goal setting, time management, and stress management. Here is something that I do, related to goal setting or time or stress management, that I would like to change:

_____

_____

_____

This is the result that I want to achieve when I take action:

_____

Here is why making this change is in my best interest:

_____

_____

Here are three strategies from the chapter that I think will help me make this change:

1. _____

2. _____

3. _____

Here is what actually happened when I put one or more of these strategies to work:

_____

_____

_____

How am I doing? **Later in the term, be accountable for your progress on page 139.**

SUGGESTED READINGS

Allen, David. *Getting Things Done: The Art of Stress-Free Productivity.* New York: Penguin Books, 2003.

Burka, Jane B., and Lenora M. Yuen. *Procrastination: Why You Do It, What to Do About It.* Cambridge, MA: Da Capo Press, 2004.

Covey, Stephen. *The Seven Habits of Highly Effective People.* New York: Free Press, 2004.

Emmett, Rita. *The Procrastinator's Handbook: Mastering the Art of Doing It Now.* New York: Walker, 2000.

Gleeson, Kerry. *The Personal Efficiency Program: How to Get Organized to Do More Work in Less Time,* 2nd ed. New York: Wiley, 2000.

Lakein, Alan. *How to Get Control of Your Time and Your Life.* New York: New American Library, 1996.

Leyden-Rubenstein, Lori. *The Stress Management Handbook.* New York: McGraw-Hill, 1999.

Sapadin, Linda, and Jack Maguire. *Beat Procrastination and Make the Grade: The Six Styles of Procrastination and How Students Can Overcome Them.* New York: Penguin USA, 1999.

Timm, Paul R. *Successful Self-Management: A Psychologically Sound Approach to Personal Effectiveness.* Los Altos, CA: Crisp Publications, 1996.

INTERNET RESOURCES

Mind Tools: Time Management (**www.mindtools.com/pages/main/newMN_HTE.htm**)

Top Achievement: Goal Setting (**www.topachievement.com**)

About.com: Stress Management (**http://stress.about.com/**)

Troubled With: Stress (**www.troubledwith.com**)

ENDNOTES

1. Background information for the discussion of cultural diversity is from Afsaneh Nahavandi and Ali Malekzadeh, *Organizational Behavior: The Person–Organization Fit,* Upper Saddle River, NJ: Prentice Hall, 1999.

2. Cited in Louis E. Boone and David L. Kurtz, *Contemporary Business Communication,* Upper Saddle River, NJ: Prentice Hall, 1994, p. 643.

3. Paul Timm, *Successful Self-Management: A Psychologically Sound Approach to Personal Effectiveness,* Los Altos, CA: Crisp Publications, 1987, pp. 22–41.

4. William E. Sydnor, "Procrastination," California Polytechnic State University Study Skills Library, based on *Overcoming Procrastination* by Albert Ellis, accessed May 2003 (**www.sas.calpoly.edu/asc/ssl/procrastination.html**). Used with permission.

5. Jane B. Burka and Lenora M. Yuen, *Procrastination: Why You Do It, What to Do About It,* Reading, MA: Perseus Books, 1983, pp. 21–22.

6. Ibid.

7. The following articles were used as sources in this section: Glenn C. Altschuler, "Adapting to College Life in an Era of Heightened Stress," *New York Times,* Education Life, Section 4A, August 6, 2000, p. 12; Carol Hymowitz and Rachel Emma Silverman, "Can Workplace Stress Get Worse?" *Wall Street Journal,* January 16, 2001, p. B1; Robert M. Sapolsky, "Best Ways to Reduce Everyday Levels of Stress . . . Bad Ol' Stress," *Bottom Line Personal,* January 15, 2000, p. 13; Kate Slaboch, "Stress and the College Student: A Debate," accessed April 4, 2001 (**www.jour.unr.edu/outpost/voices/voi.slaboch.stress.html**); University of South Florida, Counseling Center for Human Development, "Coping with Stress in College," accessed April 4, 2001 (**http://usfweb.usf.edu/counsel/self-hlp/stress.htm**); Jodi Wilgoren, "Survey Shows High Stress Levels in College Freshmen," *New York Times,* January 23, 2000, p. NA.

Gather data through all senses

"Intelligent people know that all information gets into the brain through the sensory pathways. . . . Those whose sensory pathways are open [and] alert absorb more information from the environment."

ART COSTA

GATHER DATA THROUGH ALL SENSES

When you use your senses to take in information and then observe your response, you build self-awareness. The greater your self-awareness, the better able you will be to understand how you learn and relate to others. This understanding has the potential to fuel your success in school and beyond.

Visiting a spice market in Morocco on the north coast of Africa, the senses come alive. As you smell the spices, taste the flavors, and see the colors on display, you discover what is new and different.

Your senses play the same role as you discover the new and different both among other people and within yourself. The layers of diversity *within you*—physical being, personality, talents, skills, and thinking abilities—make you a distinctive individual, with a particular style of learning. Differences *among people* include skin color, gender, ethnicity and national origin, age, physical characteristics and abilities, sexual orientation, cultural and religious beliefs and practices, education and socioeconomic status, family background, and marital and parental status.

This chapter builds your awareness of diversity, helping you to identify your learning styles, relate to others in a culturally competent way, and practice communication strategies that will promote successful relationships and add meaning to your life.

In this chapter, you explore answers to the following questions:

- How can you discover your learning styles?
- What are the benefits of knowing how you learn?
- How can you develop cultural competence?
- How can you communicate effectively?

Photo: Carol Carter

How can you discover your learning styles?

Your style of taking in, responding to, and remembering information is as unique as you are. Have you ever thought in detail about what that style is? Doing just that—working to understand your learning strengths and preferences and the primary ways in which you interact with others—will help you achieve your personal best in school and beyond.

> Do not go where the path may lead, go instead where there is no path and leave a trail.

RALPH WALDO EMERSON, WRITER, PHILOSOPHER, POET, ESSAYIST

© Olivier Salaun—Fotolia

This chapter presents two assessments designed to help you figure out how you learn and interact. The first—Multiple Pathways to Learning—focuses on learning strengths and preferences and is based on Howard Gardner's Multiple Intelligences theory. The second—the Personality Spectrum—is based on the Myers-Briggs Type Inventory® (MBTI) and helps you evaluate how you react to people and situations.

The Value of Learning Styles Assessments

Everyone has some things they do well and other things they find difficult. Successful learners maximize their strengths and compensate for their weaknesses. The first step toward that goal is knowing what those strengths and weaknesses *are*—and that's what these assessments will help you discover. With the information you gain from the Multiple Pathways to Learning and the Personality Spectrum, you can choose your own best ways to study, manage time, remember material, and much more.

Knowing how you learn will help you set specific goals for positive change. For example, instead of saying "I'm no good at math," you can strengthen your math skills with what you've learned from Multiple Pathways to Learning. You might draw diagrams of math problems if you are a visual learner or talk out problems with a study partner if you are an interpersonal learner. (You will learn about these and other learning styles later in the chapter.) The better you know yourself, the better you are able to handle different learning situations and challenges.

Gaining an understanding of *learning style*—a particular way in which the mind receives and processes information—will also enhance your ability to appreciate how people differ. When you sit in a classroom with 30 students, you can be sure that each person is learning the material in a unique way. The more you know about how others approach learning, the more you can use that understanding to improve communication and teamwork.

Putting Assessment Results in Perspective

First, remember that any assessment is simply a snapshot, a look at who you are at a given moment. Your answers can, and will, change as you and the circumstances around you change. These assessments help you look at the present—and plan for the future—by asking questions: "Who am I right now?" "How does this compare with who I want to be?"

Second, there are no "right" answers, no "best" set of scores. Think of your responses in the same way you would if you were trying on a new set of eyeglasses to correct blurred vision. The glasses will not create new paths and possibilities, but they will help you see more clearly the ones that already exist.

Following each assessment is information about the typical traits of, and appropriate study strategies for, each intelligence or personality spectrum dimension. As you will see from your scores, you have abilities in all areas, though some are more developed than others. Therefore, you will find useful suggestions under all the headings. Try different techniques, *use what your senses tell you* to evaluate how effective they are, and keep what works for you.

Assess Your Multiple Intelligences

In 1983, Howard Gardner, a Harvard University professor, changed the way people perceive intelligence and learning with his theory of Multiple Intelligences. Gardner believes that there are at least eight intelligences possessed by all people, and that every person has developed some of these intelligences more fully than others (see Key 3.1 for descriptions). He defines *intelligence* as "an ability to solve problems or fashion products that are useful in a particular cultural setting or community." According to this theory, when you find a task or subject easy, you are probably using a more fully

	Each intelligence is linked to specific abilities.	KEY 3.1

Intelligence	Description
Verbal-Linguistic	Ability to communicate through language (listening, reading, writing, speaking)
Logical-Mathematical	Ability to understand logical reasoning and problem solving (math, science, patterns, sequences)
Bodily-Kinesthetic	Ability to use the physical body skillfully and to take in knowledge through bodily sensation (coordination, working with hands)
Visual-Spatial	Ability to understand spatial relationships and to perceive and create images (visual art, graphic design, charts and maps)
Interpersonal	Ability to relate to others, noticing their moods, motivations, and feelings (social activity, cooperative learning, teamwork)
Intrapersonal	Ability to understand one's own behavior and feelings (self-awareness, independence, time spent alone)
Musical	Ability to comprehend and create meaningful sound and recognize patterns (music, sensitivity to sound and patterns)
Naturalistic	Ability to understand features of the environment (interest in nature, environmental balance, ecosystem, stress relief brought by natural environments)

Each intelligence has a set of numbered statements. Consider each statement on its own. Then, on a scale from 1 (lowest) to 4 (highest), rate how closely it matches who you are right now and write that number on the line next to the statement. Finally, total each set of six questions.

1. _____ I enjoy physical activities.
2. _____ I am uncomfortable sitting still.
3. _____ I prefer to learn through doing.
4. _____ When sitting I move my legs or hands.
5. _____ I enjoy working with my hands.
6. _____ I like to pace when I'm thinking or studying.
_____ TOTAL for **BODILY-KINESTHETIC**

1. _____ I enjoy telling stories.
2. _____ I like to write.
3. _____ I like to read.
4. _____ I express myself clearly.
5. _____ I am good at negotiating.
6. _____ I like to discuss topics that interest me.
_____ TOTAL for **VERBAL-LINGUISTIC**

1. _____ I use maps easily.
2. _____ I draw pictures/diagrams when explaining ideas.
3. _____ I can assemble items easily from diagrams.
4. _____ I enjoy drawing or photography.
5. _____ I do not like to read long paragraphs.
6. _____ I prefer a drawn map over written directions.
_____ TOTAL for **VISUAL-SPATIAL**

1. _____ I like math in school.
2. _____ I like science.
3. _____ I problem-solve well.
4. _____ I question how things work.
5. _____ I enjoy planning or designing something new.
6. _____ I am able to fix things.
_____ TOTAL for **LOGICAL-MATHEMATICAL**

1. _____ I listen to music.
2. _____ I move my fingers or feet when I hear music.
3. _____ I have good rhythm.
4. _____ I like to sing along with music.
5. _____ People have said I have musical talent.
6. _____ I like to express my ideas through music.
_____ TOTAL for **MUSICAL**

1. _____ I need quiet time to think.
2. _____ I think about issues before I want to talk.
3. _____ I am interested in self-improvement.
4. _____ I understand my thoughts and feelings.
5. _____ I know what I want out of life.
6. _____ I prefer to work on projects alone.
_____ TOTAL for **INTRAPERSONAL**

1. _____ I like doing a project with other people.
2. _____ People come to me to help settle conflicts.
3. _____ I like to spend time with friends.
4. _____ I am good at understanding people.
5. _____ I am good at making people feel comfortable.
6. _____ I enjoy helping others.
_____ TOTAL for **INTERPERSONAL**

1. _____ I enjoy nature whenever possible.
2. _____ I think about having a career involving nature.
3. _____ I enjoy studying plants, animals, or oceans.
4. _____ I avoid being indoors except when I sleep.
5. _____ As a child I played with bugs and leaves.
6. _____ When I feel stressed I want to be out in nature.
_____ TOTAL for **NATURALISTIC**

Source: Developed by Joyce Bishop, Ph. D., Golden West College, Huntington Beach, CA. Based on Howard Gardner, *Frames of Mind: The Theory of Multiple Intelligences,* New York: HarperCollins, 1993.

MULTIPLE PATHWAYS TO LEARNING

For each intelligence, shade the box in the row that corresponds with the range where your score falls. For example, if you scored 17 in Bodily-Kinesthetic intelligence, you would shade the middle box in that row; if you scored a 13 in Visual-Spatial, you would shade the last box in that row. When you have shaded one box for each row, you will see a "map" of your range of development at a glance.

A score of 20–24 indicates a high level of development in that particular type of intelligence, 14–19 a moderate level, and below 14 an underdeveloped intelligence.

	20–24 (HIGHLY DEVELOPED)	14–19 (MODERATELY DEVELOPED)	BELOW 14 (UNDERDEVELOPED)
Bodily-Kinesthetic			
Visual-Spatial			
Verbal-Linguistic			
Logical-Mathematical			
Musical			
Interpersonal			
Intrapersonal			
Naturalistic			

KEY 3.2   How to put your multiple intelligences to work for you.

Abilities and Skills Associated with Each Intelligence	Study Techniques to Maximize Each Intelligence
VERBAL-LINGUISTIC • Analyzing own use of language • Remembering terms easily • Explaining, teaching, learning, using humor • Understanding syntax and word meaning • Convincing someone to do something	**VERBAL-LINGUISTIC** • Read text; highlight no more than 10% • Rewrite notes • Outline chapters • Teach someone else • Recite information or write scripts/debates
MUSICAL-RHYTHMIC • Sensing tonal qualities • Creating/enjoying melodies, rhythms • Being sensitive to sounds and rhythms • Using "schemas" to hear music • Understanding the structure of music	**MUSICAL-RHYTHMIC** • Create rhythms out of words • Beat out rhythms with hand or stick • Play instrumental music/write raps • Put new material to songs you already know • Take music breaks
LOGICAL-MATHEMATICAL • Recognizing abstract patterns • Reasoning inductively and deductively • Discerning relationships and connections • Performing complex calculations • Reasoning scientifically	**LOGICAL-MATHEMATICAL** • Organize material logically • Explain material sequentially to someone • Develop systems and find patterns • Write outlines and develop charts and graphs • Analyze information
VISUAL-SPATIAL • Perceiving and forming objects accurately • Recognizing relationships between objects • Representing something graphically • Manipulating images • Finding one's way in space	**VISUAL-SPATIAL** • Develop graphic organizers for new material • Draw mind maps • Develop charts and graphs • Use color in notes to organize • Visualize material (method of loci)
BODILY-KINESTHETIC • Connecting mind and body • Controlling movement • Improving body functions • Expanding body awareness to all senses • Coordinating body movement	**BODILY-KINESTHETIC** • Move or rap while you learn; pace and recite • Use "method of loci" or manipulatives • Move fingers under words while reading • Create "living sculptures" • Act out scripts of material, design games
INTRAPERSONAL • Evaluating own thinking • Being aware of and expressing feelings • Understanding self in relation to others • Thinking and reasoning on higher levels	**INTRAPERSONAL** • Reflect on personal meaning of information • Visualize information/keep a journal • Study in quiet settings • Imagine experiments
INTERPERSONAL • Seeing things from others' perspectives • Cooperating within a group • Communicating verbally and nonverbally • Creating and maintaining relationships	**INTERPERSONAL** • Study in a group • Discuss information • Use flash cards with others • Teach someone else
NATURALISTIC • Deep understanding of nature • Appreciation of the delicate balance in nature	**NATURALISTIC** • Connect with nature whenever possible • Form study groups of people with like interests

Source: Adapted from David Lazear, *Seven Pathways of Learning,* Tucson: Zephyr Press, 1994.

developed intelligence. When you have trouble, you may be using a less developed intelligence.[1]

Gardner believes that the way you learn is a unique blend of intelligences, resulting from your distinctive abilities, challenges, experiences, and training. In addition, ability in the intelligences may develop or recede as your life changes. Gardner thinks that the traditional view of intelligence—based on mathematical, logical, and verbal measurements—doesn't reflect the entire spectrum of human ability:

> I believe that we should . . . look . . . at more naturalistic sources of information about how peoples around the world develop skills important to their way of life. Think, for example, of sailors in the South Seas, who find their way around hundreds, or even thousands, of islands by looking at the constellations of stars in the sky, feeling the way a boat passes over the water, and noticing a few scattered landmarks. A word for intelligence in a society of these sailors would probably refer to that kind of navigational ability.[2]

The Multiple Pathways to Learning assessment helps you determine the levels to which your eight intelligences are developed. Key 3.2, immediately following the assessment, describes specific skills associated with the eight intelligences as well as study techniques that maximize each. Finally, the Multiple Intelligence Strategies grids in chapters 5 through 11 will demonstrate how to apply your learning styles knowledge to key college success skills.

Assess Your Personality with the Personality Spectrum

Personality assessments help you understand how you respond to the world around you—including information, thoughts, feelings, people, and events. The assessment used in this chapter is based on one of the most widely used personality inventories in the world—the Myers-Briggs Type Inventory (MBTI), developed by Katharine Briggs and her daughter, Isabel Briggs Myers. It also relies upon the work of David Keirsey and Marilyn Bates, who combined the 16 Myers-Briggs types into four temperaments and developed an assessment called the Keirsey Sorter based on those temperaments.

The Personality Spectrum assessment adapts and simplifies their material into four personality types—Thinker, Organizer, Giver, and Adventurer—and was developed by Joyce Bishop. The Personality Spectrum helps you identify the kinds of interactions that are most, and least, comfortable for you. Key 3.3, which follows the assessment, shows techniques that improve performance, learning strategies, and ways of relating to others for each personality type.

Gathering data through the senses helps you learn about yourself as you react to the information your senses take in. Before you take the assessments in this chapter, use this habit of mind to describe how you react to different academic subjects and environments. In the kind of learning environment that you find comfortable or engaging, what are you seeing (setting, number of students), hearing (topics, style of lecture or conversation, background sound), touching (what you're sitting on), and smelling? What are you seeing, hearing, touching, and smelling in a learning environment that you don't like?

PERSONALITY SPECTRUM

STEP 3. Plot these numbers on the brain diagram on the next page.

STEP 1. Rank order all four responses to each question from most like you (4) to least like you (1) so that for each question you use the numbers 1, 2, 3, and 4 one time each. Place numbers in the boxes next to the responses.

1. I like instructors who
   a. ☐ tell me exactly what is expected of me.
   b. ☐ make learning active and exciting.
   c. ☐ maintain a safe and supportive classroom.
   d. ☐ challenge me to think at higher levels.

2. I learn best when the material is
   a. ☐ well organized.
   b. ☐ something I can do hands-on.
   c. ☐ about understanding and improving the human condition.
   d. ☐ intellectually challenging.

3. A high priority in my life is to
   a. ☐ keep my commitments.
   b. ☐ experience as much of life as possible.
   c. ☐ make a difference in the lives of others.
   d. ☐ understand how things work.

4. Other people think of me as
   a. ☐ dependable and loyal.
   b. ☐ dynamic and creative.
   c. ☐ caring and honest.
   d. ☐ intelligent and inventive.

5. When I experience stress I would most likely
   a. ☐ do something to help me feel more in control of my life.
   b. ☐ do something physical and daring.
   c. ☐ talk with a friend.
   d. ☐ go off by myself and think about my situation.

6. I would probably not be close friends with someone who is
   a. ☐ irresponsible.
   b. ☐ unwilling to try new things.
   c. ☐ selfish and unkind to others.
   d. ☐ an illogical thinker.

7. My vacations could be described as
   a. ☐ traditional.
   b. ☐ adventuresome.
   c. ☐ pleasing to others.
   d. ☐ a new learning experience.

8. One word that best describes me is
   a. ☐ sensible.
   b. ☐ spontaneous.
   c. ☐ giving.
   d. ☐ analytical.

STEP 2. Add up the total points for each letter.

TOTAL FOR a. ☐ Organizer b. ☐ Adventurer c. ☐ Giver d. ☐ Thinker

STEP 3. Plot these numbers on the brain diagram on the next page.

PERSONALITY SPECTRUM

SCORING DIAGRAM FOR PERSONALITY SPECTRUM

Write your scores in the four squares just outside the brain diagram—Thinker score at top left, Giver score at top right, Organizer score at bottom left, and Adventurer score at bottom right.

   Each square has a line of numbers that go from the square to the center of the diagram. For each of your four scores, place a dot on the appropriate number in the line near that square. For example, if you scored 15 in the Giver spectrum, you would place a dot between the 14 and 16 in the upper right-hand line of numbers. If you scored a 26 in the Organizer spectrum, you would place a dot on the 26 in the lower left-hand line of numbers.

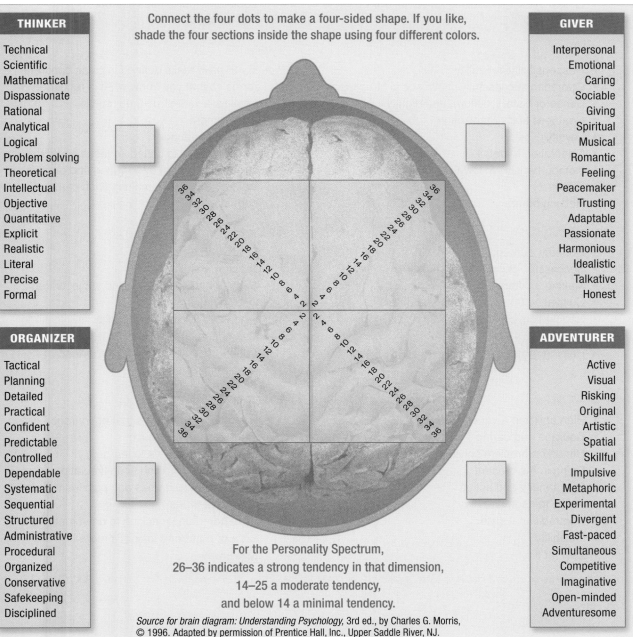

Connect the four dots to make a four-sided shape. If you like, shade the four sections inside the shape using four different colors.

THINKER

Technical
Scientific
Mathematical
Dispassionate
Rational
Analytical
Logical
Problem solving
Theoretical
Intellectual
Objective
Quantitative
Explicit
Realistic
Literal
Precise
Formal

GIVER

Interpersonal
Emotional
Caring
Sociable
Giving
Spiritual
Musical
Romantic
Feeling
Peacemaker
Trusting
Adaptable
Passionate
Harmonious
Idealistic
Talkative
Honest

ORGANIZER

Tactical
Planning
Detailed
Practical
Confident
Predictable
Controlled
Dependable
Systematic
Sequential
Structured
Administrative
Procedural
Organized
Conservative
Safekeeping
Disciplined

ADVENTURER

Active
Visual
Risking
Original
Artistic
Spatial
Skillful
Impulsive
Metaphoric
Experimental
Divergent
Fast-paced
Simultaneous
Competitive
Imaginative
Open-minded
Adventuresome

For the Personality Spectrum,
26–36 indicates a strong tendency in that dimension,
14–25 a moderate tendency,
and below 14 a minimal tendency.

Source for brain diagram: Understanding Psychology, 3rd ed., by Charles G. Morris, © 1996. Adapted by permission of Prentice Hall, Inc., Upper Saddle River, NJ.

KEY 3.3 How to put your Personality Spectrum to work for you.

Characteristics of Each Personality Type	Study Techniques to Maximize Personality Types
THINKER	**THINKER**
• Solving problems • Developing models and systems • Analytical and abstract thinking • Exploring ideas and potentials • Ingenuity • Going beyond established boundaries • Global thinking—seeking universal truth	• Find time to reflect independently on new information • Learn through problem solving • Design new ways of approaching issues • Convert material into logical charts • Try to minimize repetitive tasks • Look for opportunities to work independently
ORGANIZER	**ORGANIZER**
• Responsibility, reliability • Operating successfully within social structures • Sense of history, culture, and dignity • Neatness and organization • Loyalty • Orientation to detail • Comprehensive follow-through on tasks • Efficiency • Helping others	• Try to have tasks defined in clear, concrete terms so that you know what is required • Look for a well-structured, stable environment • Request feedback • Use a planner to schedule tasks and dates • Organize material by rewriting and organizing class or text notes, making flash cards, or carefully highlighting
GIVER	**GIVER**
• Honesty, authenticity • Successful, close relationships • Making a difference in the world • Cultivating potential of self and others • Negotiation; promoting peace • Openness • Helping others	• Study with others • Teach material to others • Seek out tasks, groups, and subjects that involve helping people • Find ways to express thoughts and feelings clearly and honestly • Put energy into your most important relationships
ADVENTURER	**ADVENTURER**
• High ability in a variety of fields • Courage and daring • Hands-on problem solving • Living in the present • Spontaneity and action • Ability to negotiate • Nontraditional style • Flexibility • Zest for life	• Look for environments that encourage nontraditional approaches • Find hands-on ways to learn • Seek people who you find stimulating • Use or develop games and puzzles to help memorize terms • Fight boredom by asking to do something extra or perform a task in a more active way

Source: Joyce Bishop, in Carol Carter, Joyce Bishop, and Sarah Lyman Kravits, *Keys to Success*, 3rd ed., Upper Saddle River, NJ: Prentice Hall, 2001.

What are the benefits of knowing how you learn?

Generally, self-knowledge helps you make choices that boost your strong areas and help you manage the weaker ones. For example, understanding what you value can help you choose friends who cheer on your successes as well as friends who broaden your horizons with their different perspectives. Likewise for learning style: When you know your multiple intelligences and personality traits, you can choose strategies that will help you learn more, remember better, and use your knowledge more successfully—in any academic or workplace situation.

Study Benefits

Knowing how you learn helps you choose study techniques that capitalize on your strengths. For example, if you learn successfully from a linear, logical presentation, you can look for order (for example, a chronology or a problem–solution structure) as you review notes. If you are a strong interpersonal learner, you can try to work in study groups whenever possible.

Learning style also points you toward strategies that help with tasks and topics that don't come so easily. An Adventurer who does *not* respond well to linear information, for example, has two choices when faced with logical presentations. She can apply her strengths to the material—for example, she might find a hands-on approach. Or she can work on her ability to handle the material by developing study skills that work well for Thinker-dominant learners.

When you study with others, an understanding of diverse learning styles will help you assign tasks effectively and learn more comprehensively. An interpersonal learner might take the lead in teaching material to others; an Organizer might be the schedule coordinator for the group; a naturalistic learner might present information in a new way that helps to solidify concepts.

Librado Romero/ *The New York Times*

These students, listening to podcasts while studying pieces at the Museum of Modern Art, are engaging verbal-linguistic and visual-spatial learning skills with the help of technology.

Classroom Benefits

Your college instructors will most likely have a range of teaching styles (an instructor's teaching style often reflects his or her dominant learning style). Your particular learning style may work well with some instructors but be a mismatch with others. After several class meetings, you should be able to assess an instructor's teaching styles (see Key 3.4). Then you can use what you know to maximize styles that suit you and compensate for those that don't.

KEY 3.4   Instructors often rely on one or more teaching styles.

Teaching Style	What to Expect in Class
Lecture, verbal focus	Instructor speaks to the class for the entire period, with little class interaction. Lesson is taught primarily through words, either spoken or written on the board, overhead projector, handouts, or text.
Group discussion	Instructor presents material but encourages class discussion.
Small groups	Instructor presents material and then breaks class into small groups for discussion or project work.
Visual focus	Instructor uses visual elements such as diagrams, photographs, drawings, transparencies.
Logical presentation	Instructor organizes material in a logical sequence, such as by time or importance.
Random presentation	Instructor tackles topics in no particular order, and may jump around a lot or digress.

Although presentation styles vary, the standard lecture is still the norm in most classrooms. For this reason, the traditional college classroom is generally a happy home for the verbal or logical learner and the Thinker and the Organizer. However, many students learn best when interacting more than a lecture allows. What can you do **when your sensory data tell you** that your styles don't match up with those of your instructor? Here are three suggestions:

■ *Play to your strengths.* For example, a musical learner with an instructor who delivers material in a random way might read lecture highlights into an MP3 player to listen to as a study tool. Likewise, a Giver taking a straight lecture course with no student-to-student contact might meet with a study group to go over the details and fill in factual gaps.

■ *Work to strengthen weaker areas.* As a visual learner reviews notes from a structured lecture course, he could outline them, allot extra time to master the material, and work with a study group. A Thinker, studying for a test from notes delivered by an Adventurer instructor, could find hands-on ways to review the material (for example, for a science course, working in the lab).

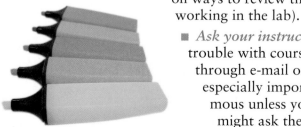

© Nicola Gavin—Fotolia

■ *Ask your instructor for additional help.* If you are having trouble with course work, communicate with your instructor through e-mail or face-to-face during office hours. This is especially important in large lectures where you are anonymous unless you speak up. The visual learner, for example, might ask the instructor to recommend graphs or figures that illustrate the lecture.

Instructors are unique. No instructor can give each of a diverse group of learners exactly what each one needs. The flexibility that you need to mesh your learning style with your instructors' teaching styles is a tool for career and life success. Just as you can't hand-pick your instructors, you will rarely, if ever, be able to choose your supervisors or their work styles.

Workplace Benefits

Knowing how you learn brings you these benefits in your career:

- *Better performance through self-awareness.* Because your learning styles are essentially the same as your working styles, knowing how you learn will help you identify career and work environments that suit you. Knowing your strengths will help you use and highlight them on the job. When a task involves one of your weaker skills, you can either take special care to accomplish it or suggest someone else who is a better fit.
- *Better teamwork.* The more attuned you are to abilities and personality traits, the better you will be at identifying the tasks you and others can best perform in team situations. For example, a Giver might enjoy helping new hires get used to the people and environment. Or a supervisor directing an intrapersonal learner might offer the chance to take material home to think about before a meeting.
- *Better career planning.* The more you know about how you learn and work, the more you will be able to focus on career paths that could work well for you. For example, strengths in logical-mathematical and interpersonal intelligence may guide a student toward specific jobs and activities while in school, such as science tutoring or participating in the math honor society, as well as help him choose career goals.

How can you develop cultural competence?

Being sensitive to your unique learning style will benefit you in ways beyond your education and career. A better understanding of your learning strengths and preferences and personality traits will help you identify, appreciate, and adapt to the diversity among people. In college you are likely to meet classmates or instructors who reflect America's growing diversity, including the following:

- Bi- or multiracial individuals or those who come from families with more than one religious tradition
- Non-native English speakers who may have emigrated from other countries
- People older than "traditional" 18- to 22-year-old students
- Persons living with various kinds of disabilities
- Persons practicing different lifestyles—often expressed in the way they dress, their interests, their sexual orientation, and their leisure activities

Being able to appreciate and adjust to differences among people is crucial to your success at school, at work, and in your personal relationships. You can

Gathering Data
Through the Senses

Courtesy of the Library of Congress

Charles Darwin collected and studied insects, birds' eggs,
seashells, and plants throughout his childhood in England.
As a man, he journeyed abroad in the early 1830s
to see native plants and animals firsthand.

Through the acuity of his observations, Darwin
revolutionized natural science when he concluded
that species evolve over time through the process of natural selection.

accomplish this goal by questioning and posing problems in a way that helps you to develop cultural competence.

As you learned in chapter 2, *cultural competence* refers to the ability to understand and appreciate differences among people and change your behavior in a way that enhances, rather than detracts from, relationships and communication. According to the National Center for Cultural Competence, to develop cultural competence you must act upon the following five steps:[3]

1. Value diversity.
2. Identify and evaluate personal perceptions and attitudes.
3. Be aware of opportunities and challenges that occur when different cultures interact.
4. Build knowledge about other cultures.
5. Use what you learn to adapt to diverse cultures as you encounter them.

As you develop cultural competence, you heighten your ability to analyze how people relate to one another. Most important, you become better equipped to connect to others by bridging the gap between who you are and who they are.[4]

Value Diversity

Valuing diversity means having a basic respect for, and acceptance of, the differences among people. Every time you meet someone new, you have a choice about how to interact. If you value diversity, you will choose to treat people with tolerance and respect, avoid assumptions about them, and grant them the right to think, feel, and believe without being judged.

Being open-minded in this way will help your relationships thrive, as shown in Key 3.5. Even though you won't like every person you meet, you can make an effort to show respect while focusing on the person as an individual.

Identify and Evaluate Personal Perceptions and Attitudes

Whereas people may value the *concept* of diversity, attitudes and emotional responses may influence how they act when they confront the *reality* of diversity in their own lives. As a result, many people have prejudices that lead to damaging stereotypes.

Prejudice

Almost everyone has some level of *prejudice*—preconceived judgment or opinion, formed without just grounds or sufficient knowledge—resulting in the prejudging of others, usually on the basis of characteristics such as gender, race, sexual orientation, and religion. People judge others without knowing anything about them because of factors like these:

■ *Influence of family and culture:* Children learn attitudes—including intolerance, superiority, and hate—from their parents, peers, and community.

KEY 3.5   Approaching diversity with an open mind builds relationships.

Your Role	Situation	Closed-Minded Actions	Open-Minded Actions
Fellow student	For an assignment, you are paired with a student old enough to be your mother.	You assume the student will be clueless about the modern world. You think she might preach to you about how to do the assignment.	You get to know the student as an individual. You stay open to what you can learn from her experiences and knowledge.
Friend	You are invited to dinner at a friend's house. When he introduces you to his partner, you realize that he is gay.	You are turned off by the idea of two men in a relationship. You make an excuse to leave early. You avoid your friend after that.	You have dinner with the two men and make an effort to get to know more about them, individually and as a couple.
Employee	Your new boss is of a different racial and cultural background from yours.	You assume that you and your new boss don't have much in common. You think he will be distant and uninterested in you.	You rein in your stereotypes. You pay close attention to how your new boss communicates and leads. You adapt to his style and make an effort to get to know him better.

- *Fear of differences:* It is human to fear the unfamiliar and to make assumptions about it.
- *Experience:* One bad experience with a person of a particular race or religion may lead someone to condemn all people with the same background.

When students react negatively to foreign-born teaching assistants, for example, they may be demonstrating prejudice rather than a genuine inability to comprehend their speech. In a recent experiment, University of Georgia professor Donald L. Rubin played the same taped lecture to two groups of undergraduate students. The lecturer, who spoke in a clear male voice, sounded like he came from middle America. As the students listened, an image of the speaker was projected at the front of the classroom. For half of the students, the projected image showed an American named "John Smith from Portland." For the other half, the image showed an Asian named "Li Wenshu from Beijing." Both men dressed in similar professional clothing. Students were then asked to fill in missing words from a transcript of the lecture. They made 20% more mistakes when looking at the image of Li Wenshu than when looking at John Smith.

To professor Rubin, these results demonstrate the impact of unconscious prejudice:

> Students who expect that non-native instructors will be poor instructors and unintelligible speakers can listen to what we know to be the most standard English speech and the most well-formed lecture, and yet experience some difficulties in comprehension. All the pronunciation improvements in the world will not by itself halt the problem of students' dropping classes or complaining about their instructors' language.[5]

Stereotypes

Prejudice is usually based on *stereotypes*—standardized mental pictures or assumptions made, without proof or critical thinking, about the characteristics of a person or group of people. Stereotyping emerges from factors such as these:

- *Desire for patterns and logic:* People often try to make sense of the world by using the labels, categories, and generalizations that stereotypes provide.
- *Media influences:* The more people see stereotypical images—the airhead beautiful blonde, the jolly fat man—the easier it is to believe that stereotypes are universal.
- *Laziness:* Labeling group members according to a characteristic they seem to have in common takes less energy than asking questions that illuminate the qualities of individuals.

Stereotypes stall the growth of relationships, because labeling a person makes it hard to see the real person underneath. Even stereotypes that seem "positive" may be untrue and may get in the way of perceiving uniqueness. Key 3.6 lists some "positive" and "negative" stereotypes.

Use critical thinking to question your own ideas and beliefs, weed out the narrowing influence of prejudice and stereotyping, and discover problems that

Stereotypes involve generalizations that may not be accurate.   **KEY   3.6**

Positive Stereotype	Negative Stereotype
Women are nurturing.	Women are too emotional for business.
African Americans are great athletes.	African Americans struggle in school.
Hispanic Americans are family oriented.	Hispanic Americans have too many kids.
White people are successful in business.	White people are cold and power hungry.
Gay men have a great sense of style.	Gay men are sissies.
People with disabilities have strength of will.	People with disabilities are bitter.
Older people are wise.	Older people are set in their ways.
Asian Americans are good at math and science.	Asian Americans are poor leaders.

need addressing. Giving honest answers to questions like the following is an essential step in the development of cultural competence:

- How do I react to differences?
- What prejudices or stereotypes come to mind when I see people, in real life or the media, who are a different color than I am? From a different culture? Making different choices?
- Where did my prejudices and stereotypes come from?
- Are these prejudices fair? Are these stereotypes accurate?
- What harm can having these prejudices and believing these stereotypes cause?

With the knowledge you build as you answer these questions, move on to the next stage: Looking carefully at what happens when people from different cultures interact.

Think about this quote (source unknown): "Stereotypes are devices for saving a biased person the trouble of learning." Now write about a time or period in your life when you felt stereotyped—in regard to gender, age, race, ethnicity, appearance, weight, financial status, disability, or some other factor. First, describe the situation or event. Then reflect in writing on the following questions: Why did this happen? How did it make you feel? What bias did one or more people hold, and how did it prevent them from learning? What have *you* learned as a result of what happened?

Be Aware of Opportunities and Challenges That Occur When Cultures Interact

Interaction among people from different cultures can promote learning, build mutual respect, and broaden perspectives. However, as history has shown, such interaction can also produce problems caused by lack of understanding, prejudice, and stereotypic thinking. At their mildest, these problems create roadblocks that obstruct relationships and communication. At their worst, they set the stage for acts of discrimination and hate crimes.

Discrimination

Discrimination refers to actions that deny people equal employment, educational, and housing opportunities, or treat people as second-class citizens. Federal law says that you cannot be denied basic opportunities and rights because of your race, creed, color, age, gender, national or ethnic origin, religion, marital status, potential or actual pregnancy, or potential or actual illness or disability (unless the illness or disability prevents you from performing required tasks and unless accommodations are not possible).

Despite these legal protections, discrimination is common and often appears on college campuses. Students may not want to work with students of other races. Members of campus clubs may reject prospective members because of religious differences. Outsiders may harass students attending gay and lesbian alliance meetings. Instructors may judge students according to their weight, accent, or body piercings.

Hate Crimes

When prejudice turns violent, it often manifests itself in *hate crimes*—crimes motivated by a hatred of a specific characteristic thought to be possessed by the victim—directed at racial, ethnic, and religious minorities and homosexuals, as in these examples:

- In Wyoming in 1998, Matthew Shepard, a gay college student, was kidnapped and tied to a fence where his captors beat and abandoned him. He died of his injuries.
- In California in 1999, Buford O. Furrow Jr. entered a community center and shot five people because they were Jewish. He then shot and killed a Filipino American letter carrier.

The increase in hate crimes in recent years is alarming. According to FBI statistics, reported hate crimes more than doubled from 1991 to 2001.[6] Incidents categorized as hate crimes include simple assault (the most common hate crime), aggravated assault, forcible sex offenses, arson, manslaughter, and murder. Because the statistics include only reported incidents, they tell just a part of the story—many more crimes likely go unreported by victims fearful of what might happen if they contact authorities.

Focusing on the positive aspect of intercultural interaction starts with awareness of the ideas and attitudes that lead to discrimination and hate crimes. With this awareness, you will be more able to push past the negative possibilities and open your mind to how you can learn and grow.

Build Cultural Knowledge

The thinking response to discrimination and hate, and the next step in your path toward cultural competence, is to gather knowledge. You have a personal responsibility to learn about people who are different from you, including those you are likely to meet on campus.

What are some ways to begin?

Keith Meyers/*The New York Times*

Building cultural knowledge can involve interacting with students from different cultures, learning a new language, or even trying an unfamiliar food.

- *Read* newspapers, books, magazines, and Web sites.
- *Ask questions* of all kinds of people, about themselves and their traditions.
- *Observe* how people behave, what they eat and wear, how they interact with others.
- *Travel internationally* to unfamiliar places where you can experience different ways of living.
- *Travel locally* to equally unfamiliar, but nearby, places that are home to a variety of people.
- *Build friendships* with fellow students or coworkers you would not ordinarily approach.

Building knowledge also means exploring yourself. Talk with family, read, seek experiences that educate you about your own cultural heritage. Then share what you know with others.

Adapt to Diverse Cultures

Here's where you take everything you have gathered—your value of diversity, your self-knowledge, your understanding of how cultures interact, your information about different cultures—and put it to work. As you question and uncover problems, you can define actions and solutions that improve how you relate to others, and perhaps even change how people relate to one another on a larger scale. Choose actions that feel right to you, that cause no harm, and that may make a difference, however small.

Martin Luther King Jr. believed that careful thinking could change attitudes. He said:

> The tough-minded person always examines the facts before he reaches conclusions; in short, he postjudges. The tender-minded person reaches conclusions before he has examined the first fact; in short, he prejudges and is prejudiced. . . . There is little hope for us until we become tough-minded enough to break loose from the shackles of prejudice, half-truths, and downright ignorance.[7]

Let the following suggestions inspire your own creative ideas about what you can do to improve how you relate to others:

- *Look past external characteristics.* If you meet a woman with a disability, get to know her. She may be an accounting major, a daughter, and a mother. She may love baseball, politics, and science fiction novels. These characteristics—not just her physical person—describe who she is.

- *Put yourself in other people's shoes.* Shift your perspective and ask questions about what other people feel, especially if there's a conflict. If you make a comment that someone interprets as offensive, for example, question why what you said was hurtful. If you can talk about it with the person, you may learn even more about how he or she heard what you said and why.

- *Adjust to cultural differences.* When you understand someone's way of being and put it into practice, you show respect and encourage communication. If a friend's family is formal at home, dress appropriately and behave formally when you visit. If an instructor maintains a lot of personal space, keep a respectful distance when you visit during office hours. If a study group member takes offense at a particular kind of language, avoid it when you meet.

- *Help others in need.* When you see or uncover a problem, do what you can to help solve it. Newspaper columnist Sheryl McCarthy wrote about an African American man who, in the midst of the 1992 Los Angeles riots, saw an Asian American man being beaten and helped him to safety. "When asked why he risked grievous harm to save an Asian man he didn't even know," she reported, "the African American man said, 'Because if I'm not there to help someone else, when the mob comes for me, will there be someone there to save me?'"[8]

- *Stand up against prejudice, discrimination, and hate.* When you hear a prejudiced remark or notice discrimination taking place, ask questions about

TAKE ACTION

Make a Difference

Put the strategies listed in the section titled "Adapt to Diverse Cultures" (see pages 88–89) to positive use. Rethink one strategy as a question—for example, "Help others in need" becomes "Who is in need? How can I help?" Then, answer the question with a specific action to which you commit. The answer to the questions in this example might be: "Students who are just beginning to master the writing process need help with papers. I can sign up to tutor in the Writing Center."

Chosen strategy:

Question(s):

Answer(s)/action(s):

Action taken on this date:

When you do what you've planned, focus on *gathering data from your senses* as much as possible. On a separate sheet of paper, describe what you saw, heard, and felt during the experience. Use what you learn from this habit of mind to clarify your reaction to the experience and to decide whether you will continue it in the future.

how to encourage a move in the right direction. You may choose to make a comment, or to get help by approaching an authority such as an instructor or dean. Sound the alarm on hate crimes—let authorities know if you suspect that a crime is about to occur, join campus protests, support organizations that encourage tolerance.

■ *Recognize that people everywhere have the same basic needs.* Everyone loves, thinks, hurts, hopes, fears, and plans. When you are trying to find common ground with diverse people, remember that you are united first through your essential humanity.

Diversity also occurs in the way people communicate. Effective communication helps people of all cultures understand one another and make connections. Understanding who you are and how you learn, and how people differ from one another, will help you communicate effectively.

How can you communicate effectively?

Clear-spoken communication promotes success at school, at work, and in relationships. Successful communicators analyze and adjust to communication styles, learn to give and receive criticism, analyze and make use of body language, and identify and resolve communication problems.

Adjust to Communication Styles

When you speak, your goal is for listeners to receive the message as you intended. Problems arise when one person has trouble "translating" a message coming from someone using a different communication style. Your knowledge of the Personality Spectrum will help you understand and analyze the ways diverse people communicate.

Identifying Communication Styles

Following are some communication styles that tend to be associated with the four dimensions of the Personality Spectrum. No one style is better than another. Successful communication depends on understanding your personal style and becoming attuned to the styles of others.

Thinker-dominant communicators focus on facts and logic. As speakers, they tend to rely on logical analysis to communicate ideas and prefer quantitative concepts to those that are conceptual or emotional. As listeners, they often do best with logical messages. Thinkers may also need time to process what they have heard before responding. Written messages—on paper or via e-mail—are often useful for these individuals because writing can allow time for them to put ideas together logically.

Organizer-dominant communicators focus on structure and completeness. As speakers, they tend to deliver well-thought-out, structured messages that fit into an organized plan. As listeners, they often appreciate a well-organized message that defines practical tasks in concrete terms. As with Thinkers, a written format is often an effective form of communication to or from an Organizer.

Giver-dominant communicators focus on concern for others. As speakers, they tend to cultivate harmony, analyzing what will promote closeness in relationships. As listeners, they often appreciate messages that emphasize personal connection and address the emotional side of an issue. Whether speaking or listening, Givers often favor in-person talks over written messages.

Adventurer-dominant communicators focus on the present. As speakers, they focus on creative ideas, tending to convey a message as soon as the idea arises and move on to the next activity. As listeners, they appreciate up-front, short, direct messages that don't get sidetracked. Like Givers, Adventurers tend to communicate and listen more effectively in person.

What is your style? Use this information as a jumping-off point for your self-exploration. Just as people tend to demonstrate characteristics from more than one dimension of the Personality Spectrum, communicators also may demonstrate different styles. Analyze your style by thinking about the communication styles associated with your dominant Personality Spectrum dimensions. Compare them to how you tend to communicate and how others seem to respond to you. Then, ask yourself questions about what works best for you as a communicator.

Speakers Adjust to Listeners

Listeners may interpret messages in ways you never intended. Think about solutions to this kind of problem as you read the following example involving a Giver-dominant instructor and a Thinker-dominant student (the listener):

Instructor: "Your essay didn't communicate any sense of your personal voice."

Student: "What do you mean? I spent hours writing it. I thought it was on the mark."

© OlgaLIS—Fotolia

- *Without adjustment:* The instructor ignores the student's need for detail and continues to generalize. Comments like "You need to elaborate" "Try writing from the heart" or "You're not considering your audience" might confuse or discourage the student.
- *With adjustment:* Greater logic and detail will help. For example, the instructor might say: "You've supported your central idea clearly, but you didn't move beyond the facts into your interpretation of what they mean. Your essay reads like a research paper. The language doesn't sound like it is coming directly from you."

Listeners Adjust to Speakers

As a listener, improve understanding by being aware of stylistic differences and translating the message into one that makes sense to you. The following example of an Adventurer-dominant employee speaking to an Organizer-dominant supervisor shows how adjusting can pay off.

Employee: "I'm upset about the e-mail you sent me. You never talked to me directly and you let the problem build into a crisis. I haven't had a chance to defend myself."

- *Without adjustment:* If the supervisor is annoyed by the employee's insistence on direct personal contact, he or she may become defensive: "I told you clearly what needs to be done. I don't know what else there is to discuss."
- *With adjustment:* In an effort to improve communication, the supervisor responds by encouraging the in-person exchange that is best for the employee: "Let's meet after lunch so you can explain to me how you believe we can improve the situation."

Know How to Give and Receive Criticism

Although adjusting to communication styles helps you speak and listen more effectively, you also need to understand, and learn how to effectively give and receive, criticism. Criticism can be either *constructive*—in other words, promoting improvement or development—or nonconstructive. Constructive criticism is a problem-solving strategy involving goodwill suggestions for improving a situation. In contrast, nonconstructive criticism focuses on what went wrong, doesn't offer alternatives or help that might help solve the problem, and is often delivered negatively, creating bad feelings.

When offered constructively, criticism can help bring about important changes. Consider a case in which someone has continually been late to study group sessions. The group leader can comment in one of two ways. Which comment would encourage you to change your behavior?

- *Constructive.* The group leader talks privately with the student, saying, "I've noticed that you've been late a lot. We count on you, because our success depends on what each of us contributes. Is there a problem that is keeping you from being on time? Can we help?"
- *Nonconstructive.* The leader watches the student arrive late and says, in front of everyone, "If you can't start getting here on time, there's really no point in your coming."

At school, instructors criticize classwork, papers, and exams. On the job, criticism may come from supervisors, coworkers, or customers. No matter the source, constructive comments can help you grow. Be open to what you hear, and remember that most people want you to succeed.

Offering Constructive Criticism

When offering constructive criticism, use the following strategies to be effective:

- *Criticize the behavior rather than the person.* Avoid personal attacks. "You've been late to five group meetings" is much preferable to "You're lazy."
- *Define the problematic behavior specifically.* Try to focus on the facts, substantiating with specific examples and minimizing emotions. Avoid additional complaints—people can hear criticisms better if they are discussed one at a time.
- *Suggest new approaches and offer help.* Talk about ways of handling the situation. Work with the person to develop creative options. Help the person feel supported.
- *Use a positive approach and hopeful language.* Express the conviction that changes will occur and that the person can turn the situation around.

Receiving Criticism

When you are on criticism's receiving end, use the following techniques:

- *Analyze the comments.* Listen carefully, then evaluate what you heard. What does it mean? What is the intent? Try to let nonconstructive comments go without responding.
- *Request suggestions on how to change your behavior.* Ask, "How would you like me to handle this in the future?"
- *Summarize the criticism and your response to it.* Make sure everyone understands the situation.
- *Use a specific strategy.* Use problem-solving skills to analyze the problem, brainstorm ways to change, choose a strategy, and take action to make it happen.

Understand Body Language

Because thoughts and feelings may be communicated nonverbally as well as verbally, you will become a more effective communicator if you understand body language. Body language has an extraordinary capacity to express people's real feelings through gestures, eye movements, facial expressions, body positioning and posture, touching behaviors, vocal tone, and use of personal space. Why is it important to know how to analyze body language?

- *Nonverbal cues shade meaning.* What you say can mean different things depending on body positioning or vocal tone. The statement "That's a great idea" sounds positive. However, said while sitting with your arms and legs crossed and looking away, it may communicate that you dislike the idea. Said sarcastically, the tone may reveal that you consider the idea a joke.
- *Culture influences how body language is interpreted.* For example, in the United States, looking away from someone may be a sign of anger or distress; in Japan, the same behavior is usually a sign of respect.
- *Nonverbal communication strongly influences first impressions.* First impressions emerge from a combination of verbal and nonverbal cues. Nonverbal elements, including tone of voice, posture, eye contact, and speed and style of movement, usually come across first and strongest.

Although reading body language is not an exact science, the following strategies will help you use it to improve communication:

- *Pay attention to what is said through nonverbal cues.* Focus on your tone, your body position, whether your cues reinforce or contradict your words. Then do the same for those with whom you are speaking. Look for the level of meaning in the physical.

- *Note cultural differences.* Cultural factors influence how individuals interpret nonverbal cues. In cross-cultural conversation, discover what seems appropriate by paying attention to what the other person does consistently, and by noting how others react to what you do.

- *Adjust body language to the person or situation.* What body language might you use when making a presentation in class? Meeting with your advisor? Confronting an angry coworker? Ask questions about how to use your physicality to communicate successfully.

Michelle V. Agins/*The New York Times*

Nonverbal cues are a significant part of communication. These medical students are participating in a program designed to boost doctors' ability to observe and interpret facial expressions and other nonverbal elements.

Body language can also be useful when speaking with someone who is struggling with your language. You can use physical cues and gestures to fill in what words can't say.

Manage Conflict

One of the biggest barriers to successful communication is conflict, which can result in anger and even violence. With effort, you can successfully manage conflict and stay away from those who cannot.

Conflicts, both large and small, arise when there is a clash of ideas or interests. You may have small conflicts with a housemate over a door left unlocked. You may have major conflicts with your partner about finances or with an instructor about a failing grade. Conflict, as unpleasant as it can be, is a natural element in the dynamic of getting along with others. Prevent it when you can—and when you can't, use problem-solving strategies to resolve it.

Conflict Prevention Strategies

The following two strategies can help you to prevent conflict from starting in the first place.

Sending "I" messages. "I" messages help you communicate your needs rather than attacking someone else. Creating these messages involves some simple rephrasing: "You didn't lock the door!" becomes "I felt uneasy when I came to work and the door was unlocked." Similarly, "You never called last night" becomes "I was worried when I didn't hear from you last night."

"I" statements soften the conflict by highlighting the effects that the other person's actions have on you, rather than focusing on the other person or the actions themselves. These statements help the receiver feel freer to respond, perhaps offering help and even acknowledging mistakes.

Being assertive. Most people tend to express themselves in one of three ways—aggressively, assertively, or passively. *Aggressive* communicators focus primarily on their own needs and can become impatient when needs are not satisfied. *Passive* communicators focus primarily on the needs of others and often deny themselves power, causing frustration. *Assertive* communicators are able to declare and affirm their own opinions while respecting the rights of others to do the same. Assertive behavior strikes a balance between aggression and passivity and promotes the most productive communication. Key 3.7 contrasts the characteristics of these three styles.

What can aggressive and passive communicators do to move toward a more assertive style of communication? Aggressive communicators might take time before speaking, use "I" statements, listen to others, and avoid giving orders. Passive communicators might acknowledge anger, express opinions, exercise the right to make requests, and know that their ideas and feelings are important.

Conflict Resolution

All too often, people deal with conflict through *avoidance* (a passive tactic that shuts down communication) or *escalation* (an aggressive tactic that often leads to fighting). Conflict resolution demands calm communication, motivation, and careful thinking. Use your thinking skills to apply the problem-solving approach you will learn in chapter 4.

Trying to calm anger is an important part of resolving conflict. All people get angry at times—at people, events, and themselves. However, excessive

	Assertiveness fosters successful communication.	KEY 3.7

Aggressive	Assertive	Passive
Loud, heated arguing	Expressing feelings without being nasty or overbearing	Concealing one's own feelings
Blaming, name-calling, and verbal insults	Expressing oneself and giving others the chance to express themselves	Feeling that one has no right to express anger
Walking out of arguments before they are resolved	Using "I" statements to defuse arguments	Avoiding arguments
Being demanding: "Do this"	Asking and giving reasons: "I would appreciate it if you would do this, and here's why . . ."	Being noncommittal: "You don't have to do this unless you really want to . . ."

anger can contaminate relationships, stifle communication, and turn away friends and family.

Manage Anger

Strong emotions can get in the way of happiness and success. It is hard to concentrate on American history when you are raging over being cut off in traffic or can't let go of your anger with a friend. Psychologists report that angry outbursts may actually make things worse. When you feel yourself losing control, try some of these anger management techniques:

- *Relax.* Breathe slowly. Repeat a calming phrase or word like "Take it easy" or "Relax."
- *Change your environment.* Take a break from what's upsetting you. Go for a walk, go to the gym, see a movie. Come up with some creative ideas about what might calm you down.
- *Think before you speak.* When angry, most people tend to say the first thing that comes to mind, even if it's hurtful. Inevitably, this escalates the hard feelings and the intensity of the argument. Instead, wait until you are in control before you say something.
- *Do your best to solve a problem, but remember that not all problems can be solved.* Instead of blowing up, think about how you can handle what's happening. Analyze a challenging situation, make a plan, resolve to do your best, and begin. If you fall short, you will know you made an effort and be less likely to turn your frustration into anger.
- *Get help if you can't keep your anger in check.* If you consistently lash out, you may need the help of a counselor. Many schools have mental health professionals available to students.

Your ability to communicate and manage anger and conflict has a major impact on your relationships with friends and family. Successful relationships are built on self-knowledge, good communication, and hard work.

MULTIPLE INTELLIGENCE STRATEGIES FOR COMMUNICATION

Using techniques corresponding to your stronger intelligences boosts your communication skills both as a speaker and as a listener.

INTELLIGENCE	SUGGESTED STRATEGIES	WHAT WORKS FOR YOU? WRITE NEW IDEAS HERE
Verbal-Linguistic	▪ Find opportunities to express your thoughts and feelings to others—either in writing or in person. ▪ Remind yourself that you have two ears and only one mouth. Listening is more important than talking.	
Logical-Mathematical	▪ Allow yourself time to think through solutions before discussing them—try writing out a logical argument on paper and then rehearsing it orally. ▪ Accept the fact that others may have communication styles that vary from yours and that may not seem logical.	
Bodily-Kinesthetic	▪ Have an important talk while walking or performing a task that does not involve concentration. ▪ Work out physically to burn off excess energy before having an important discussion.	
Visual-Spatial	▪ Make a drawing or diagram of points you want to communicate during an important discussion. ▪ If your communication is in a formal classroom or work setting, use visual aids to explain your main points.	
Interpersonal	▪ Observe how you communicate with friends. If you tend to dominate the conversation, brainstorm ideas about how to communicate more effectively. ▪ Remember to balance speaking with listening.	
Intrapersonal	▪ When you have a difficult encounter, take time alone to evaluate what happened and to decide how you can communicate more effectively next time. ▪ Remember that, in order for others to understand clearly, you may need to communicate more than you expect to.	
Musical	▪ Play soft music during an important discussion if it helps you, making sure it isn't distracting to the others involved.	
Naturalistic	▪ Communicate outdoors if that is agreeable to all parties. ▪ If you have a difficult exchange, imagine how you might have responded differently had it taken place outdoors.	

Choose Communities That Enhance Your Life

Personal relationships often take place within *communities*, or groups that include people who share your interests—for example, sororities and fraternities, athletic clubs, and political groups. The presence of the Internet has added chat rooms, blogs, and newsgroups to the scope of social communities available to you. Some colleges even put their Facebooks online and have school-sponsored online communities.

> It's amazing what ordinary people can do if they set out without preconceived notions.

CHARLES F. KETTERING, AUTHOR, *WINGS OF WISDOM*

© Piotr Sikora—Fotolia

So much of what you accomplish in life is linked to your network of personal contacts. If you affiliate with communities that are involved in positive activities, you are more likely to surround yourself with responsible and character-rich people who may become your friends and colleagues. You may find among them your future spouse or partner, your best friend, a person who helps you land a job, your doctor, accountant, real estate agent, and so on. Finding and working with a community of people with similar interests can have positive effects in personal relationships and in workplace readiness.

If you find yourself drawn toward groups that encourage negative and even harmful behavior—such as organizations that haze pledges, gangs, or mean-spirited online communities—stop and think. Analyze why you are drawn to these groups. Resist the temptation to join in. If you are already involved and want out, stand up for yourself and be determined.

I will gather data through all senses.

The senses are your pathway to the world. The only way to gather information about something or someone is through some combination of hearing, seeing, smelling, tasting, and feeling. This information is the "raw material" on which learning and relationships are built. For this reason, processing the information gathered through the senses is one of the foundations of learning about the people and world around you.

Learning more about yourself and others means staying aware of the information that comes your way as you act. When you open your sensory pathways as you participate in experiences, you become better able to discover what you enjoy or learn easily as well as what you have trouble with or dislike. These discoveries will help to lead you to the values, academic focus, personal relationships, and life choices that are right for you.

REMEMBER
THE IMPORTANT POINTS

How can you discover your learning styles?

- *Learning style* refers to how you take in, respond to, and remember information.
- Knowing your learning style helps you maximize strengths and compensate for weaknesses.
- Assess your Multiple Intelligences. Howard Gardner developed Multiple Intelligence theory; everyone has some level of ability in eight different intelligences.
- Assess your personality with the Personality Spectrum, which focuses on how you respond to people and the world around you. The four dimensions are based on the Myers-Briggs Type Inventory.

What are the benefits of knowing how you learn?

- You can choose study techniques that capitalize on strengths and help with challenges.
- In the classroom, you can adjust to instructor teaching styles.
- At work, you can have better self-awareness, teamwork, and career planning.

How can you develop cultural competence?

- Value diversity; respect and accept the differences among people.
- Identify and evaluate personal perceptions and attitudes.
  - Evaluate prejudice.
  - Look for stereotyping.
- Be aware of opportunities and challenges that occur when cultures interact.
  - Combat discrimination.
  - Avoid hate crimes.
- Learn more about other cultures.
- Adapt to diverse cultures by relating to others in active, compassionate ways.

How can you communicate effectively?

- Identify your communication style and adjust to the different styles of others.
- Know how to give constructive criticism as well as receive criticism.
- Understand how to use and analyze body language.
- Use strategies to manage and prevent conflict.
- Manage anger.
- Choose communities that enhance your life and motivate you in positive ways.

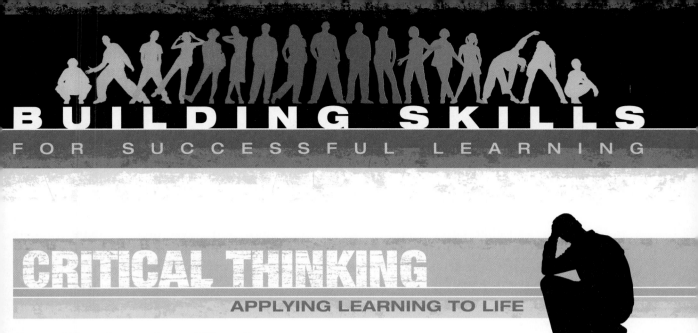

BUILDING SKILLS

FOR SUCCESSFUL LEARNING

CRITICAL THINKING

APPLYING LEARNING TO LIFE

Expand Your Perception of Diversity

Being able to respond to people as individuals requires that you become more aware of the diversity that is not always on the surface. First, brainstorm 10 words or phrases that describe you. Keep references to your ethnicity or appearance (brunette, Cuban American, wheelchair dependent, and so on) to a minimum, and primarily include characteristics others can't see at a glance (laid-back, only child, 24 years old, drummer, marathoner, interpersonal learner, and so on).

1. _____
2. _____
3. _____
4. _____
5. _____

6. _____
7. _____
8. _____
9. _____
10. _____

Second, name two values or beliefs that govern how you live.

_____

_____

Third, describe a particular choice you have made that tells something about who you are.

_____

_____

When you have finished this portion of the exercise, join with a partner in your class, preferably someone you don't know well. Your goal is to communicate to your partner what you have written here, and for your partner to communicate to you in the same way. Talk to each other for 10 minutes, and take notes on what the other person says. At the end of that period, join together as a class. Each person will describe his or her partner to the class.

On your own time, think about what you learned about your partner that surprised you or went against any assumptions you may have made about that person. Reflect on how this exercise may have altered your perspective on yourself and on others.

TEAM BUILDING

COLLABORATIVE SOLUTIONS

Ideas About Personality Types

Divide into groups according to the four types of the Personality Spectrum—Thinker-dominant students in one group, Organizer-dominant students in another, Giver-dominant students in a third, and Adventurer-dominant students in the fourth. (If you have scored the same in more than one of these types, join whatever group is smaller.) With your group, brainstorm the following lists for your type:

1. The strengths of this type
2. The struggles it brings
3. The stressors (things that cause stress) for this type
4. Career areas that tend to suit this type
5. Career areas that are a challenge for this type
6. People who clash with this type the most (often because they are strong in areas where this type needs to grow)

If there is time, each group can present this information to the entire class; this will boost understanding and acceptance of diverse ways of relating to information and people.

I recognize that my ability to **gather data through all senses** *is necessary for me to develop an accurate, useful vision of who I am as a learner and communicator. I will synthesize everything I have been exploring about myself into one comprehensive self-portrait. I will design my portrait in "think link" style, using words and visual shapes to describe my dominant Multiple Intelligences, Personality Spectrum dimensions, abilities and interests, diverse characteristics, and anything else that I have discovered through my sensory self-exploration. (Use your own paper to create a self-portrait, following the guidelines suggested here.)*

When you have finished your self-portrait, study it for a moment. What pops out to you as a significant quality or strength that will be an important tool to help you get through the term?

_____

Conversely, what emerges as a challenge that you will have to focus on this term?

_____

What learning styles- or communication-related strategies from this chapter do you plan to employ to emphasize this strength and face this challenge?

_____

_____

How am I doing? **Later in the term, be accountable for your progress on page 139.**

A "think link" is a visual construction of related ideas, similar to a map or web, which represents your thought process. Ideas are written inside geometric shapes and related ideas and facts are attached to those ideas by lines that connect the shapes (see chapter 7 for more about think links). If you want to use the style shown in Key 3.8, create a "wheel" of ideas coming off your central shape. Then, spreading out from each of those ideas (interests, communication style, and so forth),

ACTIVATE
THE HABIT OF MIND

draw lines connecting the thoughts that go along with that idea. You don't have to use the wheel image, however; you might want to design a treelike think link, a line of boxes with connecting thoughts, or anything else you like. Let your design reflect who you are, just as what you write does.

KEY 3.8 One example of a self-portrait.

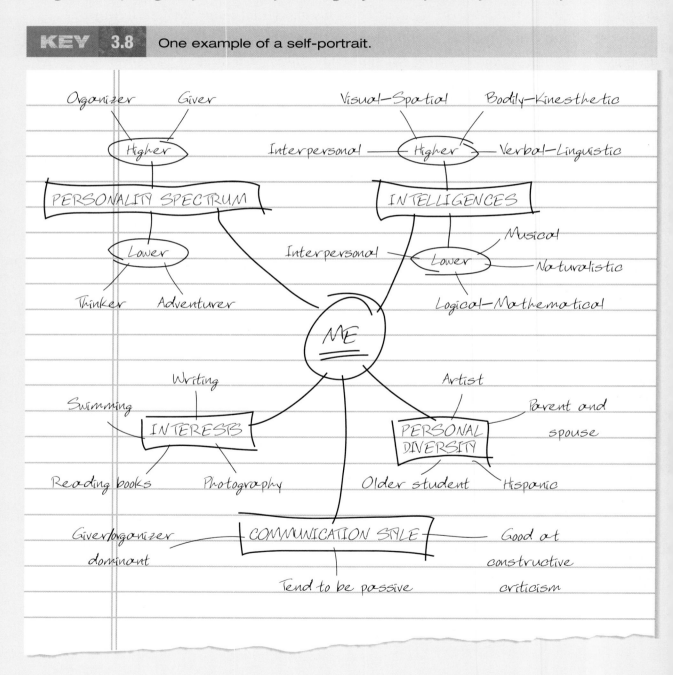

SUGGESTED READINGS

Cobb, Joyanne. *Learning How to Learn: Getting into and Surviving College When You Have a Learning Disorder*. Washington, DC: Child Welfare League of America, 2001.

College Board, ed. *The College Board Index of Majors and Graduate Degrees 2001*. New York: College Entrance Examination Board, 2000.

Gardner, Howard. *Intelligence Reframed: Multiple Intelligences for the 21st Century*. New York: Basic Books, 2000.

Fogg, Neeta, Paul E. Harrington, and Thomas F. Harrington. *The College Majors Handbook with Real Career Paths and Payoffs: The Actual Jobs, Earnings, and Trends for Graduates of 60 College Majors*. Indianapolis: Jist Works, 2004.

Keirsey, David. *Please Understand Me II: Temperament, Character, Intelligence*. Del Mar, CA: Prometheus Nemesis, 1998.

Pearman, Roger R., and Sarah C. Albritton. *I'm Not Crazy, I'm Just Not You: The Real Meaning of the 16 Personality Types*. Palo Alto, CA: Consulting Psychologists Press, 1997.

Phifer, Paul. *College Majors and Careers: A Resource Guide for Effective Life Planning*, 4th ed. Chicago: Ferguson, 2003.

Sclafani, Annette. *College Guide for Students with Learning Disabilities*. New York: Laurel Publications, 2003.

INTERNET RESOURCES

Attention Deficit Disorder Association (**www.add.org**)

Children and Adults with Attention Deficit/Hyperactivity Disorder (**www.chadd.org**)

International Dyslexia Association (**www.interdys.org**)

Keirsey Sorter and other Myers-Briggs information (**www.keirsey.com**)

Learning Disabilities Online (**www.ldonline.org**)

National Center for Learning Disabilities (**www.ncld.org**)

Prentice Hall's Student Success Supersite: Majors Exploration (**www.prenhall.com/success/MajorExp/index.html**)

ENDNOTES

1. Howard Gardner, *Multiple Intelligences: The Theory in Practice*, New York: HarperCollins, 1993, pp. 5–49.

2. Ibid, p. 7.

3. "Conceptual Frameworks/Models, Guiding Values and Principles," National Center for Cultural Competence, 2002, accessed May 2006 from the Web site of Georgetown University (**http://gucchd.georgetown.edu//nccc/framework.html**).

4. Information in the sections on the five stages of building competency is based on Mark A. King, Anthony Sims, and David Osher, "How Is Cultural Competence Integrated in Education?" accessed May 2006 from the Web site of Cultural Competence (**http://cecp.air.org/cultural/Q_integrated.htm**).

5. John Gravois, "Teach Impediment: When the Student Can't Understand the Instructor, Who Is to Blame?" *Chronicle of Higher Education*, April 8, 2005, pp. A10–A12.

6. From "Comparison of FBI Hate Crime Statistics, 1991–2001," a grid created by the Anti-Defamation League using FBI statistics, accessed May 2006 from the ADL Web site (**http://www.adl.org/99hatecrime/comp_fbi.asp**).

7. Martin Luther King, Jr., from his sermon "A Tough Mind and a Tender Heart," *Strength in Love*, Philadelphia: Fortress Press, 1986, p. 14.

8. Sheryl McCarthy, *Why Are the Heroes Always White?* Kansas City, MO: Andrews McMeel, 1995, p. 137.

CRITICAL & CREATIVE THINKING

SOLVING PROBLEMS AND MAKING DECISIONS

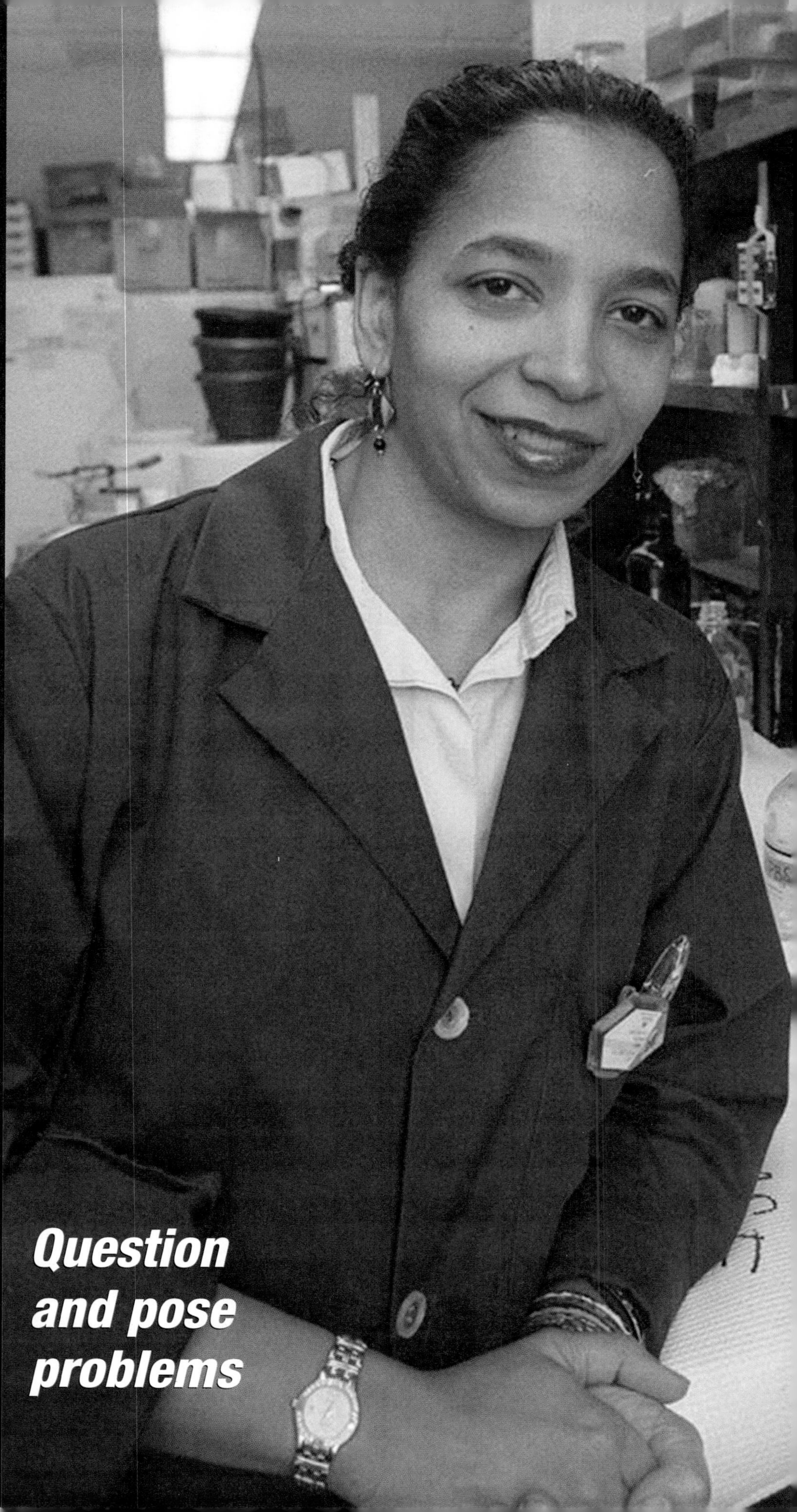

Question and pose problems

HABITS OF MIND

"One of the characteristics that distinguishes humans from other forms of life is our inclination and ability to find problems to solve. Effective problem solvers know how to ask questions to fill in the gaps between what they know and what they don't know."

ART COSTA

QUESTION AND POSE PROBLEMS

Asking questions and identifying problems is an essential part of being a creative and critical thinker. If you look at situations with an eye toward what might be improved, you will be able to ask questions that lead you to thoughtful evaluations and successful solutions.

n her training as a molecular biologist, cancer researcher Jill Bargonetti learned endless facts and figures. To pursue her goal of curing cancer through gene therapy, though, she does much more than quote data: She asks questions and works through them with critical and creative thinking. Having asked the question of how breast cancer relates to a problem with a gene labeled p53, she is determined to find ways to help this gene function correctly in breast cells.

In this chapter, you explore answers to the following questions:

- **What is important to know about thinking?**
- **How can you improve your critical thinking skills?**
- **How can you improve your creative thinking skills?**
- **How can you use your thinking skills to solve problems and make decisions?**

As with Dr. Bargonetti, your success depends on your willingness and ability to think through problems, make informed decisions, and overcome obstacles. Critical and creative thinking skills can be developed and improved with practice. This chapter will help you understand how to analyze information, come up with creative ideas, and implement problem-solving and decision-making plans. With these skills, you will be better able to challenge yourself in a way that leads to learning, goal achievement, and a more fulfilling life.

Photo: Marilynn K. Yee/ *The New York Times*

What is important to know about thinking?

As a college student, you are required to think in greater depth and complexity than ever before. Academic success involves first and foremost a combination of *critical* and *creative* thinking, which includes and goes beyond the ability to memorize and retain what you learn.

Thinking Means Asking and Answering Questions

What is thinking? According to experts, it is what happens when you ask questions and seek answers.[1] *Questioning* propels the action of thinking. "To think through or rethink anything," says Richard Paul of the Center for Critical Thinking and Moral Critique, "one must ask questions that stimulate our thought. Questions define tasks, express problems and delineate issues. . . . only students who have questions are really thinking and learning."[2]

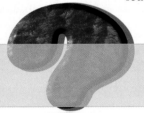

© Kerioak—Fotolia

> The one real object of education is to have a man in the condition of continually asking questions.
>
> **BISHOP MANDELL CREIGHTON**

As you answer questions, you transform raw data into information that you can use to achieve goals. A *Wall Street Journal* article titled "The Best Innovations Are Those That Come from Smart Questions" relays the story of a cell biology student, William Hunter, whose professor told him that "the difference between good science and great science is the quality of the questions posed." Later, as a doctor and the president and CEO of a pharmaceutical company, Hunter asked questions about new ways to use drugs. His questions led to the development of a revolutionary product—a drug-coated coronary stent (a slender catheter made to fit into a blood vessel) that prevents scar tissue from forming. Through seeking answers to probing questions and challenging perceived limits, William Hunter reached a significant goal.[3]

You use questions in both critical and creative thinking. Later in the chapter, you will find examples of the kinds of questions that drive each skill. Like any aspect of thinking, *questioning* is not often a straightforward process. Sometimes the answer doesn't come right away. Often the answer leads to further, and more specific, questions. Patience is key in your exploration as you search for results.

In order to ask useful questions and not move in irrelevant directions, you need to know *why* you are questioning. A general question can be your starting point for defining your purpose: "What am I trying to accomplish, and why?" As you continue your thought process, you will find more specific purposes that help you generate questions along the way.

Critical and Creative Thinking Depend on Each Other

Some tasks require only one thinking skill or ability at a time. You might use critical thinking to complete a multiple-choice quiz, or creative thinking to come up with an essay idea. However, with all but the most straightforward situations, and especially when you need to solve a problem or make a decision, you use critical and creative thinking skills together to move forward.

You need to think creatively to generate ideas and solutions; likewise, you need to think critically to evaluate the usefulness of those ideas. Inventor Wayne Kuna presents this example:

> To me as a toy inventor, critical thinking is an absolute necessity. It gives us the tools to find not just the next step, but also the step after the next step. By looking at all the things around us—the fads, the movies, the Internet—and mixing it together with what we know about how kids play . . . we begin to develop new and better ideas that no one ever thought of before.[4]

Thinking Power Is Yours to Build

You ask and answer critical and creative thinking questions every day, whether or not you realize it. For example, in deciding to pursue a college degree, you may have asked these kinds of questions as you thought through the consequences of the choice: "If I attend class full-time, what will that do to my schedule at work and at home?" "If I don't go to school, how will that affect my ability to earn a living in the short and long term?"

Other examples of students using critical and creative thinking are situations like these:

- Choosing the best term paper topic by looking at the topic list, thinking about available library and Internet sources, and considering personal interest and the instructor's approval
- Deciding between two courses by reading course descriptions and talking to your advisor
- After listening to one point of view in a class discussion, offering a solidly supported opposing opinion
- Coming up with examples that back up the central idea of a paper you are writing

You can improve your ability to think. Studies have shown that your brain will continue to develop throughout your life if you stay active in your quest to learn new things.[5] As you increase thinking skill, you increase your value both in school and on the job. Critical and creative thinkers are in demand because of their ability to apply what they know, think through a situation, innovate, and solve problems and make decisions effectively.

The "Take Action" exercises within this chapter will give you an idea of how you perceive yourself as a critical and creative thinker and encourage the development of those skills. Other chapter sets of "Take Action" exercises help you to build thinking skills and apply them to chapter topics. In short, your work throughout the book is geared toward building your thinking power.

Questioning

Christopher Reeve, best known for his Superman movie role, became paralyzed from the neck down after a catastrophic horseback riding accident.

By **continually asking what could be** and *never being satisfied with what is,* Reeve spurred research into spinal cord injuries.

LIVE IT!

How can you improve your critical thinking skills?

ritical thinking is the process of gathering information, analyzing it in different ways, and evaluating it for the purposes of gaining understanding, solving a problem, or making a decision. It is as essential for dealing with real-life problems and decisions as it is for thinking through the hypothetical questions on your chemistry homework.

Before you get into the analytical process, define your purpose by asking what you want to analyze, and why. Then gather the necessary information, analyze and clarify the ideas, and evaluate what you've found. Remember that, throughout the process, you will formulate new questions that may take you in new directions or even change your purpose.

Gather Information

Information is the raw material for thinking. Choosing what to gather requires a careful analysis of how much information you need, how much time to spend gathering it, and whether the information is relevant. Say, for instance, that your assignment is to choose a style of American jazz music and discuss its influence on a particular culture. If you gathered every available resource on the topic, the course would be over long before you got to the writing stage.

Here's how you might use analysis to effectively gather information for that paper:

Angel Franco/*The New York Times*

■ Reviewing the assignment, you learn that the paper should be 10 pages and cover at least three influential musicians.

■ At the library and online, you find lots of what appears to be relevant information.

■ You choose a jazz movement, find five or six comprehensive pieces on it, and then select three in-depth sources on each of three musicians.

Gathering data is an important step in the thinking process. Here a professor and student from Long Island University work to gather information about diamondback terrapins in Oyster Bay, New York.

In this way you achieve a subgoal—a selection of useful materials—on the way to your larger goal of writing a well-crafted paper.

Analyze and Clarify Information

Once you've gathered the information, the next step is to analyze it to determine whether the information is reliable and useful in helping you answer your questions.

Break Information into Parts

When analyzing information, you break information into parts and examine the parts so that you can see how they relate to each other and to information you already know. The following strategies help you break down information into pieces and set aside what is unclear, unrelated, or unimportant, resulting in a deeper and more reliable understanding.

Separate the ideas. If you are reading about the rise of the bebop movement, for instance, you might name events that influenced it, key musicians, facts about the sound, and ideas behind it.

Compare and contrast. Look at how things are similar to, or different from, each other. You might explore how three bebop musicians are similar in style. You might look at how they differ in what each musician intends to communicate with the music.

Examine cause and effect. Look at the possible reasons why something happened (possible causes) and its consequences (effects, both positive and negative). You might examine the causes that led up to the bebop sound as well as its effects on other non-jazz musical styles.

An important caution: Analyze carefully to seek out *true causes*—some apparent causes may not be actual causes (often called *false causes*). For example, events in the musical world and general society took place when the first musicians were developing the bebop style. Some may have led directly to the new style; some may simply have occurred at the same time.

© Richard Thorp—Fotolia

Look for themes, patterns, and categories. Note connections that form as you look at how bits of information relate to one another. A theme of "freedom versus structure," for example, might emerge out of an examination of bebop versus swing jazz. A pattern of behavior might develop as you look at how different musicians broke off from the swing movement. Musicians with different styles might fall into the bebop category based on their artistic goals.

Once the ideas are broken down, you will need to examine whether examples support ideas, to separate fact from opinion, to consider perspective, and to investigate hidden assumptions.

Examine Whether Examples Support Ideas

When you encounter an idea or claim, examine how it is supported with examples or *evidence* (facts, expert opinion, research findings, personal experience, and so on). How useful an idea is to your work may depend on whether, or how well, it is backed up with solid evidence or made concrete with examples. Be critical of the information you gather; don't take it at face value.

For example, an advertisement for a weight-loss pill, claiming that it allows users to drop a pound a day, quotes "Anne" who says that she lost 30 pounds in 30 days. The word of one person, who may or may not be telling the truth, is not adequate support. On the other hand, a medical study in the world-renowned *New England Journal of Medicine* is more reliable.

In particular reading materials, a set of connected ideas supported by examples constitutes an *argument* that a writer makes to prove or disprove a point. Through critical questioning, you work to understand the argument as you judge the quality of the evidence, whether it supports the central idea, and whether examples and ideas connect logically.

Finding credible, reliable information with which to answer questions and come up with ideas enables you to separate fact from opinion.

Distinguish Fact from Opinion

A *statement of fact* is information presented as objectively real and verifiable ("It's raining outside now"). In contrast, a *statement of opinion* is a belief, conclusion, or judgment that is inherently difficult, and sometimes impossible, to verify ("This is the most miserable rainstorm ever"). When you critically evaluate materials that you read, looking carefully at whether an argument is based on fact or opinion will help you determine how reliable it is. Key 4.1 defines important characteristics of fact and opinion.

Examine how fact and opinion differ. KEY 4.1

Opinions include statements that . . .	Facts include statements that . . .
. . . *show evaluation.* Any statement of value indicates an opinion. Words such as *bad, good, pointless,* and *beneficial* indicate value judgments. Example: "Jimmy Carter is the most successful peace negotiator to sit in the White House."	. . . *deal with actual people, places, objects, or events.* Example: "In 1978, Jimmy Carter's 13-day summit meeting with Egyptian president Anwar Sadat and Israeli prime minister Menachem Begin led to a treaty between the two countries."
. . . *use abstract words.* Words that are complicated to define, like *misery* or *success,* usually indicate a personal opinion. Example: "The charity event was a smashing success."	. . . *use concrete words or measurable statistics.* Example: "The charity event raised $5,862."
. . . *predict future events.* Statements that examine future occurrences are often opinions. Example: "Mr. Barrett's course is going to set a new enrollment record this year."	. . . *describe current events in exact terms.* Example: "Mr. Barrett's course has 378 students enrolled this semester."
. . . *use emotional words.* Emotions are by nature unverifiable. Chances are that statements using such words as *delightful* or *miserable* express an opinion. Example: "That class is a miserable experience."	. . . *avoid emotional words and focus on the verifiable.* Example: "Citing dissatisfaction with the instruction, 7 out of the 25 students in that class withdrew in September."
. . . *use absolutes.* Absolute qualifiers, such as *all, none, never,* and *always,* often point to an opinion. Example: "To pay tuition, all college students require financial aid support."	. . . *avoid absolutes,* using words like *"may," "possibly,"* and *"perhaps."* Example: "To pay tuition, some college students require financial aid support." Or "College students may require financial support to pay tuition."

Source: Adapted from Ben E. Johnson, *Stirring Up Thinking,* New York: Houghton Mifflin, 1998, pp. 268–270.

Even though facts may seem more solid, you can also make use of opinions if you determine that they are backed up with facts. However, it is important to examine opinions for their underlying perspectives and assumptions.

Examine Perspectives and Assumptions

Perspective is a characteristic way of thinking about people, situations, events, and ideas. Perspectives can be broad, such as a generally optimistic or pessimistic view of life. Or they can be more focused, such as an attitude about whether students should commute or live on campus.

Perspectives are associated with *assumptions*—judgments, generalizations, or biases influenced by experience and values. For example, the perspective that there are many successful ways to raise a family leads to assumptions such as "Single-parent homes can provide nurturing environments" and "Same-sex couples can rear well-adjusted children." Having a particular experience with single-parent homes or same-sex couples can build or reinforce a perspective.

Assumptions often hide within questions and statements, blocking you from considering information in different ways. Take this classic puzzler as an example: "Which came first, the chicken or the egg?" Thinking about this question, most people assume that the egg is a chicken egg. If you push past the limit of that assumption and come up with a new idea—such as, the egg is a dinosaur egg—then the obvious answer is that the egg came first!

Examining perspectives and assumptions is important for two reasons. First, they often affect your perception of the validity of materials you read and research. For any such materials, it is important to ask whether the source is reliable and free of bias, what particular perspective and intent the author may have, and what assumptions underlie the material. Second, your own perspectives and assumptions can cloud your interpretation of the information you encounter.

Describe your perspective on pursuing an education. (*Hint:* Consider its importance to you, what you believe is the best way to become educated, how you think it can be used, and so on.) What are your sources for this perspective? What influence does it have on how you live? If this has not always been your perspective, what was your previous perspective, and why did the change happen? How has the habit of mind of *questioning and posing problems* had an effect on your changing perspectives over time?

Perspectives and assumptions in information. Being able to determine the perspectives that underlie materials will help you separate biased from unbiased information. For example, the conclusions in two articles on federal versus state government control of education may differ radically if one appears in a politically conservative publication and one appears in a liberal publication. You may even want to acknowledge the possibility of skewed information coming from a source because of a biased perspective.

Assumptions often affect the validity of materials you read and research. A historical Revolutionary War document that originated in the colonies, for example, may assume that the rebellion against the British was entirely justified and leave out information to the contrary. Clearly understanding such a document means separating the assumptions from the facts.

Personal perspectives and assumptions. Your own preferences, values, and prejudices—which influence your perspective—can affect how accurately you view information. A student who thinks that the death penalty is wrong, for example, may have a hard time analyzing the facts and arguments in an article that supports it. Or, when researching the topic, he might use only materials that agree with his perspective.

Consider the perspectives and assumptions that might follow from your values. Then, when you have to analyze information, try to set them aside. "Anticipate your reactions and prejudices and then consciously resist their influence," says Colby Glass, professor of information research and philosophy at Palo Alto College.[6]

Evaluate Information

You've gathered and analyzed your information. You have examined its components, its evidence, its validity, its perspective, and any underlying assumptions. Now, based on an examination of evidence and careful analysis, you *evaluate* whether an idea or piece of information is important or unimportant, applicable or trivial, strong or weak, and why. You then set aside what is not useful and use the rest to form an opinion, possible solution, or decision.

For example, you're preparing a presentation on television's effects on children. You've gathered pertinent information, come up with an idea, and analyzed whether the information supports it. Now you evaluate the evidence, presenting what's useful in an organized, persuasive way. See Key 4.2 for some questions you can ask to build and use critical thinking skills.

As important as critical thinking is, it can't stand alone. Pursuing your goals, in school and in the workplace, requires not just analyzing information but also thinking creatively about how to use what you've concluded from your analysis.

How can you improve your creative thinking skills?

Some researchers define *creativity* as combining existing elements in an innovative way to create a new purpose or result. For example, in 1968 Spence Silver, a researcher for Minnesota Mining and Manufacturing Company (3M), created a weak adhesive; several years later, another 3M scientist, Arthur Fry, used it to mark pages in a book. Post-it Notes are now an office staple. Others see creativity as the art of generating ideas from taking a fresh look at how things are related (noting what ladybugs eat inspired organic farmers to bring them in to consume crop-destroying aphids).[7] Still others define it as the ability to make unusual connections—to view information in quirky ways that bring about unique results.[8]

To think creatively is to generate new ideas that often go against conventional wisdom and may bring change. For example, in the 1940s mathematician Grace Murray Hopper pioneered the effort to create computer languages that non-mathematicians could understand; her efforts opened the world of computers to a wide audience.

KEY 4.2   Ask questions like these in order to think critically.

To gather information, ask:	▢ What requirements does my goal have?
	▢ What kinds of information do I need to meet my goal?
	▢ What information is available?
	▢ Where and when is it available? Where and when can I get to it?
	▢ Of the sources I found, which ones will best help me achieve my goal?
To analyze, ask:	▣ What are the parts of this information?
	▣ What is similar to this information? What is different?
	▣ What are the reasons for this? Why did this happen?
	▣ What ideas or themes emerge from this material?
	▣ How would you categorize this information?
	▣ What conclusions can you make about this information?
To see if examples support an idea, ask:	▢ What examples, or evidence, support the idea?
	▢ Does the evidence make sense?
	▢ Does the evidence support the idea/claim?
	▢ Is this evidence key information that I need to answer my question?
	▢ Are there examples that might disprove the idea/claim?
To distinguish fact from opinion, ask:	▣ Do the words in this information signal fact or opinion? (See Key 4.1)
	▣ What is the source of this information? Is the source reliable?
	▣ How does this information compare to other facts or opinions?
	▣ If this is an opinion, is it supported by facts?
	▣ How can I use this fact or opinion?
To examine perspectives and assumptions, ask:	▢ Who is the author? What perspectives might this person have?
	▢ What might be emphasized or left out as a result of the perspective?
	▢ How could I consider this information from a different perspective?
	▢ What assumptions might lie behind this statement or material?
	▢ How could I prove, or disprove, an assumption?
	▢ What contradictory assumptions might be equally valid?
	▢ How might a personal perspective or assumption affect the way I see this material?
To evaluate, ask:	▣ Do I agree with this information?
	▣ Does this information fit what I'm trying to prove or accomplish?
	▣ Is this information strong or weak, and why?
	▣ How important, or applicable, is this information?
	▣ Which ideas or pieces of information would I choose to focus on?

Source: "Questions that Probe Reasons and Evidence" (http://ed.fnal.gov/trc/tutorial/taxonomy.html), adapted from Richard Paul, *Critical Thinking: How to Prepare Students for a Rapidly Changing World,* Santa Rosa, CA: Foundation for Critical Thinking, 1993; and Barbara Fowler, "Bloom's Taxonomy and Critical Thinking," 1996, Longview Community College (www.mcckc.edu/longview/ctac/blooms.htm).

Assess and Build Your Critical Thinking Skills

This is a two-part exercise: Part I provides insight into your ability as a critical thinker, and Part II helps you build your skill.

Part I: Assess Yourself. How do you perceive yourself as a critical thinker? For each statement, circle the number that feels right to you, from 1 for "least like me" to 5 for "most like me."

1. I tend to perform well on objective tests.   1   2   3   4   5

2. People say I'm "a thinker," "brainy," "studious."   1   2   3   4   5

3. I am not comfortable with gray areas—I prefer information to be
   laid out in black and white.   1   2   3   4   5

4. In a group setting, I like to tackle the details of a problem.   1   2   3   4   5

5. I sometimes overthink things and miss my moment of opportunity.   1   2   3   4   5

Total your answers here: _____

If your total ranges from 5 to 12, you consider your critical thinking skills to be *weak*.

If your total ranges from 13 to 19, you consider your critical thinking skills to be *average*.

If your total ranges from 20 to 25, you consider your critical thinking skills to be *strong*.

Part II: Use Critical Thinking Skills to Analyze a Statement. Put the habit of mind of *questioning and posing problems* to work. Think about this statement, then answer the questions that follow:

"The Internet is the best place to find information about any topic."

Is this statement fact or opinion? Why?

_____

_____

What examples can you think of that support or negate this statement?

_____

_____

What perspective(s) are guiding this statement?

_____

_____

(continued)

What assumption(s) underlie the statement? *Pose a problem:* What negative effects might result from accepting these assumptions and therefore agreeing with the statement?

_____

_____

As a result of your critical thinking, what is your evaluation of this statement?

_____

_____

_____

Creativity is not limited to inventions. For example, Smith College junior Meghan E. Taugher and her study group, as part of their class on electrical circuits, devised a solar-powered battery for a laptop computer. Her positive experience of putting learning to work in real life led her to generate an idea of a new major and career plan—engineering.[9]

Where does creativity come from? Some people seem to come up with inspired ideas more often than others. However, creative thinking, like critical thinking, is a skill that can be developed. Creativity expert Roger von Oech says that mental flexibility is essential. "Like race-car drivers who shift in and out of different gears depending on where they are on the course," he says, you can enhance your creativity by learning to "shift in and out of different types of thinking depending on the needs of the situation at hand."[10]

The actions discussed next will help you make those shifts and build your ability to think creatively. Because ideas often pop up randomly, writing them down as they arise will help you remember them. Keep a pen and paper by your bed, your PDA in your pocket, a notepad in your car, or a tape recorder in your backpack so that you can grab ideas before they fade.

© Chris Harvey—Fotolia

Brainstorm

Brainstorming—letting your mind free-associate to come up with different ideas or answers—is also referred to as *divergent thinking:* You start with a question and then let your mind diverge—go in many different directions—in search of solutions. Think of brainstorming as *deliberate* creative thinking—you go into it fully aware that you are attempting to create new ideas. When you brainstorm, generate and write down ideas without immediately considering how useful they are; evaluate their quality later. Brainstorming works well in groups because group members can become inspired by, and make creative use of, one another's ideas.[11]

One way to inspire ideas when brainstorming is to think of similar situations—in other words, to make *analogies.*

For example, the discovery of Velcro is a product of analogy: When imagining how two pieces of fabric could stick to each other, the inventor thought of the similar situation of a burr sticking to clothing.

When you are brainstorming ideas, don't get hooked on finding the one right answer. Questions may have many "right answers"—or many answers that have degrees of usefulness. The more possibilities you generate, the better your chance of finding the best one. Also, don't stop the process when you think you have the best answer—keep going until you are out of steam. You never know what may come up in those last gasps of creative energy.[12]

Take a New and Different Look

Just because everyone believes something doesn't make it so; just because something "has always been that way" doesn't make it good or right. If no one ever questioned established opinion, people would still think the earth was flat. Changing how you look at a situation or problem can inspire creative ideas. There are several ways to do it, including those discussed next.

Challenge assumptions. In the late 1960s, conventional wisdom said that school provided education and television provided entertainment. Jim Henson, a pioneer in children's television, asked, "Why can't we use TV to educate young children?" From that question, the characters of *Sesame Street,* and eventually a host of other educational programs, were born.

Shift your perspective. Try on new perspectives by asking others for their views, reading about new ways to approach situations, or deliberately going with the opposite of your first instinct.[13] Then use those perspectives to inspire creativity. For your English lit course, analyze a novel from the point of view of one of the main characters. For political science, craft a position paper for a presidential or senatorial candidate. Perception puzzles are a fun way to experience how looking at something in a new way can bring a totally different idea (see Key 4.3).

Ask "what if" questions. Set up hypothetical environments in which new ideas can grow: "What if I knew I couldn't fail?" "What if I had unlimited money or time?" Ideas will emerge from your "what if" questions. For example, the founders of Seeds of Peace, faced with generations of conflict in the Middle East, asked: What if Israeli and Palestinian teens met at a summer camp in Maine so that the next generation has greater understanding and respect than the last? And what if follow-up programs and reunions are set up to cement friendships so that relationships change the politics of the Middle East? Based on the ideas that came up, they created an organization to

Michelle V. Agins/*The New York Times*

Brainstorming works well in group settings, in part because people tend to be inspired by the ideas of others. This support group of South Asian women thinks through social issues together.

KEY 4.3   Use perception puzzles to experience a shift in perspective.

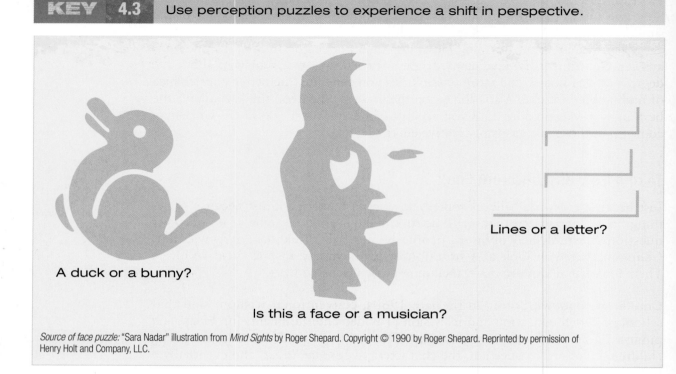

A duck or a bunny?

Is this a face or a musician?

Lines or a letter?

Source of face puzzle: "Sara Nadar" illustration from *Mind Sights* by Roger Shepard. Copyright © 1990 by Roger Shepard. Reprinted by permission of Henry Holt and Company, LLC.

prepare teenagers from the Middle East with the leadership skills needed to coexist peacefully.

Set the Stage for Creativity

Give yourself the best possible chance at generating creative ideas by employing strategies such as the ones discussed next.

Choose, or create, environments that free your mind. Find places that energize you. Play music that moves you. Paint your study walls your favorite color. Seek out people who inspire you.[14]

Be curious. Try something you consider new and different: Take a course that has nothing to do with your major, try a new sport or game, listen to a new genre of music, read a magazine or book that you've never seen before, get to know someone outside of your circle of friends. Try something you don't think you would like, in order to see if you had misjudged your reaction. Seeking out new experiences and ideas will broaden your knowledge, giving you more raw materials with which to build creative ideas.[15]

Give yourself time to "sit" with a question. American society values speed, so much so that to say someone is "quick" is to consider that person intelligent.[16] Equating speed with intelligence can stifle creativity, because many creative ideas come when you allow time for thoughts to percolate. Take breaks when figuring out a problem. Take the pressure off by getting some exercise, napping, talking with a friend, working on something else, doing something fun. Creative ideas often come when you give your brain permission to "leave the job" for a while.[17]

Take Risks

Creative breakthroughs can come from sensible risk taking.

Fly in the face of convention. Entrepreneur Michael Dell turned tradition on its ear when he took a "tell me what you want and I will build it for you" approach to computer marketing instead of a "build it and they will buy it" approach. The possibility of failure did not stop him from risking money, time, energy, and reputation to achieve a truly unique and creative goal.

Let mistakes be okay. Open yourself to the learning that comes from not being afraid to mess up. When William Hunter—the successful inventor of the drug-coated coronary stent—and his company failed to develop a particular treatment for multiple sclerosis, he said, "You have to celebrate the failures. If you send the message that the only road to career success is experiments that work, people won't ask risky questions, or get any dramatically new answers."[18]

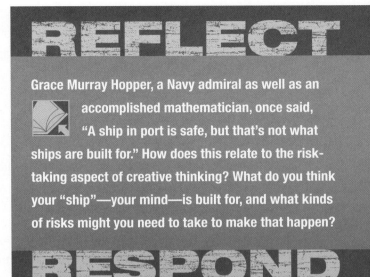

REFLECT

Grace Murray Hopper, a Navy admiral as well as an accomplished mathematician, once said, "A ship in port is safe, but that's not what ships are built for." How does this relate to the risk-taking aspect of creative thinking? What do you think your "ship"—your mind—is built for, and what kinds of risks might you need to take to make that happen?

RESPOND

As with critical thinking, *asking questions* powers creative thinking. See Key 4.4 for examples of the kinds of questions you can ask to get your creative juices flowing.

When you have a problem to solve or decision to make, creative thinking allows you to pose the right questions and generate possible solutions and choices, and critical thinking enables you to evaluate them. However, choices aren't enough and potential solutions must be tried out. You need an action plan in order to make the best solution or choice happen.

How can you use your thinking skills to solve problems and make decisions?

Since many on-paper academic problems—math problem sets, answering essay questions—can be solved with a fairly straightforward critical thinking approach, it's easy to think that critical thinking alone is your ticket to success. However, real-world problems and decisions usually aren't so clear-cut, and the stakes are often higher. Your success in a sociology class, for example, may depend as much if not more on finding a way to get along with your instructor than it does on answering multiple-choice questions correctly.

Furthermore, academic knowledge on its own isn't enough to bring you success in the workplace. You need to be able to actively apply what you know to problems and decisions that come up periodically in your work. For example, although students majoring in elementary education may successfully

KEY 4.4   Ask questions like these in order to jump-start creative thinking.

To brainstorm, ask:	
	What do I want to accomplish?
	What are the craziest ideas I can think of?
	What are 10 ways that I can reach my goal?
	What ideas or strategies have worked before and how can I apply them?
	How else can this be done?

To shift your perspective, ask:	
	How has this always been done—and what would be a different way?
	What is another way to look at this situation?
	How can I approach this task from a completely new angle?
	How would someone else do this? How would they view this?
	What if . . . ?

To set the stage for creativity, ask:	
	Where, and with whom, do I feel relaxed and inspired?
	What music helps me think out of the box?
	When in the day or night am I most likely to experience a flow of creative ideas?
	What do I think would be new and interesting to try, to see, to read?
	What is the most outrageous outcome of a situation that I can imagine?

To take risks, ask:	
	What is the conventional way of doing this? What would be a totally different way?
	What would be a risky approach to this problem or question?
	What choice would people caution me about and why?
	What is the worst that can happen if I take this risk? What is the best?
	What have I learned from this mistake?

quote child development facts on an exam, it won't mean much to their career success unless they can evaluate and address real children's needs in the classroom.

Now that you have an understanding of what it means to think critically and creatively, explore how to put your skills into action to solve problems and make decisions successfully. Problem solving and decision making follow similar paths. Both require you to identify and analyze a situation, generate possible solutions, choose one, follow through on it, and evaluate its success. Key 4.5 gives an overview of the paths, indicating how you think at each step.

How do you choose which path to follow? Understanding the differences between problem solving and decision making will help. Basically, it comes down to this:

- Problem solving generally requires more focus on coming up with possible solutions. In contrast, when you face a decision, your choices are often determined.

- Problem solving aims to remove or counteract negative effects. In contrast, decision making aims to fulfill a need.

TAKE ACTION

Assess and Build Your Creative Thinking Skills

This is a two-part exercise: Part I provides insight into your ability as a creative thinker, and Part II helps you build your skill.

Part I: Assess Yourself. How do you perceive yourself as a creative thinker? For each statement, circle the number that feels right to you, from 1 for "least like me" to 5 for "most like me."

1. I tend to resist rules and regulations.   1   2   3   4   5
2. People say I'm "expressive," "full of ideas," "innovative."   1   2   3   4   5
3. I break out of my routine and find new experiences.   1   2   3   4   5
4. In a group setting, I like to toss ideas into the ring.   1   2   3   4   5
5. If you say something is too risky, I'm all for it.   1   2   3   4   5

Total your answers here: _____

If your total ranges from 5 to 12, you consider your creative thinking skills to be *weak*.

If your total ranges from 13 to 19, you consider your creative thinking skills to be *average*.

If your total ranges from 20 to 25, you consider your creative thinking skills to be *strong*.

Part II: Gather Evidence of Your Creativity. Think about the past month; then, make a list of five creative acts you performed—small, earth-shattering, or anything in between.

1. _____
2. _____
3. _____
4. _____
5. _____

Now think of a situation for which you are currently trying to come up with an idea. It could be an essay that's due, a plan for studying for a test, a sticky situation with an instructor, or some other issue.

Time to get creative: Briefly jot down one new idea for how to deal with your situation.

_____

Now write down a second idea—but focus on the risk-taking aspect of creativity. What would be a risky way to handle the situation? How do you hope it would pay off?

_____

_____

Keep these in mind. You may want to use one soon!

KEY   4.5   Solve problems and make decisions using a plan of action.

Problem Solving	Thinking Skill	Decision Making
Define the problem—recognize that something needs to change, identify what's happening, look for true causes.	**Step 1** **Analyze**	Define the decision—identify your goal (your need) and then construct a decision that will help you get it.
Analyze the problem—gather information, break it down into pieces, verify facts, look at perspectives and assumptions, evaluate information.	**Step 2** **Analyze**	Examine needs and motives—consider the layers of needs carefully, and be honest about what you really want.
Generate possible solutions—use creative strategies to think of ways you could address the causes of this problem.	**Step 3** **Create**	Name and/or generate different options—use creative questions to come up with choices that would fulfill your needs.
Evaluate solutions—look carefully at potential pros and cons of each, and choose what seems best.	**Step 4** **Evaluate**	Evaluate options—look carefully at potential pros and cons of each, and chose what seems best.
Put the solution to work—persevere, focus on results, and believe in yourself as you go for your goal.	**Step 5** **Choose and act**	Act on your decision—go down the path and stay on target.
Evaluate how well the solution worked—look at the effects of what you did.	**Step 6** **Reevaluate**	Evaluate the success of your decision—look at whether it accomplished what you had hoped.
In the future, apply what you've learned—use this solution, or a better one, when a similar situation comes up again.	**Step 7** **Apply results**	In the future, apply what you've learned—make this choice, or a better one, when a similar decision comes up again.

See Key 4.6 for some examples. Remember, too, that whereas all problem solving requires you to make a decision (once you decide on a solution), only some decision making requires you to solve a problem.

Solving a Problem

A problem exists when a situation has negative effects. Recognizing that there is a problem—being aware of those effects—is essential before you can begin to solve it. In other words, your first move is to go from the effects ("I'm unhappy/uneasy/angry") to determining why: "My schedule is overwhelming me." "I'm over my head in this course." "My credit card debt is out of control." After you *identify the problem,* you begin the problem-solving process in earnest.

| How problems and decisions may differ. | | KEY 4.6 |

Situation	You have a problem if . . .	You need to make a decision if . . .
Planning summer activities	Your low GPA means you need to attend summer school—and you've already accepted a summer job.	You've been accepted into two summer abroad internship programs.
Declaring a major	It's time to declare but you don't have all the prerequisites for the major you want.	There are three majors that appeal to you and you quality for them all.
Relationships with instructors	You are having trouble following the lecture style of a particular instructor.	The Intro to Psychology course you want to take has seven sections taught by different instructors; you have to choose one.

But what happens if you don't solve a problem effectively? Take, for example, a student having an issue with an instructor. He may get into an argument with the instructor during class time. He may stop showing up to class. He may not make an effort with assignments. All of these choices have negative consequences for him.

Now consider how this student might work through the problem using his critical and creative thinking skills. Key 4.7 shows how his effort can pay off.

As you go through the problem-solving process, the steps discussed next will keep you on track.

Use probing questions to define problems. Focus on causes. If you are not happy in a class, for example, you could ask questions like these:

- What do I think about when I feel unhappy?
- Do my feelings involve my instructor? My classmates?
- Is the subject matter difficult? The volume of work too much?
- Is my attitude toward just this one class in particular, or toward school in general?

Chances are that how you answer one or more of these questions may lead to a clear definition—and ultimately to an effective solution.

Analyze carefully. Gather all the information you can, so that you can consider the situation comprehensively. Consider what you can learn from how the problem is similar to, or different from, other problems. Clarify facts. Note your own perspective, and ask others for theirs. Make sure you are not looking at the problem through the lens of an assumption.

KEY   4.7   Examine a problem-solving process in action.

DEFINE PROBLEM HERE	ANALYZE THE PROBLEM
I don't like my Freshman Composition instructor	We have different views and personality types— I don't feel respected or heard. I'm not interested in being there and my grades are suffering from my lack of motivation.

Use boxes below to list possible solutions:

POTENTIAL POSITIVE EFFECTS	SOLUTION #1	POTENTIAL NEGATIVE EFFECTS
List for each solution: Don't have to deal with that instructor Less stress	Drop the course	*List for each solution:* Grade gets entered on my transcript I'll have to take the course eventually; it's required for my major
Getting credit for the course Feeling like I've honored a commitment	SOLUTION #2 Put up with it until the end of the semester	Stress every time I'm there Lowered motivation Probably not such a good final grade
A chance to express myself Could get good advice An opportunity to ask direct questions of the instructor	SOLUTION #3 Schedule meetings with advisor and instructor	Have to face instructor one-on-one Might just make things worse

Now choose the solution you think is best . . .   *. . . circle it and make it happen.*

ACTUAL POSITIVE EFFECTS	ACTION TAKEN	ACTUAL NEGATIVE EFFECTS
List for each solution: Got some helpful advice from advisor Talking in person with the instructor actually promoted a fairly honest discussion I won't have to take the course again	I scheduled and attended meetings with both advisor and instructor, and opted to stick with the course.	*List for each solution:* The discussion was difficult and sometimes tense I still don't know how much learning I'll retain from this course

REEVALUATE: WAS IT A GOOD OR BAD SOLUTION?
The solution has improved things. I'll finish the course, and even though the instructor and I aren't the best of friends, we have a mutual understanding now. I feel more respected and more willing to put my time into the course.

Generate possible solutions based on causes, not effects. Addressing a cause provides a lasting solution, whereas "fixing" an effect cannot. Say, for example, that your shoulder hurts when you use your computer. Getting a friend to massage it is a nice but temporary solution, because the pain returns whenever you go back to work. Changing the height of your keyboard and mouse is a better idea, because it eliminates the cause of your pain. As you consider possible solutions, ask questions like these:

- What do I know that might apply to this situation?
- What have I seen or heard about what others have done that might help here?
- How does this situation compare to past situations I've been involved in? What has worked, or not worked, before?

Ruby Washington/*The New York Times*

One of the most important problem-solving steps is taking action. This group of students, as part of a service organization called Global Routes, helps out on the island of St. Lucia.

Be comprehensive with your final evaluation and let it lead you to future action. It's easy to skip the evaluation step when something is over and done with—but don't be tempted. From looking at how things went, you can learn valuable information that will help you repeat effective actions and avoid ineffective ones in the future. *Ask questions* like these:

- What worked well, or not so well, with my choice?
- What do I know I would do again? Why?
- What would I change if I had to do it all over again? Why?
- What effect did my actions have on others?

Making a Decision

Psychologists who have studied decision making have learned that many random factors influence the choices people make. For example, you may choose a major, not because you love the subject, but because you think your parents will approve of it. The goal is to make well-considered decisions despite factors that may derail your thinking.

What happens when you make important decisions too quickly? Consider a student trying to decide whether to transfer schools. If she makes her decision based on a reason that ultimately is not important enough to her, she may regret her choice later—most likely because she didn't consider cause and effect carefully when deciding.

Now look at how this student might make a well-considered decision. Key 4.8 shows how she worked through the parts of the process. As you use the steps in Key 4.8 to make a decision, several suggestions, discussed next, will enhance the process.

KEY 4.8   Examine a decision-making process in action.

DEFINE THE DECISION	EXAMINE NEEDS AND MOTIVES
Whether or not to transfer schools	I attend a small private college. My father has changed jobs and can no longer afford my tuition. My goal is to become a physical therapist, so I need a school with a full physical therapy program. My family needs to cut costs. I need to transfer credits.

Use boxes below to list possible solutions:

POTENTIAL POSITIVE EFFECTS	CHOICE #1	POTENTIAL NEGATIVE EFFECTS
List for each choice:		*List for each choice:*
No need to adjust to a new place or new people	Continue at the current college	Need to finance most of my tuition and costs on my own
Ability to continue course work as planned		Difficult to find time for a job
		Might not qualify for aid
	CHOICE #2	
Opportunity to connect with some high school friends	Transfer to a state college	Need to earn some money or get financial aid
Cheaper tuition and room costs		Physical therapy program is small and not very strong
Credits will transfer		
	CHOICE #3	
Many physical therapy courses available	Transfer to the community college	No personal contacts there that I know of
School is close so I could live at home and save room costs		Less independence if I live at home
Reasonable tuition; credits will transfer		No bachelor's degree available

Now make the choice you think is best . . .   *. . . circle it and act on it.*

ACTUAL POSITIVE EFFECTS	ACTION TAKEN	ACTUAL NEGATIVE EFFECTS
List for each choice:		*List for each choice:*
Money saved	Go to community college for two years; then transfer to a four-year school to get a B.A. and complete physical therapy course work.	Loss of some independence
Opportunity to spend time on studies rather than on working to earn tuition money		Less contact with friends
Availability of classes I need		

REEVALUATE: WAS IT A GOOD OR BAD CHOICE?
I'm satisfied with the decision. It can be hard being at home at times, but my parents are adjusting to my independence and I'm trying to respect their concerns. With fewer social distractions, I'm really getting my work done. Plus the financial aspect of the decision is ideal.

Look at the given options—then try to think of more. Some decisions have a given set of options. For example, your school may allow you to major, double major, or major and minor. However, when you are making your decision, you may be able to brainstorm with an advisor to come up with more options—such as an interdisciplinary major you create on your own. As with problem solving, consider similar situations you've been in or heard about, what decisions were made, and what resulted from those decisions.

Think about how your decision affects others. For example, the student thinking about a transfer considers the impact on friends and family. What she concludes about that impact may play a role in her decision about when she transfers and even the school she chooses.

Gather perspectives. Talk with others who have made similar decisions. There are more ways of doing things than one brain can possibly imagine on its own.

> The mind has exactly the same power as the hands: not merely to grasp the world, but to change it.
>
> **COLIN WILSON,** AUTHOR

Look at the long-term effects. As with problem solving, the final evaluation is a crucial part of the process. For important decisions, do a short-term evaluation and another evaluation after a period of time. Examine whether your decision has sent you down a path that has continued to bring positive effects.

As you engage your thinking skills on the road to success, keep these final tips in mind:

- *Stay motivated.* Work to persevere when you face a problem. Get started on achieving results instead of dwelling on exactly how to start. Translate thoughts into concrete actions.

- *Make the most of your personal strengths.* What you've learned in chapter 3 will help you see what you do best. Apply those strengths when you encounter problems and decisions.

- *Manage time and tasks effectively.* Use what you know from chapter 2 to plan your time in a way that promotes goal accomplishment. Avoid the pitfalls of procrastination. Accurately gauge what you can handle—don't take on too many projects, or too few.

- *Learn from your missteps.* Examine what happened when things go wrong. Learn from the experience and continue to apply what you have learned so that you don't repeat a mistake.

- *Focus on the goal.* Keep your eye on the big picture and complete what you've planned, rather than getting lost in the details or sidetracked by distractions.

- *Believe in yourself.* Have faith in your ability to go beyond your perceived capabilities and to achieve what you set out to do.

Let the obstacles come, as they will for everyone, in all aspects of life. You can face and overcome them with the power of your thinking and the ideas that you generate.

I question and pose problems.

When encountering confusion, intelligent questioners will ask the kinds of questions that will uncover a problem, should one exist: "Why did I receive that grade?" "Why didn't she understand my response?" When answering these questions reveals a problem, you then have the opportunity to solve it and thereby to improve the situation in a way that you could not have seen before your investigation.

Asking questions will power your abilities as a problem solver. The most successful problem solvers are those who use creative questions to "see" how any given solution might pan out. As a problem solver, you can empower your creative vision through asking "what if" questions: "What if I took two sciences this term?" "What if I worked part-time on campus?" "What if I designed my own major?" Use your questioning power to think through what might happen in the future and you will make the best choices for yourself today.

HABITS OF MIND

REMEMBER
THE IMPORTANT POINTS

What is important to know about thinking?

- Thinking is what happens when you ask questions and move toward answers or goals.
- Critical thinking evaluates; creative thinking generates ideas and solutions.
- You use thinking power every day and can improve thinking skill.

How can you improve your critical thinking skills?

- Critical thinking means gathering, analyzing, and evaluating information.
- Critical thinking is essential for solving problems and making decisions.
- Different ways to analyze and clarify information include these:
  - Break information into parts, seeing if examples support ideas.
  - Distinguish fact from opinion.
  - Examine perspectives and assumptions.
- Know the kinds of questions that engage critical thinking.

How can you improve your creative thinking skills?

- Creative thinking generates ideas, makes unusual connections, and takes a fresh look.
- Brainstorm when looking for choices or solutions.
- Find ways to take a new and different look at a situation.
- Use strategies to set the stage for creativity.
- Take risks and let yourself make mistakes.
- Know the kinds of questions that engage critical thinking.

How can you use your thinking skills to solve problems and make decisions?

- Problem solving addresses negative effects, but focuses on generating solutions.
  - Define problems carefully.
  - Generate possible solutions based on causes, not effects.
- Decision making aims to fulfill a need and often has predetermined choices.
  - Look at the given options and try to generate more.
  - Consider the effects of your decision on yourself and others.
- Use the step-by-step thinking path to solve problems and make decisions.

CRITICAL THINKING

APPLYING LEARNING TO LIFE

Make an Important Decision

First, describe a decision you are currently faced with. Choose an important decision that needs to be made soon.

_____

_____

Step 1: Decide on a goal. Be specific: What goal, or desired effects, do you seek from this decision? For example, if your decision is a choice between two courses, the effects you want might include credit toward a major and experience. Write down the desired effects here, prioritizing them from most important to least.

_____

_____

_____

_____

_____

Step 2: Establish needs. Who and what will be affected by your decision? If you are deciding how to finance your education and you have a family to support, for example, you must take into consideration their financial needs. List the people, things, or situations that may be affected by your decision and indicate how your decision will affect them.

_____

_____

_____

_____

Step 3: Name, investigate, and evaluate available options. Look at any options you can imagine. Consider options even if they seem impossible or unlikely; you can evaluate them later. Some decisions only have two options (to move to a new apartment or not; to get a new roommate or not); others have a wider selection of choices. List two possible options for your decision. Evaluate the potential effects of each.

Option 1: _____

Positive effects: _____

Negative effects: _____

Option 2: _____

Positive effects: _____

Negative effects: _____

Have you or someone else ever made a decision similar to the one you are about to make? If so, what can you learn from that decision that may help you?

_____

_____

_____

Step 4: Decide on a plan and take action. Taking your entire analysis into account, decide what to do. Write your decision here.

_____

_____

_____

_____

Next is perhaps the most important part of the process: Act on your decision.

Step 5: Evaluate the result. After you have acted on your decision, evaluate how everything turned out. Did you achieve the effects you wanted to achieve? What were the effects on you? On others? On the situation? To what extent were they positive, negative, or some of both? List two effects here. Name each effect, circle whether it was positive or negative, and explain your evaluation.

Effect: _____

Positive   Negative

Why? _____

_____

Effect: _____

Positive   Negative

Why? _____

_____

Final evaluation: Write a statement in reaction to the decision you made. Indicate whether you feel the decision was useful or not useful, and why. Indicate any adjustments that could have made the effects of your decision more positive.

_____

_____

_____

TEAM BUILDING

COLLABORATIVE SOLUTIONS

Solve a Problem

On a 3-by-5 card or a plain sheet of paper, each student in the class writes an academic problem—this could be a fear, a challenge, or a roadblock. Students hand these in without names. The instructor writes the list on the board.

Divide into groups of two to four. Each group chooses one problem to work on (try not to have two groups working on the same problem). Use the empty problem-solving flowchart (Key 4.9) to fill in your work.

1. *Define the problem.* As a group, look at the negative effects and state your problem specifically. Then, explore and write down the causes.

2. *Examine the problem.* Pick it apart to see what's happening. Gather information from all group members, verify facts, and go beyond assumptions.

3. *Generate possible solutions.* From the most likely causes of the problem, derive possible solutions. Record all the ideas that group members offer. After 10 minutes or so, each group member should choose one possible solution to evaluate independently.

4. *Evaluate each solution.* In thinking independently through the assigned solution, each group member should (a) weigh the positive and negative effects, (b) consider similar problems, and (c) describe how the solution affects the causes of the problem. Evaluate your assigned solution. Is it a good one? Will it work?

5. *Choose a solution.* Group members then come together, share observations and recommendations, and take a vote: Which solution is the best? You may have a tie or may want to combine two different solutions. Try to find the solution that works for most of the group. Then, together, come up with a plan for how you would put your solution to work.

6. *Evaluate your solution.* As a group, share and discuss what you had individually imagined the positive and negative effects of this solution would be. Try to come to agreement on how you think the solution would work out.

Work through a problem using this flowchart.   KEY   4.9

DEFINE PROBLEM HERE	ANALYZE THE PROBLEM

Use boxes below to list possible solutions:

POTENTIAL POSITIVE EFFECTS	SOLUTION #1	POTENTIAL NEGATIVE EFFECTS
List for each solution:		*List for each solution:*

SOLUTION #2

SOLUTION #3

Now choose the solution you think is best . . .   *. . . circle it and make it happen.*

ACTUAL POSITIVE EFFECTS	ACTION TAKEN	ACTUAL NEGATIVE EFFECTS
List for each solution:		*List for each solution:*

REEVALUATE: WAS IT A GOOD OR BAD SOLUTION?

*I recognize that my ability to **ask questions and pose problems** is an essential part of being able to move beyond my limits and achieve goals. In my opinion, I have the following specific limitation that may affect my ability to succeed in college:*

_____

_____

Here is how I would reword this limitation in order to pose it as a problem:

_____

_____

Here are two examples of how this problem has caused school-related issues:

_____

_____

Now I will ask the question: What are some ideas about how I can push past this limit and be more successful? (Write down at least three.)

1. _____

2. _____

3. _____

Finally, I commit to trying to put one into action. Which one is it?

_____

_____

How am I doing? **Later in the term, be accountable for your progress on page 139.**

SUGGESTED READINGS

Cameron, Julia, with Mark Bryan. *The Artist's Way: A Spiritual Path to Higher Creativity.* New York: Putnam, 2002.

deBono, Edward. *Lateral Thinking: Creativity Step by Step.* New York: Perennial Library, 1990.

Sark, *Sark's New Creative Companion: Ways to Free Your Creative Spirit.* Berkeley, CA: Celestial Arts, 2005.

Treffinger, Donald J., Scott G. Isaksen, and K. Brian Dorval. *Creative Problem Solving: An Introduction.* Austin, TX: Prufrock Press, 2000.

von Oech, Roger. *A Kick in the Seat of the Pants.* New York: Harper & Row, 1986.

von Oech, Roger. *A Whack on the Side of the Head.* New York: Warner Books, 1998.

INTERNET RESOURCES

Roger von Oech's Creative Think Web site (**www.creativethink.com**)

Tim van Gelder's Critical Thinking on the Web (**www.austhink.org/critical/**)

The Thinking Page (**www.thinking.net**)

ENDNOTES

1. Vincent Ruggiero, *The Art of Thinking,* 2001, quoted in "Critical Thinking," accessed July 2006 from the Web site of Oregon State University, Academic Success Center (**http://success.oregonstate.edu/criticalthinking.html**).

2. Richard Paul, "The Role of Questions in Thinking, Teaching, and Learning," 1995, accessed April 2004 from the Web site of the Center for Thinking and Learning (**http://www.criticalthinking.org/resources/articles/the-role-of-questions.shtml**).

3. "The Best Innovations Are Those That Come From Smart Questions," *Wall Street Journal,* April 12, 2004, p. B1.

4. *Keys to Lifelong Learning Telecourse* (videocassette), directed by Mary Jane Bradbury, Intrepid Films, 2000.

5. Lawrence F. Lowery, "The Biological Basis of Thinking and Learning," 1998, accessed April 2004 from the Full Option Science System at the University of California at Berkeley (**http://lhsfoss.org/newsletters/archive/pdfs/FOSS_BBTL.pdf**).

6. Colby Glass, "Strategies for Critical Thinking," March 1999, accessed April 2004 from the Web site of the Alamo Community College District (**www.accd.edu/pac/philosop/phil1301/ctstrategies.htm**).

7. Charles Cave, "Definitions of Creativity," accessed April 2003 (**http://members.ozemail.com.au/~caveman/Creative/Basics/definitions.htm**).

8. Robert J. Sternberg, *Successful Intelligence,* New York: Plume, 1997, p. 189.

9. Elizabeth F. Farrell, "Engineering a Warmer Welcome for Female Students: The Discipline Tries to Stress Its Social Relevance, an Important Factor for Many Women," *Chronicle of Higher Education,* February 22, 2002, accessed July 2006 from the Web site of Old Dominion University, Frank Batten College of Engineering and Technology (**www.eng.odu.edu/womengineers/bank_15.shtml**).

10. Roger von Oech, *A Kick in the Seat of the Pants,* New York: Harper & Row, 1986, pp. 5–21.

11. Dennis Coon, *Introduction to Psychology: Exploration and Application,* 6th ed., St. Paul: West, 1992, p. 295.

12. Roger von Oech, *A Whack on the Side of the Head,* New York: Warner Books, 1990, pp. 11–168.

13. J. R. Hayes, *Cognitive Psychology: Thinking and Creating,* Homewood, IL: Dorsey, 1978.

14. Sternberg, *Successful Intelligence,* p. 219.

15. Adapted from T. Z. Tardif and R. J. Sternberg, "What Do We Know About Creativity?" in *The Nature of Creativity,* R. J. Sternberg, ed., London: Cambridge University Press, 1988.

16. Sternberg, *Successful Intelligence,* p. 212.

17. Hayes, *Cognitive Psychology.*

18. "The Best Innovations," p. B1.

■ MULTIPLE CHOICE

Circle or highlight the answer that seems to fit best.

1. A "habit of mind" is defined as
   A. a regular study time and set of strategies.
   B. a set of solutions to problems.
   C. a disposition toward behaving intelligently when confronted with problems.
   D. a problem to be solved.

2. All of the following are considered plagiarism *except:*
   A. summarizing a key point and citing the source.
   B. submitting a paper copied from a Web site.
   C. copying material from a source without a citation.
   D. handing in a paper written by a fellow student.

3. It is important to link daily and weekly goals with long-term goals because
   A. the process will help you focus your day-to-day activities on the big-picture values and goals that are most important to you.
   B. short-term goals have no meaning if they are not placed in a longer time frame.
   C. the process will help you eliminate frivolous activities.
   D. others expect you to know how everything you do relates to what you want to accomplish in life.

4. A learning style is
   A. the best way to learn when attending classes.
   B. a particular way of being intelligent.
   C. an affinity for a particular job choice or career area.
   D. a way in which the mind receives and processes information.

5. The activity that lies at the heart of critical thinking is
   A. solving problems.
   B. taking in information.
   C. reasoning.
   D. asking questions.

6. The problem-solving process is complete after you have
   A. chosen and executed the solution you think is best.
   B. evaluated how your chosen solution worked out and refined it for future use.
   C. brainstormed possible solutions.
   D. identified the problem.

▨ TRUE/FALSE

Place a T or an F beside each statement to indicate whether you think it is true or false.

1. _____ Attention deficit disorder (ADD) and attention deficit hyperactivity disorder (ADHD) are classified as learning disabilities.
2. _____ According to studies, students who join organizations tend to persist in their studies more than students who do not branch out.
3. _____ Keeping your values in mind will help you choose a major and career that is meaningful to you.
4. _____ Your personal time profile has no effect on what time of day you function best in class.
5. _____ Stereotypes are preconceived notions or judgments, formed without just grounds or sufficient knowledge.
6. _____ A statement of opinion is a belief, conclusion, or judgment that is inherently difficult, and sometimes impossible, to verify.

▨ FILL-IN-THE-BLANK

Complete the following sentences with the appropriate word(s) or phrase(s) that best reflect what you learned in part I. Choose from the items that follow each blank.

1. A student who commits to _____ (academic excellence, academic success, academic integrity) behaves according to five values—honesty, trust, fairness, _____ (respect, motivation, commitment), and _____ (timeliness, equality, responsibility).
2. When you set _____ (long-term goals, short-term goals, priorities) you focus on the goals that are most important at that moment.
3. One way to look at learning style is to divide it into two equally important aspects: _____ and _____ (learning preferences/personality traits, verbal/visual, interests/abilities).
4. The ability to understand and appreciate differences, and behave in ways that enhance communication among people, is referred to as _____ (acculturation, culture shock, cultural competence).
5. A broad range of interests and a willingness to take risks are two common characteristics of _____ (creativity, critical thinking, cause and effect).
6. When you _____ (brainstorm, cooperate, innovate), you generate ideas without immediately evaluating whether they are good or useful.

▨ ESSAY QUESTION

The following essay question will help you learn to organize and communicate your ideas in writing, just as you must do on an essay test. Before you begin answering a question, spend a few minutes planning (brainstorm possible approaches, write a thesis statement, jot down main thoughts in outline or think link form). To prepare yourself for actual test conditions, limit your writing time to no more than 20 minutes.

> This part of the text, encompassing chapters 1 through 4, is titled "Getting Ready to Learn." Define what it means to be prepared to learn. Discuss the roles that the major chapter topics play in preparing to learn, being sure to include the habits of mind. Evaluate how prepared you feel to learn throughout your college career, and explain your evaluation. Finally, discuss how you plan to continue your preparation throughout the term.

BE ACCOUNTABLE FOR YOUR HABITS OF MIND FROM PART I

Look back at the "Activate the Habit of Mind" exercises in chapters 1 through 4 (pages 32, 66, 101–102, and 134), and specifically at your plans for incorporating each habit into your study routine. On a separate sheet of paper, write a short journal entry that assesses the progress you've made on each habit. Consider questions such as the following:

- Have I put into action the strategies I planned to use?
- How have the strategies helped or changed how I work?
- Do I feel that I now "own" each habit of mind? In what way?
- What is my plan going forward to further develop and use these habits of mind?

PART II
TARGETING SUCCESS IN SCHOOL AND LIFE

Reading and Studying
FOCUSING ON CONTENT

5

Listening and Memory
TAKING IN AND REMEMBERING INFORMATION

6

Taking Notes
RECORDING CONCEPTS AND INFORMATION

7

Test Taking
SHOWING WHAT YOU KNOW

8

Quantitative Learning
BECOMING COMFORTABLE WITH MATH AND SCIENCE

9

Effective Writing
COMMUNICATING YOUR MESSAGE

10

Creating Your Life
BUILDING A SUCCESSFUL FUTURE

11

Apply past knowledge to new situations

HABITS OF MIND

"Intelligent human beings learn from experience. When confronted with a new and perplexing problem, they . . . call upon their store of knowledge and experience for sources of data and for processes that will help them solve each new challenge."

ART COSTA

APPLY PAST KNOWLEDGE TO NEW SITUATIONS

As a reader, you bring the knowledge you have gained from all you have read and experienced in the past to the material you are now reading. By applying past knowledge to new situations, you are able to place what is new and different in the context of what you know and understand.

Active learning means more than just storing information in your brain. You grow by applying what you already know to new situations. Recalling how blowing bubbles held his attention and interest as a child, this man is able to take a break from his standard way of thinking to approach business challenges from a new perspective.

In every college course, reading and studying are essential to learning. Becoming more proficient in these skills requires a step-by-step approach linked to specific techniques. This chapter will help you learn reading and studying strategies to increase your efficiency and depth of understanding. By the end of the chapter, every hour you spend with your books will become more valuable as you learn and retain more and apply your knowledge to new situations, having the ability to approach and understand them in your own way.

In this chapter, you explore answers to the following questions:

- What will improve your reading comprehension?
- How can SQ3R help you own what you read?
- How do you customize your text with highlighting and notes?

Photo: Don Ipock/The New York Times

What will improve your reading comprehension?

R eading is a process that requires you to master concepts in a personal way. Your familiarity with a subject, your background and life experiences, and even your personal interpretation of words and phrases affect understanding. Because of this, you are using this chapter's habit of mind—*applying past knowledge to new situations*—every time you open a book.

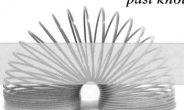

A mind once stretched by a new idea never regains its original dimension.

OLIVER WENDELL HOLMES, EARLY 20TH CENTURY
SUPREME COURT JUSTICE

© Stephen Coburn—Fotolia

Because past knowledge is different for everyone, reading experiences are unique. If, for example, your family owns a hardware store where you worked during summers, you will read a retailing chapter in a business text in the context of your background. While you are comparing text concepts to your family's business practices, your classmates may be reading for basic ideas and vocabulary.

The goal of reading comprehension is *understanding*. This is crucial in college where you will be asked to master material on your own and use what you learn as a foundation in upper-level courses. When you struggle through and master concepts that you considered impossible the first time you read them, you'll be proud of your ability to overcome obstacles instead of giving up. This pride will motivate you every time you read.

Henry David Thoreau, the 19th century American author, poet, and philosopher, made the following observation: "How many a man has dated a new era in his life from the reading of a book." What do you think Thoreau meant? Discuss why this statement may be especially meaningful to you now as you begin college. How do you think Thoreau's statement relates to the habit of mind of *applying past knowledge to new situations?*

Set Your Expectations

On any given day, you may be faced with reading assignments like these:

- A textbook chapter on the history of South African apartheid (world history)
- An original research study on the relationship between sleep deprivation and the development of memory problems (psychology)
- The first 30 pages in John Steinbeck's classic novel, *The Grapes of Wrath* (American literature)
- A technical manual on the design of computer antivirus programs (computer science, software design)

This material is rigorous by anyone's standards. In fact, many students are surprised at how much reading there is in college, and that they are often expected to learn concepts that are never covered in class.

If you have a reading disability, if English is not your primary language, or if you have limited reading skills, seek out the support programs your college offers at reading and tutoring centers (see chapter 1 for more on learning disabilities and support services). Your ability to succeed is linked to your willingness to ask for help.

Take an Active Approach to Difficult Texts

Because college texts are generally written to challenge the intellect, even well-written texts may be tough going. Generally, the further you advance in school, the more complex your readings will be. You may encounter concepts and terms that are foreign to you. This is often the case when assignments are from *primary sources*—original documents, including academic journal articles and scientific studies, rather than another writer's interpretation of these documents.

Some academic writing has earned the reputation of being difficult for the sake of difficulty—an observation that motivated novelist George Orwell to write a parody of how a passage from the Old Testament would read if it were translated into academic prose (see Key 5.1).

Your challenge is to approach difficult material actively and positively. The strategies discussed next will help.

Look for order and meaning in seemingly chaotic reading materials. Use SQ3R and the critical reading strategies introduced later in this chapter to discover patterns and connections.

Don't expect to master material on the first pass. Instead, create a multistep plan: On your first reading, your goal is to gain an overview of key concepts and interrelationships. On subsequent readings, you grasp ideas and relate them to what you already know. By your last reading, you master concepts and details and can apply the material to problems.

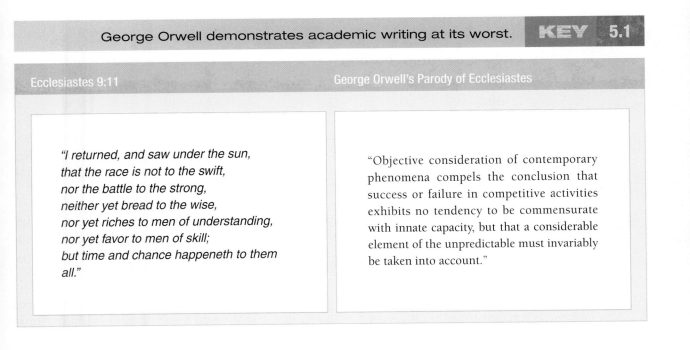

George Orwell demonstrates academic writing at its worst.   KEY   5.1

Ecclesiastes 9:11	George Orwell's Parody of Ecclesiastes
"I returned, and saw under the sun, that the race is not to the swift, nor the battle to the strong, neither yet bread to the wise, nor yet riches to men of understanding, nor yet favor to men of skill; but time and chance happeneth to them all."	"Objective consideration of contemporary phenomena compels the conclusion that success or failure in competitive activities exhibits no tendency to be commensurate with innate capacity, but that a considerable element of the unpredictable must invariably be taken into account."

Know that some texts require extra work and concentration. You may have to look back at last term's text to refresh your memory so that you can apply what you have learned to new material. If the material still doesn't click, scan background material for information that will help you understand. Set a goal to make your way through the material, whatever it takes. If you want to learn, you will.

Define unclear concepts and words. Consult resources—instructors, study group partners, and reference materials—for help. Build a library of texts in your major and minor areas of study and refer to them when needed, and bookmark helpful Web sites.

Ask yourself questions. Engage in an internal question-and-answer session before reading a chapter. Look at the chapter outline or chapter headings and then think about what the material means and why it is being presented in this way. Write down your thoughts. Then read the chapter summary to see if your questions are answered. (Questioning is at the heart of the SQ3R study system, as you will learn later in this chapter.)

Think critically. Ask yourself, "Do I understand what I just read? Are ideas and supporting evidence clear? Am I able to explain the material to someone else?"

Build knowledge through reading and studying. More than any other factor, what you already know before you read provides a context for new material. Getting in the habit of mind of *applying what you know to new situations* will help you grow intellectually.

Think positively. Instead of telling yourself that you cannot understand, think positively. Tell yourself, "I can learn this material. I am a good reader. I can succeed."

Have an open mind. Be careful not to prejudge assignments as impossible or boring or a waste of time and energy before you begin.

Choose the Right Setting

Finding a place and time that minimize distractions will help you focus on your reading.

Select the right company (or no company at all). If you prefer to read alone, establish a relatively interruption-proof place and time, such as an out-of-the-way spot at the library. Even if you don't mind activity nearby, try to minimize distractions.

Select the right location. Many students study at a library desk. Others prefer an easy chair at the library, in their dorm, or at home. Still others prefer spreading out papers on the floor. Avoid studying in bed, since you are likely to fall asleep. After choosing a spot, adjust the heat and light to do your best work.

Select a time when you are alert and focused. Eventually, you will associate certain times with focused reading. Pay attention to your natural body rhythms and study when your energy is high. Whereas night owls are productive when everyone else is sleeping, for example, morning people have a hard time working during late-night sessions.

Students with young children have an additional factor to consider when they are thinking about when, where, and how to read. Key 5.2 explores some ways that parents or others caring for children can maximize their study efforts.

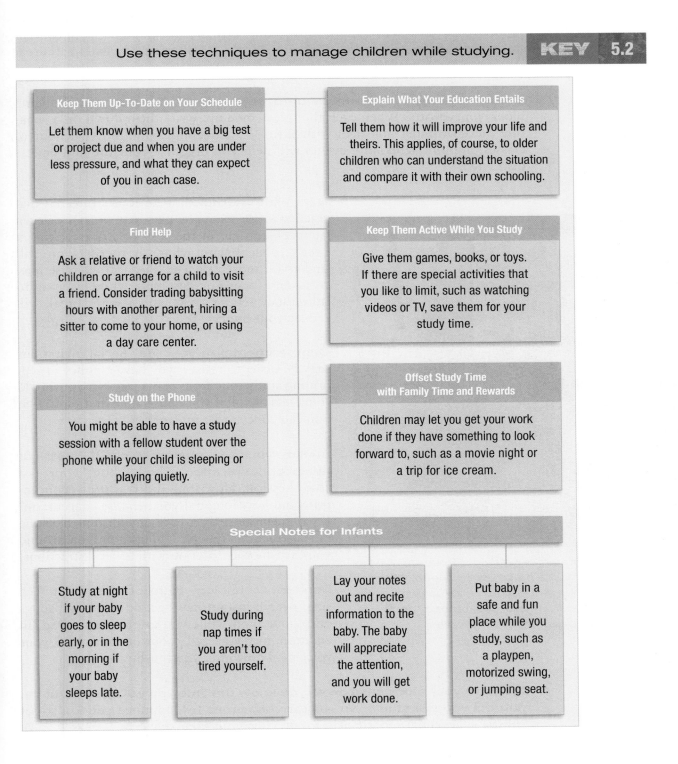

Use these techniques to manage children while studying. **KEY 5.2**

Keep Them Up-To-Date on Your Schedule

Let them know when you have a big test or project due and when you are under less pressure, and what they can expect of you in each case.

Explain What Your Education Entails

Tell them how it will improve your life and theirs. This applies, of course, to older children who can understand the situation and compare it with their own schooling.

Find Help

Ask a relative or friend to watch your children or arrange for a child to visit a friend. Consider trading babysitting hours with another parent, hiring a sitter to come to your home, or using a day care center.

Keep Them Active While You Study

Give them games, books, or toys. If there are special activities that you like to limit, such as watching videos or TV, save them for your study time.

Study on the Phone

You might be able to have a study session with a fellow student over the phone while your child is sleeping or playing quietly.

Offset Study Time with Family Time and Rewards

Children may let you get your work done if they have something to look forward to, such as a movie night or a trip for ice cream.

Special Notes for Infants

Study at night if your baby goes to sleep early, or in the morning if your baby sleeps late.

Study during nap times if you aren't too tired yourself.

Lay your notes out and recite information to the baby. The baby will appreciate the attention, and you will get work done.

Put baby in a safe and fun place while you study, such as a playpen, motorized swing, or jumping seat.

Learn to Concentrate

When you focus your attention on one thing and one thing only, you are engaged in the act of *concentration*. Without concentration, you are likely to remember little as your mind wanders. Following are active learning methods for remaining focused as you study.

Be intensely involved. Tell yourself that what you are doing is important and needs your full attention—no matter what is going on around you. It might help to place a purpose statement at the top of your desk. For example: "I'm concentrating on the U.S. Constitution because it is the basis for our laws and because it will be on Friday's exam."

Banish extraneous thoughts onto paper. Don't let unrelated thoughts block your efforts. When such thoughts come up, write them down on a separate piece of paper and deal with them later. Keeping a monthly calendar of classes, appointments, and events will help you organize your life and be less distracted.

Marilynn K. Yee/*The New York Times*

An important part of reading success is making sure you have the materials you need. Check your syllabi for required reading materials and acquire them from your bookstore or copy center at the beginning of the term.

Deal with internal distractions. Internal distractions—for example, personal worries or even hunger—can get in the way of work. Taking a break to deal with what's bothering you will make you more efficient. Physical exercise may relax and focus you, studying while listening to music may relieve stress, and a snack break will reduce your hunger.

Compartmentalize your life. Social invitations may be easier to resist if you have a policy of separating study time from play time. No one should think less of you if you refuse an invitation so that you can concentrate on work.

Analyze your environment to see if it helps or hurts concentration. Think about your last study session. How long did you *try* to concentrate and how long did you *actually* concentrate? If you spent more than 10% of your time blocking out distractions (people, things going on around you), try another location with fewer distractions.

Don't let technology distract you. Don't Web surf, e-mail, instant message, or download songs onto your iPod while you are trying to read. In addition, turn your cell phone off, and check your voice mail only after you finish your work.

Structure your study session so you know the time you will spend and the material you will study. No one can concentrate for unlimited periods, so set realistic goals and a specific plan for dividing your time.

Linking the Past to the Future

AP Wide World Photos

Bill Cosby became a serious spokesperson for African American youth after the murder of his son.

He asks young people to accept and value their past as they *build a future through education and hard work,* instead of viewing themselves as victims, dropping out of school, and rejecting personal responsibility.

Plan a reward. Make sure you have something to look forward to, because you deserve it!

The strongest motivation to concentrate comes from within—not from the fear of failing a test, or disappointing a teacher. When you see the connection between what you study and your short- and long-term goals, you will be better able to focus on your readings, to remember, to learn, and to apply.

Become Emotionally Involved

You are more likely to remember material that evokes an emotional response than material that does not affect you at all. Student success expert Eric Jensen explains:

> The stronger you feel about something you read the more likely you are to remember it and make sense out of it. The good thing about this is that it works both ways; hating something or disagreeing with something works just as well as liking something or strongly agreeing with it.[1]

How do you surround normally "dry" text material with emotions? These suggestions might help:

- Stop and think about your reaction to ideas, to the author's point of view and writing style, to chapter features and text design, and even to the chapter order.
- Discuss specific points with classmates and have a heated discussion when you disagree. This will also help you understand the material.
- Think through the implications of a concept when it is applied in the real world.

Define Your Reading Purpose

When you define your purpose, you ask yourself *why* you are reading particular material. One way to do this is by completing this sentence: "In reading this material, I intend to define/learn/answer/achieve . . . " *Write your goal down before you begin and look at it whenever you lose focus or get bogged down in details.* With a clear purpose you can decide how much time and effort to expend on various assignments. Nearly 375 years ago, Francis Bacon, the great English philosopher, made this observation:

> Some books are to be tasted, others to be swallowed, and some few to be chewed and digested; that is, some books are to be read only in parts, others to be read but not curiously; and some few to be read wholly, and with diligence and attention.

Bacon's advice is particularly true in college where you may be overwhelmed by assignments unless you prioritize. Later in this chapter, you will find suggestions for evaluating and prioritizing the readings on your plate.

Achieving your reading purpose also requires adapting to different materials. Being a flexible reader—adjusting your strategies and pace—will help you get what you want from each assignment. You are in control.

© Liudmila Korsakova—Fotolia

Purpose Determines Reading Strategy

Following are four reading purposes, examined briefly. You may have one or more for any "reading event."

■ *Purpose 1: Read for understanding.* Studying involves reading to comprehend concepts and details. Details help explain or support general concepts, and concepts provide a framework for remembering details.

■ *Purpose 2: Read to evaluate critically.* Critical evaluation involves understanding. It means approaching material with an open mind, examining causes and effects, evaluating ideas, and asking questions that test the writer's argument and assumptions. Critical reading brings a level of understanding that goes beyond basic information recall.

■ *Purpose 3: Read for practical application.* Here you gather usable information to apply toward a specific goal. When you read a textbook preface or an instruction booklet for new software, your goal is to learn how to do or use something. Reading and action usually go hand in hand.

■ *Purpose 4: Read for pleasure.* Some materials you read for entertainment, such as *Sports Illustrated* magazine or the latest page-turner by *DaVinci Code* author Dan Brown.

Use your class syllabus to help you define your purpose for each assignment. If, for example, you know that the topic of inflation will be discussed in your next economics class, read the assigned chapter, targeting what your instructor will expect you to know and do with the material. He may expect you to master definitions, economic models, causes and consequences, government intervention strategies, and historical examples and to be able to apply what you know to economic problems. In this case, depending on what your instructor expects, you have three reading purposes—understanding, critical evaluation, and practical application. If you are confused about your purpose, e-mail your instructor for clarification. He is likely to be impressed with your motivation to stay on top of your assignments.

Purpose Determines Pace

As Key 5.3 shows, good readers link the pace of reading to their reading purpose.

Spend Enough Time

You'll need more than good intentions to finish assignments on schedule. You'll have to put in hours of work every day. One formula for success is this: For every hour you spend in the classroom each week, spend at least two hours preparing for the class. For example, a course load of 15 credit hours means that you should spend 30 hours per week studying and doing homework outside of class. Students who fall far short of this goal are likely to have a hard time keeping up. Check your syllabus for the dates that reading assignments are due, and give yourself enough time to complete every reading. (The syllabus on pages 9–10 specifies reading assignments and due dates.)

KEY 5.3   Link your reading pace to your reading purpose.

Type of Material	Reading Purpose	Pace
Academic readings ■ Textbooks ■ Original sources ■ Articles from scholarly journals ■ Online publications for academic readers ■ Lab reports ■ Required fiction	■ Critical analysis ■ Overall mastery ■ Preparation for tests	Slow, especially if the material is unfamiliar
Manuals ■ Instructions ■ Recipes	Practical application	Slow to medium
Journalism and nonfiction for the general reader ■ Nonfiction books ■ Newspapers ■ Magazines ■ Online publications for the general public	Understanding of general ideas, key concepts, and specific facts for personal understanding and/or practical application	Medium to fast
Nonrequired fiction	Understanding of general ideas, key concepts, and specific facts for enjoyment	Variable, but tending toward faster speeds

Source: Adapted from Nicholas Reid Schaffzin, *The Princeton Review Reading Smart,* New York: Random House, 1996, p. 15.

Expand Your Vocabulary

As your reading materials become more complex, how much you comprehend—and how readily you do it—is influenced by your vocabulary. Use the following techniques to learn unfamiliar words as you encounter them.

Analyze Word Parts

Often, if you understand part of a word, you can figure out what the entire word means. This is true because many English words combine Greek and Latin pre-fixes, roots, and suffixes. *Prefixes* are word parts that are added to the beginning of a root. The *root* is the central part or basis of a word around which prefixes and/or suffixes are added to produce different words. *Suffixes* are added to the end of the root. When you use word parts to grow your vocabulary, you are *applying past knowledge to new situations*.

Key 5.4 contains just a few of the prefixes, roots, and suffixes you will encounter as you read, but there are literally thousands more. Taking the time to memorize these verbal building blocks will help you grow your vocabulary, as you will encounter them in many different words. (Keep in mind that although prefixes, roots, and suffixes are reliable language tools, they do not always apply to words with complex origins.)

Build your vocabulary with common prefixes, roots, and suffixes.   KEY 5.4

Prefix	Primary Meaning	Example
a-, ab-	from	abstain, avert
ad-, af-, at-	to	adhere, affix, attain
con-, cor-, com-	with, together	convene, correlate, compare
di-	apart	divert, divorce
il-	not	illegal, illegible
ir-	not	irresponsible
post-	after	postpone, postpartum
pro-	before	prologue
sub-, sup-	under	subordinate, suppose

Root	Primary Meaning	Example
logue	to speak	dialogue
com	fill	incomplete
strict	bind	restriction
cept	take	receptacle
chron	time	synchronize
ann	year	biannual
sper	hope	desperate
clam	cry out	proclamation
voc	speak, talk	convocation

Suffix	Primary Meaning	Example
-able	able	recyclable
-arium	place for	aquarium, solarium
-cule	very small	molecule
-ist	one who	pianist
-meter	measure	thermometer
-ness	state of	carelessness
-sis	condition of	hypnosis
-y	inclined to	sleepy

Use a Dictionary

When reading a textbook, the first "dictionary" to search is the glossary. Textbooks often include an end-of-book glossary that explains technical words and concepts. The definitions there are usually limited to the meaning of the term as it is used in the text.

Standard dictionaries provide broader information such as word origin, pronunciation, part of speech, synonyms, antonyms, and multiple meanings. Buy a standard dictionary, keep it nearby, and consult it for help in understanding unfamiliar words. You may even want to invest in an electronic handheld dictionary, which you can take wherever you go. If you prefer an online version, investigate Web sites like Dictionary.com. The following suggestions will help you make the most of your dictionary.

Read every meaning, not just the first. Think critically about which meaning suits the context of the word in question, and choose the one that makes the most sense to you.

Say the word out loud—then write it down to make sure you can spell it. Check your pronunciation against the dictionary symbols as you say each word. Speaking and writing new words will boost recall.

Use your chosen definition. Imagine, for example, that you encounter the following sentence and do not know what the word *indoctrinated* means:

> The cult indoctrinated its members to reject society's values.

In the dictionary, you find several definitions, including *brainwashed* and *instructed*. You decide that the one closest to the correct meaning is *brainwashed*. With this term, the sentence reads as follows:

> The cult brainwashed its members to reject society's values.

Restate the definition in your own words. When you can do this with ease, you know that you understand the meaning and are not merely parroting a dictionary definition.

Try to use the word in conversation in the next 24 hours. Not only does this demonstrate that you know how the word is used, but it also aids memorization.

Learn Specialized Vocabulary

As you learn a subject, you will encounter specialized vocabulary (see Key 5.5 for examples from four college texts). Most of these words, phrases, and acronyms may be unfamiliar unless you have studied the topics before. Even if you feel like you are diving into a foreign language, know that continual exposure will create mastery as the term progresses.

KEY 5.5   Every text includes specialized vocabulary.

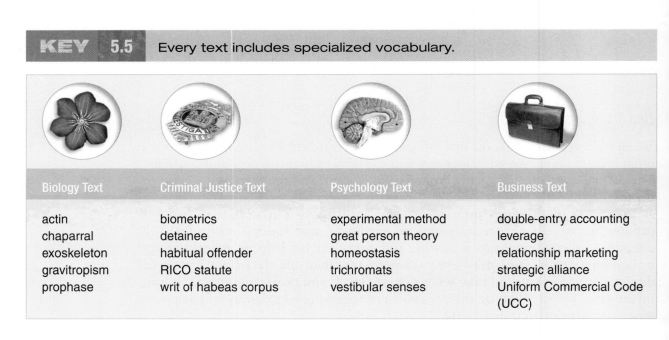

Biology Text	Criminal Justice Text	Psychology Text	Business Text
actin	biometrics	experimental method	double-entry accounting
chaparral	detainee	great person theory	leverage
exoskeleton	habitual offender	homeostasis	relationship marketing
gravitropism	RICO statute	trichromats	strategic alliance
prophase	writ of habeas corpus	vestibular senses	Uniform Commercial Code (UCC)

Apply a basic vocabulary-building approach to learn these terms. Understand words in the context of the chapter; then turn to the glossary for a review, record definitions in your notes, create vocabulary flashcards, use terms in your own sentences, and more. Don't rush through unfamiliar words. Rather, look them up, ask other students about them, and relate them to concepts you already know.

Your instructors will test you on your ability to define and use course-specific vocabulary, so make sure you understand terms well enough to define them correctly on short-answer tests and to use them on essay exams.

Use Memory Aids to Ensure Recall

Most students find that their most important vocabulary-building tool is the flash card. Your efforts will pay off if you study several cards a day and push yourself to use your new words in conversation and writing. You may also want to work together with another student to review each other's cards. Memorization tools, including mnemonic devices and flash cards, are discussed in chapter 6.

How can SQ3R help you own what you read?

SQ3R stands for *survey, question, read, recite,* and *review.* Developed more than 60 years ago by Francis Robinson, this textbook reading technique is still used today because it works.[2]

As you move through the stages of SQ3R, you will skim and scan your text. *Skimming* involves the rapid reading of such chapter elements as section introductions and conclusions, boldfaced or italicized terms, pictures and charts, and chapter summaries. The goal of skimming is a quick construction of the main ideas. In contrast, *scanning* involves the careful search for specific facts and examples. You might use scanning during the review phase of SQ3R to locate particular information.

Approach SQ3R as a flexible framework on which to build your study method. When you bring your personal learning styles and study preferences to the system, it will work better than if you follow it rigidly. For example, you and another classmate may focus on elements in a different order when you survey, write different types of questions, or favor different sets of review strategies. Explore the strategies, evaluate what works, and then make the system your own. (Note that SQ3R is not appropriate for literature.)

Survey

Surveying, the first stage in SQ3R, is the process of previewing, or pre-reading, a book before you study it. Compare it to looking at a map before starting a road trip; determining the route and stops along the way in advance will save time and trouble while you travel.

Most textbooks include elements that provide a big-picture overview of the main ideas and themes. You need the big picture to make sense of the thousands of information nuggets contained in the text and to learn the order of topics and the amount of space allotted to each.

Front Matter

Skim the *table of contents* for the chapter titles, the main topics in each chapter, and the order in which they will be covered, as well as special features. Then skim the *preface,* which is a personal note from the author that tells you what the book will cover and its point of view. For example, the preface for the American history text *Out of Many* states that it highlights "the experiences of diverse communities of Americans in the unfolding story of our country."[3] This tells you that cultural diversity is a central theme.

Chapter Elements

Generally, every chapter includes devices that structure the material and highlight important content. Among these are the following:

- Chapter title, which establishes the topic and often the author's perspective
- Chapter introduction, outline, list of objectives, or list of key topics
- First-, second-, and third-level headings, including those in question form
- Information in the margins including definitions, quotes, questions, and exercises
- Tables, charts, photographs, and captions that express important concepts
- Side-bar boxed features that are connected to text themes
- Particular styles or arrangements of type (**boldface,** *italics,* <u>underlining,</u> larger fonts, bullet points, boxed text) that call attention to vocabulary or concepts
- An end-of-chapter summary that reviews chapter content
- Review questions and exercises that help you analyze and master content

In Key 5.6, a typical page from the college textbook *Psychology: An Introduction* by Charles G. Morris and Albert A. Maisto, how many elements do you recognize? How do these elements help you grasp the subject even before reading it?[4]

How does reading assigned textbook material enrich your classroom experience? What aspects of your favorite text this term make it a helpful learning tool for you? After reading about text survey techniques, what techniques do you intend to use as you study?

Back Matter

Some texts include a *glossary* that defines text terms. You may also find an *index* to help you locate topics and a *bibliography* that lists additional readings.

Question

Now that you have surveyed your text, your next step is to *ask questions* about your assignment. The process of asking questions leads you to discover knowledge on your own, which is the essence of critical thinking (see chapter 4). As you pose questions and discover the answers in your text, you teach yourself the material.

Various survey elements are included on this text page. KEY 5.6

Classical (or Pavlovian) condition-ing The type of learning in which a response naturally elicited by one stimu-lus comes to be elicited by a different, formerly neutral stimulus.

Unconditioned stimulus (US) A stimulus that invariably causes an organ-ism to respond in a specific way.

Unconditioned response (UR) A response that takes place in an organism whenever an unconditioned stimulus occurs.

Conditioned stimulus (CS) An origi-nally neutral stimulus that is paired with an unconditioned stimulus and eventually produces the desired response in an organism when presented alone.

Conditioned response (CR) After conditioning, the response an organism produces when only a conditioned stimu-lus is presented.

you are experiencing insight. When you imitate the steps of professional dancers you saw last night on television, you are demonstrating observational learning. Like conditioning, cognitive learning is one of our survival strategies. Through cognitive processes, we learn which events are safe and which are dangerous without having to experience those events directly. Cognitive learning also gives us access to the wisdom of people who lived hundreds of years ago, and it will give people living hundreds of years from now some insight into our experiences and way of life.

Our discussion begins with *classical conditioning*. This simple kind of learning serves as a convenient starting point for examining what learning is and how it can be observed.

Classical Conditioning

How did Pavlov's discovery of classical conditioning help to shed light on learning?

Ivan Pavlov (1849–1936), a Russian physiologist who was studying digestive processes, discovered classical conditioning almost by accident. Because animals salivate when food is placed in their mouths, Pavlov inserted tubes into the salivary glands of dogs to measure how much saliva they produced when they were given food. He noticed, however, that the dogs salivated before the food was in their mouths: The mere sight of food made them drool. In fact, they even drooled at the sound of the experimenter's footsteps. This aroused Pavlov's curiosity. What was making the dogs salivate even before they had the food in their mouths? How had they learned to salivate in response to the sound of the experimenter's approach?

To answer these questions, Pavlov set out to teach the dogs to salivate when food was not present. He devised an experiment in which he sounded a bell just before the food was brought into the room. A ringing bell does not usually make a dog's mouth water but, after hearing the bell many times just before getting fed, Pavlov's dogs began to salivate as soon as the bell rang. It was as if they had learned that the bell signaled the appearance of food, and their mouths watered on cue even if no food followed. The dogs had been conditioned to salivate in response to a new stim-ulus—the bell—that would not normally have prompted that response (Pavlov, 1927). Figure 5–1, shows one of Pavlov's procedures in which the bell has been replaced by a touch to the dog's leg just before food is given.

Elements of Classical Conditioning

Generally speaking, **classical (or Pavlovian) conditioning** involves pairing an *involuntary* response (for example, salivation) that is usually evoked by one stimulus with a different, formerly neutral stimulus (such as a bell or a touch on the leg). Pavlov's experiment illustrates the four basic elements of classical conditioning. The first is an **unconditioned stimulus (US)**, such as food, which invariably prompts a certain reaction—salivation, in this case. That reaction—the **unconditioned response (UR)**—is the second element and always results from the unconditioned stimulus: Whenever the dog is given food (US), its mouth waters (UR). The third element is the neutral stimulus—the ringing bell—which is called the **conditioned stimulus (CS)**. At first, the conditioned stimulus is said to be "neutral" with respect to the desired response (salivation), because dogs do not salivate at the sound of a bell unless they have been conditioned to react in this way by repeatedly presenting the CS and US together. Frequent pairing of the CS and US produces the fourth element in the classical conditioning process: the **conditioned response (CR)**. The conditioned response is the behavior that the animal has learned in response to the conditioned stimulus. Usually, the unconditioned response and the conditioned

Step 1: Ask Yourself What You Know About the Topic

Before you begin reading, take a few minutes to summarize in writing what you already know about the topic, if anything. As you perform this task, you delve into your knowledge base, preparing yourself to *apply what you know to new reading material.*

TAKE ACTION

Survey a Text

Practice will improve your surveying skills. So start now with this text or another you are currently using.

Skim the front matter, including the table of contents and preface. What does this material tell you about the theme? About the book's approach and point of view?

_____

_____

Are there unexpected topics listed in the table of contents? Are there topics you expected to see but are missing?

_____

_____

Now look at a typical text chapter. List the devices that organize the structure and content of the material.

_____

_____

After skimming the chapter, what do you know about the material? What elements helped you skim quickly?

_____

_____

Finally, skim the back matter. What back matter elements can you identify?

_____

_____

How do you plan to use each of these elements when you begin studying?

_____

_____

How does surveying help activate the habit of mind of _applying past knowledge to new situations?_

_____

_____

Thinking about your current knowledge is especially important in your major, where the concepts you learn in one course prepare you for those you will learn in subsequent courses. For example, while your first business course may introduce the broad concept of marketing research, an upper-level marketing course may explore, in depth, how marketing research analyzes consumer behavior according to age, education, income, economic status, and attitudes. Learning this advanced material depends on understanding the basics.

Step 2: Write Questions Linked to Chapter Headings

Next, examine the chapter headings and, on a separate page or in the text margins, write questions linked to them. When you encounter an assignment without headings, divide the material into logical sections, and then develop questions based on what you think is the main idea of each section.

Key 5.7 shows how this works. The column on the left contains primary- and secondary-level headings from a section of *Out of Many*. The column on the right rephrases these headings in question form. There is no "correct" set of questions. Given the same headings, you could create different questions. Your goal is to engage the material as you begin to think critically about it.

Use Bloom's taxonomy to formulate questions. Educational psychologist Benjamin Bloom developed *Bloom's taxonomy* because he believed that not all questions are created equal and that the greatest learning results from rigorous inquiry.[5] While some questions ask for a simple recall, said Bloom, others ask for higher levels of thinking. Key 5.8 shows the six levels of questions identified by Bloom: knowledge, understanding, application, analysis, synthesis, and evaluation. It also identifies verbs that are associated with each level. As you read, using these verbs to formulate specific questions will help you learn. Recognizing these verbs on an essay test will help you develop complete, comprehensive answers.

KEY 5.7 Creating questions from headings.

Heading	Question
The Meaning of Freedom	What did freedom mean for both slaves and citizens in the United States?
Moving About	Where did African Americans go after they were freed from slavery?
The African American Family	How did freedom change the structure of the African American family?
African American Churches and Schools	What effect did freedom have on the formation of African American churches and schools?
Land and Labor After Slavery	How was land farmed and maintained after slaves were freed?
The Origins of African American Politics	How did the end of slavery bring about the beginning of African American political life?

KEY 5.8   Use Bloom's taxonomy to formulate questions at different cognitive levels.

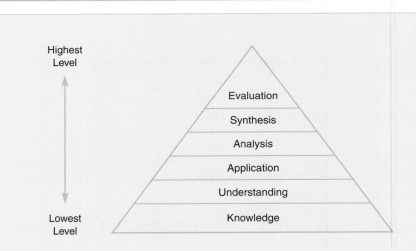

Verbs That Indicate Each Level

1. *Knowledge:* arrange, define, duplicate, label, list, memorize, name, order, recognize, relate, recall, repeat, reproduce, state.

2. *Understanding:* classify, describe, discuss, explain, express, identify, indicate, locate, recognize, report, restate, review, select, translate.

3. *Application:* apply, choose, demonstrate, dramatize, employ, illustrate, interpret, operate, practice, schedule, sketch, solve, use, write.

4. *Analysis:* analyze, appraise, calculate, categorize, compare, contrast, criticize, differentiate, discriminate, distinguish, examine, experiment, question, test.

5. *Synthesis:* arrange, assemble, collect, compose, construct, create, design, develop, formulate, manage, organize, plan, prepare, propose, set up, write.

6. *Evaluation:* appraise, argue, assess, attach, choose, compare, defend, estimate, judge, predict, rate, score, select, support, value, evaluate.

Read

Your text survey and questions give you a starting point for *reading,* the first R in SQ3R. Retaining what you read requires an active approach, as follows:

- *Focus on the key points of your survey.* Pay special attention to points raised in headings, in boldface type, in chapter objectives, and in the summary.

- *Focus on your Q stage questions.* Read the material with the purpose of answering each question. Write down or highlight ideas and examples that relate to your questions.

- *Mark up your text and take text notes.* You may want to write notes in the margins or on separate paper, circle key ideas, or highlight key points to remind you of what's important. These cues will help you study for exams. Text-marking and note-taking techniques will be examined later in the chapter.

- *Create text tabs.* Place plastic index tabs or adhesive notes at the start of different chapters to help you flip back and forth with ease.

TAKE ACTION

Turn Chapter Headings into Questions

Put pencil to paper with the one primary-level heading and eight secondary-level headings from the "Groups and Organization" chapter of the 10th edition of *Sociology* by John J. Macionis. Create questions that will make you think about the subject—even if you know nothing about it right now.

Headings in Macionis's "Groups and Organization" chapter	Questions that will help you think critically about the material
SOCIAL GROUPS	
Primary and Secondary Groups	
Group Leadership	
Group Conformity	
Reference Groups	
In-Groups and Out-Groups	
Group Size	
Social Diversity: Race, Class, and Gender	
Networks	

Source: John J. Macionis, *Sociology*, 10th ed., Upper Saddle River, NJ: Prentice Hall, 2005, pp. 162–170.

Find the Main Idea

Understanding what you read depends on your ability to recognize *main ideas* and link other ideas to them. Here are places you are likely to find these core ideas:

- In a topic sentence at the beginning of the paragraph, stating the topic of the paragraph and what about that topic the author wants to communicate, followed by support
- At the end of the paragraph, following supporting details that lead up to it
- Buried in the middle of the paragraph, sandwiched between supporting details
- In a compilation of ideas from various sentences, each of which contains a critical element—sometimes leaving it up to you to piece these elements together to find the main idea
- Never explicitly stated, but implied in the passage

When the main idea of a passage is not clear, how do you decide what it is? Ophelia H. Hancock, a reading-skills specialist, suggests a three-step approach:[6]

1. *Search for the topic of the paragraph.* The topic of the paragraph is not the same as the main idea. Rather, it is the broad subject being discussed—for example, former President John F. Kennedy, hate crimes on campus, or the Internet.

2. *Identify the aspect of the topic that is the paragraph's focus.* If the general topic is President Kennedy, the author may focus on any of thousands of aspects of that topic, such as his health problems, his civil rights policies, or his effectiveness as a public speaker.

3. *Find what the author wants you to know about that specific aspect; this is the main idea.* The main idea of a paragraph dealing with President Kennedy as a public speaker may be this:

> President Kennedy was a charismatic speaker who used his charm and intelligence to make the presidency accessible during regularly televised news conferences.

Prioritize Your Reading Assignments

Ask yourself what is important and what you have to remember. According to Adam Robinson, cofounder of *The Princeton Review,* successful students can tell the difference between information worthy of study, information they should know in a general way, and information they should ignore. Says Robinson: "The only way you can effectively absorb the relevant information is to ignore the irrelevant information. . . . Trying to digest and understand all the information in a textbook is . . . an excellent way to become quickly and hopelessly confused."[7]

The following questions will help you determine if text material is important enough to study in depth:

- Is the material stressed in headings, charts, tables, captions, key terms, and definitions? In mid-chapter and end-of-chapter exercises? In the chapter introduction and summary? (Surveying before reading will enable you to answer these questions.)

- Is the material a definition, a crucial concept, an example, an explanation of a variety or type, a critical relationship or comparison?

- Does it spark questions and reactions as you read?

- Does it surprise or confuse you?

- Did your instructor stress the material in class? Does your assignment ask you to focus on something specific?

When trying to figure out what to study and what to skim, ask yourself whether your instructor would expect you to know the material. If you are unsure and if the topic is not on your syllabus, e-mail your instructor and ask for clarification.

Recite

Once you finish reading a topic, stop and answer the questions you raised in the Q stage of SQ3R. *Even if you have already done this during the reading phase, do it again now—with the purpose of learning and committing the material to memory.*

You may decide to *recite* each answer aloud, silently speak the answers to yourself, "teach" the answers to another person, or write your ideas and answers in note form. Whatever recitation method you choose, make sure you know how ideas connect to one another and to the general concept being discussed.

Writing is the most effective way to learn new material. Using your own words to explain new concepts gives you immediate feedback: When you can do it effectively, you know the material. When you can't, you still need work with the text or with a study partner. Whatever you do, don't get discouraged. Just go back and search for what you missed.

Bill Greene/*Boston Globe*

Writing comprehensive responses at this stage can save time later. As you record responses to your Q stage questions, you can compare what you write to your text and make adjustments, a process that will help you digest the material. Your responses then become a study tool for review.

Keep your learning styles in mind when you explore different strategies (see chapter 3). For example, an intrapersonal learner may prefer writing, while an interpersonal learner may choose to recite answers aloud to a class-

Reciting aloud to another person is one of the best ways to solidify your knowledge of what you are reading.

mate. A logical-mathematical learner may benefit from organizing material into detailed outlines or charts, while a musical learner might want to chant information aloud to a rhythm.

When do you stop to recite? Waiting for the end of a chapter is too late; stopping at the end of a paragraph is too soon. The best plan is to recite at the end of each text section, right before a new text heading. Repeat the question-read-recite cycle until you complete the chapter.

If you find yourself fumbling for thoughts, you may not yet own the ideas. Reread the section that's giving you trouble until you master its contents.

Review

Review soon after you finish a chapter. Reviewing both immediately and periodically in the days and weeks after you read will help you learn and memorize material as it prepares you for exams. If you close the book after reading it once, chances are that you will forget almost everything, which is why students who read material for the first time right before a test often do poorly. Reviewing is your key to learning.

Reviewing the same material over time will also help you identify knowledge gaps. It's natural to forget material between study sessions, especially if it's confusing or complex. When you come back after a break, you can focus on your deficits.

Here are some reviewing techniques. Try them all, and use what works best.

- Reread your notes. Then summarize them from memory.
- Review and summarize in writing the text sections you highlighted or bracketed. Try to condense the material so that you can focus on key ideas.

- Answer the end-of-chapter review, discussion, and application questions.
- Reread the preface, headings, tables, and summary.
- Recite important concepts to yourself, or record and play them back on a tape player.
- Make flash cards with a word or concept on one side and a definition, examples, or other related information on the other. Test yourself.
- Quiz yourself, using the questions you raised in the Q stage. If you can't answer a question, scan the text for the answer.
- Discuss the concepts with a classmate or in a study group. Use Q stage questions to help one another learn.
- Finally, ask your instructor for help with difficult material. Define exactly what you want to discuss, and then schedule a meeting during office hours or e-mail your questions.

All this effort takes time, but the potential payoff is huge if you're motivated to work hard. Although at times it may be tempting to photocopy a classmate's text notes instead of reading and taking your own notes, you will learn only if you do the work yourself.

Refreshing your knowledge is easier and faster than learning it the first time. Make a review schedule—for example, once a week—and stick to it until you're sure of your knowledge. Use different reviewing techniques as you work toward mastering the material.

Key 5.9 summarizes how SQ3R turns you into an active reader.

KEY 5.9	Use SQ3R to become an active reader and learn new concepts.

Stage of SQ3R	Description
Survey	Pre-reading a book before studying it—skimming and scanning as you examine the front matter, chapter elements, and back matter for clues about text content and organization
Question	Developing questions linked to chapter headings and to what you already know about the topic—engaging your critical thinking skills
Read	Reading the material to answer the questions formulated in the Q stage and finding main ideas—taking notes as you read or highlighting key ideas and information in your text
Recite	Answering, perhaps for a second time, your Q stage questions—reciting the answers aloud or silently to yourself, teaching them to a study partner, or recording them in writing
Review	Using various techniques to learn the material before an exam—becoming actively involved with the material through summarizing notes, answering study questions, writing outlines or think links, reciting concepts, using flash cards, thinking critically, and so on

How do you customize your text with highlighting and notes?

Textbooks are designed and written with students in mind, but they are not customized to meet your unique reading and studying needs. It is up to you to do that for yourself through text highlighting and notes. Transforming your textbook into a valuable work tool through highlighting and notes will help you make the most of study time as you set the stage for review.

How to Highlight a Text

Highlighting involves the use of special highlighting markers or regular pens or pencils to flag important passages. When used correctly, highlighting is an essential study technique. Here are some techniques that will help you transform highlighting into a learning tool:

- *Develop a highlighting system and stick to it.* For example, decide in advance if you will use different colored markers for different elements, brackets for long passages, or pencil underlining. Make a key that identifies each notation.
- *Consider using a regular pencil or pen instead of a highlighter pen.* The copy will be cleaner and look less like a coloring book than a textbook.
- *Read an entire paragraph before you begin to highlight, and don't start until you have a sense of what is important.* Only then put pencil or highlighter to paper as you pick out key terms, phrases, and ideas.
- *Highlight key terms and concepts.* Mark examples that explain and support important ideas.
- *Avoid overmarking.* A phrase or two in any paragraph is usually enough. Enclose long passages with brackets rather than marking every line. Avoid underlining entire sentences, when possible. The less color the better.

Michelle V. Agins/*The New York Times*

Marking materials with a highlighter can be effective if you highlight selectively.

Although these techniques will help you highlight effectively, they won't help you learn the material and, ironically, they may actually obstruct learning as you diligently add color to the page. Experts agree that you will not learn what you highlight unless you *interact* with the material through surveying, questioning, reciting, and review. Without this interaction, all you are doing is marking your book.

How to Take Text Notes

When you combine highlighting with marginal notes or text flags, you remind yourself what a particular passage is about and why you consider it important. This combination customizes your text, which helps you study for exams. Going

© Piotr Przeszlo—Fotolia

a step further by taking a full set of text notes is an excellent way to commit material to memory.

As you will also see in chapter 7, note taking on texts and in class is critical because material is cumulative—that is, what you learn today builds on what you learned yesterday and the day before since the beginning of the term. Notes will help you master what you need to know and review effectively for midterms and finals.

Taking Marginal Notes

Here are some tips for taking marginal notes right on the pages of your text:

- Use pencil so you can erase comments or questions that are answered as you read.
- Write your Q questions from SQ3R in the margins right next to text headings.
- Mark critical sections with marginal notations, such as "def." for definition, "e.g." for helpful example, or "concept" for an important concept.
- Write notes at the bottom of the page connecting the text to what you learned in class or in research. If you don't have enough room, attach adhesive notes with your comments.

Key 5.10 shows how to highlight effectively and take marginal notes in a business textbook that introduces the concept of target marketing and market segmentation.

Your customized text will be uniquely yours; no one else will highlight or take text notes as you do because no one else has your knowledge, learning style, or study techniques. Because text customization is so important to mastering course material, you may encounter a problem if you buy used texts that are heavily highlighted or filled with marginal notations. Even if the previous owner was a good student, he or she is not you—and that fact alone may make a huge difference in your ability to master content.

Taking Full-Text Notes

Taking a full set of notes on assigned readings helps you learn as you summarize main ideas in your own words. Taking notes makes you an active participant as you think about how material fits into what you already know and how to capture key points.

To construct a summary, focus on the main ideas and the examples that support them. Don't include any of your own ideas or evaluations at this point. Your summary should simply condense the material, making it easier to focus on concepts and how they relate to one another when you review.

Here are suggestions for creating effective full-text summaries:

- Try to use your own words, because repeating the author's words may mean simply parroting concepts you do not understand. When studying a technical subject with precise definitions, you may have little choice but to use text wording.
- Try to make your notes simple, clear, and brief. Include what you need to understand about the topic, while eliminating less important details.
- Consider outlining the text so you can see the interrelationship among ideas.

- Before you write, identify the main idea of a passage.
- Once that idea ends and another begins, begin taking notes from memory, using your own words. Go back into the text, as needed, to cull information that you didn't get on first reading.

Underlining and taking marginal notes help you master content. KEY 5.10

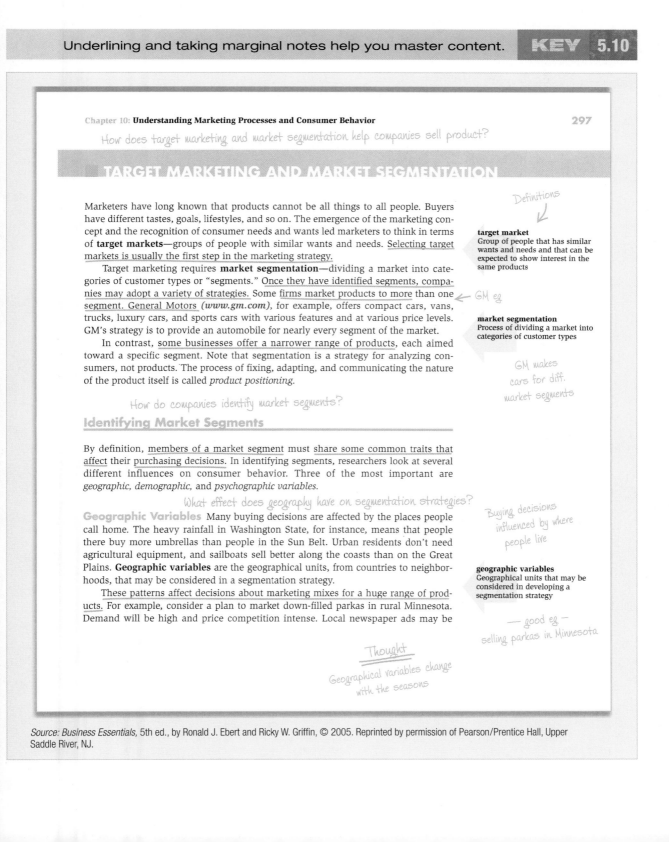

Chapter 10: **Understanding Marketing Processes and Consumer Behavior** 297

How does target marketing and market segmentation help companies sell product?

TARGET MARKETING AND MARKET SEGMENTATION

Marketers have long known that products cannot be all things to all people. Buyers have different tastes, goals, lifestyles, and so on. The emergence of the marketing concept and the recognition of consumer needs and wants led marketers to think in terms of **target markets**—groups of people with similar wants and needs. Selecting target markets is usually the first step in the marketing strategy.

Target marketing requires **market segmentation**—dividing a market into categories of customer types or "segments." Once they have identified segments, companies may adopt a variety of strategies. Some firms market products to more than one segment. General Motors (*www.gm.com*), for example, offers compact cars, vans, trucks, luxury cars, and sports cars with various features and at various price levels. GM's strategy is to provide an automobile for nearly every segment of the market.

In contrast, some businesses offer a narrower range of products, each aimed toward a specific segment. Note that segmentation is a strategy for analyzing consumers, not products. The process of fixing, adapting, and communicating the nature of the product itself is called *product positioning*.

How do companies identify market segments?

Identifying Market Segments

By definition, members of a market segment must share some common traits that affect their purchasing decisions. In identifying segments, researchers look at several different influences on consumer behavior. Three of the most important are *geographic, demographic,* and *psychographic variables.*

What effect does geography have on segmentation strategies?

Geographic Variables Many buying decisions are affected by the places people call home. The heavy rainfall in Washington State, for instance, means that people there buy more umbrellas than people in the Sun Belt. Urban residents don't need agricultural equipment, and sailboats sell better along the coasts than on the Great Plains. **Geographic variables** are the geographical units, from countries to neighborhoods, that may be considered in a segmentation strategy.

These patterns affect decisions about marketing mixes for a huge range of products. For example, consider a plan to market down-filled parkas in rural Minnesota. Demand will be high and price competition intense. Local newspaper ads may be

Handwritten margin notes:

Definitions ↓

target market
Group of people that has similar wants and needs and that can be expected to show interest in the same products

← *GM eg*

market segmentation
Process of dividing a market into categories of customer types

GM makes cars for diff. market segments

Buying decisions influenced by where people live

geographic variables
Geographical units that may be considered in developing a segmentation strategy

— *good eg* —
selling parkas in Minnesota

Thought
Geographical variables change with the seasons

Source: *Business Essentials,* 5th ed., by Ronald J. Ebert and Ricky W. Griffin, © 2005. Reprinted by permission of Pearson/Prentice Hall, Upper Saddle River, NJ.

TAKE ACTION

Mark Up a Page to Learn a Page

Below, the text material in Key 5.10 continues. Put your own pencil to paper as you highlight concepts and take marginal notes. Compare your efforts to those of your classmates to see how each of you approached the task and what you can learn from their methods.

KEY 5.10 Continued

effective, and the best retail location may be one that is easily reached from several small towns.

Although the marketability of some products is geographically sensitive, others enjoy nearly universal acceptance. Coke, for example, gets more than 70 percent of its sales from international markets. It is the market leader in Great Britain, China, Germany, Japan, Brazil, and Spain. Pepsi's international sales are about 15 percent of Coke's. In fact, Coke's chief competitor in most countries is some local soft drink, not Pepsi, which earns 78 percent of its income at home.

demographic variables
Characteristics of populations that may be considered in developing a segmentation strategy

Demographic Variables Demographic variables describe populations by identifying such traits as age, income, gender, ethnic background, marital status, race, religion, and social class. For example, several general consumption characteristics can be attributed to certain age groups (18–25, 26–35, 36–45, and so on). A marketer can, thus, divide markets into age groups. Table 10.1 lists some possible demographic breakdowns. Depending on the marketer's purpose, a segment can be a single classification (aged 20–34) or a combination of categories (aged 20–34, married with children, earning $25,000–$34,999). Foreign competitors, for example, are gaining market share in U.S. auto sales by appealing to young buyers (under age 30) with limited incomes (under $30,000). Whereas companies such as Hyundai (www.hyundai.net), Kia (www.kia.com), and Daewoo (www.daewoous.com) are winning entry-level customers with high quality and generous warranties, Volkswagen (www.vw.com) targets under-35 buyers with its entertainment-styled VW Jetta.[4]

psychographic variables
Consumer characteristics, such as lifestyles, opinions, interests, and attitudes, that may be considered in developing a segmentation strategy

Psychographic Variables Markets can also be segmented according to such **psychographic variables** as lifestyles, interests, and attitudes. Take, for example, Burberry (www.burberry.com), whose raincoats have been a symbol of British tradition since 1856. Burberry has repositioned itself as a global luxury brand, like Gucci (www.gucci.com) and Louis Vuitton (www.vuitton.com). The strategy, which recently resulted in a 31-percent sales increase, calls for attracting a different type of customer—the top-of-the-line, fashion-conscious individual—who shops at such stores as Neiman Marcus and Bergdorf Goodman.[5]

Psychographics are particularly important to marketers because, unlike demographics and geographics, they can be changed by marketing efforts. For example, Polish companies have overcome consumer resistance by promoting the safety and desirability of using credit rather than depending solely on cash. One product of changing attitudes is a booming economy and the emergence of a robust middle class.

TABLE 10.1
Demographic Variables

Age	Under 5, 5–11, 12–19, 20–34, 35–49, 50–64, 65+
Education	Grade school or less, some high school, graduated high school, some college, college degree, advanced degree
Family life cycle	Young single, young married without children, young married with children, older married with children under 18, older married without children under 18, older single, other
Family size	1, 2–3, 4–5, 6+
Income	Under $9,000, $9,000–$14,999, $15,000–$24,999, $25,000–$34,999, $35,000–$45,000, over $45,000
Nationality	African, American, Asian, British, Eastern European, French, German, Irish, Italian, Latin American, Middle Eastern, Scandinavian
Race	Native American, Asian, Black, White
Religion	Buddhist, Catholic, Hindu, Jewish, Muslim, Protestant
Sex	Male, female

- Take notes on tables, charts, photographs, and captions; these visual presentations may contain information presented nowhere else in the text.
- Use shorthand symbols to write quickly (see chapter 7).
- Create notes in visual form (more details in chapter 7):
  - Construct your own charts, tables, and diagrams that visually express the concepts in the written text.
  - Devise a color-coding system to indicate level of importance of different ideas, and then mark up your notes with these colors.
  - Devise symbols and numbers and use them consistently to indicate the level of importance of different ideas.

It used to be doctors and research scientists who faced the challenge of lifelong learning, but now all of us do. Embrace it or be left by the wayside.

DONALD ASHER, AUTHOR AND CAREER CONSULTANT

© Harris Shiffman—Fotolia

I apply past knowledge to new situations.

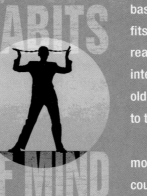

Your mind is not a blank slate. On the contrary, it is filled with information, ideas, and practical applications you have gained from a lifetime of experience and reading. Just as there is no need to relearn the alphabet every time you open a book, there is no need to start from ground zero—the absence of knowledge—when you encounter new ideas in your texts. Your challenge is to place these ideas in the context of what you already know.

The successful use of SQ3R depends on this habit of mind. When you approach a new assignment, ask yourself what you already know about the material. Similarly, when you develop questions that expand your knowledge base, ask yourself how this new material fits into what you already know. Critical readers understand that knowledge is interconnected—and that integrating the old with the new will bring understanding to the next level.

This habit of mind is essential as you move from lower-level to higher-level courses in your major—for example, from an introduction to business to a marketing course. Embracing this habit will also enrich your learning in seemingly unrelated courses. By understanding 20th century world history, for example, you will be better able to appreciate the paintings of Frida Kahlo, the novels of Richard Wright, and the music of Bob Dylan.

MULTIPLE PATHWAYS TO LEARNING

MULTIPLE INTELLIGENCE STRATEGIES FOR READING

Use selected reading techniques in Multiple Intelligence areas to strengthen your ability to read for meaning and retention.

INTELLIGENCE	SUGGESTED STRATEGIES	WHAT WORKS FOR YOU? WRITE NEW IDEAS HERE
Verbal-Linguistic	▪ Mark up your text with marginal notes while you read. ▪ When tackling a chapter, use every stage of SQ3R, taking advantage of each writing opportunity (writing Q stage questions, writing summaries, and so on).	
Logical-Mathematical	▪ Read material in sequence. ▪ Think about the logical connections between what you are reading and the world at large; consider similarities, differences, and cause-and-effect relationships.	
Bodily-Kinesthetic	▪ Take physical breaks during reading sessions—walk, stretch, exercise. ▪ Pace while reciting important ideas.	
Visual-Spatial	▪ As you read, take particular note of photos, tables, figures, and other visual aids. ▪ Make charts, diagrams, or think links illustrating difficult concepts you encounter in your reading.	
Interpersonal	▪ With a friend, have a joint reading session. One should read a section silently and then summarize aloud the important concepts for the other. Reverse the order of summarizer and listener for each section. ▪ Discuss reading material and clarify important concepts in a study group.	
Intrapersonal	▪ Read in a solitary setting and allow time for reflection. ▪ Think about how a particular reading assignment makes you feel, and evaluate your reaction by considering the material in light of what you already know.	
Musical	▪ Play music while you read. ▪ Recite important concepts in your reading to rhythms, or write a song to depict those concepts.	
Naturalistic	▪ Read and study in a natural environment. ▪ Before reading indoors, imagine your favorite place in nature in order to create a relaxed frame of mind.	

REMEMBER
THE IMPORTANT POINTS

1

What will improve your reading comprehension?

- Approach difficult texts in an active way and with a will to succeed.
- Improve concentration by minimizing internal and external distractions.
- Use a systematic approach like SQ3R.
- Become emotionally involved with the material.
- Know which of four reading purposes you have before you begin.
- Build your vocabulary every day.

2

How can SQ3R help you own what you read?

- SQ3R, a reading/studying system, moves readers through five learning stages: surveying, questioning, reading, reciting, and reviewing.
- Surveying involves previewing a text before studying it.
- Questioning requires that you think about and question what you read.
- Reading—the first R in SQ3R—actively involves you in pinpointing main ideas.
- Reciting—the second R in SQ3R—requires an active approach to answer your Q stage questions.
- Reviewing—the third R in SQ3R—should be done soon after you finish a chapter and on a regular basis during the semester.

3

How do you customize your text with highlighting and notes?

- Highlight to mark key terms and concepts, not the entire page.
- Take marginal notes to personalize your text even more.
- Take full-text notes to summarize main points.

CRITICAL THINKING

APPLYING LEARNING TO LIFE

Studying a Text Page

The following page is from the chapter "Groups and Organizations" in the sixth edition of John J. Macionis's *Sociology*.[8] Apply SQ3R as you read the excerpt. Using what you learned in this chapter about study techniques, complete the questions that follow (some questions ask you to mark the page itself).

Step 1. Think it through: Gather information and analyze it.

First gather: Skim the excerpt. Identify the headings on the page and the relationships among them. Mark primary-level headings with a #1, secondary headings with a #2, and tertiary (third-level) headings with a #3.

Then analyze: Which heading serves as an umbrella for the rest?

_____

What do the headings tell you about the content of the page?

_____

What are three concepts that seem important to remember?

1. _____

2. _____

3. _____

Step 2. Think out of the box: Create useful study questions. Based on the three concepts you pulled out, write three study questions that you can review with an instructor, a teaching assistant, or a fellow student.

1. _____

2. _____

3. _____

SOCIAL GROUPS

Virtually everyone moves through life with a sense of belonging; this is the experience of group life. A **social group** refers to *two or more people who identify and interact with one another*. Human beings continually come together to form couples, families, circles of friends, neighborhoods, churches, businesses, clubs, and numerous large organizations. Whatever the form, groups encompass people with shared experiences, loyalties, and interests. In short, while maintaining their individuality, the members of social groups also think of themselves as a special "we."

Groups, Categories, and Crowds

People often use the term "group" imprecisely. We now distinguish the group from the similar concepts of category and crowd.

Category. A *category* refers to people who have some status in common. Women, single fathers, military recruits, homeowners, and Roman Catholics are all examples of categories.

Why are categories not considered groups? Simply because, while the individuals involved are aware that they are not the only ones to hold that particular status, the vast majority are strangers to one another.

Crowd. A *crowd* refers to a temporary cluster of individuals who may or may not interact at all. Students sitting in a lecture hall do engage one another and share some common identity as college classmates; thus, such a crowd might be called a loosely formed group. By contrast, riders hurtling along on a subway train or bathers enjoying a summer day at the beach pay little attention to one another and amount to an anonymous aggregate of people. In general, then, crowds are too transitory and impersonal to qualify as social groups.

The right circumstances, however, could turn a crowd into a group. People riding in a subway train that crashes under the city streets generally become keenly aware of their common plight and begin to help one another. Sometimes such extraordinary experiences become the basis for lasting relationships.

Primary and Secondary Groups

Acquaintances commonly greet one another with a smile and the simple phrase, "Hi! How are you?" The response is usually a well scripted, "Just fine, thanks, how about you?" This answer, of course, is often more formal than truthful. In most cases, providing a detailed account of how you are *really* doing would prompt the other person to beat a hasty and awkward exit.

Sociologists classify social groups by measuring them against two ideal types based on members' genuine level of personal concern. This variation is the key to distinguishing *primary* from *secondary* groups.

According to Charles Horton Cooley (1864–1929), a **primary group** is a *small social group whose members share personal and enduring relationships*. Bound together by primary relationships, individuals in primary groups typically spend a great deal of time together, engage in a wide range of common activities, and feel that they know one another well. Although not without periodic conflict, members of primary groups display sincere concern for each other's welfare. The family is every society's most important primary group.

Cooley characterized these personal and tightly integrated groups as *primary* because they are among the first groups we experience in life. In addition, the family and early play groups also hold primary importance in the socialization process, shaping attitudes, behavior, and social identity.

Step 3. Make it happen: Read and remember. Read the excerpt putting SQ3R to work. Using a marker pen, highlight key phrases and sentences. Write short marginal notes to help you review the material later. After reading this page thoroughly, write a short summary paragraph.

_____

_____

_____

_____

_____

TEAM BUILDING

COLLABORATIVE SOLUTIONS

Join with your study partners to sharpen your highlighting skills. The following technique will help group members help each other.[9]

- *Step 1*: Photocopy a three- to four-page section from an introductory text, and ask everyone to highlight the important material. Then compare versions, asking group members to explain why they highlighted certain words, phrases, and sentences and not others. Your goal is to learn from each other and to get in the habit of using critical thinking as you highlight.

- *Step 2*: Each group member should then pledge to use, over a period of a week, two new highlighting techniques from step 1.

- *Step 3*: At the end of the week, come together and discuss the results. Each person should answer this question: "Am I a better highlighter as a result of this exercise, and am I learning more content in the process?"

I recognize that being a successful student requires that I build an ever-broadening base of knowledge as I move from introductory-level to advanced courses in my major. With this in mind, I can see why certain courses are prerequisites for others.

Looking at the course catalog, I will name a course I am now taking and two higher-level courses I am likely to take. I realize that doing well in the upper-level courses requires that I master the material in my current course.

Introductory course (name, number, and brief description):

_____

First upper-level course (name, number, and brief description):

_____

Second upper-level course (name, number, and brief description):

_____

*I will use three reading and studying strategies I learned in this chapter to help me master material as I **apply past knowledge to new content**.*

Strategy 1: _____

Strategy 2: _____

Strategy 3: _____

I will get in the habit of trying to connect what I learn in one course with what I learn in other courses that are indirectly related or seemingly not related at all. Here are the courses I am taking this term in which I will look for knowledge links.

Course 1: _____

Course 2: _____

Course 3: _____

Finally, I will describe two specific knowledge links that I found in these courses.

Knowledge link #1: _____

_____

Knowledge link #2: _____

_____

How am I doing? **Later in the term, be accountable for your progress on page 377.**

SUGGESTED READINGS

Armstrong, William H., and M. Willard Lampe II. *Barron's Pocket Guide to Study Tips: How to Study Effectively and Get Better Grades.* New York: Barron's Educational Series, 1990.

Bernard, George. *Studying at University: How to Adapt Successfully to College Life.* New York: Routledge, 2003.

Chesla, Elizabeth. *Reading Comprehension Success: In 20 Minutes a Day*, 2nd ed. Garden Grove, CA: Learning Express, 1998.

Luckie, William R., Wood Smethurst, and Sarah Beth Huntley. *Study Power Workbook: Exercises in Study Skills to Improve Your Learning and Your Grades.* Cambridge, MA: Brookline Books, 1999.

Rooks, Clay D. *The Quick College Guide: Reading, Writing, and Studying.* New York: Longman, 2002.

Silver, Theodore. *The Princeton Review Study Smart: Hands-On, Nuts and Bolts Techniques for Earning Higher Grades.* New York: Villard Books, 1996.

INTERNET RESOURCES

Academictips.org (www.academictips.org)

How to Study (www.howtostudy.com)

Prentice Hall's Student Success Supersite: Study Skills (**www.prenhall.com/success/StudySkl/index.html**)

ENDNOTES

1. Eric Jensen, *Student Success Secrets*, 5th ed., New York: Barron's Educational Series, 2003, p. 88.

2. Francis P. Robinson, *Effective Behavior*, New York: Harper & Row, 1941.

3. John Mack Faragher, Mary Jo Buhle, Daniel Czitrom, and Susan H. Armitage, *Out of Many*, 3rd ed., Upper Saddle River, NJ: Prentice Hall, 2000, p. xxxvii.

4. Charles G. Morris and Albert A. Maisto, *Psychology: An Introduction*, 12th ed., Upper Saddle River, NJ: Prentice Hall, 2005, p. 186.

5. Benjamin S. Bloom, *Taxonomy of Educational Objectives, Handbook I: Cognitive Domain.* New York: Longman, 1956.

6. Ophelia H. Hancock, *Reading Skills for College Students*, 5th ed., Upper Saddle River, NJ: Prentice Hall, 2001, pp. 54–59.

7. Adam Robinson, *What Smart Students Know*, New York: Three Rivers Press, 1993, p. 82.

8. John J. Macionis, *Sociology*, 6th ed., Upper Saddle River, NJ: Prentice Hall, 1997, p. 174.

9. Technique suggested by Mel Levine, *A Mind at a Time*, New York: Simon & Schuster, 2002, pp. 67–68.

Listen with understanding and empathy

HABITS OF MIND

6

"People with this habit of mind are able to take on the diverse perspectives of others. They gently demonstrate their understanding and empathy by recapping, building on, clarifying, or giving examples."

ART COSTA

LISTEN WITH UNDERSTANDING AND EMPATHY

When you appreciate the words of others through their perspectives, not your own, you are engaged in empathetic listening. As an empathetic listener, you will hear what others fail to hear—and the knowledge and insight you gain will add immeasurably to your education.

To listen with empathy means to have, and convey, real understanding—and to bring your understanding to an even deeper level as you listen. This firefighter who lost a brother on September 11, 2001, and this construction worker who has labored on the site since that day are able to listen to each other with empathy and to grow from what they hear.

Skilled, active listening enables you to take in information during lectures, labs, and class discussions. You are then challenged to remember much of what you hear for tests, and also because it may be important to your future studies and career. Bringing empathy to the table will help what you hear matter more and stay with you longer. This chapter encourages you to take an active learning approach to listening and remembering so that you can learn new material and hang on to it for the long term.

In this chapter, you explore answers to the following questions:

- How can you become a better listener?
- How can you maximize the power of your memory?
- How can mnemonic devices boost recall?

Photo: James Estrin/*The New York Times*

How can you become a better listener?

The act of hearing isn't the same as the act of listening. *Hearing* refers to sensing spoken messages from their source. *Listening* involves a complex process of communication. Successful listening occurs when the listener understands the speaker's intended message. In school and at work, poor listening may cause communication breakdowns, while skilled listening

KEY   6.1   Barriers may interfere with listening at every stage.

A peer group is a social group made up of members with a lot in common. During adolescence, common interests often center on dating, popular music, clothing, and sports.

"Peer groups!" I've heard that term before. I'd better take notes; it'll probably be on the test.

The appeal of the group often comes from the fact that adults would not approve of what group members are doing. As a result, illicit activities—such as car racing, alcohol abuse, and drugs—are often the most popular.

What's this guy saying? That my friends and I do things just because our parents would object? Yeah, I guess I want to be different, but gimme a break! I don't drink and drive. I don't do drugs. I don't ignore my school work. Anyway, I'd better remember the connection between peer group popularity and adult disapproval. What were his exact words? I wish I remembered . . . on second thought maybe he has a point. I know kids who do things just to get a rise out of their parents.

Peer groups exert such a strong influence during adolescence because they give students the opportunity to form social relationships that are separate and apart from the one they have with their families. This is a time of rebellion and breaking away: a rough time for both adolescents and their parents.

Is it lunchtime yet? I'm really hungry! Stop thinking of food and start listening . . . back to work! Yeah, he's right, social relationships that have nothing to do with my family are important to me. I'd better write this down.

The good news for parents is that peer group pressure is generally strongest during adolescence. Teens achieve a greater balance between the influence of family and friends as the years pass. This doesn't make it any easier for parents trying to persuade their sons and daughters not to dye their hair green or pierce their eyebrows, but at least it tells them that the rebellion is temporary.

Why is he talking down to us? Why is he reassuring parents instead of focusing on how hard it is for teens to deal with life? He must be a parent himself . . . I wish those guys behind me would stop talking! I can't hear the lecture . . . there's a generation gap coming from the front of the room that's the size of the Grand Canyon! What's wrong with green hair and pierced eyebrows? He sounds like he knows all the answers and that we'll eventually see the light. I'm going to ask him how teens are supposed to act when they believe that their parents' values are wrong. Now, how should I word my question . . .

promotes progress and success. The good news is that listening is a teachable—
and learnable—skill.

To see how complex listening can be, look at Key 6.1. The left-hand column
contains an excerpt from a typical classroom lecture on peer group influence
during adolescence, and the right-hand column records what an 18- or 19-year-
old student might be thinking while the instructor is speaking. The column on
the right reveals the complexity of listening as well as some of the barriers that
block communication.

It's only through listening that you learn, and I never want to stop learning.

DREW BARRYMORE, FILM ACTRESS

© Mehmet Dilsiz—Fotolia

As Key 6.1 shows, this student doesn't focus consistently on the information
presented. Instead, she reacts to specific parts of the message and gets caught
up in evaluations and judgments. Understanding the listening process and why
people may have trouble listening well can help you overcome barriers.

Know the Stages of Listening

Listening is made up of four stages that build on one another: sensation, interpretation, evaluation, and reaction. These stages take the message from the speaker
to the listener and back to the speaker (see Key 6.2).

- During the *sensation* stage (also known as hearing) your ears pick up sound
  waves and transmit them to the brain. For example, you are sitting in class
  and hear your instructor say, "The only opportunity to make up last week's
  test is Tuesday at 5:00 P.M."

The listening process moves messages along a listening loop.   **KEY** 6.2

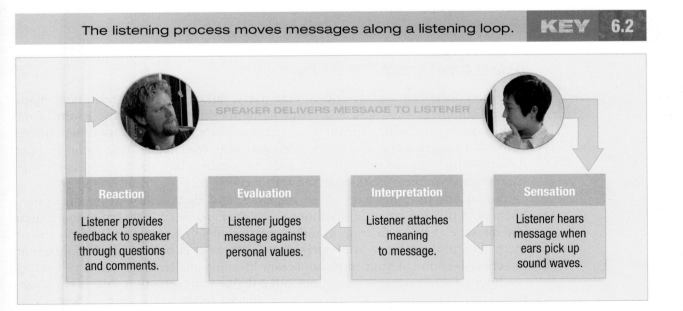

Reaction	Evaluation	Interpretation	Sensation
Listener provides feedback to speaker through questions and comments.	Listener judges message against personal values.	Listener attaches meaning to message.	Listener hears message when ears pick up sound waves.

SPEAKER DELIVERS MESSAGE TO LISTENER

- In the *interpretation* stage, listeners attach meaning to a message. This involves understanding what is being said and relating it to what you already know. You relate this message to your knowledge of the test, whether you need to make it up, and what you are doing on Tuesday at 5:00.

- In the *evaluation* stage, you decide how you feel about the message—whether, for example, you like it or agree with it. This involves evaluating the message as it relates to your needs and values. If the message goes against your values or does not fulfill your needs, you may reject it, stop listening, or argue in your mind with the speaker. In this example, if you need to make up the test but have to work Tuesday at 5:00, you may evaluate the message as less than satisfactory. *Empathy* occurs during the evaluation stage as you think about what the speaker is saying from his position rather than your own. As Key 6.1 showed, what happens during the evaluation phase can interfere with listening.

- The final stage of listening is a *reaction* to the message in the form of direct feedback. In a classroom, direct feedback often comes in the form of questions and comments. Your reaction, in this case, may be to ask the instructor if she can schedule another test time. If the student in Key 6.1 actually asks a question, she will give the instructor the opportunity to clarify the lecture or add information.

Improving your listening skills involves two primary actions involving self-awareness and skill building: managing listening challenges (maximizing the sensation stage) and becoming an active listener (maximizing the interpretation and evaluation stages). Although becoming a better listener will help in every class, it is especially important in subjects that challenge you.

Manage Listening Challenges

Classic studies have shown that immediately after listening, students are likely to recall only half of what was said. This low retention rate is partly due to such listening challenges as divided attention and distractions, the tendency to shut out the message, the inclination to rush to judgment, and partial hearing loss or learning disabilities.[1]

Divided Attention and Distractions

Imagine yourself at a noisy end-of-year party, talking with a friend about plans for the summer, when you hear your name mentioned across the room. Your name was not shouted, and you weren't consciously listening to anything outside your own conversation. However, once you hear your name, you strain to hear more as you now listen with only half an ear to what your friend is saying. Chances are you hear neither person very well.

Situations like this happen all the time, and they demonstrate the consequences of divided attention. Although you are capable of listening to more than one message at the same time, you may not completely hear or understand any of them. Learning to focus your attention—even as it is being pulled in different directions—is one of your most important listening challenges.

Internal and external distractions often divide your attention. *Internal distractions* include anything from hunger to headache to personal worries. Something the speaker says may also trigger a recollection that may cause your mind to drift. In contrast, *external distractions* include noises and excessive heat or cold. Your goal is to reduce distractions so you can concentrate.

You'll listen better if you are relaxed, comfortable, and awake. Get enough sleep to stay alert, eat enough to avoid hunger pangs, and dress comfortably. In addition, try to save worrying about personal problems for time outside of class.

Work to eliminate external distractions during class by sitting near the front of the room and moving away from others who are chatting. If there's a chance that the classroom will be over- or under-heated, bring an extra layer that you can put on or take off.

Shutting Out the Message

Although instructors are responsible for communicating information, they cannot force you to listen. The responsibility to listen consistently is in your hands. If students perceive that a subject is difficult or uninteresting, they may tune out and miss information that forms the foundation for what comes next. Many students also fall into the trap of focusing on specific points and shutting out the rest of the message. It's tough to refocus after these kinds of listening lapses.

One way to avoid this is to remind yourself that what your instructors say is valuable even if it is not obvious or in the textbook. Instructors often present material in class that is not in the textbook and include that material on tests. If you work to take in the whole message, you will be able to read over your notes later, combine your class and text notes, and think critically about what is important. If you experience a listening lapse, the best strategy is to refocus quickly instead of worrying about what you missed. After class, ask to see a classmate's notes to fill in the gaps.

The Rush to Judgment

As Key 6.1 illustrates, people may stop listening when they hear something they don't like. Their focus turns to their personal reactions and away from the message. When students disagree, they often spend valuable class time figuring out how to word a question or comment in response.

Judgments also involve reactions to the speakers themselves. If you do not like your instructors or if you have preconceived notions about their ideas or cultural background, you may decide that their words have little value or that you don't understand them. Anyone whose words have ever been ignored because of race, ethnic background, gender, sexual preference, or disability understands how prejudice can interfere with listening. Activating the habit of mind of *listening with understanding and empathy* will help lessen the tendency to pass judgment without a fair evaluation.

Before you give in to your inclination to tune out, consider these points:

Stephen Crowley/*The New York Times*

Effective listening depends on being open-minded, refraining from judgment, and taking time afterwards to think critically about what you've heard.

- An important part of your education involves using critical thinking to evaluate other points of view—even those radically different from your own. Be open to the possibility that your instructor may say something to change your mind.

■ You are under no obligation to like every instructor. However, academic integrity requires that you listen respectfully. It benefits you to listen with an open mind.

Describe what goes through your head while you listen to an instructor with whom you disagree. Do you stop listening? Do you get caught up in an internal argument? Do you spend your time figuring out how to respond? Do your feelings hinder your ability to focus? Do you try to *listen with understanding and empathy* so you can view the world through your instructor's perspective? Brainstorm ways of listening effectively the next time this occurs.

Listening with understanding and empathy will help you perceive your education as a continuing search for evidence, regardless of whether that evidence supports or negates your point of view.

Partial Hearing Loss and Learning Disabilities

If you have a hearing loss, seek out special services, including tutoring and equipment, that can help you listen in class. For example, listening to a taped lecture at a higher-than-normal volume can help you hear things you missed. Ask your instructors if digitalized recordings are available, which you can download onto your computer or iPod. Meeting with your instructor outside of class to clarify your notes may also help, as will sitting near the front of the room.

Other disabilities, such as attention deficit disorder (ADD) or a problem with processing spoken language, can add to listening difficulties. People with these problems may have trouble paying attention or understanding what they hear. If you have a disability that creates a listening challenge, seek help through the services available at your college.

Become an Active Listener

On the surface, listening seems like a passive activity: You sit back as someone else speaks. Effective listening, however, is really an active process that involves being a presence in class, setting a listening purpose, focusing on understanding, asking questions, paying attention to verbal signposts, and knowing what helps and hinders listening.

Ironically, passive listeners may think they are actually learning material when all they are doing is taking it in on a surface level. They have not challenged themselves to understand, organize, or digest the material on their own, but simply rely on their instructor's rendering. Many of these students experience a rude awakening when they have trouble with exams or assignments that test their active, analytical knowledge.

Be There

Being an active listener requires that you show up on time—preferably a few minutes before class is scheduled to start. Instructors often make important

Empathetic Listening

AP Wide World Photos

Eleanor Roosevelt was the First Lady of the United States during World War II.

In the dark days of the war, Roosevelt urged her husband to remember people on the margins—the poor and homeless in America, the Jews who were being slaughtered in Nazi Germany. She was their voice because *she heard their pleas* and never forgot their pain.

announcements during the first few minutes of class and may also summarize the last lecture. You goal is to be settled in your seat with your notebook open when the instructor starts speaking.

Set Purposes for Listening

In any situation, establish what you want to achieve through listening, such as understanding the material better or mastering a specific task. Many instructors state their purpose at the start of the class. A political science instructor might say, for example, "Today, we're going to discuss how lobbyists impact the passage of legislation." Listening carefully to the purpose and writing it down will help you focus on the message.

Accomplishing your purpose requires that you read assignments before class (your syllabus will tell you when assignments are due; see the syllabus on pages 9–10 for an example) and review your notes from the previous class. This preparation will allow you to follow the lecture successfully, helping you to differentiate between material to take notes on and material that is less important. Without it, you may find yourself scrambling to take down every word (see chapter 7 for more on note taking).

Making your purpose for listening *personal* will motivate you to listen closely. As you prepare for class, ask yourself how the material relates to your academic goals and interests and to other material you need to know. You will be motivated to block out internal and external distractions if you come to class with the mind-set that what you hear will help *you*.

An implicit purpose of listening is to learn what your instructor considers important about a topic. Often, instructors ask students to provide information and analysis that supplements their own presentation, so don't stop listening when a classmate starts talking. In fact, you can learn as much from classmates as you can from instructors. Listening to classmates with an open mind sets the stage for developing an *empathetic habit of mind.*

Focus on Understanding

Listening without understanding has no value, so make sure you understand what you hear. Rather than taking notes on everything, record information only when you can say to yourself, "I get it!" If you miss important material, leave holes in your notes and return later. Your instructor may repeat the point you missed, or another comment may help you piece it together.

Ask Questions

A willingness to ask questions shows a desire to learn and is the mark of an active listener, says education professor Paul Eggen of the University of North Florida:

> Successful students are constantly looking for links between what they are learning and other information. Less successful students tend to learn information in isolation through cramming. In most cases, this information will stay with them for a short time because it isn't linked to anything else. When you listen to a lecture, ask yourself questions: What is this part of? What's the bigger idea? How is it similar to the topic we dealt with in the last class? How is it different? By identifying similarities and differences, you're associating the ideas you are trying to learn with other memories and making it more likely that you will remember.[2]

Although questions and comments turn you into an active participant, they may sometimes divert your attention from the speaker. One way to avoid this is to jot down your questions quickly and come back to them during a discussion period.

Pay Attention to Verbal Signposts

Instructors' choice of words may tell you a lot about what they consider important and help you predict test questions. For example, an idea described as "new and exciting" or "classic" is more likely to be on a test than one described as "interesting." *Verbal signposts*—words or phrases that call your attention to what you will hear next—help organize information, connect ideas, and indicate what is important and what is not. Let phrases like those in Key 6.3 direct your attention to the material that follows.

Over time, you will also learn your instructor's nonverbal speaking style. For example, after a few classes, you may realize that when she looks at her notes before speaking, she is probably telling you something important. You may also learn that when he asks questions about the same topic, he is repeating for emphasis, or when she gets excited about a question she is flagging both the question and answer as crucial.

Know What Helps and Hinders Listening

Ralph G. Nichols, a pioneer in listening research, defined the characteristics of successful and unsuccessful listeners by studying 200 freshmen at the University of Minnesota over a nine-month period. His findings, summarized in Key 6.4, demonstrate that effective listening depends as much on a positive attitude as on specific skills.[3]

Engage Professor Nichols's strategies to turn on and tune up your listening when you take a class that doesn't interest you. With a positive attitude, you may learn something important and even grow to like the material.

Through effective listening, you acquire knowledge—but acquisition is not enough. You must also retain what you learn, whether you learn it in the classroom, through reading, or via direct experience. As you will see next, a good memory improves with practice and the use of specific strategies.

Cornell University Photography

Being a good listener can serve you well in many career areas. This acoustic biologist is listening to recorded sounds of elephant calls in their native habitat, and analyzing what the sounds indicate about elephant behavior.

How can you maximize the power of your memory?

Your accounting instructor is giving a test tomorrow on key taxation concepts. You feel confident because you spent hours last week memorizing your class and text notes. Unfortunately, as you start the test, you realize that you have forgotten almost everything you learned. This is not surprising, since most forgetting occurs within minutes after memorization.

KEY 6.3   Pay attention to verbal signposts.

Signals Pointing to Key Concepts	Signals of Support
A key point to remember . . .	A perfect example, . . .
Point 1, point 2, etc. . . .	Specifically, . . .
The impact of this was . . .	For instance, . . .
The critical stages in the process are . . .	Similarly, . . .
Signals Pointing to Differences	**Signals that Summarize**
On the contrary, . . .	From this you have learned, . . .
On the other hand, . . .	In conclusion, . . .
In contrast, . . .	As a result, . . .
However, . . .	Finally, . . .

KEY 6.4   Effective listening is linked to attitude and skill.

Listening is helped by . . .	Listening is hindered by . . .
. . . making a conscious decision to work at listening; viewing difficult material as a listening challenge.	. . . caring little about the listening process; tuning out difficult material.
. . . fighting distractions through concentration.	. . . refusing to listen at the first distraction.
. . . continuing to listen when a subject is difficult or dry, in the hope that one might learn something interesting.	. . . giving up as soon as one loses interest.
. . . withholding judgment until hearing everything.	. . . becoming preoccupied with a response as soon as a speaker makes a controversial statement.
. . . focusing on the speaker's theme by recognizing organizational patterns, transitional language, and summary statements.	. . . getting sidetracked by unimportant details.
. . . adapting a note-taking style to the unique style and organization of the speaker.	. . . always taking notes in outline form, even when a speaker is poorly organized, leading to frustration.
. . . pushing past negative emotional responses and forcing oneself to continue to listen.	. . . letting an initial emotional response disrupt listening.
. . . using excess thinking time to evaluate, summarize, and question what one just heard and anticipate what will come next.	. . . thinking about other things and, as a result, missing much of the message.

TAKE ACTION

Change Your Listening Habits

Think about your personal listening habits in the classroom. Then complete the following:

Look again at Key 6.4. Which habits, helpful or not so helpful, are part of your listening pattern?

_____

_____

How do you react when you strongly disagree with something your instructor says—when you are convinced that you are "right" and your instructor is "wrong"?

_____

_____

If one of the purposes of a college education is to open you to new ideas and opinions, how do feelings of being "right" affect your education?

_____

_____

List two changes you could make in your listening to activate the habit of mind of *listening with understanding and empathy*.

1. _____
2. _____

If forgetting is so common, why do some people have better memories than others? Some may have an inborn talent for remembering. More often, though, they succeed because they take an active approach and have mastered techniques for improving recall.

How Your Brain Remembers: Short-Term and Long-Term Memory

Learning is a physical process—your brain undergoes physical changes when you hear, interpret, and work to remember information. Understanding how your brain commits information to memory will motivate actions that strengthen your ability to remember.

Memories are stored in three different "storage banks" in your brain. The first, called *sensory memory,* holds an exact copy of what you see and hear and lasts for only a second or less. Certain information is then selected from sensory memory and moved into *short-term memory,*

© William Berry—Fotolia

TAKE ACTION

Analyze the Link Between Memorization and Critical Thinking

Identify the course you are most interested in this term and the role memorization and critical thinking are likely to play in your efforts to do well. Then complete the following:

Describe some material you will have to memorize.

_____

_____

_____

Describe the specific ways in which you will use critical thinking to help you learn and retain the material.

_____

_____

_____

Evaluate whether or not the material you have to remember for this course will be important to your working and/or personal life after college.

_____

_____

a temporary information storehouse that lasts no more than 10 to 20 seconds. You are consciously aware of material in short-term memory. Unimportant information is quickly dumped. Important information is transferred to *long-term memory*—the mind's more permanent storehouse.

Targeting long-term memory will solidify learning the most. "Short-term—or working—memory is useful when we want to remember a phone number until we can dial or an e-mail address until we can type it in to the computer," says biologist James Zull. "We use short-term memory for these momentary challenges, all the time, every day, but it is limited in capacity, tenacity, and time."[4] Zull explains that short-term memory can only hold small amounts of information for brief periods. In addition, it is unstable—a distraction can easily bump out information. As you learn new material, your goal is to anchor information in long-term memory. Memory strategies will help you succeed.

Memory Strategies Improve Recall

The following strategies will help improve your ability to remember what you learn.

Have Purpose, Intention, and Emotional Connection

Why can you remember the lyrics to dozens of popular songs but not the functions of the pancreas? Perhaps this is because you *want* to remember the lyrics or you have an emotional tie to them. To achieve the same results at school, try to create in yourself the purpose and will to remember. This is often linked to your emotional involvement with the material.

For example, as a student in a city-planning course, it may be easier for you to remember the complex rules surrounding housing subsidies if you think about the families who benefit from these programs. If someone you know lives in a city housing project, the personal connection will probably make it easier to remember these rules.

Genuine interest and passion for a subject are invaluable memory tools. When you care about something, your brain responds differently, and learning is easier.

Understand What You Memorize

Something that has meaning is easier to recall than something that makes little sense. This basic principle applies to everything you study. Determine the logical connections in the information, and use these connections to help you learn. For example, in a plant biology course, memorize plant families; in a history course, memorize events by linking them in a cause-and-effect chain.

The best way to guarantee that concepts become part of your long-term memory is to understand them inside and out. With a depth of learning comes the framework on which to place related concepts. Thus, if you are having trouble remembering something new, think about how the new idea fits into what you already know.

A simple example: If you continually forget the definition of a new vocabulary word, try to identify the word's root, prefix, or suffix. Knowing that the root *bellum* means "war" and the prefix *ante* means "before" will help you recognize and remember that *antebellum* means "before the war."

Use Critical Thinking

Critical thinking encourages you to associate new information with what you already know. Imagine that you have to remember information about a specific historical event—for example, the signing of the Treaty of Versailles, the agreement that ended World War I. You might use critical thinking in the following ways:

- Recall everything that you know about the topic.
- Think about how this event is similar to other events in history.
- Consider what is different and unique about this treaty in comparison to other treaties.
- Explore the causes that led up to this event, and look at the event's effects.
- From the general idea of treaties that ended wars, explore other examples of such treaties.
- Think about examples of what happened during the treaty signing, and from those examples come up with ideas about the tone of the event.
- Looking at the facts of the event, evaluate how successful you think the treaty was.

By critically exploring the Treaty of Versailles in this fashion, you are more likely to remember the specific facts and overarching concepts associated with it.

Limit and organize the items you are processing

This involves three key activities:

- *Separate main points from unimportant details.* Ask yourself, "What is the most important information?" Highlight only the key points in your texts, and write notes in the margins about central ideas. See the example in Key 5.10 on page 167.

- *Divide material into manageable sections.* Generally, when material is short and easy to understand, studying it from start to finish improves recall. With longer material, however, you may benefit from dividing it into logical sections, mastering each section, putting all the sections together, and then testing your memory of all the material.

- *Use organizational tools.* Rely on an outline, a think link, or another organizational tool to record material and the logical connections among the elements (see chapter 7 for more on these note-taking techniques). These tools will expose gaps in your understanding as they help you study and learn.

Recite, Rehearse, and Write

When you *recite* material, you repeat key concepts aloud, in your own words, to aid memorization. You also summarize these concepts. *Rehearsing* is similar to reciting but is done silently. *Writing* is reciting on paper. All three processes actively involve you in learning and remembering material.

You will get the greatest benefit if you separate your learning into the following steps:

- Focus as you read on the key points you want to remember. These are usually found in the topic sentences of paragraphs. Then recite, rehearse, or write the ideas down.

- Convert each main idea into a key word, phrase, or visual image—something that is easy to recall and that will set off a chain of memories that will bring you back to the original information. Write each key word or phrase on an index card.

- One by one, look at the key words on your cards and recite, rehearse, or write all the associated information you can recall. Check your recall against your original material.

Michelle V. Agins/*The New York Times*

The rehearsing that this circus performer does builds her memory of the routines through repetition and physical action.

These steps are part of the process for consolidating and summarizing your lecture and text notes as you study (see chapter 7).

Reciting, rehearsing, and writing involve much more than simply rereading material and then parroting words out loud, in your head, or on paper. Because rereading does not necessarily require any involvement, you can reread without learning.

However, you cannot help but think and learn as you convert text concepts into key points, rewrite key points as key words and phrases, and judge your learning by assessing what you know and what you still need to learn.

Study During Short, Frequent Sessions

Research has shown that you can improve your chances of remembering material if you learn it more than once. Spread your study sessions over time: A pattern of short sessions, say three 20-minute study sessions, followed by brief periods of rest is more effective than continual studying with little or no rest. With this in mind, try studying during breaks in your schedule, and even consider using these time slots to study with classmates. Although studying between classes isn't for everyone, you may find that it can help you remember more information.

Sleep can actually aid memory because it reduces interference from new information. Because you can't always go to sleep immediately after studying for an exam, however, try postponing the study of other subjects until your exam is over. When studying for several tests at once, avoid studying two similar subjects back-to-back. Your memory is likely to be more accurate when you study history right after biology rather than chemistry after biology.

Practice the Middle

When you are trying to learn something, you usually study some material first, attack other material in the middle of the session, and approach still other topics at the end. The weak link is likely to be the material you study midway. It pays to give this material special attention in the form of extra practice.

Create Groupings

When items do not have to be remembered in any particular order, the act of *grouping*—forming digestible information segments that are easy to remember— can help you recall them better. Say, for example, that you have to memorize these five 10-digit numbers:

   9806875087   9876535703   7636983561   6724472879   3122895312

It may look nearly impossible. If you group the numbers to look like telephone numbers, however, the job may become more manageable:

   (980) 687-5087   (987) 653-5703   (763) 698-3561   (672) 447-2879   (312) 289-5312

In general, try to limit groups to 10 items or fewer. It's hard to memorize more at one time.

Use Flash Cards

Flash cards are a great visual memory tool. They give you short, repeated review sessions that provide immediate feedback, and they are portable, which gives you the flexibility to use them wherever you go. Use the front of a 3-by-5-inch index card to write a word, idea, or phrase you want to remember. Use the back for a definition, explanation, and other key facts. Key 6.5 shows two flash cards used to study for a pychology exam.

KEY   6.5   Flash cards help you memorize important facts.

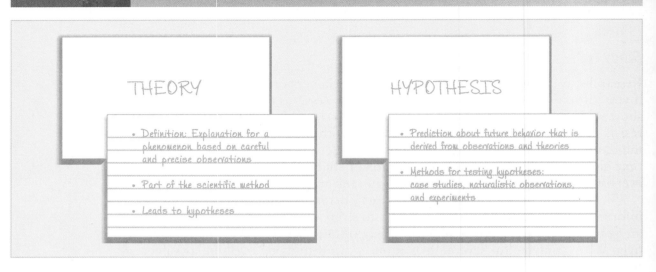

Here are some suggestions for making the most of your flash cards:

- *Use the cards as a self-test.* As you go through them, divide them into two piles—the material you know and the material you are learning.
- *Carry the cards with you and review them frequently.* You'll learn the most if you start using cards early in the course, well ahead of exam time.
- *Shuffle the cards and learn the information in various orders.* This will help you avoid putting too much focus on some items and not enough on others.
- *Test yourself in both directions.* First, look at the terms and provide the definitions or explanations. Then turn the cards over and reverse the process.
- *Reduce the stack as you learn.* You can eliminate cards as you are certain of your knowledge. Watching the pile get smaller is a reward that reinforces your motivation. As test time approaches, put all the cards together again for a final review.

Use a Tape Recorder

Questions on tape can work like audio flash cards. One method is to record short-answer study questions, leaving 10 to 15 seconds between questions for you to answer out loud. Recording the correct answer after the pause will give you immediate feedback. For example, part of a recording for a writing class might say, "Three elements that require analysis before writing are . . . (10–15 seconds) . . . topic, audience, and purpose."

Use the Information

In the days after you learn something new, try to use the information in every way you can. Think about other contexts in which it applies and link it to new problems. Then test your knowledge to make sure the material is in long-term memory. "Don't confuse recognizing information with being able to recall it," says learning expert Adam Robinson. "Be sure you can recall the information without looking at your notes for clues. And don't move on until you have created some sort of sense-memory hook for calling it back up when you need it."[5]

Choose the strategies that are likely to help you the most in different memory challenges. As you will see next, mnemonic devices create sense-memory hooks that are difficult to forget.

How can mnemonic devices boost your recall?

Certain performers entertain audiences by remembering the names of 100 strangers or flawlessly repeating 30 ten-digit numbers. Although these performers probably have superior memories, they also rely on memory techniques, known as *mnemonic devices* (pronounced neh-MAHN-ick), for assistance.

Mnemonic devices depend on vivid associations (relating new information to other information) that engage your emotions. Instead of learning new facts by *rote* (repetitive practice), associations give you a "hook" on which to hang these facts and retrieve them later. Mnemonic devices make information familiar and meaningful through unusual, unforgettable mental associations and visual pictures.

There are different kinds of mnemonic devices, including visual images and associations and acronyms. Study how these devices work, then apply them to your own memory challenges. As you will see, these devices take time and effort to create, and you'll have to be motivated to remember them. Because of this, it is smart to use mnemonic devices only when you really need them—for instance, to distinguish confusing concepts that consistently trip you up or to recall items in order.

Create Visual Images and Associations

Turning information into mental pictures helps improve memory, especially for visual learners. To remember that the Spanish artist Picasso painted *The Three Women,* you might imagine the women in a circle dancing to a Spanish song with a pig and a donkey (pig-asso). The more outlandish the image the better, as such images are the most memorable. The best mental images involve bright colors, three dimensions, action scenes, inanimate objects with human traits, and humor.

Here is another example: Say you are trying to learn some basic Spanish vocabulary, including the words *carta, río,* and *dinero.* Instead of trying to learn these words by rote, you might come up with mental images such as those in Key 6.6.

© Paha_L—Fotolia

Use Visual Images to Remember Items in a List

Using the *mental walk* strategy, you imagine that you store new ideas in familiar locations. Say, for example, that for your biology course you have to remember the major endocrine glands, starting in the brain and working downward

KEY 6.6		Visual images aid recall.
Spanish Word	**Definition**	**Mental Image**
carta	letter	A person pushing a shopping cart filled with letters into a post office.
río	river	A school of sharks rioting in the river. One of the sharks is pulling a banner inscribed with the word *riot*. A killer shark bites off the *t* in riot as he takes charge of the group. "I'm the king of this river," he says.
dinero	money	A man eating lasagna at a diner. The lasagna is made of layers of money.

through the body. To do this, think of your route to the library. You pass the college theater, the science center, the bookstore, the cafeteria, the athletic center, and the social science building before reaching your destination. At each spot along the way, you "place" the concept you want to learn. You then link the concept with a similar-sounding word that brings to mind a vivid image (see Key 6.7):

- At the campus theater, you imagine bumping into the actor Brad **Pitt**, who is holding **two** cell phones and has a **terri**ble cold (pituitary gland).
- At the science center, you visualize Mr. Universe with bulging **thighs**. When you are introduced, you learn that his name is **Roy** (thyroid gland).
- At the campus bookstore, you envision a second Mr. Universe with his **thighs** covered in **mus**tard (thymus gland).
- In the cafeteria, you see an **ad** for **Dean Al** for president (adrenal gland).
- At the athletic center, you visualize a student throwing a ball into a **pan** and **crea**tures applauding from the bleachers (pancreas).
- At the social science building, you imagine receiving a standing **ova**tion (ovaries).
- And at the library, you visualize sitting at a table taking a **test** that is **easy** (testes).

Create a Vocabulary Cartoon

Visual cartoons use the *DAP method*—definition, association, and picture—to harness the power of humor to help you remember challenging vocabulary. The recall is accomplished through the following steps:

Step 1. Write down the new vocabulary word followed by its pronunciation and *definition*. For example:

word: histrionic

pronunciation: (his tree AHN ik)

definition: overly dramatic, theatrical

A mental walk mnemonic helps you remember items in a list.   KEY   6.7

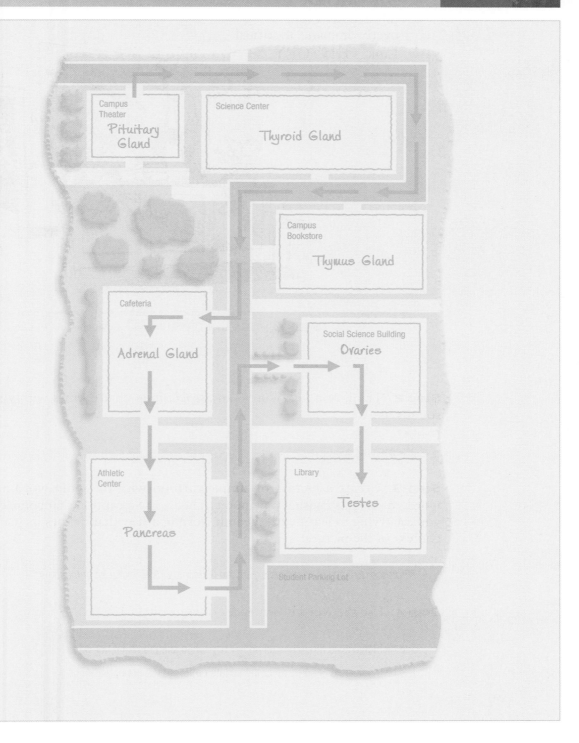

HISTRIONIC
(his tree AHN ik)
overly dramatic, theatrical
Link: HISTORY

Source: Sam Burchers, *Vocabulary Cartoons: Building an Educated Vocabulary with Visual Mnemonics,* Punta Gorda, FL: New Monic Books, 1997, p. 40. Reprinted with permission.

Step 2. Think of a link word—an *association*—that rhymes with your word or sounds like it:

association: history

Step 3. Create a *picture* or simple cartoon with the main word and the link word, to serve as a visual mnemonic. Then write a caption that connects the word you are trying to learn with the link word in a way that defines its meaning in the context of the picture:

"Professor Bradley liked his history on the histrionic side—with a lot of theatrics."

Step 4. Use the word in sentences of your own:

The histrionic child threw herself on her bed when she didn't get her way.

The histrionic actor's portrayal of the sedate professor did not ring true.

Create Acronyms

Another helpful association method involves the use of the *acronym*, a word formed from the first letters of a series of words created in order to help you remember the series. In history class, you can remember the Allies during World War II—Britain, America, and Russia—with the acronym BAR. This is an

TAKE ACTION

Create Your Own Mnemonic

Identify specific content you have to memorize for a course. Then complete the following:

Create a mnemonic to help you memorize all the details. (If you need more space, use a separate sheet of paper.)

_____

_____

Describe the types of visual images you used in the mnemonic. Were they humorous, ridiculous, or colorful?

_____

_____

Why do you think these types of images help you retain information?

_____

_____

example of a *word acronym,* because the first letters of the items you want to remember spell a word. The word (or words) spelled don't necessarily have to be real words; see Key 6.8 for an acronym—the name Roy G. Biv—that will help you remember the colors of the spectrum.

Other acronyms take the form of an entire sentence in which the first letter of each word in each sentence stands for the first letter of the memorized term. This is called a *list order acronym.* For example, when astronomy students wanted to remember the list of planets in order of their distance from the sun (Mercury, Venus, Earth, Mars, Jupiter, Saturn, Uranus, Neptune, and Pluto), they learned the sentence:

My very elegant mother just served us nine pickles.

Here's another example, from music. Use this phrase to remember the notes that correspond to the lines on the treble clef (E, G, B, D, and F):

Every Good Boy Does Fine

You can create your own acronyms. Suppose you want to remember the names of the first six U.S. presidents. You notice that the first letters of their

KEY   6.8   Use this acronym to remember the colors of the spectrum.

red
orange
yellow
green
blue
indigo
violet

R O Y G B I V

last names—Washington, Adams, Jefferson, Madison, Monroe, and Adams—together read W A J M M A. To remember them, first you might insert an e after the J and create a short nonsense word: *wajemma*. Then, to make sure you don't forget the nonsense word, you might picture the six presidents sitting in a row and wearing pajamas.

Use Songs or Rhymes

Some of the classic mnemonic devices are rhyming poems that tend to stick in your mind effectively. One you may have heard is the rule about the order of "i" and "e" in spelling.

> I before E, except after C, or when sounded like A as in "neighbor" and "weigh." Four exceptions if you please: either, neither, seizure, seize.

Make up your own poems or songs, linking familiar tunes or rhymes with information you want to remember. Thinking back to the "wajemma" example from the previous section, imagine that you want to remember the presidents' first names as well. You might set those first names—George, John, Thomas, James, James, and John—to the tune of "Happy Birthday." Or, to extend the history theme, you might use the first musical phrase of the National Anthem.

Haverford College physics professor Walter Smith hosts a Web site—**www.PhysicsSongs.org**—dedicated to helping students enjoy physics and learn essential concepts by putting them to music. Here, for example, is "The Gauss's

MULTIPLE PATHWAYS TO LEARNING

MULTIPLE INTELLIGENCE STRATEGIES FOR MNEMONIC DEVICES

Tap into these Multiple Intelligence strategies to develop more effective mnemonics.

INTELLIGENCE	SUGGESTED STRATEGIES	WHAT WORKS FOR YOU? WRITE NEW IDEAS HERE
Verbal-Linguistic	▪ Develop a story line for the mnemonic first, then work on the visual images. ▪ Choose language-based mnemonics such as word- or list-order acronyms.	
Logical-Mathematical	▪ Think of a mnemonic device that flows logically from the material. ▪ Develop three or four mnemonic device structures and use them repeatedly with different content.	
Bodily-Kinesthetic	▪ Create a storyboard for your mnemonic on large pieces of paper. Tape the paper up on your walls as you memorize the material. ▪ Record the mnemonic onto a tape and learn it as you walk between classes.	
Visual-Spatial	▪ Focus on visual mnemonics such as mental walks and idea chains. ▪ Use markers to add color to the images.	
Interpersonal	▪ Work with a study partner to develop helpful mnemonics for the course. ▪ Use the mnemonic to test each other on specific content.	
Intrapersonal	▪ Take time alone to brainstorm ideas for the mnemonic. ▪ After you develop the mnemonic, find a quiet spot to memorize the material.	
Musical	▪ Play music while you are brainstorming ideas. ▪ Create a mnemonic in the form of a musical rhyme.	
Naturalistic	▪ Include images from nature in your mnemonic. ▪ Learn the mnemonic while sitting outdoors.	

Law Song," written by Professor Smith and Marian McKenzie and sung to the tune of "East Side, West Side:"

> Inside, outside, count the lines to tell—
> If the charge is inside, there will be net flux as well.
> If the charge is outside, be careful and you'll see
> The goings in and goings out are equal perfectly.
> If you wish to know the field precise,
> And the charge is symmetric,
> you will find this law is nice—
> Q upon a constant—eps'lon naught they say—
> Equals closed surface integral of E dot n dA.

© 2001 Walter Fox Smith[6]

REFLECT

How do you react to the following statement:

"We retain 10% of what we read, 20% of what we hear, 30% of what we see, 50% of what we hear and see, 70% of what we say, 90% of what we say and do." How can you use this insight to improve your ability to retain information?

RESPOND

Professor Smith's students credit musical mnemonics for helping them retain complex equations. Student Katie Baratz went one step further and started writing her own songs. For her final project in Professor Smith's class she paired lyrics titled "In My Mind, I've Got Physics Equations" with the James Taylor tune "Carolina in My Mind." When friends asked her why she was spending so much time on the PhysicsSongs.org Web site, she explained that she was having fun.[7]

Improving your memory requires energy, time, and work. It also helps to master SQ3R, the textbook study technique that was introduced in chapter 5. By going through the steps in SQ3R and using the specific memory techniques described in this chapter, you will be able to learn more in less time—and remember what you learn long after exams are over. These techniques will be equally valuable when you start a career.

Own only what you can carry with you; know language, know countries, know people.
Let your memory be your travel bag.

ALEXANDER SOLZHENITSYN, RUSSIAN NOVELIST AND POLITICAL EXILE, WINNER OF THE 1970 NOBEL PRIZE FOR LITERATURE

I listen with understanding and empathy.

Think for a moment about what you hope to learn in school: Are you eager to gain new perspectives as you see things in new ways, or are you content to stay in your comfort zone, perhaps out of a reluctance to entertain ideas that challenge your values and beliefs? College is the place to stretch your mind—to go places intellectually that you never knew existed and to see things from the perspective of others, even those with whom you disagree.

The rewards of reining in your personal biases as you listen are immeasurable. Listening with understanding and empathy is a habit of mind that will help you become aware of other perspectives as you pursue your education. For example, although you will never be able to change your skin color or country of origin, you can get a sense of what others experience by paying attention to what they say and to the emotional tone of their words.

It may take years to fine-tune your listening skills, even though, on the surface, listening comes naturally. Why? Because the best listeners focus on what is "said" beneath the words to uncover the essence of the person speaking. Start now, as you begin college, on this mind-expanding journey of uncovering deeper meaning as you interact with others.

REMEMBER
THE IMPORTANT POINTS

How can you become a better listener?

- Listening skills can be improved with knowledge and strategy.
  - Improvement starts with understanding the four stages of the listening process: sensation, interpretation, evaluation, and reaction.
  - Learning to handle different listening challenges, including internal and external distractions, will aid listening.
  - Become an active listener by being ready to concentrate, defining your listening purpose, focusing on understanding, using critical thinking and questioning, and paying attention when the instructor signals important thoughts.

How can you maximize the power of your memory?

- Understand the function of the three memory storage banks: sensory memory, short-term memory, and long-term memory.
- Use different memory strategies to improve recall.
  - Become passionate about what you are learning.
  - Focus on understanding the material.
  - Recite, rehearse, and write to increase your active involvement.
  - Study the material more than once, practice the middle, create groupings, and use flash cards and tape recordings to study.
  - Use the material often and link it to what you know and to new facts and problems.

How can mnemonic devices boost recall?

- Use mnemonic devices to create vivid associations that engage your emotions and aid recall.
  - A mental imagery technique that will help you remember items in a list is known as taking a mental walk in a familiar place.
  - When you use vocabulary cartoons to link funny cartoons and captions to new vocabulary, you will create unforgettable visual images.
  - Use acronyms.
  - Use mnemonic devices that are in song or rhyme form.

CRITICAL THINKING
APPLYING LEARNING TO LIFE

Optimum Listening Conditions

Think of a recent situation (during this or last term) in which you were able to understand and retain most of what you heard in the classroom.

Describe the environment (course title, type of classroom setting, and so forth):

_____

_____

Describe the instructor's style (lecture, group discussion, Q&A):

_____

_____

Describe your level of preparation for the class:

_____

_____

Describe your attitude toward the course:

_____

_____

Describe any barriers to listening that you had to overcome in this situation:

_____

_____

Now think of a classroom situation you recently experienced where you feel you did not retain information well.

Describe the environment (course title, type of classroom setting, and so forth):

_____

_____

Describe the instructor's style (lecture, group discussion, Q&A):

_____

_____

Describe your level of preparation for the class:

_____

_____

Describe your attitude toward the course:

_____

_____

Describe any barriers to listening that were present in this situation:

_____

_____

Examine the two situations. Based on your descriptions, name two conditions that seem crucial for you to listen effectively and retain information:

_____

_____

Describe one way in which you could have improved your listening and retention in the more difficult situation:

_____

_____

Finally, using what you learned about mnemonic devices, create a mnemonic that allows you to remember what you consider the most important principles of listening. Write your mnemonic here.

_____

_____

TEAM BUILDING

COLLABORATIVE SOLUTIONS

Assess Your Memory and Then Boost Its Power

Gather as a class if there are fewer than 20 people, or divide into two groups if it is larger. Then do the following:

- Each person in your group should contribute at least one item to lay on a table (try to avoid repeats). When all the items are laid out, allow one minute to look at them (use a watch or clock to time yourselves).

- Then cover the items, and, allowing five minutes, have each person list on paper as many items as possible.

- Compare lists to the actual items to see how you did.

- Talk as a group about the results, what you didn't remember and why, and what helped you remember. List your observations here and on a separate sheet, if necessary.

_____

_____

_____

Now repeat the exercise using a mnemonic device. For example, create a new group of items, and then allow five minutes to look at them and to develop an acronym or idea chain in that time. Then cover the items and make lists again. Finally, talk about whether this helped you remember more items. Write your findings here.

_____

_____

_____

*I recognize that the more I use the habit of mind of **listening with understanding and empathy,** the more effective I will be as a student and a learner. With this in mind, I will follow Professor Art Costa's advice on page 179 to recap, build on, clarify, and give examples in order to appreciate the words of others through their perspective.*

The next time I attend a controversial lecture, I will take these steps after the lecture to cut through listening barriers (working alone or with a classmate, write your thoughts on a separate sheet of paper):

I will recap: What did the speaker say? What was her thesis and point of view? What was her evidence and logic?

I will build on: What do I already know that supports or refutes the speaker?

I will clarify: I will put confusing and abstract concepts in terms that make sense to me.

I will give examples: I will link the speaker's thoughts to actual real-world examples.

Now I will analyze how taking these steps changed me as a listener. In what ways did they enable me to be more empathetic and understanding?

_____

_____

_____

*I will try to use my growing ability to **listen with understanding and empathy** in my personal relationships as well. Here is a specific way I think it will help me:*

_____

_____

_____

How am I doing? **Later in the term, be accountable for your progress on page 377.**

SUGGESTED READINGS

Burley-Allen, Madelyn. *Listening: The Forgotten Skill: A Self-Teaching Guide* (Wiley Self-Teaching Guides). New York: Wiley, 1995.

Fogler, Janet, and Lynn Stern. *Improving Your Memory: How to Remember What You're Starting to Forget.* Baltimore: Johns Hopkins University Press, 2005.

Higbee, Kenneth L. *Your Memory: How It Works and How to Improve It.* New York: Marlowe, 2001.

Lorayne, Harry. *Super Memory—Super Student: How to Raise Your Grades in 30 Days.* Boston: Little, Brown, 1990.

Lorayne, Harry. *The Memory Book: The Classic Guide to Improving Your Memory at Work, at School, and at Play.* New York: Ballantine Books, 1996.

Robbins, Harvey A. *How to Speak and Listen Effectively.* New York: AMACOM Books, 1992.

Roberts, Billy. *Educate Your Memory: Improvement Techniques for Students of All Ages.* London: Allison & Busby, 2000.

Zull, James E. *The Art of Changing the Brain: Enriching Teaching by Exploring the Biology of Learning.* Sterling, VA: Stylus, 2002.

INTERNET RESOURCES

About Memory (**www.memory-key.com**)

ForgetKnot: A Source for Mnemonic Devices (**http://members.tripod.com/~ForgetKnot**)

ENDNOTES

1. Ralph G. Nichols, "Do We Know How to Listen? Practical Helps in a Modern Age," *Speech Teacher,* March 1961, pp. 118–124.

2. From *Keys to Lifelong Learning Telecourse* (videocassette), directed by Mary Jane Bradbury, Intrepid Films, 2000.

3. Nichols, "Do We Know How to Listen?"

4. James Zull, *The Art of Changing the Brain: Enriching Teaching by Exploring the Biology of Learning,* Sterling, VA: Stylus, 2002, p. 180.

5. Adam Robinson, *What Smart Students Know: Maximum Grades, Optimum Learning, Minimum Time,* New York: Three Rivers Press, 1993, p. 118.

6. Walter Smith and Marian McKenzie, "The Gauss's Law Song," © 2001, accessed March 28, 2005, from PhysicsSongs.org (**www.haverford.edu/physics-astro/songs/Gauss**).

7. Christopher Conkey, "It's All Relative: Songs to Make Physics Easier," *Wall Street Journal,* March 17, 2005, p. B1.

"Flexible people draw upon a repertoire of problem-solving strategies and tailor their style to the situation, knowing when to be broad and global in their thinking and when to apply detailed precision."

ART COSTA

THINK FLEXIBLY

One of the hallmarks of a successful student is flexibility in the classroom. Your job is to learn from your instructors, no matter their teaching styles. To do this effectively, you'll learn to tailor your notes to what is happening around you—a challenge you can readily accomplish, but a challenge nonetheless.

World champion skater Michelle Kwan is the picture of flexibility. Beyond being physically flexible, she also must *think* flexibly at every turn. If she misses a required jump, for example, she has to quickly decide where else to fit it into her program, all while continuing to skate through move after difficult move.

Every time you go to class, what you learn depends upon your ability to listen actively and think flexibly as you take in and absorb new information. Your success in retaining that information also depends on taking notes actively, recording information that you can study later. Similarly, when you conduct library or Internet research, note-taking skills will enable you to capture information that will form the basis for papers and other assignments. With its focus on taking class and research notes, this chapter will help you master the note-taking skills you will need to succeed in college.

In this chapter, you explore answers to the following questions:

- **How will taking notes help you succeed in college?**
- **What note-taking system should you use?**
- **How can you make the most of class notes?**
- **How do you combine class and text notes to create a master set?**
- **What can you do to take notes faster?**
- **What are research notes and how can you use them?**

Photo: Barton Silverman/*The New York Times*

How will taking notes help you succeed in college?

Note taking can be a challenge, especially when it gets in the way of listening to your instructor or studying what is written on the board. It's even more of a challenge when you're having trouble with difficult concepts or when, no matter how fast you write, you can't keep up with the instructor's pace.

© Vladimir Kondrachov—Fotolia

Taking notes forces you to think about concepts as you select and transcribe the instructor's thoughts. Like a high performance automobile, you're running on all eight cylinders instead of just two.

STEPHEN REID, PROFESSOR OF ENGLISH, COLORADO STATE UNIVERSITY

These problems may leave you wondering whether notes are that important after all, especially since you have your text and other assigned materials to study. Don't be fooled: *The truth is that the act of note taking involves you in the learning process in ways you cannot do without.* Taking notes makes you an active class participant—even when you don't say a word—and provides you with study materials for tests. What's on the line, in many classes, is nothing short of your academic success (see Key 7.1).

Class notes have two primary purposes: (1) to serve as a record of what happened in class and (2) to use for studying, alone and in combination with your text notes. Because it is virtually impossible to take notes on everything you hear, note taking encourages you to think critically and evaluate what is worth remembering.

KEY   7.1   Taking effective class notes leads to academic success.

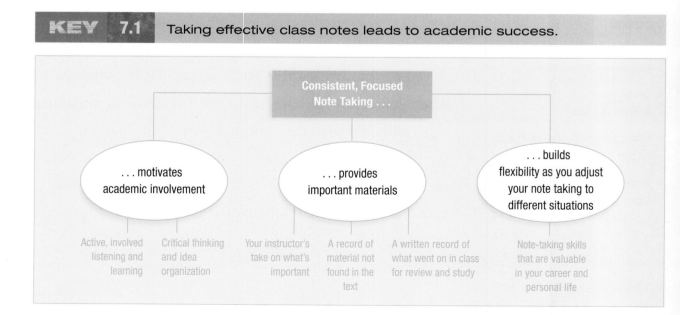

Consistent, Focused Note Taking . . .

. . . motivates academic involvement

. . . provides important materials

. . . builds flexibility as you adjust your note taking to different situations

Active, involved listening and learning

Critical thinking and idea organization

Your instructor's take on what's important

A record of material not found in the text

A written record of what went on in class for review and study

Note-taking skills that are valuable in your career and personal life

Asking yourself questions like the following will help you judge what is important enough to write down.

- Is this information important to the academic discipline I am studying, for my success in the course, and for my broad education and career success?
- Do I recognize its connections to what I already know?
- Do I want to learn it for myself?

Choosing the right note-taking system is an essential first step in becoming a better note taker.

What note-taking system should you use?

You will benefit most from a note-taking system that is comfortable and makes the most sense for the course content. The most common note-taking systems are outlines, the Cornell system, and think links. The more familiar you are with each, the more likely you are to develop your ability to *think flexibly* as you try it in your own work.

Consider trying a note-taking strategy you have never used before. For example, how willing are you to try the Cornell system or a think link if you have always used an outline? How willing are you to give a new system a fair test over a period of weeks or months? Brainstorm ways of opening yourself to new strategies that may improve your note taking and other study skills. How does trying different note-taking strategies demonstrate a willingness to activate a *flexible thinking* habit of mind?

Take Notes in Outline Form

When a lecture seems well organized, you may choose to take notes in outline form. Outlining allows you to show the interrelationships and levels of importance among general concepts and supporting details.

Formal Versus Informal Outlines

Formal outlines indicate concepts and examples with Roman numerals, uppercase and lowercase letters, and numbers. In contrast, *informal outlines* show the same associations but replace the formality with a system of consistent indentations and dashes. Key 7.2 shows the difference between the two outline forms. Many students prefer using informal outlines to take class notes. Key 7.3 demonstrates how an informal outline is used to record notes on civil rights legislation.

Outlines are difficult to use with disorganized instructors, making flexibility important. You may have to abandon its structure when the presentation becomes chaotic. Focus instead on taking down whatever information you can as you try to connect key topics. After class, do your best to restructure your notes and, if possible, rewrite them in outline form. If you are unclear about how ideas link, review the concept in your text or ask a classmate or your instructor for help.

KEY   7.2   Outlines show levels of importance as they link details to main ideas.

Formal Outline	Informal Outline
TOPIC	TOPIC
I. First Main Idea	First Main Idea
A. Major supporting fact	—Major supporting fact
B. Major supporting fact	—Major supporting fact
1. First reason or example	—First reason or example
2. Second reason or example	—Second reason or example
a. First supporting fact	—First supporting fact
b. Second supporting fact	—Second supporting fact
II. Second Main Idea	Second Main Idea
A. Major supporting fact	—Major supporting fact
1. First reason or example	—First reason or example
2. Second reason or example	—Second reason or example
B. Major supporting fact	—Major supporting fact

Guided Notes

From time to time, an instructor may give you a guide, usually in the form of an outline, to help you take notes. Although *guided notes* help you follow the lecture and organize your thoughts, they do not replace your own notes. Because they are usually no more than a basic topic outline, they require that you fill in the details. If your mind wanders because you think that the guided notes are all you need, you may miss vital information.

When you receive guided notes on paper, write directly on the paper if there is room. If not, use a separate sheet to write the outline categories that structure the guided notes. If the guided notes are on the board or overhead, copy them down but leave plenty of space for the information that comes up during the presentation. When you receive these notes online, be sure to take a printed copy to class.

Use the Cornell Note-Taking System

The *Cornell note-taking system,* also known as the *T-note system,* was developed by Walter Pauk at Cornell University and is now used throughout the world.[1] The system consists of three sections on ordinary notepaper, as follows:

- *Section 1,* the largest section, is on the right. Record your notes here in whatever form is most comfortable for you. Skip lines between topics so you can clearly see where a section begins and ends.

- *Section 2,* to the left of your notes, is the cue column. Leave it blank while you read or listen, and then fill it in later as you review. You might insert key words or comments that highlight main ideas, clarify meaning, suggest examples, or link ideas and examples. You can even draw diagrams. Many students use this column to raise questions, which they answer when they study.

An informal outline is excellent for taking class notes.   **KEY** **7.3**

Civil Rights Legislation: 1860–1968

—Post-Civil War Era
  —Fourteenth Amendment, 1868: equal protection of the law for all citizens
  —Fifteenth Amendment, 1870: constitutional rights of citizens regardless
    of race, color, or previous servitude
—Civil Rights Movement of the 1960s
  —National Association for the Advancement of Colored People (NAACP)
    —Established in 1910 by W.E.B. DuBois and others
    —Legal Defense and Education fund fought school segregation
  —Martin Luther King Jr., champion of nonviolent civil rights action
    —Led bus boycott: 1955–1956
    —Marched on Washington, D.C.: 1963
    —Awarded NOBEL PEACE PRIZE: 1964
    —Led voter registration drive in Selma, Alabama: 1965
  —Civil Rights Act of 1964: prohibited discrimination in voting, education,
    employment, and public facilities
  —Voting Rights Act of 1965: gave the government power to enforce desegregation
  —Civil Rights Act of 1968: prohibited discrimination in the sale or rental of
    housing

■ *Section 3*, at the bottom of the page, is known as the summary area. Here
you reduce your notes to only the most critical points. Restating your
instructor's points in your own words will help you learn. Use this section
to provide an overview of what the notes say.

Create this note-taking structure before class begins. Picture an upside-down
letter T as you follow these directions:

■ Start with a sheet of $8\frac{1}{2}$-by-11-inch lined paper. Label it with the date and
title of the lecture.

■ To create the cue column, draw a vertical line about $2\frac{1}{2}$ inches from the
left side of the paper. End the line about 2 inches from the bottom of
the sheet.

■ To create the summary area, start at the point where the vertical line ends
(about 2 inches from the bottom of the page) and draw a horizontal line
that spans the entire paper.

Key 7.4 shows how the Cornell system is used in a business course.

KEY 7.4   The Cornell system has space for notes, comments, and a summary.

October 3, 200x, p. 1

UNDERSTANDING EMPLOYEE MOTIVATION

Why do some workers have a better attitude toward their work than others?	Purpose of motivational theories
	  —To explain role of human relations in motivating employee performance
	  —Theories translate into how managers actually treat workers

Some managers view workers as lazy; others view them as motivated and productive.	2 specific theories
	  —Human resources model, developed by Douglas McGregor, shows that managers have radically different beliefs about motivation.
	    —Theory X holds that people are naturally irresponsible and uncooperative
	    —Theory Y holds that people are naturally responsible and self-motivated

Maslow's Hierarchy
 	
self-actualization needs (challenging job)
esteem needs (job title)
social needs (friends at work)
security needs (health plan)
physiological needs (pay)
	—Maslow's Hierarchy of Needs says that people have needs in 5 different areas, which they attempt to satisfy in their work.
	  —Physiological need: need for survival, including food and shelter
	  —Security need: need for stability and protection
	  —Social need: need for friendship and companionship
	  —Esteem need: need for status and recognition
	  —Self-actualization need: need for self-fulfillment
	Needs at lower levels must be met before a person tries to satisfy needs at higher levels.
	  —Developed by psychologist Abraham Maslow

Two motivational theories try to explain worker motivation. The human resources model includes Theory X and Theory Y. Maslow's Hierarchy of Needs suggests that people have needs in 5 different areas: physiological, security, social, esteem, and self-actualization.

Create a Think Link

A *think link*, also known as a *mind map* or *word web*, is a visual form of note taking that encourages flexible thinking. When you draw a think link, you diagram ideas by using shapes and lines that link ideas and supporting details and examples. The visual design makes the connections easy to see, and shapes and pictures extend the material beyond just words.

Use a think link to connect ideas visually.   **KEY 7.5**

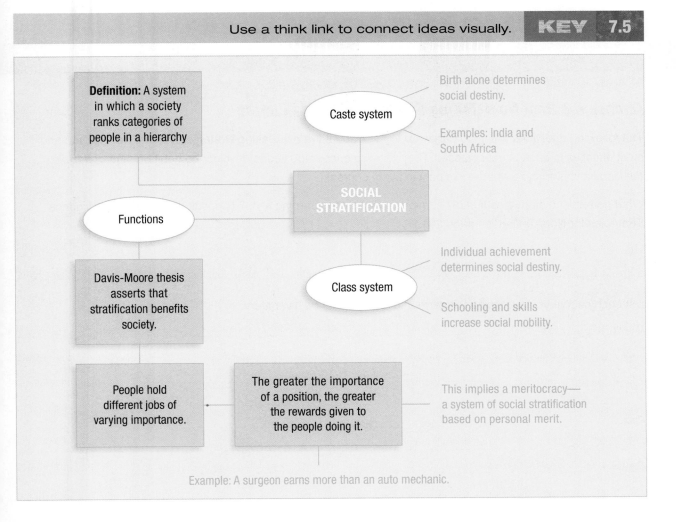

To create a think link, start by circling or boxing your topic in the middle of a sheet of paper. Next, draw a line from the topic and write the name of one major idea at the end of the line. Circle that idea also. Then, jot down specific facts related to the idea, linking them to the idea with lines. Continue the process, connecting thoughts to one another by using circles, lines, and words. Key 7.5, a think link on the sociological concept called *stratification*, follows this particular structure.

Examples of think link designs include stair steps showing connected ideas that build toward a conclusion, and a tree with trunk and roots as central concepts and branches as examples. Key 7.1 is another type of think link called a "jellyfish."

A think link may be difficult to construct in class, especially if your instructor talks quickly. In this case, transform your notes later when you review.

Use Other Visual Note-Taking Strategies

Several other note-taking strategies will help you organize information and are especially useful to visual learners. These strategies may be too involved to complete quickly during class, so you may want to use them when taking text notes or combining class and text notes for review.

TAKE ACTION

Choose the Best Note-Taking Strategy for Every Course

The following questions will encourage you to think about the note-taking strategies that are best for you and most effective in each of your classes. They will also encourage you to develop the habit of mind of *flexible thinking* as you analyze what works best in every course.

What note-taking strategies fit most comfortably with your learning style? (Consult the "Multiple Intelligence Strategies for Note-Taking" on page 221.)

_____

_____

List each course you are taking this term and briefly describe its content:

Course 1: _____

Course 2: _____

Course 3: _____

Course 4: _____

Briefly explain the instructor's teaching style for each course:

Course 1: _____

Course 2: _____

Course 3: _____

Course 4: _____

With these factors in mind, name the best note-taking system for each course:

Course 1: _____

Course 2: _____

Course 3: _____

Course 4: _____

Time lines. Use a time line to organize information into chronological order. Draw a vertical or horizontal line on the page and connect each item to the line, in order, noting the dates and basic event descriptions.

Tables. Use the columns and rows of a table to organize information as you condense and summarize your class and text notes. Many tables are included in this text, including the "Multiple Pathways to Learning" presentation in many chapters.

Hierarchy charts. Charts showing an information hierarchy can help you visualize how pieces fit together. You can use a hierarchy chart to show levels within a government bureaucracy or levels of scientific classification of animals and plants.

You can improve your skill as a note taker and the value of your notes as a study tool by defining note taking as a three-stage process to master material.

How can you make the most of class notes?

Eighteenth century German playwright Johann von Goethe said, "If you miss the first buttonhole, you will not succeed in buttoning up your coat." Describe how this quote applies to effective note taking and especially to the preparation you do before class. How will your first note-taking steps, including choosing the right note-taking style, affect your success?

Like learning to ride a bicycle, taking good class notes improves with practice—practice preparing, practice doing, and practice reviewing.

Prepare for Note Taking

Showing up for class on time with pad and pen in hand is important preparation, but it's only the beginning.

Preview your reading material. More than anything else you can do, reading the text and other assigned materials before class will give you the background to take effective notes. Check your class syllabi daily for when assignments are due, and plan your reading time with these deadlines in mind. (The syllabus on pages 9–10 shows when specific reading assignments are due.)

Try to get a sense of how each lecture relates to your reading assignment by comparing the lecture topic listed on the syllabus with the topic in the text. If the lecture material is not found in the text, you know you have a different kind of

Michelle V. Agins/ *The New York Times*

Being in class and involved will help you become more able to take comprehensive and helpful notes.

listening and note-taking challenge than if the material is in the text. Why? Because hearing material for the first time is more difficult than hearing what is familiar.

Coming to class fully prepared also gives you note-taking flexibility. Say, for example, your instructor defines a word on the blackboard—a sure sign of its importance—but before you are through writing the definition, she presents an example that requires your full attention. If you read the text before class and know that you will find the definition there, you can listen carefully to the example.

Review what you know. Taking 15 minutes before class to review your notes from the previous class and your reading assignment notes for that day will give you the context to follow the lecture from the start. Without this preparation, you may find yourself flipping back in your notebook instead of listening to new information.

Before your instructor begins, write down one or two questions about the material to put yourself in an active listening frame of mind. If you know nothing about the topic, think about why learning it is important. If your preparatory questions are not answered during the lecture, *ask them*. Not only will this help you be an attentive listener, but it will tell your instructor that you are prepared for class and willing to participate.

Gather your supplies. Use a separate notebook for each course, and start a new page for each class. (Always put your name, phone number, and e-mail address in every notebook, in case of loss.) If you use a three-ring binder, punch holes in handouts and insert them immediately after your notes for that day. If you take notes on a laptop, open the file containing your class notes right away.

Location, location, location. Find a comfortable seat that is away from friends to minimize distractions. Be ready to write as soon as the instructor begins speaking.

Choose the best note-taking system. Select a system from those discussed earlier in this chapter that will work best in each class. Take the following factors into account when making your choices:

- *The instructor's style* (which will be clear after a few classes): In the same term, you may have an instructor who is organized and speaks slowly, another who jumps from topic to topic and talks rapidly, and a third who goes off on tangents in response to questions. Your challenge is to be flexible enough to adapt your note taking to each situation.
- *The course material:* You may decide that an informal outline works best for a highly structured lecture, but that a think link is right when the presentation is looser. Try a note-taking system for several classes, then adjust if necessary.
- *Your learning style:* Choose strategies that make the most of your strong points and help compensate for weaknesses. A visual-spatial learner might prefer think links or the Cornell system; a thinker type might be comfortable with outlines; an interpersonal learner might use the Cornell system and fill in the cue column in a study group (see chapter 3 for a discussion of learning styles). You might even find that one system is best in class and another in review sessions.

Gather support. In each class, set up a support system with one or two students so that you can look at their notes when you're absent.

MULTIPLE INTELLIGENCE STRATEGIES FOR NOTE TAKING

Note taking is a critical learning tool. The tips below will help you retain information for both the short and long term.

INTELLIGENCE	SUGGESTED STRATEGIES	WHAT WORKS FOR YOU? WRITE NEW IDEAS HERE
Verbal-Linguistic	▪ Rewrite important ideas and concepts in class notes from memory. ▪ Write summaries of your notes in your own words.	
Logical-Mathematical	▪ Organize the main points of a lecture or reading using outline form. ▪ Make charts and diagrams to clarify ideas and examples.	
Bodily-Kinesthetic	▪ Make note taking as physical as possible—use large pieces of paper and different colored pens. ▪ When in class, choose a comfortable spot where you have room to spread out your materials and shift body position when you need to.	
Visual-Spatial	▪ Take notes using colored markers. ▪ Rewrite lecture notes in think link format, focusing on the most important and difficult points from the lecture.	
Interpersonal	▪ Whenever possible, schedule a study group right after a lecture to discuss class notes. ▪ Review class notes with a study buddy. See what you wrote that he or she missed and vice versa.	
Intrapersonal	▪ Schedule some quiet time as soon as possible after a lecture to reread and think about your notes. If no class is meeting in the same room after yours and you have free time, stay in the room and review there.	
Musical	▪ Play music while you read your notes. ▪ Write a song that incorporates material from one class period's notes or one particular topic. Use the retain to emphasize the most important concepts.	
Naturalistic	▪ Read or rewrite your notes outside. ▪ Review notes while listening to a nature CD—running water, rain, forest sounds.	

TAKE ACTION

Prepare to Take Notes in Your Most Challenging Class

In the spaces below, record the specific steps you will take to prepare to take notes in what you consider your most challenging course.

Course name and date of next class:

_____

Consult your course syllabus, and then list all the readings you must complete before the next class (include pages from text and supplemental sources):

_____

_____

List three strategies you intend to use to focus your attention and minimize distractions during the class:

1. _____

2. _____

3. _____

Which note-taking system is best suited for the class? Why?

_____

_____

How will developing a *flexible* note-taking habit of mind help you take comprehensive notes?

_____

_____

Write the names and e-mail addresses of two classmates whose notes you can borrow if you miss a class or if you are confused about material:

1. _____

2. _____

Record Information Effectively During Class

The following suggestions will help you record what is important in a format that you can review later. Identifying the best approach for each situation requires flexible thinking.

- Date and identify each page. When you take several pages of notes, add an identifying letter or number to the date: 11/27A, 11/27B, for example, or 11/27—1 of 2, 11/27—2 of 2. This will help you keep track of page order.

© Honda Vita—Fotolia

- Add the specific topic of the lecture at the top of the page (for example: 11/27A—U.S. Immigration Policy After World War II) so that it's easy to gather and organize all your notes when it's time to study.

- If your instructor jumps from topic to topic during a single class, it may help to start a new page for each new topic.

- Record whatever your instructor emphasizes by paying attention to verbal and nonverbal cues (see Key 7.6).

- Write down all key terms and definitions.

- Try to capture explanations of difficult concepts by noting relevant examples, applications, and links to other material.

- Write down every question your instructor raises, since these questions may be on a test.

- Be organized, but not fussy. Remember that you can always improve your notes later as long as you understand what you've written.

- Write quickly but legibly, perhaps using a personal shorthand (shorthand suggestions are presented later in this chapter). In addition, use short phrases instead of full sentences.

- Leave one or more blank spaces between points so that when you review you can easily see where one topic ends and another begins. (This suggestion does not apply if you are using a think link.)

Instructors signal important material in a variety of ways.   KEY 7.6

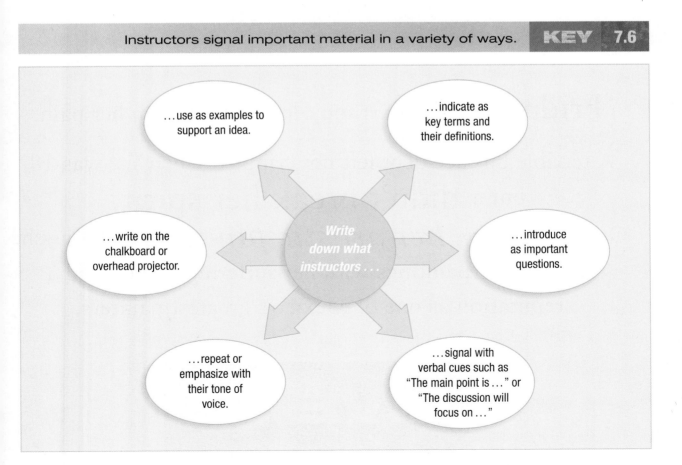

...use as examples to support an idea.

...indicate as key terms and their definitions.

...write on the chalkboard or overhead projector.

Write down what instructors...

...introduce as important questions.

...repeat or emphasize with their tone of voice.

...signal with verbal cues such as "The main point is..." or "The discussion will focus on..."

Flexible Thinking

Nickolas Muray/Getty Images Inc.—Hulton Archive Photos

Frida Kahlo's art took inspiration from her pain.

A terrible bus accident left her crippled when she was 18, but it didn't break her spirit.
On the contrary, *her artistic power grew* as she infused her paintings with her suffering and earned a reputation as one of Mexico's greatest painters.

- Draw pictures and diagrams to illustrate ideas.
- Indicate important material with a star or by underlining. Don't try to highlight, since it takes too much time. Rather, use your highlighter pen as a tool to focus on the important parts of your notes during review sessions.
- Consistency is important. Use the same system for indicating importance—such as indenting, spacing, or underlining—on each page. This will help you perceive key information with a minimum of effort.
- If you have trouble understanding a concept, record as much as you can, leaving space for an explanation later, and then flag the margin with a large question mark. After class, try to clarify your questions in the text; work with a classmate who understands the material better; or ask your instructor for help.
- Consider that your class notes are part, but not all, of what you need to learn. As you will see later in this chapter, you will learn best when you combine your text and class notes into a comprehensive master set.

Your challenge is to keep mentally involved and active—even if you are having trouble following the material, the presentation is boring, or your instructor's voice makes listening difficult. Remember, you will need to know the information, regardless of the circumstances.

Taking Notes During Extended Class Discussions

Classroom discussions yield some of the most important information you will learn all term. One student may say something, then another, and finally the instructor may summarize the comments or link them to make a new point. Frequently, class discussions have tremendous value, but just as frequently information is presented in a disorganized, sometimes chaotic way. Here are suggestions for getting the most from these discussions. Thinking flexibly will help you make the most of these discussions.

- Listen carefully to everyone, since noting what other students say may give you a new perspective.
- Listen for idea threads that weave through the comments. These threads may signal an important point.
- Listen for ideas the instructor reinforces and emphasizes and for encouraging comments, such as "You make a great point," "I like your idea," and so on.
- Take notes when the instructor rephrases and clarifies a student's point. The intensity and articulation of the instructor's voice often indicates the significance of a discussion point.
- Try using a think link as your note-taking system, as discussions often take the form

Michelle V. Agins/ *The New York Times*

Visual aids sometimes help to support the information that you learn from the lecture. Students in this anatomy class can refer to an anatomical model as they take notes.

of brainstorming sessions. A think link will help you connect ideas that come from different perspectives and in different voices.

- Take careful notes during discussion sessions with teaching assistants, since it is the purpose of these sessions to clarify difficult material.

Review and Revise Your Notes

By their very nature, class notes are imperfect and require revision. They may be incomplete in some places, confusing in others, and illegible in still others. That is why it is critical that you review and revise your notes as soon as possible after class. This will enable you to fill in gaps with information that you still remember, to clarify sloppy handwriting, or to raise questions about confusing material. (This process reemphasizes the importance of leaving space between major points or ideas.)

Reviewing and revising your class notes prepares you for the vital step of combining class and text notes.

How do you combine class and text notes to create a master set?

Studying from a single, comprehensive set of notes is more efficient than flipping back and forth between multiple sets. Furthermore, studying from either text or class notes alone is not enough, because your instructor may present material in class that is not in your text or may gloss over topics that your text covers in depth. So take the time to combine your class and text notes into a master set that reflects everything you should know.

The process of combining class and text notes engages you in active studying. As you combine material, you may see patterns and relationships among ideas, find examples that explain difficult concepts, identify key conceptual differences, and much more. All of this helps activate the *flexible thinking* habit of mind.

Be Creative

Your goal is to create notes that help you learn and remember. You can boost recall with a creative visual approach, as college learning specialist Eric Jensen explains: "Your brain stores information as pictures, sounds, and feelings very well. That means put as much sensory information as possible into your notes and they'll work better for you."[2]

Be flexible as you find different relationships within the material and format your notes based on these relationships. For instance, instead of following the structure of the text or lecture on the topic of hate crimes, you might choose an alternate organizational structure and divide your notes into different categories, such as statistics, opinions, events, definitions, and so forth.

© Piotr Przeszlo—Fotolia

Take a Step-by-Step Approach

When you combine your class and text notes, the five steps described next will simplify and enhance the process.

Step 1: Act Quickly

Try to combine your class and reading notes into a logical, comprehensive presentation while the material is fresh in your mind. See the "Take Action" feature below.

Step 2: Focus on What's Important by Condensing to the Essence

Now, reduce your combined notes so they contain only key terms and concepts. (You are likely to find repetition in your class and reading notes, which will make it easy to reduce the material.) Tightening and summarizing forces you to critically evaluate which ideas and examples are most important and to rewrite your notes with only this material. As you begin to study, move back and forth between the full set and the reduced set. Key 7.7 shows a comprehensive outline and a reduced key term outline of the same material on the topic of freedom and equality in the American democracy.

Step 3: Recite What You Know

As you approach exam time, use the terms in your bare-bones notes as cues for reciting everything you know about a topic. Many students assume that they know concepts simply because they understand what they read. What they are

TAKE ACTION

GET PREPARED

Combine Class and Text Notes

Following are two presentations on the same topic: The first is an excerpt on hate crimes from a sociology textbook and the second presents class notes based on a lecture on the same topic. As you read, think about how you would combine the material into a master set.

Excerpt on Hate Crimes from *Sociology,* 10th edition, by John J. Macionis

The term **hate crime** refers to *a criminal act against a person or a person's property by an offender motivated by racial or other bias.* A hate crime may express hostility toward someone's race, religion, ancestry, sexual orientation, or physical disability. The federal government records about 10,000 incidents of hate crimes each year.

Most people were stunned by the brutal killing in 1998 of Matthew Shepard, a gay student at the University of Wyoming, by two men filled with hate toward homosexuals. The National Gay and Lesbian Task Force reports that one in five lesbians and gay men is physically assaulted and that more than 90 percent are verbally abused because of sexual orientation (cited in Berrill, 1992:19–20). Victims of hate-motivated violence are especially likely to be people who contend with multiple stigmas, such as gay men of color. Yet hate crimes can victimize anyone: A recent study found that about 25 percent of the hate crimes based on race targeted white people (Jenness & Grattet, 2001).

By 2002, forty-five states and the federal government had enacted legislation that increased penalties for crimes motivated by hatred. Supporters are gratified, but opponents charge that such laws punish "politically incorrect" thoughts.[3]

(continued)

NOTES FROM SOCIOLOGY CLASS ON HATE CRIMES

What are hate crimes?
— also called bias crimes
— defined in a 1990 federal law as an offense "in which the defendant's conduct was motivated
    by hatred, bias, or prejudice, based on the actual or perceived race, color, religion, national
    origin, ethnicity, gender, or sexual orientation of another individual or group of individuals."
        — Congress passed 2nd law in 1994 that focused on "crimes of violence motivated by gender."
        These crimes are committed because of the victim's gender and are punished as felonies.
            — The same law declared as hate crimes offenses motivated by bias against people with
                disabilities
            — Recent examples: Matthew Shepard was murdered in 1998 because he was gay;
                James Byrd Jr, was murdered in 1999 because of his race
Controversy over whether hate crimes should be punished more severely than crimes not motivated
by bias?
        — One side says they should:
            — offender's motives have always been considered in weighing criminal responsibility
            — hate crimes inflame the public more than non-hate crimes and punishment should be given
                with that in mind
            — hate crime victims often have greater injury than victims of other crimes
        — Critics disagree
            — it is difficult to separate hard-core racism from impulsive acts, especially if the offender
                is a young person
            — hate-crime laws are a potential threat to 1st Amendment guarantees of free speech in
                that hate-crime laws may lead to courts convicting people because of their attitudes
                and words, not their actions.

List three key facts found in the class notes, but not in the text:

1. _____

2. _____

3. _____

What does this tell you about the importance of studying from a combination of class and text notes?

_____

On a separate piece of paper, combine these class and text notes into a comprehensive presentation on hate
crimes. Be creative as you consider using one of the note-taking systems presented earlier in this chapter.

Reducing a full set of notes into key-term notes will help you master content.

KEY 7.7

MASTER SET OF CLASS AND TEXT NOTES

Different Views of Freedom and Equality in the American Democracy

I. U.S. democracy based on 5 core values: freedom and equality, order and stability, majority rule, protection of minitory rights, and participation.

   A. U.S. would be a "perfect democracy" if it always upheld these values.

   B. U.S. is less than perfect; so it is called an "approaching democracy."

II. Freedom and Equality

   A. Historian Isaiah Berlin defines freedom as either positive or negative.

     1. Positive freedoms allow us to exercise rights under the Constitution, including right to vote.

     2. Negative freedoms safeguard us from government actions that restrict certain rights, such as the right to assemble. The 1st Amendment restricts government action by declaring that "Congress shall make no law . . ."

   B. The value of equality suggests that all people be treated equally, regardless of circumstance. Different views on what equality means and the implications for society.

     1. Equality of opportunity implies that everyone has the same chance to develop inborn talents.

       a. But life's circumstances—affected by factors like race and income—differ. This means that people start at different points and have different results. E.g., a poor, inner-city student will be less prepared for college than an affluent, suburban student.

       b. It is impossible to equalize opportunity for all Americans.

     2. Equality of result seeks to eliminate all forms of inequality, including economic differences, through wealth redistribution.

   C. Freedom and equality are in conflict, say text authors Berman and Murphy: "If your view of freedom is freedom from government intervention, then equality of any kind will be difficult to achieve. If government stays out of all citizen affairs, some people will become extremely wealthy, others will fall through the cracks, and economic inequality will multiply. On the other hand, if you wish to promote equality of result, then you will have to restrict some people's freedoms—the freedom to earn and retain an unlimited amount of money, for example."[*]

KEY-TERM OUTLINE OF THE SAME MATERIAL

Different Views of Freedom and Equality in the American Democracy

I. America's 5 core values: freedom and equality, order and stability, majority rule, protection of minority rights, and participation.

   a. "Perfect democracy"

   b. "Approaching democracy"

II. Value #1—Freedom and equality

   a. Positive Freedoms and Negative Freedoms

   b. Different views of equality: equality of opportunity versus equality of result

   c. Conflict between freedom and equality centers on differing views of government's role

[*] Larry Berman and Bruce Allen Murphy, *Approaching Democracy: Portfolio Edition,* Upper Saddle River, NJ: Prentice Hall, 2005, pp. 6–8.

actually demonstrating is a passive understanding that doesn't necessarily mean that they know the material well enough to recreate it in their own words on an exam or apply it to problems. Make the process more active by reciting out loud during study sessions, writing your responses on paper, making flash cards, or working with a study partner.

Step 4: Use Critical Thinking

Now toss around ideas in your mind as you reflect on your combined notes—both the comprehensive and reduced sets. Working with material in the following ways will help you learn it fully as you develop *flexible thinking*:

- Brainstorm and write down examples from other sources that illustrate central ideas. Write down new ideas or questions that come up as you review.
- Think of ideas from your readings or from something your instructor said that support or clarify your notes.
- Consider what in your class notes differed from your reading notes and why.
- Apply concepts to problems at the end of text chapters, to problems posed in class, or to real-world situations.

Step 5: Review and Review Again

To ensure learning and to prepare for exams, expound on your key word summary and critical thinking questions until you demonstrate a solid knowledge of every topic. "Few of us are gifted with the kind of memory that allows us to reproduce something new and difficult after one exposure," explain study skills experts James and Ellin K. Deese.[4]

Try to vary your review methods—focusing on active involvement. Recite the material to yourself, have a Q&A session with a study partner, take a practice test. Another helpful technique is to summarize your notes in writing from memory after you review them. This is a good indication that you'll be able to recall the same information on a test. You may even want to summarize as you read, then summarize from memory, and compare the two summaries.

Step up your efforts before a test. Schedule longer review sessions, call a study group meeting, and review more frequently. Shorter sessions of intense review interspersed with breaks may be more effective than long hours of continuous studying.

A word of warning about comparing notes with study group partners: Don't be surprised if each of you has a radically different take on what went on in class, especially if the material was difficult or the presentation confusing. When this happens, work together to reconstruct critical information and, if necessary, bring in other perspectives.

What can you do to take notes faster?

Personal shorthand can help you push your pen faster. Because you are the only intended reader, you can misspell and abbreviate words in ways that only you understand.

A danger of using shorthand is that you might forget what your writing means. To avoid this problem, review your notes while your abbreviations and symbols are fresh in your mind. If you are confused, spell out words as you review.

Another danger is forgetting to remove shorthand from work you hand in. This can happen when you use the same system for class notes as you do when talking to friends online. For example, when students take notes in Instant Messenger language, they may be so accustomed to omitting apostrophes and commas, using acronyms, and replacing long words with incorrect contractions that they may forget to correct their final work. Therefore, in order to avoid being penalized, take care not to hand in a paper with *2* instead of *too,* or *thru* instead of *through.*

Here are some suggestions that will help you master personal shorthand. Many of these techniques will be familiar and, in fact, you may already use them to speed up your e-mail and instant messaging.

Ruth Fremson/ *The New York Times*

You never know how quickly an instructor will talk, or change gears, during class. Personal shorthand will help you keep up when the information is coming faster than you can write it all out.

w/	with		cf	compare, in comparison to
w/o	without		ff	following
→	means; resulting in		Q	question
←	as a result of		p.	page
↑	increasing		*	most importantly
↓	decreasing		<	less than
∴	therefore		>	more than
∵ or b/c	because		=	equals
≈	approximately		%	percent
+ or &	and		Δ	change
−	minus; negative		2	to; two; too
No. or #	number		vs	versus; against
i.e.	that is,		e.g.	for example
etc.	and so forth		c/o	care of
ng	no good		lb	pound

1. Use standard abbreviations in place of complete words.
2. Shorten words by removing vowels from the middle of words.

   prps = purpose
   lwyr = lawyer
   cmptr = computer

3. Substitute word beginnings for entire words.

   assoc = associate; association
   info = information
   subj = subject

4. Form plurals by adding *s* to shortened words.

   prblms = problems
   drctrys = directories
   prntrs = printers

5. Make up your own symbols and use them consistently.

   b/4 = before
   4tn = fortune
   2thake = toothache

6. Use standard or informal abbreviations for proper nouns such as places, people, companies, scientific substances, events, and so on.

   DC = Washington, D.C.
   H_2O = water
   Moz. = Wolfgang Amadeus Mozart

7. If you know that a particular word or phrase will be repeated, write it out once, and then establish an abbreviation for the rest of your notes. For example, if you are taking notes in a political science class on the search for weapons of mass destruction in Iraq, you might start by writing *weapons of mass destruction (WMD)*, and then use *WMD* as you continue.

8. Write only what is essential. Include only the information nuggets you want to remember, even if your instructor says much more. Do this by paring down your writing. Say, for example, your instructor had this to say on the subject of hate crimes:

   "After the terrorist attacks on September 11, 2001, law enforcement officials noted a dramatic shift in the nature of hate crimes. For the first time, replacing crimes motivated by race as the leading type of hate crime were crimes that targeted religious and ethnic groups and particularly Muslims."[5]

   Your notes, which include some shorthand, might look something like this:

   —After 9/11 HCs Δ focus & targeted religious and ethnic groups, esp. Muslims.
   —Reduction of HC based on race.

Finally, remember that the primary goal of your note taking is to generate material that will help you learn and remember information. No matter how popular a note-taking strategy may be, it won't do you any good if it doesn't help you reach that goal. Keep a close eye on what works for you and stick to it.

If you find that your notes aren't comprehensible, legible, or focused, think critically about how you might improve them. Can't read your notes? You might have been sleepy, been careless in your handwriting, or used a leaky pen that smudged the page. Lots of confusing gaps? You might be distracted in class, have an instructor who goes off on tangents, or have holes in your knowledge base. Put your problem-solving skills to work to address your challenge, brainstorming solutions from the strategies in this chapter. With a little time and effort, your notes will become a helpful learning tool in school and beyond.

As you will see next, doing research at the library and on the Internet will require that you learn how to take effective research notes.

What are research notes and how can you use them?

Your *research notes*—the notes you take while gathering information to answer a research question—take two forms: source notes and content notes. Both help you organize your work, keep track of sources, and avoid plagiarism.

Source notes are the preliminary notes you take, usually on index cards, as you review research. They include vital bibliographic information, as well as a short summary and critical evaluation of the work. Write these notes when you consider a book or article interesting enough to look at again. They do not signal that you have read a source carefully, only that you plan to review it later.

Each source note should include the author's full name; the title of the work; the edition (if any); the publisher, year, and city of publication; the issue and/or volume number when applicable (such as for a magazine); and the page numbers you consulted. See Key 7.8 for an example of how you can write source notes on index cards.

The second type of research notes is *content notes*. Unlike source notes, content notes provide an in-depth look at the source, taken during a thorough reading. Use them to record the information you need to write your draft. Here are some suggestions for taking effective content notes:

- When a source looks promising, begin reading it and summarizing what you read. Use standard notebook paper that fits into a three-ring binder. This gives you space to write, as well as the flexibility to rearrange the pages into any order that makes sense. (If you prefer using large index cards for content notes, choose 5-by-6-inch or 5-by-8-inch sizes.)
- Include bibliographic information and page numbers for every source.

KEY 7.8 Create source note cards as you review research.

> LORENZ, KONRAD. *King Solomon's Ring*, New York: Crowell, 1952, pp. 102–122.
>
> Summary: Descriptions of the fascinating habits of various animals and birds.
>
> Evaluation: Although this book is old, it's a classic! Added pluses: the author can be funny and provocative.

- Limit each page to a single source.
- If you take notes on more than one subject from a single source, create a separate page for each subject.
- If the notes on a source require more than one page, label the pages and number them sequentially. For example, if the source is *Business Week* magazine, your pages might be labeled BW1, BW2, and so on.
- Identify the type of note that appears on each page. State whether it is a summary in your own words, a quotation, or a paraphrase.
- Write your summary notes in any of the note-taking systems described earlier in the chapter.

The map is not the journey and the notes are not the course. Take notes, but don't try to be a stenographer.

SCOTT WOELFEL, GRADUATE OF THE UNIVERSITY OF MISSOURI

© Kirill Putchenko—Fotolia

Notations that you make directly on photocopies of sources, including marginal notes, highlighting, and underlining, can supplement your content notes as they detail your immediate reactions to key points. If you use photocopies as your primary reference without making any of your own content notes, you may have more work to do when you begin writing a paper because you will need to spend time putting the source material in your own words. Writing paraphrases and summaries in content notes ahead of time will save you some work later in the process.

I think flexibly.

In the best of all possible worlds, every instructor would come to class ready to deliver a well-organized presentation and have a dynamic speaking style that captures your interest. In this same ideal world, every instructor's style would mesh perfectly with your note-taking style so that you can comfortably record everything of value.

The reality of the classroom is often very different. Throughout college, you will meet a range of instructors who have good days and bad days—just like anyone else. Moreover, even gifted instructors may sometimes use a stream-of-consciousness style that leaves you scribbling ferociously as you try to take notes that make sense.

Your success in the classroom depends, in part, on recording key concepts, on taking down examples and supporting data, and on writing down problems and solutions. Taking effective notes during a freewheeling presentation is possible only with flexibility. Open yourself up to different note-taking techniques, even if you've used one technique for as far back as you can remember. Having the flexibility to adjust your note-taking style to the situation will help ensure that your notes will help you learn.

REMEMBER

THE IMPORTANT POINTS

1 **How will taking notes help you succeed in college?**

- Taking notes makes you an active participant and provides you with study materials for tests.
- Use critical thinking to decide if something is important enough to write down.

2 **What note-taking system should you use?**

- Use either a formal outline or an informal outline to show relationships among ideas.
- Guided notes, provided by instructors, are a bare-bones lesson, not complete notes.
- The Cornell note-taking system has a section to record information, a cue section for comments, and a summary section.
- Think links translate verbal concepts into visual diagrams that connect ideas and evidence.
- Other forms of note taking include time lines, tables, and hierarchy charts.

3 **How can you make the most of class notes?**

- Preparation is critical for effective note taking. Strategies include previewing reading material, choosing a good location, and selecting the right note-taking system.
- Use strategies to record information effectively. Be organized; indicate the importance of material and mark difficult concepts; use creative approaches to aid understanding; and indicate material your instructor emphasizes.
- It is important to continue to take notes during class discussions.

4 **How do you combine class and text notes to create a master set?**

- Studying from a comprehensive set of notes will increase your efficiency as it helps you learn.
- Reduce your combined notes to key terms and concepts.
- Use the terms in your bare-bones notes as cues for reciting what you know.
- Use critical thinking questions to reflect as you learn.
- Review again by expounding on the keyword summary and critical thinking questions.

5 **What can you do to take notes faster?**

- Use personal shorthand to speed up your in-class notes.

6 **What are research notes and how can you use them?**

- Notes you take while conducting research include source notes and content notes.
  - Source notes—your preliminary research notes, usually taken on index cards—include bibliographic information and may also include a short summary and evaluation.
  - Content notes provide an in-depth look at the source taken during a thorough reading.

BUILDING SKILLS
FOR SUCCESSFUL LEARNING

CRITICAL THINKING
APPLYING LEARNING TO LIFE

Using Your Combined Class and Text Notes to Study for an Exam

To evaluate the role your combined class and text notes play when you are learning information for an exam, take the following steps in one of your courses. (Well in advance of these steps, make sure you understand what will be covered on the exam. Ask your instructor for clarification if necessary.)

1. Check your syllabus for when the material on the exam will be covered. Then read your textbook and use SQ3R to learn the material. Finally, take notes during the class meetings that deal with the material.

2. Next, follow the directions on pages 226–230 to create a combined set of notes.

3. Use these notes to study for your exam. As needed, look back at your text to review concepts and learn material.

After you learn the material—but before your exam—evaluate the role your combined class and text notes played in your studying:

How important were your notes in learning the material?

_____

_____

Did your combined notes clarify important text concepts, did they cover material not found in the text, or both?

_____

_____

What does your answer to the previous question tell you about your instructor's teaching style and expectations?

_____

_____

Your next step is to take the exam and evaluate the role your combined class and text notes played in your performance. The following will guide your analysis:

Evaluate how much of the test material was based on class lectures and discussions rather than on the text. Then analyze how you did on class-based questions. What does this analysis tell you about the effectiveness of your notes?

_____

_____

Evaluate how much of the test was based on your text. Then analyze how you did on these questions. What does this analysis tell you about the effectiveness of your method for studying your text?

_____

_____

Based on your analysis, describe one way to improve your combined notes before the next exam.

_____

_____

Finally, describe one way to improve your method of *studying* your combined notes.

_____

TEAM BUILDING

COLLABORATIVE SOLUTIONS

Create a Note-Taking Team

In this course or another, come together with two or three study group partners to review the quality and style of each other's class notes. Your goal is to strengthen your techniques by assessing the strengths and weaknesses of other notes.

- Start by passing around the class notes you took on a specific day. Try to choose a day when a lot of new material was covered and when student comments were important. Allow as much time as needed to review each other's work. (Make sure you reread your own notes as part of this step.)
- Then make a list of the strengths and weaknesses of each set of notes. As you assess the material, think back to what you considered important in the class and how you included that material in your own notes.
- Next, discuss each other's evaluations. Your goal is to pinpoint techniques that work well and to think about ways to incorporate them into your own note taking. Among the techniques you might consider are choice of note-taking system, effectiveness of shorthand, comprehensiveness of notes (material included and material omitted), and usefulness of the notes as a study tool.
- Finally, each person should choose what he or she considers the three best techniques and start using them right away. In a week, assess your progess in turning these techniques into note-taking habits.

*I recognize that my ability to **think flexibly** as I take notes is a habit of mind that will help me get the most out of every class. To improve my flexibility, I commit to using three note-taking strategies I learned in this chapter:*

Strategy 1: _____

Strategy 2: _____

Strategy 3: _____

I will focus on one of these strategies (circle the strategy) that I believe will help me most to become a flexible note taker. Using this strategy, I will:

Describe my goal—what I want to gain.

_____

_____

_____

Describe in detail how I plan to use the strategy to gain flexibility.

_____

_____

_____

_____

Describe how I will measure my progress toward the goal this term.

_____

_____

_____

*I will apply my growing ability to **think flexibly** to other important study skills, such as reading and listening. Here are some specific ways I will be more flexible in two different areas:*

Area #1: _____

_____

Area #2: _____

_____

How am I doing? **Later in the term, be accountable for your progress on page 377.**

SUGGESTED READINGS

DePorter, Bobbi, and Mike Hernacki. *Quantum Notes: Whole-Brain Approaches to Note-Taking.* Chicago: Learning Forum, 2000.

Dunkel, Patricia A., Frank Pialorsi, and Joane Kozyrez. *Advanced Listening Comprehension: Developing Aural and Note-Taking Skills.* Boston: Heinle & Heinle, 1996.

Kesselman-Turkel, Judi, and Franklynn Peterson. *Note-Taking Made Easy.* Madison: University of Wisconsin Press, 2003.

Klein, Brock, and Matthew Hunt. *The Essential Workbook for Library and Internet Research Skills.* New York: McGraw-Hill, 1999.

Lebauer, R. Susan. *Learn to Listen, Listen to Learn: Academic Listening and Note-Taking.* Upper Saddle River, NJ: Prentice Hall, 2000.

Levin, Leonard. *Easy Script Express: Unique Speed Writing Methods to Take Fast Notes and Dictation.* Chicago: Legend, 2000.

INTERNET RESOURCES

Study Skills Guide: College of Saint Benedict, Saint John's University (**http://www.csbsju.edu/academicadvising/helplist.htm**)

Study Skills Library: Notetaking Systems, California Polytechnic State University, San Luis Obispo (**www.sas.calpoly.edu/asc/ssl/notetaking.systems.html**)

ENDNOTES

1. Walter Pauk, *How to Study in College,* 7th ed., Boston: Houghton Mifflin, 2001, pp. 236–241.

2. Eric Jensen, *Student Success Secrets,* 5th ed., Hauppauge, NY: Barron's Educational Series, 2003, p. 124.

3. John J. Macionis, *Sociology,* 10th ed., Upper Saddle River, NJ: Prentice Hall, 2005, pp. 203–204.

4. James Deese and Ellin K. Deese, *How to Study and Other Skills for Success in College,* 4th ed., New York: McGraw-Hill, 1994, p. 28.

5. Information from Frank Schmalleger, *Criminal Justice Today,* 8th ed., Upper Saddle River, NJ: Prentice Hall, 2005, p. 71.

Take responsible risks

"Flexible people tend to go beyond established limits; they 'live on the edge' of their competence. . . . However, they do not behave impulsively. Their risks are calculated. They draw on past knowledge, are thoughtful about consequences, and have a well-trained sense of which risks are worthwhile."

ART COSTA

TAKE RESPONSIBLE RISKS

Every time you register for a new course, you are taking a responsible risk that may result in success or disappointment on class tests. Despite the risk, it is worth it to put yourself out there. If you are committed to learning, you will succeed by studying hard and mastering helpful test-taking techniques.

People who enjoy roller coasters like this classic wood coaster on Coney Island know how to take responsible risks. Even as they fly wildly up, down, and around, they are secured by metal and straps and protected by the promise that the amusement park maintains a high safety standard.

Although test taking may seem risky, being prepared to the top of your ability makes that risk a responsible one, as well as a productive one. When you successfully show what you know on tests, you develop the ability to perform well again and again. Exams also help you gauge your progress and, if necessary, improve or adjust your efforts. Most importantly, the test-preparation, test-taking, and test-evaluation skills you acquire today will help you face risks responsibly and productively through your life.

As you will see in this chapter, test taking is about preparation, persistence, and strategy. It is also about conquering fears, focusing on details, learning from mistakes, and having an indomitable spirit of success.

In this chapter, you explore answers to the following questions:

- How can preparation improve test performance?

- How can you work through test anxiety?

- What general strategies can help you succeed on tests?

- How can you master different types of test questions?

- How can you learn from test mistakes?

Photo: Nicole Bengiveno/The New York Times

How can preparation improve test performance?

You prepare for exams every day you are in school—by attending class, staying on top of assignments, completing readings, papers, and projects, and participating in class discussions. You are actively learning and retaining the knowledge you need to do well on exams. The following additional measures will enhance your test preparation.

Far better it is to dare mighty things, to win glorious triumphs even though checkered by failure, than to rank with those poor spirits who neither enjoy nor suffer much because they live in the gray twilight that knows neither victory nor defeat.

THEODORE ROOSEVELT, 26TH PRESIDENT OF THE UNITED STATES

Identify Test Type and Material Covered

Before you begin studying, find out as much as you can about the test, including:

- *Topics that will be covered.* Will it cover everything since the course began, or will it be limited to a narrow topic?
- *Material you will be tested on.* Will the test cover only what you learned in class and in the text, or will it also include outside readings? Will you be given material to work with—for example, will you be asked to analyze a poem?
- *Types of questions.* Will the questions be objective (multiple-choice, true/false, sentence completion), subjective (essay), or a combination?
- *How the test will be graded.* Will partial credit be given for short-answer questions? Do you need to show your thought processes to receive full credit? What sections of the exam are worth more—the essay or multiple choice, for example?

Your instructors may answer many of these questions. They may tell you the question format and the topics that will be on the test. Some instructors may even drop hints about possible questions, either directly ("I might ask a question on this subject on your next exam") or more subtly ("One of my favorite theories is . . ."). If you skip class or space out in the back of the room, you will miss these vital hints.

As you begin thinking about the test, remember that not all tests are created equal—a quiz is not as important as a midterm or final. Learn to prioritize as you link the time and energy you put into studying to the test's value, realizing as you do that the accumulated grades you get on small quizzes add up and can make a difference in your final grade. Your class syllabus will tell you when quizzes and tests are scheduled throughout the term (see the syllabus on pages 9–10 for an example).

Following are other practical strategies for predicting what may be on a test. Combine these with the strategies you have learned throughout *Keys to Effective Learning* to prepare.

Use SQ3R to identify what's important. Often, the questions you write and ask yourself when you read assigned materials may be part of the test. Textbook study questions—or variations of them—are also good candidates.

Listen for clues at review sessions. Many instructors offer review sessions before midterms and finals in order to answer last-minute questions. Bring your own questions to these sessions and listen to the questions others ask. They may cover material you thought you knew, but actually need to review or learn more about.

Make an appointment to see your instructor. Spending a few minutes talking about the test one-on-one may clarify misunderstandings and help you focus on what to study.

Talk to people who already took the course. Try to get a sense of test difficulty, whether tests focus primarily on assigned readings or class notes, what materials are usually covered, and what types of questions are asked. If you learn that the instructor pays close attention to specific facts, for example, use flash cards to drill yourself on details. If she emphasizes a global overview, focus on big-picture concepts.

Examine old tests, if the instructor makes them available. You may find old tests in class, online, or on reserve in the library. (Make sure you have the instructor's permission to consult them.) Old tests will help you answer questions like these:

- Do tests focus on examples and details, general ideas and themes, or a combination?
- Are the questions straightforward, or confusing and sometimes tricky?
- Will you be asked to integrate facts from different areas in order to draw conclusions?
- Will you be asked to apply principles to new situations and problems?

After taking the first exam in a course, you will have a better idea of what to expect.

Create a Study Schedule and Checklist

Now choose what you will study. Go through your notes, texts, related primary sources, and handouts, and set aside anything you don't need. Then prioritize the remaining materials. Your goal is to focus on information that is most likely to be on the exam.

Next, use the time-management and goal-setting skills from chapter 2 to prepare a schedule. Consider all of the relevant factors—your study materials, the number of days until the test, your ongoing responsibilities, and the time you can study each day. If you establish your schedule ahead of time and write it in a planner, you are more likely to follow it.

Andrea Mohin/ *The New York Times*

Using time-management skills to schedule individual review sessions and study group meetings is part of successful test preparation.

Use a checklist to assign specific tasks to particular study times and sessions. That way, not only do you know when you have time to study, but you also have defined goals for each study session.

Try to build flexibility into your schedule. If it takes longer to study than you originally planned, you may have to rearrange your priorities to get everything done.

Prepare Through Careful Review

A thorough, *active* review is the best way to master material for an exam. The following strategies will ensure that your preparation is active.

Use SQ3R. The reading method you studied in chapter 5 provides an excellent structure for reviewing your reading materials.

Actively review your combined class and text notes. One of the best ways to review for an exam is to combine and condense your text and class notes—a process that gets you actively involved with the material (see chapter 7). Work with this combined note set to prepare for exams using these strategies.

- *As exam time nears, go through your key terms and concepts outline, and recite everything you know about a topic.* Remember that reading your notes is not enough. Learning takes place only if you express content in your own words and apply it to problems using these strategies.

- *Use critical thinking to increase active involvement.* As you review, think about examples that illustrate concepts, ideas from outside readings and experiences that demonstrate points, and divergent ideas and opinions. Finally, use what you know to solve problems.

- *Continue to actively review until you demonstrate a solid knowledge of every topic.* Use varied techniques that get you involved with the material—take a practice test, have your study partner question you, answer your SQ3R questions in writing one more time. Don't stop until you are sure of your ability to apply concepts to new material.

Take a Pretest

Use end-of-chapter text questions to create your own pretest. Or tap into the technology that accompanies your text, expecially CD-ROMs and the text Web site with sample quizzes. If your course doesn't have an assigned text, develop your own questions from your notes and assigned outside readings.

Old homework problems will also help you target topics. The best questions integrate different topics in ways that make you think. When you are able to answer them correctly, you establish that you understand the material and can

TAKE ACTION

Organize for Test Success

Complete the following checklist for each exam to define your study goals, get organized, and stay on track. Make extra copies so that they're ready to fill out as soon as an exam is announced.

Course: _____ *Instructor:* _____

Date, time, and place of test: _____

Type of test (Is it a midterm or a minor quiz?) _____

What instructor said about the test, including types of test questions, test length, and how much the test counts toward your final grade: _____

_____

_____

Topics to be covered on the test, in order of importance:

1. _____
2. _____
3. _____
4. _____
5. _____

Study schedule, including materials you plan to study (texts, class notes, homework problems, and so forth) and dates you plan to complete each:

MATERIAL   **COMPLETION DATE**

1. _____   _____
2. _____   _____
3. _____   _____
4. _____   _____
5. _____   _____

Materials you are expected to bring to the test (textbook, sourcebook, calculator):

_____

_____

(continued)

Special study arrangements (study group meetings, meeting with the instructor, outside tutoring), including scheduled times:

_____

_____

Life-management issues (such as rearranging work hours to study with a classmate):

_____

_____

Source: Adapted from Ron Fry, *"Ace" Any Test*, 3rd ed., Franklin Lakes, NJ: Career Press, 1996, pp. 123–24.

apply it in different ways. Take pretests under test-like conditions—in a quiet place, with no books or notes to help you (unless the exam is open book), and with a clock to tell you when time is up.

Prepare Physically

Most tests ask you to work at your best under pressure, so a good night's sleep will leave you rested and alert. It will also improve your ability to remember what you studied the night before.

Eating a light, well-balanced meal is also important. Avoid carbohydrates, including candy and cakes, and focus on protein instead (eggs, milk and yogurt, meat and fish, nuts, and peanut butter). When time is short, grab a quick-energy snack such as a banana, orange juice, or a high-protein granola bar—and *never* skip breakfast.

Make the Most of Last-Minute Cramming

Cramming—studying intensively and around the clock right before an exam—often results in information going into your head and popping right back out shortly after the exam is over. If learning is your goal, cramming is not a good idea. The reality, however, is that nearly every student crams during college, especially during midterms and finals. Use the following hints to make the most of this intensive study time:

- *Focus on crucial concepts.* Summarize the most important points and try to resist reviewing notes or texts page by page.
- *Create a last-minute study sheet.* On a single sheet of paper, write down key facts, definitions, formulas, and so on. If you prefer visual notes, use think links to map out ideas and supporting examples. You can also put these items on flash cards and review them right before the test.
- *Arrive early.* Review your study sheet until you are asked to clear your desk.

A practical warning about cramming: Thousands of well-meaning students who study until four in the morning sleep through the sound of their alarm clocks and miss their exams. To prevent this from happening to you, place several clocks on distant tables. This will force you to get out of bed to stop the noise.

After your exam, evaluate how cramming affected your performance. Did it help, or did it load your mind with disconnected details? Did it increase or decrease your anxiety when the test began? Then evaluate how cramming affected your recall. Within a few days, you will probably remember very little—a reality that will work against you in advanced courses that build on this knowledge and in careers that require it. Think ahead about how you can start studying earlier to prepare for your next exam.

How can you work through test anxiety?

A certain amount of stress can be a good thing. Your body is alert, and your energy motivates you to do your best. Some students, however, experience incapacitating stress before and during exams, especially midterms and finals.

Test anxiety can cause sweating, nausea, dizziness, headaches, and fatigue. It can reduce your ability to concentrate, make you feel overwhelmed, and cause you to "blank out" during the exam. As a result, test anxiety often contributes to lower grades that may not reflect what you really know. To minimize anxiety, prepare thoroughly and build a positive attitude.

Reminding yourself that most students are feeling similar anxiety may help you relax. It also helps to remember that test taking is a *responsible type of risk taking*—a habit of mind worth developing. Putting yourself out there for a test will prepare you to take calculated risks, and benefit from them, in the future.

REFLECT

Do you experience test anxiety? Describe how tests generally make you feel (you might include an example of your feelings during a recent test). Identify your specific test-taking fears, and write out your plan to overcome them. If test anxiety isn't a problem, what do you think contributes to your pretest calm? Finally, how do you respond to the statement that putting yourself out there for a test helps you learn to *take responsible academic risks?*

RESPOND

Prepare and Have a Positive Attitude

Finding out what to expect on the exam will add to your sense of control. Similarly, creating and following a detailed study plan will build knowledge and a sense of mastery. The following suggestions will help you build a positive attitude:

- *See tests as opportunities to learn.* Instead of thinking of tests as contests that you either "win" or "lose," think of them as signposts along the way to mastering material.

- *Understand that tests measure performance, not personal value.* Your grade reflects neither your ability to succeed nor your self-worth. Whether you get an A or an F, you are the same person.

Barton Silverman / *The New York Times*

To help calm test anxiety, use positive mental images. Picture yourself at the "finish line" of your test, having achieved your goal as this long-distance runner did at the 2000 Olympics in Sydney, Australia.

- *Appreciate that instructors are on your side.* Your instructors want you to do well, even when they give challenging tests, so contact them during office hours or via e-mail.

- *Seek study partners who challenge you.* Find study partners who inspire you to do your best. Try to avoid people who are also anxious, because you may pick up on one another's fears and negativity. (For more on study groups, see chapter 1.)

- *Practice relaxation.* When you feel test anxiety mounting, breathe deeply, close your eyes, and visualize positive mental images such as getting a good grade and finishing with time to spare. Try to ease muscle tension—stretch your neck, tighten and then release your muscles.

- *Shut out negative vibrations.* If you arrive at the testing room early for a last-minute review, pick a seat far away from others who are nervously discussing the test.

- *Practice positive self-talk.* Tell yourself that you can do well and that it is normal to feel anxious, particularly before an important exam.

- *Remind yourself of your goals.* Connecting the test to your long-term goals will help you calm down as you focus on what's important.

Math exams are a special problem for many students. Dealing with the anxieties associated with these exams will be examined in chapter 9.

Finally, a good attitude involves being prepared for different test-taking challenges than you experienced in high school. The exams that you take in college may ask you to critically analyze and apply material in ways that you never did before. For example, your history instructor may give you a new primary source and ask you to place it in its historical context. Prepare for these challenges as you study by continually asking critical thinking questions (see chapter 4).

Test Anxiety and the Returning Student

If you're returning to school after years away, you may wonder how well you will handle exams. To deal with these feelings, focus on what you have learned through life experience, including the ability to handle work and family pressures. Without even knowing it, you may have developed the time-management, planning, organizational, and communication skills needed for college success.

In addition, your life experiences will give real meaning to abstract classroom ideas. For example, workplace relationships may help you understand social psychology concepts, and refinancing your home mortgage may help you grasp the importance of interest rate swings—a key concept in economics.

Responsible Risk Taking

Reuters/Molly Riley/Corbis

Bono, the world-famous lead singer of U2, raises billions to restore dignity to those afflicted with malaria and AIDS.

"This can be a generation that can **end extreme poverty,**" he said. He has *risked his reputation and career* to fight poverty and illness around the world.

Parents who have to juggle child care with study time can find the challenge especially difficult before a test. Here are some suggestions that might help:

- *Find help.* Join a babysitting cooperative, switch off with a neighbor, post a sign for a part-time babysitter at the local high school.
- *Plan activities.* With younger children, have a supply of games, books, and videos. Give your young artists a new box of markers and an unlimited supply of paper. Then tell them to draw scenes of their family, their home, their friends—all in brilliant color.
- *Explain the time frame.* Tell school-aged children your study schedule and test date. Then reward them for cooperating with a trip to the movies or their favorite pizza restaurant.

What general strategies can help you succeed on tests?

Even though every test is different, there are general strategies that will help you handle almost all tests, including short-answer and essay exams.

Choose the Right Seat

Your goal is to choose a seat that will put you in the right frame of mind and minimize distractions. Finding a seat near a window or next to a wall or in the front row will enable you to look off into the distance without being suspected of looking at another paper. It's smart to avoid sitting near friends.

Write Down Key Facts

Before you even look at the test, write down key information, including formulas, rules, and definitions, that you don't want to forget. (Use the back of the question sheet so your instructor knows that you made these notes after the test began.)

Begin with an Overview

Although exam time is precious, spend a few minutes at the start gathering information about the questions—how many there are in each section, what types, and their point values. Use this information to schedule your time. For example, if a two-hour test is divided into two sections of equal value—an essay section with four questions and a short-answer section with 60 questions—you might spend an hour on the essays (15 minutes per question) and an hour on the short-answers (one minute per question).

Take level of difficulty into account as you parcel out your time. For example, if you think you can get through the short-answer questions in 45 minutes and sense that the writing section will take longer, you can budget an hour and a quarter for the essays.

Read Test Directions

Reading test directions carefully can save you trouble. For example, although a history test of 100 true/false questions and one essay may look straightforward, the directions may tell you to answer 80 of the 100 questions or that the essay is optional. If the directions indicate that you are penalized for incorrect answers—meaning that you would lose points instead of simply not gaining points—avoid guessing unless you're fairly certain.

When you read directions, you may learn that some questions or sections are weighted more heavily than others. For example, the short-answer questions may be worth 30 points, whereas the essays are worth 70. In this case, it's smart to spend more time on the essays than the short answers.

Mark Up the Questions

Mark up instructions and key words to avoid careless errors. Circle qualifiers, such as *always, never, all, none, sometimes,* and *every;* verbs that communicate specific instructions; and concepts that are tricky or need special attention.

Marking up your question sheet may help you process the questions and avoid careless mistakes. On multiple-choice exams, for example, write one or two words next to the choices you reject indicating why they are wrong, circle the correct answer, and finally mark it in the specified place.

Take Special Care on Machine-Scored Tests

Use the right pencil (usually a #2) on machine-scored tests, and mark your answer in the correct space, filling it completely. (Use a ruler or your pencil as a straight edge to focus on the correct line for each question.) Periodically, check the answer number against the question number to make sure they match. If you mark the answer to question 4 in the space for question 5, not only will your response to question 4 be wrong, but also your responses to all subsequent questions will be off by a line. When you plan to return to a question and leave a space blank, put a small dot next to the number on the answer sheet. Neatness counts on these tests because the computer may misread stray pencil marks or partially erased answers.

© Jason Stitt—Fotolia

Work from Easy to Hard

Begin with the easiest questions, and answer them as quickly as you can without sacrificing accuracy. This will boost your confidence and leave more time for questions that require greater focus and effort. Mark tough questions as you reach them, and return to them after answering the questions you know.

According to study-skills expert Adam Robinson, a common mistake of students is spending the most time trying to answer questions about which they know the least instead of spending more time on the questions they can ace. When you know material well, expecially on an essay test, explains Robinson, "the favorable impression your answer will make in your teacher's mind will earn you the benefit of the doubt on the other questions."[1]

Watch the Clock

Keep track of how much time is left and how you are progressing. Some students are so concerned about time that they rush through the test and have time left over. If this happens to you, spend the remaining time refining and checking your work instead of leaving early. You may be able to correct mistakes, change answers, or add information to an essay. If, on the other hand, midway through the test you realize that you are falling behind, reevaluate to determine the best use of the remaining time. Remaining flexible will help you during a time crunch.

Take a Strategic Approach to Questions You Cannot Answer

Even if you are a diligent student, you may be faced with questions you do not understand or cannot answer. What do you do in this situation?

- If your instructor is proctoring the exam, ask for clarification. Sometimes a simple rewording will make you realize that you really know the material.
- If this doesn't work, skip the question and come back to it later. Letting your subconscious mind work on the question sometimes makes a difference.
- Use what you do know about the topic to build logical connections that may lead you to the answer. Take a calculated risk.
- Try to remember where the material was covered in your notes and text. Creating this kind of visual picture may jog your memory about content as well.
- Start writing—even if you think you're going in the wrong direction and not answering the question that was asked. The act of writing about related material may help you recall the targeted information. You may want to do this kind of "freewriting" on a spare scrap of paper, think about what you've written, and then write your final answer on the test paper or booklet. Put yourself out there.
- If you think of an answer at the last minute but are short on time, write on the paper that you only have minutes left to answer the question, so you are putting your answer in outline form. While most instructors will deduct points for this approach, they may also give you partial credit because you showed that you know the material.

Master the Art of Intelligent Guessing

When you are unsure of an answer on a short-answer test, you can leave it blank or guess. As long as you are not penalized for incorrect answers, the risk you take in guessing may help you. When you take advantage of what you know in order to try to figure out what you don't know, you have a reasonable chance of getting the answer right.

When you check your work at the end of the test, decide whether you would make the same guesses again. Chances are that you will leave your answers alone because your first instincts are usually the best, but you may notice something that changes your mind—a qualifier that affects meaning, for example—or you may recall information that you couldn't remember the first time around.

Maintain Academic Integrity

Cheating as a strategy to pass a test or get a better grade robs you of the opportunity to learn, which, ultimately, is your loss. Cheating also jeopardizes your future if you are caught. You may be seriously reprimanded—or even expelled—if you violate your school's code of academic integrity. You should also know that employers don't hire, promote, or reward cheaters, especially in the post-Enron era when companies have become more vigilant than ever.

In recent years, cheating has become high-tech, with students using their cell phones, iPods, personal digital assistants (PDAs), graphing calculators, and Internet-connected laptops to share information with other test takers through text messaging or to search the Internet. Because high-tech cheating can be difficult to discover when exams are administered in large lecture halls, some instructors ban all electronic devices from the room.

How can you master different types of test questions?

Every type of test question has a different way of finding out how much you know about a subject. For *objective questions,* you choose or write a short answer, often making a selection from a limited number of choices. Multiple-choice, fill-in-the-blank, matching, and true/false questions fall into this category. *Subjective questions* demand the same information recall as objective questions, but they also require you to plan, organize, draft, and refine a response. All essay questions are subjective.

Key 8.1 shows samples of real test questions from Western civilization, macroeconomics, Spanish, and biology college texts published by Pearson Education. Included are multiple-choice, true/false, fill-in-the-blank, matching, and essay questions, including a short-answer essay. Analyzing the types, formats, and complexity of these questions will help you gauge what to expect when you take your exams.

As you study the suggestions that follow, you'll see that some are repeated in various sections. This is no accident. It is done to reinforce the importance of these suggestions and their application to different types of test questions.

James Estrin/ *The New York Times*

Having good test-taking skills helps you handle high-pressure situations both at school and on the job. Here a student disassembles a watch while observed by other students in training to be watchmakers.

KEY   8.1   Real test questions from real college texts.

From Chapter 29, "The End of Imperialism," in *Western Civilization: A Social and Cultural History,* 2nd edition.

■ **MULTIPLE-CHOICE QUESTION**

India's first leader after independence was:

A. Gandhi   B. Bose   C. Nehru   D. Sukharno   *(answer: C)*

■ **FILL-IN-THE-BLANK QUESTION**

East Pakistan became the country of _____ in 1971.

A. Burma   B. East India   C. Sukharno   D. Bangladesh   *(answer: D)*

■ **TRUE/FALSE QUESTION**

The United States initially supported Vietnamese independence.   T   F   *(answer: false)*

■ **ESSAY QUESTION**

Answer one of the following:

1. What led to Irish independence? What conflicts continued to exist after independence?

2. How did Gandhi work to rid India of British control? What methods did he use?

From Chapter 6, "Unemployment and Inflation," in *Macroeconomics: Principles and Tools,* 3rd edition.

■ **MULTIPLE-CHOICE QUESTION**

If the labor force is 250,000 and the total population 16 years of age or older is 300,000, the labor-force participation rate is

A. 79.5%   B. 83.3%   C. 75.6%   D. 80.9%   *(answer: B)*

■ **FILL-IN-THE-BLANK QUESTION**

Mike has just graduated from college and is now looking for a job, but has not yet found one. This causes the employment rate to _____ and the labor-force participation rate to _____.

A. increase; decrease   C. stay the same; stay the same

B. increase; increase   D. increase; stay the same   *(answer: C)*

■ **TRUE/FALSE QUESTION**

The Consumer Price Index somewhat overstates changes in the cost of living
because it does not allow for substitutions that consumers might
make in response to price changes.   T   F   *(answer: true)*

■ **ESSAY QUESTION**

During a press conference, the Secretary of Employment notes that the unemployment rate is 7.0%. As a political opponent, how might you criticize this figure as an underestimate? In rebuttal, how might the Secretary argue that the reported rate is an overestimate of unemployment?

(Possible answer: The unemployment rate given by the secretary might be considered an underestimate because discouraged workers, who have given up the job search in frustration, are not counted as unemployed. In addition, full-time workers may have been forced to work part-time. In rebuttal, the secretary might note that a portion of the unemployed have voluntarily left their jobs. Most workers are unemployed only briefly and leave the ranks of the unemployed by gaining better jobs than they had previously held.)

From *Mosaicos: Spanish as a World Language,* 3rd edition.

■ **MATCHING QUESTION**

You are learning new words and your teacher asks you to think of an object similar to or related to the words he says. His words are listed below. Next to each word, write a related word from the list below.

| el reloj | el cuaderno | el pupitre | una computadora |
| el televisor | la tiza | el lápiz | la mochila |

1. el escritorio ————————————
2. el bolígrafo ————————————
3. la videocasetera ————————————

4. la pizarra ————————————
5. el libro ————————————

*(answers: 1 el pupitre; 2. el lápiz;
3. el televisor; 4. la tiza; 5. el cuaderno)*

■ **ESSAY QUESTION**

Your mother always worries about you and wants to know what you are doing with your time in Granada. Write a short letter to her describing your experience in Spain. In your letter, you should address the following points:

1. What classes you take
2. When and where you study
3. How long you study every day

4. What you do with your time (mention three activities)
5. Where you go during your free time (mention two places)

From Chapter 13, "DNA Structure and Replication," in *Biology: A Guide to the Natural World,* 2nd edition.

■ **MULTIPLE-CHOICE QUESTION**

What units are bonded together to make a strand of DNA?

A. chromatids   B. cells   C. enzymes   D. nucleotides   E. proteins   *(answer: D)*

■ **TRUE / FALSE QUESTION**

Errors never occur in DNA replication, because the DNA polymerases edit out mistakes.   T   F

(answer: false)

■ **FILL-IN-THE-BLANK QUESTION**

In a normal DNA molecule, adenine always pairs with _____ and cytosine always pairs with _____.

(answers: thymine; guanine)

■ **MATCHING QUESTION**

Match the scientists and the approximate time frames (decades of their work) with their achievements.

Column 1

_____ 1. Modeled the molecular structure of DNA

_____ 2. Generated X-ray crystallography images of DNA

_____ 3. Correlated the production of one enzyme with one gene

Column 2

_____ A. George Beadle and Edward Tatum, 1930s and 1940s

_____ B. James Watson and Francis Crick, 1950s

_____ C. Rosalind Franklin and Maurice Wilkins, 1950s

(answers: 1–B; 2–C; 3–A)

Sources: [*Western Civilization* test items] Margaret L. King, *Western Civilization: A Social and Cultural History,* 2nd ed., Upper Saddle River, NJ: Pearson Education, 2003. Questions from *Instructor's Manual* and *Test Item File* by Dolores Davison Peterson. Used with permission. [*Macroeconomics* test items] Arthur O'Sullivan and Steven M. Sheffrin, *Macroeconomics: Principles and Tools,* 3rd ed., Upper Saddle River, NJ: Pearson Education, 2003. Questions from *Test Item File 2* by Linda Ghent. Used with permission. [*Mosaicos* test items] Matilde Olivella de Castells, Elizabeth Guzmán, Paloma Lupuerta, and Carmen García, *Mosaicos: Spanish as a World Language,* 3rd ed., Upper Saddle River, NJ: Prentice Hall, 2002. Questions from *Testing Program* by Mark Harpring. Used with permission. [*Biology* test items] David Krogh, *Biology: A Guide to the Natural World,* 2nd ed., Upper Saddle River, NJ: Prentice Hall, 2002. Questions from *Test Item File* edited by Dan Wivagg. Used with permission.

Multiple-Choice Questions

Multiple-choice questions are the most popular type of question on standardized tests. Using the following strategies will help you answer them.

Read the directions carefully. Directions tell you precisely what to do. For example, whereas most test items ask for a single correct answer, some may give you the option of marking several choices that are correct. For some tests, you might be required to answer only a certain number of questions.

Read each question thoroughly and try to think of the answer before looking at the choices. Then read the choices and make your selection. When the answer you thought of matches one of the choices, it is most likely correct. Do not second-guess!

Underline key words and phrases. If the question is complicated, try to break it down into small sections that are easy to understand.

Make sure you read every word of every answer. Instructors have been known to include answers that are correct, except for a single word. Focus especially on qualifying words such as *always, never, tend to, most, often,* and *frequently.* Look also for negatives in a question ("Which of the following is *not . . .*").

Once you read every word, take the question on face value. Don't spend time reading between the lines to figure out what the instructor is *really* asking.

If you don't know the answer, eliminate answers that you know or suspect are wrong. If you can leave yourself with two possible answers, at least you will have a 50-50 chance of making the right choice. To narrow down, ask questions like these about each of the choices:

- *Is the choice accurate on its own terms?* If there's an error in the choice—for example, a term that is incorrectly defined—the answer is wrong.
- *Is the choice relevant?* An answer may be accurate, but unrelated to the question.
- *Are there any qualifiers?* Absolute qualifiers like *always, never, all, none,* or *every* often signal an exception that makes a choice incorrect. For example, the statement "Normal children *always* begin talking before the age of 2" is untrue (most normal children begin talking before age 2, but some start later). Analysis has shown that choices containing conservative qualifiers like *often, most, rarely,* or *may sometimes be* are often correct.
- *Do the choices give clues?* Does a puzzling word remind you of a word you know? Do any parts of an unfamiliar word—its prefix, suffix, or root—ring a bell?

When questions are linked to a reading passage, read the questions first. This will help you focus on the information you need to answer the questions.

Here are examples of the kinds of multiple-choice questions you might encounter in an introductory psychology course (the correct answer follows each question):

1. Arnold is at the company party and has had too much to drink. He releases all of his pent-up aggression by yelling at his boss, who promptly fires him. Arnold normally would not have yelled at his boss, but after drinking heavily he yelled because

    a. parties are places where employees are supposed to be able to "loosen up"

    b. alcohol is a stimulant

    c. alcohol makes people less concerned with the negative consequences of their behavior

    d. alcohol inhibits brain centers that control the perception of loudness   *(answer: C)*

2. Which of the following has not been shown to be a probable cause of or influence in the development of alcoholism in our society?

    a. intelligence   c. personality

    b. culture   d. genetic vulnerability   *(answer: A)*

3. Geraldine is a heavy coffee drinker who has become addicted to caffeine. If she completely ceases her intake of caffeine over the next few days, she is likely to experience each of the following *except:*

    a. depression   c. insomnia

    b. lethargy   d. headaches   *(answer: C)*

Source: Gary W. Piggrem and Charles G. Morris, *Test Item File* for *Understanding Psychology,* 3rd ed., 1996. Reprinted by permission of Pearson Education, Inc., Upper Saddle River, NJ.

True/False Questions

Read true/false questions carefully to evaluate what they are asking. If you're stumped, guess (unless you're penalized for wrong answers).

Look for qualifiers in true/false questions—such as *all, only,* and *always* (the absolutes that often make a statement false) and *generally, often, usually,* and *sometimes* (the conservatives that often make a statement true)—that can make a true statement false and vice versa. For example, "The grammar rule '*i* before *e* except after *c*' is *always* true" is false, whereas "The grammar rule '*i* before *e* except after *c*' is *usually* true" is true. The qualifier makes the difference.

© Nikonite—Fotolia

Be sure to read *every* word of a true/false question to avoid jumping to an incorrect conclusion. Common problems in reading too quickly include missing negatives (*not, no*) that would change your response and deciding on an answer before reading the complete statement. You will lose full credit if you mark a statement as true when only a part of it is true.

Matching Questions

Matching questions ask you to match the terms in one list with the terms in another list, according to the directions. For example, the directions may tell you to match a communicable disease with the microorganism that usually causes it. The following strategies will help you handle these questions.

Here are some examples of the kinds of true/false questions you might encounter in an introductory psychology course (the correct answer follows each question):

Are the following questions true or false?

1. Alcohol use is clearly related to increases in hostility, aggression, violence, and abusive behavior.   *(true)*
2. Marijuana is harmless.   *(false)*
3. Simply expecting a drug to produce an effect is often enough to produce the effect.   *(true)*
4. Alcohol is a stimulant.   *(false)*

Source: Gary W. Piggrem and Charles G. Morris, *Test Item File* for *Understanding Psychology,* 3rd ed., 1996. Reprinted by permission of Pearson Education, Inc., Upper Saddle River, NJ.

Make sure you understand the directions. The directions tell you whether each answer can be used only once or more than once.

Work from the column with the longest entries. The left-hand column usually contains terms to be defined or questions to be answered, while the right-hand column contains definitions or answers. As a result, entries in the right-hand column are usually longer than those on the left. Reading the items on the right only once will save time as you work to match them with the shorter phrases on the left.

Start with the matches you know. On your first run-through, mark the matches you know with a penciled line, waiting to finalize your choices after you've completed all the items. Keep in mind that if you can use an answer only once, you may have to change answers if you reconsider a choice.

Finally, tackle the matches you're not sure of. On your next run-through, focus on the more difficult matches. Look for clues and relationships you might not have considered. Think back to your class lectures, text notes, and study sessions as you try to visualize the correct response. If one or more phrases seem to have no correct answer, look back at your easy matches to be sure that you did not jump too quickly. Consider the possibility that one of your sure-thing answers is wrong.

Fill-in-the-Blank Questions

Fill-in-the-blank questions, also known as sentence-completion questions, ask you to supply one or more words or phrases with missing information that completes the sentence. The following strategies will help you make successful choices.

Be logical. Insert your answer; then reread the sentence from beginning to end to be sure it makes sense and is factually and grammatically correct. Consider thinking of the right answer *before* looking at the choices, then finding the choice that most closely matches.

Note the length and number of the blanks. These are important clues but not absolute guideposts. If two blanks appear right after one another, the instructor is probably looking for a two-word answer. If a blank is longer than

Here are examples of fill-in-the-blank questions you might encounter in an introductory astronomy course (correct answers follow questions):

1. A _____ is a collection of hundreds of billions of stars.   *(galaxy)*
2. Rotation is the term used to describe the motion of a body around some _____.   *(axis)*
3. The solar day is measured relative to the sun; the sidereal day is measured relative to the _____.   *(stars)*
4. On December 21, known as the _____ _____ , the sun is at its _____ _____.   *(winter solstice; southernmost point)*

Source: Eric Chaisson and Steve McMillan, *Astronomy Today,* 3rd ed., 1999. Reprinted by permission of Pearson Education, Inc., Upper Saddle River, NJ.

usual, the correct response may require additional space. However, if you are certain of an answer that doesn't seem to fit the blanks, trust your knowledge and instincts.

Pay attention to how blanks are separated. If there is more than one blank in a sentence and the blanks are widely separated, treat each one separately. Answering each as if it were a separate sentence-completion question increases the likelihood that you will get at least one answer correct.

Think outside the box. If you can think of more than one correct answer, take the risk of putting them both down. Your instructor may be impressed by your assertiveness and creativity.

If you are uncertain of an answer, make an educated guess. Have faith that after hours of studying, the correct answer is somewhere in your subconscious mind and that your guess is not completely random.

Essay Questions

Essay questions ask you to express your knowledge and views in a less structured way than short-answer questions. With freedom of thought and expression comes the challenge to organize your ideas and write well under time pressure. The following steps will help improve your responses to essay questions.

Start by reading the questions. Decide which to tackle (if there's a choice). Use critical thinking to identify exactly what the question is asking.

Map out your time. Use the techniques you learned earlier in this chapter to schedule your time, remembering that things don't always go as planned. Try to remain flexible if an answer takes longer than expected.

Watch for action verbs. Action verbs, like those in Key 8.2 (p. 263), tell you what your instructor wants you to do as you answer the question. Underline these words as you read and use them to guide your writing.

Develop Strategies for Test Success

You have just studied strategies for taking objective tests. Think about five that will help improve your performance on upcoming tests. Write these strategies here:

1. _____
2. _____
3. _____
4. _____
5. _____

Over the next month, evaluate whether these strategies worked well, whether they had no impact, or whether they actually caused problems. Write your evaluation here:

_____
_____
_____

Evaluate whether any of the successful strategies encouraged the habit of mind of *taking responsible risks*. Write your thoughts here:

_____
_____

For the strategies that worked, name three actions you will take to transform them into habits:

Action 1: _____

Action 2: _____

Action 3: _____

Plan. Think carefully about what the question is asking and what you know about the topic. On a piece of scrap paper, create an informal outline or a think link to map your ideas and supporting evidence. Then come up with a thesis statement that defines your content and point of view. If necessary—and if you have the time—reorganize your planning notes into an exact writing roadmap.

The biggest mistake students make is to skip the planning stage and start writing without thinking through or organizing their answer. Not only does planning result in a better essay, but it also reduces stress. Instead of scrambling for ideas as you write, you are in the position of carrying out an organized plan.

Focus on action verbs on essay tests. **KEY 8.2**

analyze—Break into parts and discuss each part separately.

compare—Explain similarities and differences.

contrast—Distinguish between items being compared by focusing on differences.

criticize—Evaluate the issue, focusing on its problems or deficiencies.

define—State the essential quality or meaning.

describe—Paint a complete picture; provide the details of a story or the main characteristics of a situation.

diagram—Present a drawing, chart, or other visual.

discuss—Examine completely, using evidence and often presenting both sides of an issue.

enumerate/list/identify—Specify items in the form of a list.

evaluate—Give your opinion about the value or worth of something, usually by weighing positive and negative effects, and justify your conclusion.

elaborate on—Start with information presented in the question, and then add new material.

explain—Make the meaning of something clear, often by discussing causes and consequences.

illustrate—Supply examples.

interpret—Explain your personal views and judgments.

justify—Discuss the reasons for your conclusions or for the question's premise.

outline—Organize and present main and subordinate points.

prove—Use evidence and logic to show that something is true.

refute—Use evidence and logic to show that something is not true, or how you disagree with it.

relate—Connect items mentioned in the question, showing, for example, how one item influenced the other.

review—Provide an overview of ideas and establish their merits and features.

state—Explain clearly, simply, and concisely.

summarize—Give the important ideas in brief, without comments.

trace—Present a history of the way something developed, often by showing cause and effect.

Here are some examples of essay questions you might encounter in an interpersonal communication course. In each case, notice the action verbs from Key 8.2.

1. Summarize the role of the self-concept as a key to interpersonal relationships and communication.
2. Explain how internal and external noise affects the ability to listen effectively.
3. Describe three ways that body language affects interpersonal communication.

To answer the third essay question in the example above, one student created the planning outline shown in Key 8.3. Notice how abbreviations and shorthand help the student write quickly. Writing "Roles of BL in IC" is much faster than "Roles of Body Language in Interpersonal Communication (see chapter 7 for shorthand notes strategies).

Draft. Unlike writing a paper, when you can go through a series of drafts before your final version, your first draft on an exam essay is usually the one you hand in. If you take enough time and effort in the planning stage, you will have enough material to construct a suitable answer.

Use the following guidelines as you draft your answer:

- Start by stating your thesis, and then get right to the evidence that backs it up. You won't have time for an extensive introduction, and your instructor won't expect one.
- Pay close attention to how you organize your ideas and how well you support them with evidence. Try to structure your essay so that each paragraph presents an idea that supports the thesis.

KEY 8.3   Create an informal outline during essay tests.

Roles of BL in IC
1. To contradict or reinforce words
   — e.g., friend says "I'm fine"
2. To add shades of meaning
   — saying the same sentence in 3 diff. ways
3. To make lasting 1st impression
   — impact of nv cues and voice tone greater than words
   — we assume things abt person based on posture, eye contact, etc.

■ Use clear language and tight logic to link ideas to your thesis and to create transitions between paragraphs.

■ Look back at your outline periodically to make sure you cover everything.

■ Wrap it up with a short, to-the-point conclusion.

Pay attention to the test directions when drafting your answer. Your essay may need to be of a certain length, for example, or may need to take a certain form (for example, a particular format such as a business letter). Finally, write on only one side of the page to give the grader the best chance of reading your response.

Revise. Take a few moments to evaluate your word choice, paragraph structure, and style. Although you may not have the time or opportunity to rewrite your entire answer, you can certainly improve it with minor deletions or additions in the margin. If you find a hole in your work—an idea without support, for example, or some unnecessary information—add the new material in the margins and cross out what you don't need. When adding material, you can indicate with an arrow where it fits or note that inserts can be found on separate pages. If you have more than one insert, label each to avoid confusion (for example, Insert #1, Insert #2). Be neat as you make changes.

As you check over your essay, ask yourself these questions:

■ Have I answered the question?

■ Does my essay begin with a clear thesis statement, and does each paragraph start with a strong topic sentence that supports the thesis?

■ Have I provided the support necessary in the form of examples, statistics, and relevant facts to prove my argument?

■ Is my logic sound and convincing?

■ Have I covered all the points in my original outline?

■ Is my conclusion an effective wrap-up?

■ Does every sentence effectively communicate my point?

Edit. Check for mistakes in grammar, spelling, punctuation, and usage. No matter your topic, the correct use of language leaves a positive impression and eliminates problems that may lower your grade. Key 8.4 shows the student's completed response to the essay on body language, including the word changes and inserts she made while revising the draft.

Neatness is a crucial factor in essay writing. No matter how good your ideas are, if your instructor can't read them, your grade will suffer. If your handwriting is a problem, try printing or skipping every other line, and be sure to write on only one side of the page. Students with illegible handwriting might ask to take the test on a computer.

The purpose of a test is to see how much you know, not merely to get a grade. Embrace this attitude to learn from your mistakes and to develop the habit of mind of *taking responsible academic risks.*

KEY 8.4 Response to an essay question with revision marks.

QUESTION: Describe three ways that body language affects interpersonal communication.

Body language plays an important role in interpersonal communication and helps shape the impression you make. Two of the most important functions of body language are to contradict and reinforce verbal statements. When body language contradicts verbal language, the message ~~conveyed~~ *delivered* by the body is dominant. For example, if a friend tells you that she is feeling "fine," but her posture is slumped, and her facial expression troubled, you have every reason to wonder whether she is telling the truth. If the same friend tells you that she is feeling fine and is smiling, walking with a bounce in her step, and has direct eye contact, her body language is ~~telling the truth.~~

, especially when you meet someone for the first time

her eye contact minimal,

accurately reflecting and reinforcing her words.

The nonverbal cues that make up body language also have the power to add shades of meaning. Consider this statement: "This is the best idea I've heard all day." If you were to say this three different ways—in a loud voice while standing up; quietly while sitting with arms and legs crossed and looking away; and while ~~maintaining~~ *maintaining* eye contact and taking the receiver's hand—you might send three different messages.

Finally, the impact of nonverbal cues can be greatest when you meet someone for the first time. When you meet someone, you tend to make assumptions based on nonverbal behavior such as posture, eye contact, gestures, and speed and style of movement.

Although first impressions emerge from a combination of nonverbal cues, tone of voice, and choice of words, nonverbal elements (cues and tone) usually come across first and strongest.

In summary, nonverbal communication plays a ~~crusial~~ *crucial* role in interpersonal relationships. It has the power to send an accurate message that may ~~destroy~~ *belie* the speaker's words, offer shades of meaning, and set the tone of a first meeting.

How can you learn from test mistakes?

As painful as test mistakes can be, they are valuable learning tools if you approach them with an open mind. With exam in hand, use the following strategies to reduce the likelihood of making the same errors again. (If your instructor posts grades but does not hand exams back, ask to see your paper.)

MULTIPLE PATHWAYS TO LEARNING

MULTIPLE INTELLIGENCE STRATEGIES FOR OBJECTIVE AND ESSAY EXAMS

These tips will help you handle different types of test questions and situations.

INTELLIGENCE	SUGGESTED STRATEGIES	WHAT WORKS FOR YOU? WRITE NEW IDEAS HERE
Verbal-Linguistic	▪ Read carefully to understand every word of every question. ▪ Do language-oriented questions first, saving extra time for questions involving visual or quantitative elements.	
Logical-Mathematical	▪ Focus on quantitative and/or objective questions first, saving extra time for more subjective work such as essays. ▪ Use logic to narrow choices in multiple-choice and matching questions.	
Bodily-Kinesthetic	▪ Select an area and/or seat in the testing location where you feel comfortable. ▪ Take brief breaks to stretch your muscles at your seat.	
Visual-Spatial	▪ Focus on the length and number of the blanks in fill-in-the-blank questions. ▪ Create think links to map out responses to essay questions.	
Interpersonal	▪ Replay study group conversations in your mind to remember key facts. ▪ Think through an answer to an essay test by imagining you are explaining it to someone.	
Intrapersonal	▪ If you encounter a difficult question, take a deep breath and focus on what you know about the topic. ▪ Visualize answering every question correctly.	
Musical	▪ Remember the rhymes and tunes you created to help you learn material. Recite them to yourself to recall an answer.	
Naturalistic	▪ Instructor and weather permitting, take your exam outdoors.	

Ask yourself global questions that may help you identify correctable patterns. Here are some suggestions:

- Can you generalize about your biggest problems on the test? Did you get nervous; did you misread the question; did you fail to study enough; did you study incorrectly; did you focus on memorizing material instead of understanding and applying it?
- Did your instructor's comments clarify what you failed to do? Did your answer lack specificity; did you fail to support your thesis with concrete examples; was your analysis weak?
- Were you surprised by the questions? For example, did you expect them all to be from the text instead of coming from the text and a supplemental reading?
- Did you make careless errors? Did you misread the question or directions; did you blacken the wrong box on the answer sheet; did you skip a question; did you write illegibly?
- Did you make conceptual or factual errors? Did you misunderstand a concept; did you fail to master facts or concepts; did you skip part of the text or miss classes in which ideas were covered?

Your answers to these questions will help you change the way you study for the next exam.

Rework the questions you got wrong. Based on instructor feedback, try to rewrite an essay, recalculate a math problem from the original question, or redo questions following a reading selection. If you discover a pattern of careless errors, redouble your efforts to be more careful and save time to double-check your work.

After reviewing your mistakes, fill in your knowledge gaps. If you made mistakes because of a lack of understanding, develop a plan to learn the material. Solidifying your knowledge can help you on future exams and in work and life situations that involve the subject you're studying.

Talk to your instructor. Talk with your instructor about specific mistakes on short-answer questions or about a weak essay. The fact that you care enough to review your errors will leave a positive lasting impression. If you are not sure why you were marked down on an essay, ask what you could have done to improve your grade. If you feel that an essay was unfairly graded, ask your instructor to reread it.

As long as there are tests, there will be prayer in schools.

AUTHOR UNKNOWN

Rethink the way you studied. Make changes to avoid repeating your errors. Use the varied techniques in *Keys to Effective Learning* to study more effectively so that you can show yourself and your instructor what you are really capable of doing. The earlier in the term you make positive adjustments, the better—so working hard to learn from early mistakes will help you throughout the term.

If you fail a test, don't throw it away. Use it as a way to review troublesome material, especially if you will be tested on it again. You might also want to keep it as a reminder that you can improve if you have the will to succeed. When you compare a failure to later successes, you'll see how far you've come.

REFLECT

Lao-tzu, the Chinese Taoist philosopher who lived around 600 B.C.E., said the following: "Failure is the foundation of success, and the means by which it is achieved." What do you think Lao-tzu meant, and how is it related to the habit of mind of *responsible risk taking?* How do you think the statement will help you the next time you do poorly on a test? As you write, think about the importance of a positive attitude and perseverance in overcoming your obstacles.

RESPOND

TAKE ACTION

GET PREPARED

Learn from Your Mistakes

Examine what went wrong on a recent exam to build knowledge for next time.

Look at an exam on which your performance fell short of expectations. If possible, choose one that contains different types of objective and subjective questions. With the test and answer sheet in hand, use critical thinking to answer the following questions:

1. Identify the types of questions on which you got the most correct answers (for example, matching, essay, multiple choice).

   _____

2. Identify the types of questions on which you made the greatest number of errors.

   _____

3. Analyze your errors to identify patterns—for example, did you misread test instructions, or did you ignore qualifiers that changed the questions' meaning? What did you find?

   _____

   _____

4. Finally, list two practical steps you are prepared to take during your next exam to avoid the same problems:

   Action 1: _____

   Action 2: _____

I take responsible risks.

There is a voice inside nearly every student's head that expresses reluctance to take on new academic challenges because of the fear of failing tests: "If you don't try it, you won't be wrong," the voice says, "but if you try it and you are wrong, you will look stupid." If this voice sounds familiar, think for a moment about why you are in school. Are you there to get an A on every test, or are you there to master new concepts, gain competence in new areas, and enrich your mind and your potential? Your answer should reflect what is in your long-term best interest.

Because testing is an inherent part of your education, responsible risk taking is too. That is, on every test, you put your knowledge—and a bit of yourself—on the line. Ironically, taking tests moves you forward even as it causes you to feel unbalanced.

Take comfort in knowing that test anxiety is understandable as you are asked to show mastery of new and often difficult material. Work to overcome this anxiety by learning the concrete test-taking skills presented in this chapter. These skills will help you gain the significant rewards that can come from the risks you have taken.

REMEMBER
THE IMPORTANT POINTS

1

How can preparation improve test performance?

- Effective preparation is the key to better performance on tests.
- Helpful strategies include identifying test type and coverage, choosing appropriate study materials, setting a study plan and schedule, reviewing, taking a pretest, preparing yourself physically, and making the most of last-minute studying.

2

How can you work through test anxiety?

- Test anxiety may reduce your effectiveness and grade, even when you know the material.
- Helpful strategies to ease anxiety include strong preparation, finding out what will be covered, learning the types of questions and the length of the test, creating a study plan, and having a positive attitude.

3

What general strategies can help you succeed on tests?

- You can improve your test performance by using certain techniques consistently.
    - Write down key information as soon as the test begins.
    - Take time to skim the exam to get an overview.
    - Read the directions.
    - Work from the easiest questions to the hardest.
    - Keep track of time as you work.
    - Use intelligent guessing.
    - Know how to complete machine-scored tests.
    - Use critical thinking to avoid errors.

4

How can you master different types of test questions?

- Objective questions (multiple-choice, true/false, matching, and fill-in-the-blank) use a short-answer format to test your ability to recall, compare, and contrast information.
- Subjective questions—essay questions—require you to express your knowledge and perspective, usually in written form.

5

How can you learn from test mistakes?

- Test mistakes can highlight weaknesses in your knowledge and study approach.
    - To learn from test errors, look for careless errors, as well as those involving concepts and facts.
    - Treat your errors as an opportunity to understand the material and to avoid repeating your mistakes.

CRITICAL THINKING

APPLYING LEARNING TO LIFE

Analysis of How You Perform on Tests

First, look at the potential problems listed here. Circle the ones that you feel are factors that hurt your performance on exams. Fill in the blanks with any key problems not listed.

Incomplete preparation　　　　　　　*Confusion about directions*

Fatigue　　　　　　　　　　　　　　*Test anxiety*

Feeling rushed during the test　　　　_____

Weak understanding of concepts　　　_____

Poor guessing techniques

Pick your two most significant problems. For each, brainstorm ways to minimize the problem as you move forward. Include specific strategies you learned in this chapter.

Problem 1: _____

_____

Solutions: _____

_____

_____

_____

Problem 2: _____

_____

Solutions: _____

_____

_____

_____

TEAM BUILDING

COLLABORATIVE SOLUTIONS

Benchmark to Improve Your Test-Preparation Habits

Benchmarking is a business practice that involves assessing how other companies do something and adopting the best practices. You can use benchmarking right now to learn how others prepare for exams—and to adopt what will work for you. Here's how:

Step 1: Form a study group with two or three other students in one of your academic courses, setting a meeting time that fits into each student's schedule. Ask each group member to record everything he or she does to prepare for the next exam. Among the items on the lists may be:

- Making a study checklist and posting it on my bulletin board
- Spending two hours a day studying at the library in the week before the exam
- Learning what to expect on the test (topics and material that will be covered, types of questions that will be asked)
- Getting a partner to drill me on multiple-choice questions from old tests
- Using SQ3R to review material
- Recording information on an iPod and listening to it between classes
- Having a pretest breakfast with a study group
- Getting to sleep by midnight the night before the exam

Step 2: After the exam, come together to compare preparation regimens. What important differences can you identify in routines? How might different routines have affected test performance and outcome?

Step 3: On a separate piece of paper, for your own reference, write down what you learned from the habits of your study mates that may help you as you prepare for upcoming exams.

I recognize that my willingness to take increasingly more difficult courses and to be tested on my mastery of material is a way of challenging myself. I understand that this is important and plan to take the following three challenging courses in the next year (I will consult the course catalog for specific course titles):

Course 1: _____

Course 2: _____

Course 3: _____

*I know what it is like to feel unsure of myself before a big exam, especially in a challenging course. I will take three steps to ease my fears. These actions will empower me to **take responsible academic risks:***

Step 1: _____

Step 2: _____

Step 3: _____

*I will generalize from my growing ability to **take responsible risks** to other important study skills, such as note taking and reading. Here are some specific ways I will take responsible risks in three different areas:*

Area #1: _____

_____

Area #2: _____

_____

Area #3: _____

_____

How am I doing? **Later in the term, be accountable for your progress on page 377.**

SUGGESTED READINGS

Browning, William G., Ph.D. *Cliffs Memory Power for Exams.* Lincoln, NE: Cliffs Notes, 1990.

Frank, Steven. *Test Taking Secrets: Study Better, Test Smarter, and Get Great Grades.* Holbrook, MA: Adams Media, 1998.

Fry, Ron. *"Ace" Any Test,* 3rd ed. Franklin Lakes, NJ: Career Press, 1996.

Hamilton, Dawn. *Passing Exams: A Guide for Maximum Success and Minimum Stress.* Herndon, VA: Cassell Academic, 1999.

Kesselman, Judy, and Franklynn Peterson. *Test Taking Strategies.* New York: NTC/Contemporary, 1981.

Luckie, William R., and Wood Smethurst. *Study Power: Study Skills to Improve Your Learning and Your Grades.* Cambridge, MA: Brookline Books, 1997.

Rozakis, Laurie. *Test Taking Strategies and Study Skills for the Utterly Confused.* New York: McGraw-Hill, 2003.

INTERNET RESOURCES

Prentice Hall's Student Success Supersite: Test Taking (**www.prenhall.com/success/StudySkl/testtake.html**)

Florida State University—List of sites offering information on test-taking skills (**http://osi.fsu.edu/hot/testtaking/skills.htm**)

Test Taking Tips—Help for studying (**www.testtakingtips.com**)

University of Minnesota–Duluth: Study Strategies Homepage (**www.d.umn.edu/kmc/student/loon/acad/strat/study_strat_enr.html**)

ENDNOTES

1. Adam Robinson, *What Smart Students Know: Maximum Grades, Optimum Learning, Minimum Time.* New York: Three Rivers Press, 1993, p. 189.

Strive for precision and accuracy

"People who value accuracy, precision, and craftsmanship take time to check over their products. They review the rules by which they are to abide and the models and visions they are to follow . . . and confirm that their finished product conforms exactly."

ART COSTA

STRIVE FOR PRECISION AND ACCURACY

Approaching math and science with precision and a focus on accuracy will get you far. You will have the best chance at solving a numerical problem if you approach it with care and deliberateness—focus on the rules, work to be accurate, and carefully check your work.

As you might expect, striving for accuracy and precision is an everyday task for chess grandmaster Maurice Ashley. It may surprise you to know, however, that math and science skills will serve you in less obvious tasks and areas of study. Working with numbers trains your mind to solve problems as it builds your ability to think actively and work through processes logically. In addition, quantitative skills are increasingly valuable in a workplace dominated by technology, the exchange of information, and finance.

This chapter will give you an overview of quantitative thinking and offer basic problem-solving strategies. You will also explore how to approach math and science in an open-minded, positive way, both in your course work and during tests. Many students experience math anxiety, and a positive attitude is crucial to building a successful relationship with numbers. Finally, you will expand your understanding of the value of math and science learning in today's workplace and in your adult life overall.

In this chapter, you explore answers to the following questions:

- **How are math and science part of your daily life?**
- **How can you master math and science basics?**
- **How can you overcome math anxiety?**
- **How can you "read" visual aids?**
- **How will math and science learning be an important part of your future?**

Photo: Librado Romero/ The New York Times

How are math and science part of your daily life?

Numbers are a part of life. You use aspects of *quantitative thinking* often—basic calculations in your checkbook, geometrical thinking for how to pack a collection of items into the trunk of your car, figuring ratios for allowable deductions on a tax return, and so forth. Everyday functioning requires a certain level of comfort and competence in quantitative skills. These skills can be broken down into several broad areas.

> Mathematics, even in its present and most abstract state, is not detached from life. It is just the ideal handling of the problems of life.

CASSIUS JACKSON KEYSER, MATHEMATICS PROFESSOR AND PHILOSOPHER

© iwka—Fotolia

Arithmetic. Many everyday tasks, especially those involving money, require *arithmetic* (numerical computations such as addition, subtraction, multiplication, and division, plus the use of fractions, percentages, and other ratios). You are using arithmetic when you calculate how much tuition you can cover in a year or figure out what to tip in a restaurant. You also use arithmetic when you interpret ingredient amounts and percentages on food labels in the effort to eat more healthfully.

Algebra. A knowledge of *algebra*—a generalization of arithmetic in which letters representing unknown quantities are combined, often with other numbers, into equations according to mathematical rules—is needed almost as frequently as arithmetic. Algebra involves determining an unknown value using known values. You use algebra when you figure out the interest on a loan or compute what score you need on an exam in order to achieve a particular final grade in a course.

Geometry. The most common uses of *geometry*—the mathematics of the properties, measurement, and relationships of points, lines, angles, surfaces, and solids—occur in determining areas and volumes. However, geometric ideas occur in many other forms. You make use of geometric principles without even thinking about it when, for example, you determine how closely you can pass a car or how to pack a suitcase so that it can close.

Probability and statistics. A knowledge of basic *probability* (the study of the chance that a given event will occur) and *statistics* (collection, analysis, and interpretation of numerical data) is needed for understanding the relevance and importance of the overwhelming amount of statistical information you encounter. For example, a woman's knowledge of probability can help her determine her risk of getting breast cancer; a student's understanding of statistics can help him analyze his chances of getting into a particular college as a transfer student.

Sciences. Biology, anatomy, and other sciences directly related to the human body can help you to manage your health through a greater understanding of how your body works. Chemistry can help you figure out how to substitute ingredients in a recipe or become aware of possible interactions between medications you are taking. A knowledge of physics can help you load items safely on the roof of a car for a family outing to minimize wind resistance and increase gas mileage.

Ultimately, both math and science are relevant to other subjects because they aid problem solving and critical thinking as they move you from questions to solutions. When you put your brain through the paces of mathematical and scientific problem solving, you are building critical thinking, *precision,* and *accuracy*—skills that you can apply to problem solving in any subject.

How can you master math and science basics?

Math and science are interrelated. Sciences such as chemistry, physics, and astronomy are quite often problem-solving courses. There are also classes in geology, anthropology, and biology that fall into this category. You can apply the strategies you work with in your math courses to these sciences. "Math is the empowering skill that underlies all science," says Don Pierce, executive director of education at Heald Colleges. "Without it, you can't succeed as a scientist. The scientific process depends on your ability to analyze, interpret, and attach meaning to data, so math and science are intrinsically linked."[1]

For example, in beginning chemistry, you will usually have to balance chemical equations. This may involve writing an equation, drawing a diagram, or perhaps working backwards. In physics, the study of forces involves applying problem-solving strategies developed from vector calculus. In fact, the most common strategy to solve force problems involves drawing a diagram called a force diagram. The key thing to remember is that although these strategies are listed as mathematical strategies, the actual process of applying them is far more wide-ranging, helping you to develop into a more precise critical thinker and problem solver.

Certain thinking strategies will help improve your ability to think quantitatively. Mastering math and science basics is easier when you take a critical approach to the classroom, the textbook, studying and homework, and word problems.

Classroom Strategies

When you are taking a math or science class, there are two primary ingredients for success:

- *Be prepared.* Before class, read the material that will be covered that day. This allows you to build a base of knowledge, providing a context in which to ask questions about the material. Also before class, review homework problems and mark any that gave you trouble. When you are prepared, you will be more able to retain and understand what you hear and see in class.

- *Be in class.* Take notes, focusing on central ideas and connecting supporting examples (especially sample problems) to those ideas. Highlight items or examples that confuse you so that you can go back and focus on them later.

Also, take responsibility for addressing any confusion you have: *Ask questions*. Participating actively through questioning will help you clarify, retain, and use what you are learning. Finally, immediately after class, briefly review the information you just learned.

College math and science are quite different from high school courses—and the differences require you to be more focused and diligent about attending class and keeping up with homework. Among the differences you may notice are the following:

- Courses are faster-paced.
- Assignments are crucial (although they may not always be collected).
- Class time may be more focused on theories and ideas than on problem solving.
- Class size might be considerably larger, with smaller lab sections. (If this is the case, you will most likely be working directly on problems only in your lab section.)
- Technological proficiency may be important; for example, you may need to know how to use a graphing calculator for your work in a particular course.

How to Approach Your Textbook

Math and science textbooks move sequentially (later chapters build on concepts and information introduced in previous chapters). Your command of later material depends on how well you learned material in earlier chapters. Use the following strategies to get the most from your textbooks.

Interact with math material actively through writing. Math textbooks are problem-and-solution based. As you read, highlight important information and take notes of examples on a pad of paper. If problem steps are left out, as they often are, work them out on your pad or right in the book if there is room. Draw sketches as you read to help visualize the material. Try not to move on until you understand the example and how it relates to the central ideas. Write down questions you want to ask your instructor or fellow students.

Pay attention to formulas. In any math or science textbook, note the *formulas*—general facts, rules, or principles usually expressed in mathematical symbols—that are given. Evaluate whether these formulas are important and recall whether the instructor emphasized them. Whether you gather formulas through reading or classroom lecture, make sure you understand formulas clearly and know how to apply them. Read the assigned material to prepare for homework.

Use memory skills with science material. Science textbooks are often packed with vocabulary specific to that particular science (for example, a chapter in a psychobiology course may give medical names for the parts of the brain). To remember what you read, use mnemonic devices, test yourself with flash cards, and rehearse aloud or silently (see chapter 6). Selective highlighting and writing summaries of your readings, perhaps in table format, will also help (see chapter 5).

Because many sciences rely on a base of mathematical knowledge, your math reading strategies will help you understand and remember the formulas that may appear in your science reading. As with math, make sure you understand the principles behind each formula, and do as many problems as you can to solidify your knowledge.

Studying and Homework

When it comes to studying and doing homework in math and science courses, action gets results.

Review materials. Review your class notes as soon as possible after each class. Have the textbook alongside and compare the lecture information to the book. Fill in missing steps in the instructor's examples before you forget them. You may want to write the instructor's examples in the book by the corresponding topics.

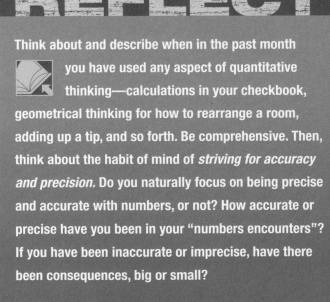

Think about and describe when in the past month you have used any aspect of quantitative thinking—calculations in your checkbook, geometrical thinking for how to rearrange a room, adding up a tip, and so forth. Be comprehensive. Then, think about the habit of mind of *striving for accuracy and precision.* Do you naturally focus on being precise and accurate with numbers, or not? How accurate or precise have you been in your "numbers encounters"? If you have been inaccurate or imprecise, have there been consequences, big or small?

Do problems, problems, and more problems. Working through problems is critical for math courses, as well as math-based science courses such as chemistry and astronomy, because it provides examples that will help you understand concepts and formulas. Plus, becoming familiar with a group of problems and related formulas will help you apply what you know to similar problems on other assignments and tests. Strive for *precision* as you work through problems; you want to make sure you are performing the procedures *accurately.*

Fight frustration with action. Do not expect to complete every problem without effort. If you are stuck on a problem, go on to another one. If you repeatedly get a wrong answer, look at the steps you've taken and see if anything doesn't make sense. If you hit a wall, take a break to clear your head. If you have done the assigned homework but still don't feel secure, do additional problems.

Work with others. Even if your math and science classes have lab sessions, try to set up study groups outside of class. Do as much of your homework as you can and then meet to discuss the homework and work through additional problems. Be open to other perspectives, and don't hesitate to ask other students to explain their thought processes in detail. Sometimes students will do a problem differently but get the same correct answer; looking at alternative approaches to problems helps broaden your perspective on how the problems work. As you explain problems to one another, everyone builds understanding.

Focus on learning styles. Use strategies that activate your strengths. For example, a visual learner might draw pictures to illustrate problems, and an interpersonal learner might organize a study group. Musical learners might even

Joyce Dopkeen/ *The New York Times*

Give yourself time to focus when you are working to understand a math or science concept. Stop and think, do additional problems, and take breaks when you get stuck.

make up songs describing math concepts—Barbara Aaker wrote 40 of them for her students at the Community College of Denver, and they have helped musical learners retain difficult concepts. Key 9.1 presents one of her algebra songs. The Multiple Pathways to Learning feature on page 297 offers more ideas for working with numbers.

Strive for accuracy and precision. Although *accuracy and precision* are important in many different subjects, they have particular value in math and science. Complete a step of an algebra problem inaccurately, and your answer will be incorrect. Complete a step of a biology lab project imprecisely, and your results will be off. In class, of course, the consequences of inaccuracy are reflected in low grades; in life, the consequences could show in more profound ways such as in a patient's health, in the strength of a bridge, or in the calculation of widely used data such as jobless rates. Check over the details of your work and strive for the right answers.

Word Problems

Because word problems are the most common way you will encounter quantitative thinking throughout your life, being able to solve them is crucial. Word problems can be tough, however, because they force you to translate between two languages—one expressed in words, and one expressed in numbers and symbols. Although math is a precise language, English and other living languages tend to leave more room for interpretation. This difference in precision makes the process of translating difficult.

Steps to Solving Word Problems

Translating English or any other language into math takes a lot of practice. George Polya, in his 1945 classic *How to Solve It,* devised a four-step method for attacking word problems.[2] The basic steps reflect the general problem-solving process you explored in chapter 4, and they will work for any word problem, whether in a math or science course:

1. *Understand the individual elements of the problem.* Read the problem carefully. Understand what it is asking. Know what information you have. Know what information is missing. Draw a picture, if possible. Translate the given information from words into mathematical language (numbers, symbols, formulas).

2. *Name and explore potential solution paths.* Think about similar problems that you understand and how those were solved. Consider whether this problem is an example of a mathematical idea that you know. In your head, try out different ways to solve the problem to see which may work best.

3. *Choose a solution path and solve the problem.* As you carry out your plan, check the *precision* of each of your steps.

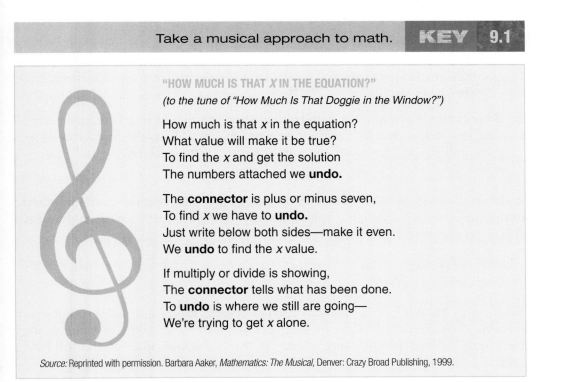

Take a musical approach to math.   **KEY   9.1**

"HOW MUCH IS THAT X IN THE EQUATION?"
(to the tune of "How Much Is That Doggie in the Window?")

How much is that x in the equation?
What value will make it be true?
To find the x and get the solution
The numbers attached we **undo.**

The **connector** is plus or minus seven,
To find x we have to **undo.**
Just write below both sides—make it even.
We **undo** to find the x value.

If multiply or divide is showing,
The **connector** tells what has been done.
To **undo** is where we still are going—
We're trying to get x alone.

Source: Reprinted with permission. Barbara Aaker, *Mathematics: The Musical,* Denver: Crazy Broad Publishing, 1999.

4. *Review your result.* Check your answer for ***accuracy,*** if possible. Make sure you've answered the question the problem is asking. Does your result seem logical in the context of the problem? Are there other ways to do the problem?

Different problem-solving strategies will be useful to you when solving word problems. On a given problem, evaluate which strategy will work best and then apply it. The following discussion outlines several problem-solving strategies by working through word problem examples.[3]

Problem-Solving Strategies

Strategy 1: Look for a pattern. G. H. Hardy (1877–1947), an eminent British mathematician, described mathematicians as makers of patterns and ideas. The search for patterns is one of the best strategies in problem solving. When you look for a pattern, you think inductively, observing a series of examples and determining the general idea that links the examples together.

Example: Find the next three entries in each of the following:

a. 1, 2, 4, _____, _____, _____
b. 0, T, T, F, F, S, S, _____, _____, _____

Solutions to example:

a. When identifying patterns, you may find a different pattern than someone else. This doesn't mean yours is wrong. This example actually has several possible answers. Here are two:

- Each succeeding term of the sequence is twice the previous term. In that case, the next three values would be 8, 16, 32.

■ The second term is 1 more than the first term and the third term is 2 more than the second. This might lead you to guess the fourth term is 3 more than the third term, the fifth term is 4 more than the fourth term, and so on. In that case, the next three terms are 7, 11, 16.

b. This example is a famous pattern that often appears in puzzle magazines. The key to it is that "O" is the first letter of *one*, "T" is the first letter of *two*, and so on. Therefore, the next three terms would be E, N, and T for *eight*, *nine*, and *ten*.

Strategy 2: Make a table. A table can help you organize and summarize information. This may enable you to see how examples form a pattern that leads you to an idea and a solution.

Example: How many ways can you make change for a half dollar using only quarters, dimes, nickels, and pennies?

Solution to example: You might construct several tables and go through every possible case. You could start by seeing how many ways you can make change for a half dollar without using a quarter, which would produce the following tables:

Quarters	0	0	0	0	0	0	0	0	0	0	0	0	0	0	0	0	0	0
Dimes	0	0	0	0	0	0	0	0	0	0	0	1	1	1	1	1	1	1
Nickels	0	1	2	3	4	5	6	7	8	9	10	0	1	2	3	4	5	6
Pennies	50	45	40	35	30	25	20	15	10	5	0	40	35	30	25	20	15	10

Quarters	0	0	0	0	0	0	0	0	0	0	0	0	0	0	0	0	0	0
Dimes	1	1	2	2	2	2	2	2	2	3	3	3	3	3	4	4	4	5
Nickels	7	8	0	1	2	3	4	5	6	0	1	2	3	4	0	1	2	0
Pennies	5	0	30	25	20	15	10	5	0	20	15	10	5	0	10	5	0	0

There are 36 ways to make change for a half dollar without using a quarter. Using one quarter results in this table:

Quarters	1	1	1	1	1	1	1	1	1	1	1	1
Dimes	0	0	0	0	0	0	1	1	1	1	2	2
Nickels	0	1	2	3	4	5	0	1	2	3	0	1
Pennies	25	20	15	10	5	0	15	10	5	0	5	0

Using one quarter, you get 12 different ways to make change for a half dollar. Lastly, using two quarters, there's only one way to make change for a half dollar. Therefore, the solution to the problem is that there are 36 + 12 + 1 = 49 ways to make change for a half dollar using only quarters, dimes, nickels, and pennies.

Strategy 3: Identify a subgoal. Breaking the original problem into smaller and possibly easier problems may lead to a solution to the original problem. This is often the case in writing a computer program.

Example: Arrange the nine numbers 1, 2, 3, . . . , 9 into a square subdivided into nine sections in such a way that the sum of every row, column, and main diagonal is the same. This is called a *magic square.*

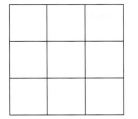

Solution to example: The sum of any individual row, column, or main diagonal has to be one-third the sum of all nine numbers (or else they wouldn't be the same). The sum of $1 + 2 + 3 + 4 + 5 + 6 + 7 + 8 + 9 = 45$. Therefore, each row, column, and main diagonal needs to sum to $45 \div 3 = 15$. Now, you need to see how many ways you can add three of the numbers from 1 to 9 and get 15. When you do this, you should get:

$9 + 1 + 5 = 15$	$8 + 3 + 4 = 15$
$9 + 2 + 4 = 15$	$7 + 2 + 6 = 15$
$8 + 1 + 6 = 15$	$7 + 3 + 5 = 15$
$8 + 2 + 5 = 15$	$6 + 4 + 5 = 15$

Now, looking at your magic square, notice that the center position will be part of four sums (a row, a column, and the two main diagonals). Looking back at your sums, you see that 5 appears in four different sums; therefore 5 is in the center square:

	5	

Now, in each corner, the number there appears in three sums (row, column, and a diagonal). Looking through your sums, you find that 2, 4, 6, and 8 each appear in three sums. Now, you need to place them in the corners in such a way that your diagonals add up to 15:

2		6
	5	
4		8

Then, to finish, all you need to do is fill in the remaining squares so that 15 is the sum of each row, column, and main diagonal. The completed square is as follows:

2	7	6
9	5	1
4	3	8

Strategy 4: Examine a similar problem. Sometimes a problem you are working on has similarities to a problem you've already read about or solved. In that case, it is often possible to use a similar approach to solve the new problem.

Example: Find a magic square using the numbers 3, 5, 7, 9, 11, 13, 15, 17, and 19.

Solution to example: This problem is very similar to the example for strategy 3. Approaching it in the same fashion, you find that the row, column, and main diagonal sum is 33. Writing down all the possible sums of three numbers to get 33, you find that 11 is the number that appears four times, so it is in the center:

	11	

The numbers that appear three times in the sums and will go in the corners are 5, 9, 13, and 17. This now gives you:

13		17
	11	
5		9

Finally, completing the magic square gives you:

13	3	17
15	11	7
5	19	9

Strategy 5: Work backward. With some problems, you may find it easier to start with the perceived final result and work backward.

> *Example:* In the game of "Life," Carol had to pay $1,500 when she was married. Then, she lost half the money she had left. Next, she paid half the money she had for a house. Then, the game was stopped, and she had $3,000 left. How much money did she start with?

Solution to example: Carol ended up with $3,000. Right before that she paid half her money to buy a house. Because her $3,000 was half of what she had before her purchase, she had 2 × $3,000 = $6,000 before buying the house. Prior to buying the house, Carol lost half her money. This means that the $6,000 is the half she didn't lose. So, before losing half her money, Carol had 2 × $6,000 = $12,000. Prior to losing half her money, Carol had to pay $1,500 to get married. This means she had $12,000 + $1,500 = $13,500 before getting married. Because this was the start of the game, Carol began with $13,500.

Strategy 6: Draw a diagram. Drawing a picture is often an aid to solving problems, especially for visual learners. Although pictures are especially useful for geometrical problems, they can be helpful for other types of problems as well.

> *Example:* There were 20 women at a round table for dinner. Each woman shook hands with the woman to her immediate right and left. At the end of the dinner, each woman got up and shook hands with everybody except those who sat on her immediate right and left. How many handshakes took place after dinner?

Solution to example: To solve this with a diagram, it might be a good idea to examine several simpler cases to see if you can determine a pattern of any kind that might help. Starting with two or three people, you can see there are no handshakes after dinner because everyone is adjacent to everyone else.

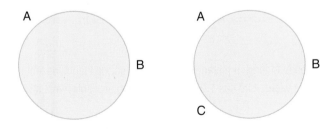

Now, in the case of four people, we get the following diagram, connecting those people who shake hands after dinner:

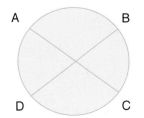

In this situation, you see there are two handshakes after dinner, AC and BD. In the case of five people, you get this picture:

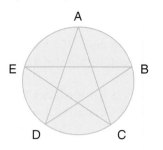

In this case, you have five after-dinner handshakes: AC, AD, BD, BE, and CE. Six people seated around a circle gives the following diagram:

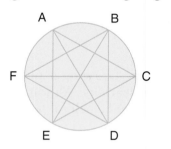

In this diagram, there are now a total of nine after-dinner handshakes: AC, AD, AE, BD, BE, BF, CE, CF, and DF. By studying the diagrams, you realize that if there are N people, each person would shake $N - 3$ people's hands after dinner. (They don't shake their own hands or the hands of the two people adjacent to them.) Because there are N people, that would lead to $N(N - 3)$ after-dinner handshakes. However, this would double-count every handshake, because AD would also be counted as DA. Therefore, there are only half as many actual handshakes. So, the correct number of handshakes is $[N(N - 3)] \div 2$. So finally, if there are 20 women, there would be $20(17) \div 2 = 170$ after-dinner handshakes.

Strategy 7: Translate words into an equation. This strategy is often used in algebra.

Example: A farmer needs to fence a rectangular piece of land. He wants the length of the field to be 80 feet longer than the width. If he has 1,080 feet of fencing available, what should the length and width of the field be?

Solution to example: The best way to start this problem is to draw a picture of the situation and label the sides:

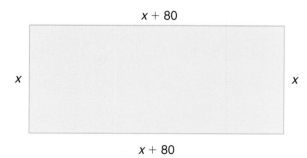

Let x represent the width of the field and $x + 80$ represent the length of the field. The farmer has 1,080 feet of fencing and he will need $2x + 2(x + 80)$ feet of fencing to fence his field. This gives you the equation: $2x + 2(x + 80) = 1080$. Then:

Multiplying out: $2x + 2x + 160 = 1,080$

Simplifying and subtracting 160: $4x = 920$

Dividing by 4: $x = 230$

Therefore, $x + 80 = 310$

As a check, you find that $2(230) + 2(310) = 1,080$

These sample problems are designed to boost your ability to think critically through some basic math strategies. If these or other quantitative problems make you feel anxious, however, you may benefit from some information about math anxiety.

TAKE ACTION

GET PREPARED

Tackle a Word Problem

Read this word problem:

When using a stair climber; Eric burns 9.6 calories per minute. When he walks on the treadmill, he burns 5.3 calories per minute. If Eric has 50 minutes to exercise and wants to burn 350 calories, how many minutes should he spend on each machine?

Work through the problem here, focusing on the habit of mind of *striving for accuracy and precision.* Use additional pages if you need to. Indicate the equation you came up with. Finally, name the strategy or strategies that you used.

_____

_____

_____

_____

_____

_____

_____

_____

_____

[The answer can be found on the last page of this chapter.]

Source: Adapted from The Math Forum @ Drexel, an online community for mathematics education (http://mathforum.org/).

Precision
and Accuracy

NASA/Johnson Space Center

Ellen Ochoa has literally reached for the stars during four space shuttle missions lasting 978 hours.

As an inventor of optical systems, she holds three patents. As the *first female Hispanic American astronaut,* she has put her degrees in physics and electrical engineering to work, specializing in robotics and solar and atmospheric studies.

How can you overcome math anxiety?

*M*ath anxiety refers to any kind of uncomfortable, high-stress feeling that appears in relation to quantitative thinking. It occurs most commonly right before or during an exam. A student getting ready to take a test or reading a particular problem on a test experiences rising anxiety or even what can be described as "blanking out." Math anxiety also plagues people in class or lab sessions, if they have to work through a problem in front of others or with others, or even when doing math and science homework outside of the classroom.

Understand Myths and Facts About Math

Math anxiety stems in large part from misconceptions about math. Such assumptions are untrue as well as damaging to the thought processes of students who might otherwise succeed in math and science courses. Here are some commonly held misconceptions:

Myth: *People are born with or without an ability to think quantitatively; in other words, you either have it or you don't.*

Fact: *Quantitative thinking skills can be improved.* Everyone is born with a unique set of natural talents; some people will naturally have more aptitude or interest in math and science than others. However, anyone can take his or her own aptitude and improve on it. As with critical thinking or other intellectual skills, quantitative thinking skills can be increased with hard work and practice. Working with numbers in a personal area of interest may also build aptitude; for example, students pursuing degrees in medicine or computers may find that they are more motivated in quantitative courses that relate to their career pursuits.

Myth: *Everyone is either a words person or a numbers person; you can't excel in both areas.*

Fact: *People can and do excel in both quantitative and verbal areas of study.* Mathematician and math anxiety expert Sheila Tobias reports: "No evidence exists, whatsoever, that writing ability and mathematics ability are mutually exclusive. In fact, people who show high capability on both the mathematical and verbal sections of the SAT are more likely to succeed in math than those who have a severely skewed score, strong only in quantitative skills."[4]

Myth: *Women aren't as capable as men of succeeding in math and science.*

Fact: *Gender does not determine quantitative aptitude.* The ability to succeed in math and science does not rely on gender.

Marilynn K. Yee/*The New York Times*

Women who excel in math and science have increasing career opportunities. This graduate student is working on a report about monkeys and mosquitoes for the science journal Chemical Ecology.

KEY 9.2   Women are taking advantage of math and science opportunities in college.

Of graduates receiving degrees in math and science, academic year 2001–2002, percentages who are women.

	Bachelor's	Master's	Doctorates
Health sciences	85.5%	77.5%	63.3%
Biological sciences	60.8%	57.8%	44.3%
Mathematics	46.7%	42.4%	29.0%
Computer science	27.6%	33.2%	22.8%
Engineering	18.9%	21.4%	17.3%

Source: Adapted from W. Michael Cox and Richard Alm, "Scientists Are Made, Not Born," *New York Times,* February 28, 2005, p. A19.

"Scientists are made, not born," say economist W. Michael Cox and economics writer Richard Alm: "Scientific knowledge requires years of education at the college level and beyond. . . . What matters are the choices and opportunities open to young women at our universities."[5] In the last 30 years, such opportunities have grown, and women have increasingly taken advantage of them. For example, in 1971, only 0.8% of undergraduate women earned bachelor's degrees in engineering; in 2001, women made up 18.9% of those graduating with bachelor's degrees in engineering. In 1971, 16.5% of the recipients of doctoral degrees in the health sciences were women; by 2001–2002, the percentage rose to 63.3%.[6]

Key 9.2 details how many women are now receiving degrees in math and science.

The stereotype that women do poorly in math, even if it is false, can cause damage. Women who believe in the stereotype may create a self-fulfilling prophecy that harms their ability to perform successfully in math and science courses. All students should combat this stereotype by taking an honest look at their relationship to math and science, independent of gender.

One final assumption that many make about math is that it is boring or scary. Some of this attitude stems from the way in which math and science are taught, especially in the younger years. Sheila Tobias points out that math skills have to be practiced extensively in the grade school years so that students can develop the level of proficiency needed to be more creative about math. Such practice, usually involving problems for which there is only one right answer, most often leave no room for subjective debate such as one might find in an English or a history class. This can frustrate students. In addition, teachers have to present a series of math rules to students and rarely offer opportunities to question such rules and formulas; some students react to this by turning off.[7]

Finally, the fear that people feel can be real. Says Tobias:

> Few people can think clearly and well with a clock ticking away. It is hard to perform at the blackboard with thirty sets of eyes watching you. No one likes a subject that is presented rigidly and uncompromisingly. And most people do not do well when they are scared. Some years ago, my colleagues and I came to suspect that math inability may not be the result of a failure of intellect but rather of nerve.[8]

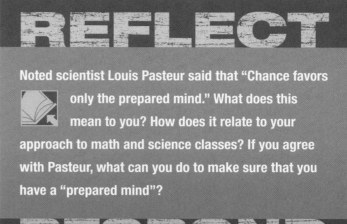

Noted scientist Louis Pasteur said that "Chance favors only the prepared mind." What does this mean to you? How does it relate to your approach to math and science classes? If you agree with Pasteur, what can you do to make sure that you have a "prepared mind"?

Negative feelings stemming from any of these assumptions become "static," as Tobias calls it, interfering with the brain's ability to work. Emotional static can clog the mental pathways that a person uses to reason through a problem and come to a conclusion. Even though the static is often the primary issue, many people interpret their difficulties to a lack of brain power instead. As a result, confidence dwindles, and students stop trying.[9] Many students carry negative feelings about math and science from experiences back in high school or even earlier.

Think about your attitude toward quantitative learning. If it has been affected by these false assumptions, or any other negative ideas, you may experience some level of math anxiety. Read on to discover what you can do about it.

Use Strategies to Combat Math Anxiety

Strategies that help include building self-knowledge, practice, using your resources, taking responsibility for your quantitative learning, understanding your rights as a quantitative learner, and taking your time.

Know yourself as a quantitative learner. Self-knowledge is essential to working through math anxiety. Which subjects make sense to you, and which give you trouble? Which strategies help or do not help you? Which processes can you do more easily, and which require increased focus? What events, courses, instructors, or other people have influenced what you think of your math and science abilities, and how? You may want to put your thoughts in writing. The more you know about yourself as a quantitative learner, the more you will be able to identify—and deactivate—your emotional static, giving your brain a chance to do good work.

Practice. The best way to overcome test-time anxiety is to practice quantitative thinking to increase your confidence. Keeping up with your homework, attending class, preparing well for tests, and doing extra problems alone and with others will help you feel confident because they increase your familiarity with the material. Key 9.3 shows additional ways to reduce math anxiety.

Use resources. Most schools have math or science learning labs, tutors, or computer programs that can help you practice difficult quantitative processes. You can visit your instructor during office hours or ask a lab assistant or TA questions. Sometimes there will be an extra review session set up by an instructor or TA so that students can ask questions before a major test. You can even find

KEY   9.3   Ten ways to reduce math anxiety.

1. Overcome your negative self-image about math.

2. Ask questions of your teachers and your friends, and seek outside assistance.

3. Math is a foreign language—practice it often.

4. Don't study mathematics by trying to memorize information and formulas.

5. *Read* your math textbook.

6. Study math according to your personal learning style.

7. Get help the same day you don't understand something.

8. Be relaxed and comfortable while studying math.

9. "Talk" mathematics. Discuss it with people in your class. Form a study group.

10. Develop a sense of responsibility for your own successes and failures.

Source: Adapted from Ellen Freedman, "Ten Ways to Reduce Math Anxiety," accessed from Professor Freedman's Math Help Web site (www.mathpower.com/reduce.htm).

© Cyril Serpault—Fotolia

help online; for example, you can submit a question to "Dr. Math" through the question-and-answer service on The Math Forum Web site (**www.mathforum.org/dr.math**). Don't hesitate to make the most of any and all helpful resources available to you.

Take responsibility. Even though math anxiety is a real problem, students must take some responsibility for their responses to quantitative thinking. You can't change the math experiences you have had in the past, but you can make choices about how to respond to quantitative material from here on out. The following responsibilities are worded as intention statements; use them for focus and motivation.[10]

- I will attend all classes and do my homework.
- I will seek extra help when necessary, from an instructor, a tutor, or a fellow student.
- I will speak up in class when I have questions.
- I will be realistic about my abilities and will work to improve them.
- I will approach quantitative thinking with an open mind, not assuming the worst.

Know your rights. Along with being a responsible student, you also have rights regarding your mathematical learning. These include:[11]

- The right to learn at your own pace
- The right to ask questions
- The right not to understand
- The right to be treated as a competent person
- The right to believe you are capable of thinking quantitatively

Be persistent and take your time. Do not expect that you will be able to solve every problem in the wink of an eye. Speed does not necessarily translate into success when it comes to working with numbers. In fact, says Tobias, successful quantitative learners "never quit because they recognized long ago that progress in mathematics very often involves making just a little headway, one step at a time. They do not judge themselves as harshly as we judge ourselves when answers do not come out right. They are patient, tenacious, and rarely very fast."[12]

TAKE ACTION

GET PREPARED

Assess Your Level of Math Anxiety

Rate your answers from 1 (strongly disagree) to 5 (strongly agree); add them up and check your score below.

1. I cringe when I have to go to math class. **1 2 3 4 5**
2. I am uneasy about going to the board in a math class. **1 2 3 4 5**
3. I am afraid to ask questions in math class. **1 2 3 4 5**
4. I am always worried about being called on in math class. **1 2 3 4 5**
5. I understand math now, but I worry that it's going to get really difficult soon. **1 2 3 4 5**
6. I tend to zone out in math class. **1 2 3 4 5**
7. I fear math tests more than any other kind. **1 2 3 4 5**
8. I don't know how to study for math tests. **1 2 3 4 5**
9. It's clear to me in math class, but when I go home it's like I was never there. **1 2 3 4 5**
10. I'm afraid I won't be able to keep up with the rest of the class. **1 2 3 4 5**

Check Your Score:

40–50 You suffer from full-blown math anxiety.

30–39 You are coping, but you're not happy about mathematics.

20–29 You're doing okay.

10–19 Loose as a goose! You have very little problem with anxiety.

Now, combine the results of this assessment with what you know about yourself as a quantitative learner. On a separate sheet of paper, create a portrait of yourself as a quantitative learner in a journal entry. Include thoughts about your attitude toward math and science, your level of success in those areas through your educational career, events and people that have influenced you, how math and science might be (or are) part of your working life, and how you want to approach math and science in the future.

Source for assessment: Ellen Freedman, "Do You Have Math Anxiety?" March 1997, accessed May 2006 from Professor Freedman's Math Help Web site (www.mathpower.com/anxtest.htm).

Beyond working to control your math anxiety, several other techniques will help you do your very best when you are tested on your math skills.

Reduce Math Anxiety at Test Time

In addition to the general strategies for test taking that you explored in chapter 8, here are several additional actions that can help you achieve better results on math and science exams:

- *Put key information in front of you.* Before you open the exam, write down any formulas that you just studied and don't want to forget (writing down formulas after a test is given out is *not* cheating). Use the back of the test if you don't have scrap paper.
- *Read through the exam first.* When you first get an exam, read through every problem quickly. Make notes on how you might attempt to solve the problem, if something occurs to you immediately.
- *Analyze problems carefully.* Categorize problems according to type. Take all the "givens" into account, and write down any formulas, *theorems* (mathematical statements proposed or accepted as demonstrable truth), or definitions that apply before you begin your calculations. Focus on what you want to find or prove. If some problems seem easier than others, do them first in order to boost your confidence.
- *Estimate before you begin to come up with an approximate solution.* To *estimate* means to make a rough or preliminary calucation. Then, work the problem and check the solution against your guess. The two answers should be close. If they're not, recheck your calculations. You may have made a simple calculation error.
- *Break the calculation into the smallest possible pieces.* Go step-by-step and don't move on to the next step until you are clear about what you've done so far. Focus only on the information you need to solve the problem.
- *Recall how you solved similar problems.* Past experience can give you valuable clues to how a particular problem should be handled.
- *Draw a picture to help you see the problem.* This can be a diagram, a chart, a probability tree, a geometric figure, or any other visual image that relates to the problem at hand.
- *Try not to rush.* Precison demands concentration. Take the time you need to reach an accurate solution.
- *Be neat.* When it comes to numbers, mistaken identity can mean the difference between a right and a wrong answer. A 4 that looks like a 9, for example, can mean trouble.
- *Use the opposite operation to check your work.* When you come up with an answer, work backward to see if you are right. Use subtraction to check your addition, use division to check multiplication, and so on.
- *Look back at the questions to be sure you did everything that was asked.* Did you answer every part of the question? Did you show all required work? Be as complete as you possibly can. If you have time, rework problems on a scrap piece of paper and see if you arrive at the same answers.

MULTIPLE PATHWAYS TO LEARNING

MULTIPLE INTELLIGENCE STRATEGIES FOR WORKING WITH NUMBERS

When math and science get tough, look to your strongest multiple intelligences to figure out ways to cope.

INTELLIGENCE	SUGGESTED STRATEGIES	WHAT WORKS FOR YOU? WRITE NEW IDEAS HERE
Verbal-Linguistic	▪ Whenever possible, write out word problem versions of numerical problems and formulas. ▪ When you have word problems, convert them into numbers to help solidify the relationship between words and the numbers they signify.	
Logical-Mathematical	▪ Practice using math games and puzzles. ▪ Focus on process. Make sure you understand any formula you use; then, carefully work through each step of the problem-solving process.	
Bodily-Kinesthetic	▪ Find physical representations of problems. Use pennies; cut up an apple; measure lengths; drive distances. ▪ For hands-on experience, look for science classes with a strong laboratory component. ▪ When several instructors teach sections of the course, find out who is best at concrete examples.	
Visual-Spatial	▪ Draw visual representations of problems—geometrical shapes, grids, charts, matrices—and use plenty of space. ▪ Circle important items in the description of the problem. ▪ Write out formulas when working word problems.	
Interpersonal	▪ Go over homework problems with a study group each week. Pass around your solutions and discuss them. ▪ Take advantage of your instructor's office hours. Schedule a time to talk about concepts that are giving you trouble.	
Intrapersonal	▪ Find a solitary spot to do your reading or homework. ▪ Take quiet breaks when you hit a roadblock. Take a walk or a nap; see if this helps you think of a new approach.	
Musical	▪ Listen to, and study, music whenever possible. The rhythms and notes of music are based in mathematics; musical experience can enhance quantitative abilities.	
Naturalistic	▪ When you need science credits, look for courses in biological sciences and/or botany. ▪ Find patterns and categorize the information whenever possible.	

How can you "read" visual aids?

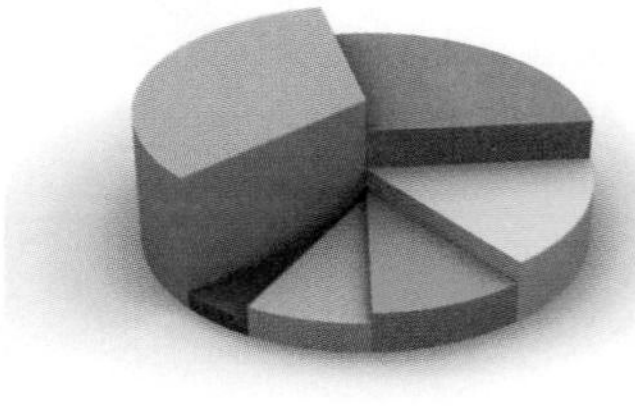

isual aids present data in tables, charts, illustrations, maps, and photographs. Their purpose is to present, clarify, or summarize information in a form that shows comparisons and that is easy to read and understand. Visual aids save space and speed up reading. A table or chart can present information more concisely than if the information were presented in paragraph form.

Visual aids are in nearly every college text and are a staple of business documents, including e-mail. Their popularity has spread because PowerPoint and other software programs make them so easy to create. Visual aids highlight statistical comparisons that show the following:

- *Trends over time* (for example, the number of computers with Internet connections per household in 2006 as compared to the number in 2001)
- *Relative rankings* (for example, the size of the advertising budgets of four major consumer products companies)
- *Distributions* (for example, student performance on standardized tests by geographic area)
- *Cycles* (for example, the regular upward and downward movement of the nation's economy as defined by periods of prosperity and recession)

Knowing what to look for in visual aids will help you learn to "read" the information they present. The most common types of visual aids are tables and charts.

Tables. The two basic types of tables are *data tables* and *word tables*. Data tables present numerical information—for example, the number of students taking a standardized test in 50 states. Word tables summarize and consolidate complex information, making it easier to study and evaluate. Look at Key 10.2 on page 320 for an example of a word table. Key 9.2 in this chapter is a data table.

Charts. Also known as graphs, *charts* show statistical comparisons in visual form. They present *variables,* which are numbers that can change, often along *vertical*—top to bottom—and *horizontal*—side to side—axes. Types of charts include pie charts, bar charts, and line charts. The *pie chart* presents data as wedge-shaped sections of a circle to show the relative size of each item as a percentage of the whole. *Bar charts* consist of horizontal bars of varying lengths to show the relative as well as absolute quantities. Whereas pie charts compare individual parts to the whole, bar charts compare items to one another. Finally, *line charts* show trends. The horizontal axis often shows a span of time, and the vertical axis frequently represents a specific measurement such as dollars.

Key 9.4 gives an example of each type of chart. The pie chart shows the political views of college freshmen during a particular academic year. The bar chart shows probable majors chosen by freshmen at four-year colleges in the fall of 2003. Finally, the line chart shows the number of immigrants to the United States from 1821 to 2010 (projected).

Tables and charts help you to understand quantitative information. They are valuable study aids that can enhance your comprehension of what you read in school and in the workplace.

A sample pie chart, bar chart, and line chart.   **KEY   9.4**

(a) Sample pie chart

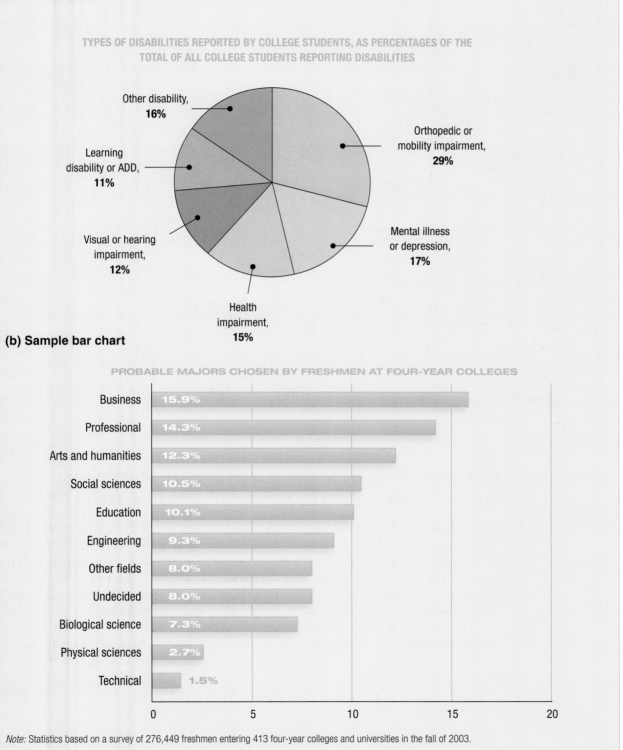

TYPES OF DISABILITIES REPORTED BY COLLEGE STUDENTS, AS PERCENTAGES OF THE
TOTAL OF ALL COLLEGE STUDENTS REPORTING DISABILITIES

Other disability, **16%**

Orthopedic or mobility impairment, **29%**

Learning disability or ADD, **11%**

Mental illness or depression, **17%**

Visual or hearing impairment, **12%**

Health impairment, **15%**

(b) Sample bar chart

PROBABLE MAJORS CHOSEN BY FRESHMEN AT FOUR-YEAR COLLEGES

Major	Percentage
Business	15.9%
Professional	14.3%
Arts and humanities	12.3%
Social sciences	10.5%
Education	10.1%
Engineering	9.3%
Other fields	8.0%
Undecided	8.0%
Biological science	7.3%
Physical sciences	2.7%
Technical	1.5%

0   5   10   15   20

Note: Statistics based on a survey of 276,449 freshmen entering 413 four-year colleges and universities in the fall of 2003.

(continued)

(c) Sample line chart

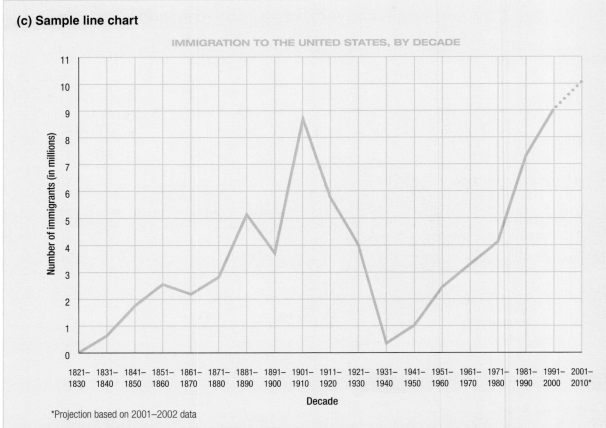

IMMIGRATION TO THE UNITED STATES, BY DECADE

*Projection based on 2001–2002 data

Sources: (a) [Pie chart] J. Wirt, S. Choy, S. Provasnik, P. Rooney, A. Sen, and R. Tobin, *The Condition of Education 2003,* Washington, D.C: National Center for Education Statistics, June, 2003, p. 68. (b) [Bar chart] Data from "The American Freshman: National Norms for Fall 2003," American Council on Education and the University of California–Los Angeles, Higher Education Research Institute, reprinted in *Chronicle of Higher Education:* Almanac Issue 2004–05, August 27, 2004, p. 19. (c) [Line chart] Data from U.S. Citizenship and Immigration Services, 2003.

How will math and science learning be an important part of your future?

In a workplace increasingly dominated by statistics and information technology, people in nearly every profession need some level of skill in math and science. "Mathematics is no longer just an entry-level prerequisite for engineering, the physical sciences, and statistics," says Sheila Tobias. "Its principles and techniques, along with computers, have become part of almost all areas of work, and its logic is used in thinking about almost everything."[13]

The Mathematical Association of America has defined the level of *quantitative literacy* that every college graduate should have in order to succeed on the job (see Key 9.5). With competence in these areas, you will be able to tackle quantitative challenges at work and in your personal life.

Following are some specifics about the role of math and science in workplace success.

Certain careers require study in specific math and science disciplines. Careers such as actuarial or genetic science demand a strong background in probability and statistics, and some areas of business, economics, and engineering require strong skills as well. Medical careers require study in biology, chemistry,

Know and build the skills that constitute quantitative literacy.   KEY 9.5

"A quantitatively literate college graduate should be able to:

- Interpret mathematical models such as formulas, graphs, tables, and schematics, and draw inferences from them.

- Represent mathematical information symbolically, visually, numerically, and verbally. Use arithmetical, algebraic, geometric, and statistical methods to solve problems.

- Estimate and check answers to mathematical problems in order to determine reasonableness, identify alternatives, and select optimal results.

- Recognize that mathematical and statistical methods have limits.

In addition, college students should be expected to go beyond routine problem solving to handle problem situations of greater complexity and diversity, and to connect ideas and procedures more readily with other topics both within and outside mathematics."

Source: "What Is Quantitative Literacy?" Quantitative Skills Program, Bowdoin College, accessed August 2006 (http://academic.bowdoin.edu/qskills/).

---

anatomy, and other sciences. Calculus and differential equations are needed for most engineering fields, business and economics, physics, and astronomy. Says Evelyn Hu-DeHart of the University of Colorado at Boulder:

> One of the chief problems for students who opt out of mathematics too early is that they foreclose certain careers. If a student doesn't continue in mathematics through calculus or pre-calculus while still in high school—perhaps for lack of early interest in pursuing a career in science or engineering—that student will need to do a lot of catching up if he or she discovers later on that indeed, science and engineering are interesting after all.[14]

Modern businesses demand quantitatively literate workers. To succeed in business, prospective employees need to be competent in two areas: use of numbers and problem solving.

- *Numbers:* People who work in any business, large or small, perform mathematical functions to budget income and expenses. For example, a corporate lawyer in charge of a five-person staff must submit a yearly budget that includes salaries, benefits, building overhead, and other expenses. "Business wants new employees from the educational system who can do mathematics accurately, within benchmark time periods, and frequently with the use of a calculator," says C. J. Shroll of the National Coalition for Advanced Manufacturing.[15]

- *Problem solving:* In business, the ability to set up and analyze a problem is even more

Joyce Dopkeen/ *The New York Times*

Ways that you can apply math and science knowledge in the workplace may surprise you. This computer science researcher found that some aspects of his computer calculations can be used to help fight forest fires.

important than performing the calculations that emerge from that analysis. Shroll says, "In the world of work, [problem solving] means dealing with real, unpredictable, and unorganized situations where the first task is to organize the information and only then calculate to find an answer. . . . Organizing the information is the most important aspect."[16]

Quantitatively based visuals play a crucial role in the workplace. Due to the increased need for communication across language and cultural lines, visuals are becoming more and more important, as is the ability to use software programs such as PowerPoint to create and present complex data. As C. J. Shroll explains:

> Charts, graphs, diagrams, etc., are the evolving language of business, made necessary because of the significant problems associated with communication based only on words, written or oral. The ideal situation is when someone has the ability to communicate in many different ways including charts, graphs, words, symbols, and more. Employees are most likely to understand a complex idea when it is presented in different ways. This is true for all people—in life as well as in work. Employers are often frustrated that many people coming to them have only learned to communicate with words.[17]

© Rogelio Bautista—Fotolia

> I advise my students to listen carefully the moment they decide to take no more mathematics courses. They might be able to hear the sound of closing doors.

JAMES CABALLERO, MATHEMATICIAN

Most important is the way math and science learning build critical-thinking power, which is crucial to success in any job or career area. As Tobias puts it: "Just as college students' ability to think more complex thoughts is enhanced every time they learn a new word or phrase, so their ability to understand abstract concepts will be enriched when they master such mathematical constructs as 'limits,' 'nonlinear,' and 'exponential growth.'"[18]

I strive for accuracy and precision.

Although accuracy and precision are important in many subjects, they have particular value in math and science. If there is an error in any step of an algebra problem, for instance, the final answer will be incorrect. If any step of a chemistry lab project is imprecise, the results will be off. Math and science must be approached with a focus on accuracy and precision.

Working accurately and precisely with numbers requires time, focus, attention to detail, and striving for high quality. Lots of practice with problems—essential for developing precision—requires that you take your time. Checking over the details of your work—key for assuring accuracy—demands focus. Furthermore, consistently striving for high quality will help you to base your work on solid understanding of concepts rather than counting on guesses. The quality you are capable of will shine through if you focus on precision and accuracy in your work.

REMEMBER
THE IMPORTANT POINTS

1

How are math and science part of your daily life?

- You use math such as arithmetic, algebra, and geometry for routine tasks.
- You estimate using probability and statistics.
- You use scientific methods and facts in a variety of daily activities.
- Most importantly, math and science build problem-solving and critical-thinking abilities.

2

How can you master math and science basics?

- Two ingredients for success in class are: Be prepared by reading materials and doing problems. Be in class and participate actively by asking questions.
- With textbooks: Make notes, note formulas, work problems, and use memory strategies.
- Take an active approach to studying and homework by reviewing frequently, doing problems, working with others, and thinking about learning styles.
- Use the basic four-step method for word problems.
- When they apply, use one or more of the seven word problem strategies.

3

How can you overcome math anxiety?

- Math anxiety is any kind of high-stress feeling related to quantitative thinking.
- Push past the myths about math. Remember that quantitative thinking skills can be improved; people can and do excel in both quantitative and verbal areas of study; and gender does not determine quantitative aptitude.
- Work through your negative assumptions, or "static," that can clog mental pathways.
- Use specific strategies to combat math anxiety.

4

How can you "read" visual aids?

- Visual aids present, clarify, or summarize information in an easy-to-understand format.
- Visual aids highlight trends over time, relative rankings, distributions, and cycles.
- Look for tables, pie charts, bar charts, and line charts.

5

How will math and science learning be an important part of your future?

- All workers should have the skills that constitute quantitative literacy.
- Many growing careers require study in specific math and science disciplines.
- Math and science build problem-solving ability, necessary in any workplace.

CRITICAL THINKING
APPLYING LEARNING TO LIFE

Get the Most from Your Textbook

From a textbook in a math or science course you are now taking, choose a chapter that you are about to cover in class. Do the following to maximize your understanding of the material:

1. Read the chapter now, before its material is covered in class. Take notes. Check this box when you have read it through: ☐

2. Identify and work through two difficult concepts or formulas. Develop a game plan to understand and learn each concept, basing your plan on what will help most—memory techniques, study groups, practice with problems, asking your instructor for help, and so forth.

Note the first concept or formula here:

_____

Briefly describe your game plan:

_____

_____

Check the box when you have put your plan into action, and indicate whether it helped.

Work done?   ☐

How did your plan help? _____

_____

_____

Note the second concept or formula here:

_____

Briefly describe your game plan:

_____

_____

Check the box when you have put your plan into action, and indicate whether it helped.

Work done?   ☐

How did your plan help? _____

_____

_____

TEAM BUILDING
COLLABORATIVE SOLUTIONS

Take a Study Group Approach to Quantitative Learning

Choose one or two people from one of your math or science classes—fellow students with whom you feel comfortable working. Use problems from your assigned text.

1. Choose one problem. Each of you work on the same problem separately. After finishing the problem, come together to share your methods. Discuss how each of you approached the problem. What steps did you each take in solving the problem? What strategies did you use? How did you check to see if your procedures were correct?

2. Now pick a different problem on which to work together. After solving it, discuss your problem-solving process. Did you learn more or less by working together, as compared to working separately? Were you able to solve the problem faster by working together than when you worked alone? Did you gain a better understanding of the problem by working together?

I recognize that my ability to **strive for accuracy and precision** is essential in order to successfully work with numbers in any setting. As I know from the chapter, precision and accuracy take time and focus. Planning to work on three problems from a math or science course, I will first put myself into a setting that will maximize my ability to concentrate:

- Generous block of time: When during the day do I have the most time? _____
- Quiet location where I can spread out: Where do I prefer to work? _____
- Necessary supplies: What do I need other than a pencil, paper, and my text?

_____

_____

- Any other important factor: What else helps me focus? _____

Next I will work through the problems in this setting. I will take my time, focusing on accuracy and precision with each step, until I reach the correct answers. (Work through the problems on separate sheets of paper in the setting that you have described above.)

Finally, I will evaluate: Was my work accurate and precise? What about my setup helped me to focus? _____

_____

How am I doing? **Later in the term, be accountable for your progress on page 377.**

SUGGESTED READINGS

Hart, Lynn, and Deborah Najee-Ullich. *Studying for Mathematics*. New York: HarperCollins College Publishers, 1997.

Lerner, Marcia. *Math Smart: Essential Math for These Numeric Times*. New York: Villard Books, 1995.

Polya, George. *How to Solve It*. London: Penguin Books, 1990.

Schmidt, Philip, and Frank Ayres. *Schaum's Outline of College Mathematics*. New York: McGraw-Hill, 2003.

INTERNET RESOURCES

Algebra Online (**www.algebra-online.com**)

Professor Freedman's Math Help (**www.mathpower.com**)

Math.com: The World of Math Online (**www.math.com**)

The Math Forum @ Drexel (**http://mathforum.org**)

ENDNOTES

1. Quoted in *Keys to Lifelong Learning Telecourse* (videocassette), directed by Mary Jane Bradbury, Intrepid Films, 2000.

2. George Polya, *How to Solve It,* New ed., London: Penguin Books, 1990.

3. Rick Billstein, Shlomo Libeskind, and Johnny W. Lott, *A Problem Solving Approach to Mathematics for Elementary School Teachers,* pp. 5–22, 24–26, 28–36. Copyright © 2004 Pearson Education, Inc. Reproduced by permission of Pearson Education, Inc. All rights reserved.

4. Sheila Tobias, "Math Anxiety: Author's Update," Spring 1990, accessed May 2005 (**www.mathanxiety.net**).

5. W. Michael Cox and Richard Alm, "Scientists Are Made, Not Born," *New York Times,* February 28, 2005, p. A19.

6. Ibid.

7. Tobias, "Math Anxiety."

8. Ibid.

9. Ibid.

10. Adapted from Kathy Acker, "Math Anxiety Code of Responsibilities," March 1997, accessed March 1998 (**http://fc.whyy.org/CCC/alg1/code.htm**).

11. Sheila Tobias, *Overcoming Math Anxiety,* New York: Norton, 1993, pp. 226–227.

12. Tobias, "Math Anxiety."

13. Ibid.

14. Quoted in "Interviews About Quantitative Literacy," June 22, 1999, accessed March 2005 from College Board Online (**www.stolaf.edu/other/ql/intv.html**).

15. Ibid.

16. Ibid.

17. Ibid.

18. Tobias, "Math Anxiety."

ANSWER TO TAKE ACTION

Here is the solution to the word problem on page 289:

30 minutes on the treadmill

20 minutes on the stair climber

EFFECTIVE WRITING

COMMUNICATING YOUR MESSAGE

Communicate with clarity and precision

"Language and thinking are closely entwined. . . . Intelligent people strive to communicate accurately in both written and oral form, taking care to define terms and to use precise language, correct names, universal labels, and apt analogies."

ART COSTA

The benefits of clear, precise writing are immeasurable—not only in school, but in everything you do. When you write clearly, you show others that you care enough to use language properly and to organize your thoughts. You leave a lasting impression of intelligence.

W riting is about communication, and successful communication requires clarity. It is part of Rene Alegria's job as editorial director of Rayo, an imprint of publisher HarperCollins, to make sure that the books Rayo publishes communicate clearly to readers.

Words, shaped to present information and argue positions, have enormous power. Whether you write a research paper, a short essay, a memo to a supervisor, or an extensive report, words take ideas out of the realm of thought and give them a form that has an impact on others. In class or at work, writing clearly and well will help you understand what you take in and communicate what you learn.

This chapter will reinforce many writing basics that you may also study in your English composition course. They appear here as well because effective writing is that important to your academic and career success.

In this chapter, you explore answers to the following questions:

- **What are the elements of effective writing?**
- **What is the writing process?**
- **How can you deliver an effective oral presentation?**

Photo: Chester Higgins Jr./The New York Times

What are the elements of effective writing?

This chapter's habit of mind—***thinking and communicating with clarity and precision***—empowers you to present information and argue positions. Becoming an effective writer requires that you understand that every writing situation depends on three elements:

- *Your purpose:* What do you want your work to accomplish?
- *Your audience:* What do you need to know about your readers to meet your communication purposes and theirs?
- *Your topic:* What is the subject about which you will write?

> How can I know what I think until I read what I write?
>
> **JAMES RESTON,** *NEW YORK TIMES* COLUMNIST, DURING THE 1962 NEWSPAPER STRIKE

© Adam Borkowski—Fotolia

Consider your purpose and audience even before you start planning your document. Consider your topic during the early stage of planning.

Define Your Writing Purpose

Writing without a clear *purpose* is like driving without a destination. You'll get somewhere, but chances are it won't be the right place. Therefore, when you write, always decide what you want to accomplish before you start.

When you are assigned a research paper, your purpose is to uncover material others have written and present your findings in one of two ways:

- As an *expository paper,* which presents information without arguing a viewpoint: Your work may include analyzing and synthesizing material from different sources and presenting it in a clear, unbiased way.

- As a *persuasive paper,* which presents and argues a point of view to prove a thesis: Your goal is to convince readers that your views and evidence are correct.

Identify a piece of writing you recently read that captured your attention. (It could be a work of literature, a biography, a magazine or newspaper article, or even a section from one of your college texts.) Describe, in detail, why it was effective. Did it communicate ideas you never thought of before? Did it arouse buried or unfamiliar feelings? Did it inspire you to action? Why? What can you learn from this piece that you can apply to your own writing?

Identify Your Audience

As a writer, you speak to an *audience* of readers—a group or a single individual. Knowing who your readers are helps you communicate effectively.

Clear Thinking

Courtesy of the Library of Congress

Winston Churchill said, "Never give in. Never give in. ever, never, never, never—in nothing great or small, large or petty— never give in, except to convictions of honor and good sense."

He lived by these words even when his countrymen abandoned him during the days preceding World War II. Churchill persisted with *clear, persuasive speaking and writing* that still inspire his nation today.

When you hand in a paper, your audience is usually an instructor who takes the role of either an *uninformed reader,* who knows little about your topic, or an *informed reader.* The following questions will help you determine how much information your reader needs:

- Who are my readers? Are they instructors or fellow students or both?
- How much do they know about my topic? Are they experts or beginners?
- Are they interested, or do I have to convince them to read my material?
- Can I expect readers to have open or closed minds about my topic?

Begin to Define Your Topic

Depending on your instructor, you may be assigned a *specific topic* for your paper ("Write a five-page paper describing provisions of the federal Family and Medical Leave Act, FMLA, passed by Congress in 1993, guaranteeing workers 12 weeks of unpaid leave for family emergencies."), a *general topic* that gives you some choice ("Write a five-page paper on the impact of FMLA on working Americans."), or a *broad topic* ("Write a five-page paper on the difficulties workers are facing as they juggle career and family responsibilities."). The remainder of this chapter will look at writing assignments in which you are given a general topic and told to choose a specific aspect for your paper.

What is the writing process?

The *writing process*—planning, drafting, revising, and editing—enables you to express what you want to say in the way you want to say it. Your goal is to produce a research paper that addresses your purpose, topic, and audience; that comes in on schedule; and that represents your best work.

Planning

When planning to write, use critical thinking to evaluate the assignment. Go over the logistics of the assignment, brainstorm for topic ideas, use prewriting strategies to define and narrow your topic, conduct research, write a thesis statement, and write a working outline. Although these steps are listed here in sequence, in real life they often overlap.

Pay Attention to Logistics

Avoid biting off more than you can chew. Start planning by asking questions to determine the feasibility of different topics:

1. *How much depth does my instructor expect?* Does she want a basic introduction, or a more sophisticated, high-level presentation?
2. *How much time do I have to write the paper?* Consider your other course assignments as well as personal responsibilities, such as part-time work.
3. *How long should the paper be?* Going too far above or below the number of pages your instructor specifies can count against you.
4. *What kind of research is needed?* Your topic and purpose may determine your research sources, and some sources are harder to get than others.

5. *Is it a team project, or am I research-ing and writing alone?* If you are working with others, determine what each person will do and whether others can deliver their work on time.

6. *Am I interested enough in the topic to live and breathe it for an extended period?* Ask yourself whether the material will bring out the best in you or whether you will quickly tire of it.

Answering questions like these will help you decide on a topic and depth of coverage.

Open Your Mind to Topic Ideas Through Brainstorming

Start the process of choosing a topic for an expository paper with *brainstorming*—a creative technique to generate ideas with-out making judgments about their worth (see chapter 4):

Michelle V. Agins/ *The New York Times*

Technology helps when you use the library to perform research for a writing assignment. You may access library holdings using an online catalog, or you may connect with Internet resources using a library computer terminal.

- Begin by writing down anything on the assigned subject that comes to mind, in no particular order. To jump-start your thoughts, scan your textbook, look at your notes, check general references at the library, or meet with your instructor to discuss ideas.

- Next, organize that list into a logical outline or think link that helps you see the possibilities more clearly.

Key 10.1 shows a portion of an outline constructed from a brainstorming list. The assignment, for an introduction to business class, is to choose an aspect of business ethics and write a short expository research paper on it. Because the student's research is only preliminary, many ideas are in question form.

Narrow Your Topic Through Prewriting Strategies

Prewriting strategies, including brainstorming, freewriting, and asking journalists' questions,[1] help you decide which possible topic you would most like to pursue. Use them to narrow your topic, focusing on the specific sub-ideas and examples from your brainstorming session.

Brainstorming. The same process you used to generate ideas will help you narrow your topic. Write down your thoughts about one or more of the possibilities you have chosen, do some more research, and then organize your thoughts into categories, noticing patterns that appear. See if any of the sub-ideas or examples might make good topics. Asking critical-thinking questions can spark ideas and help you focus on what to write.

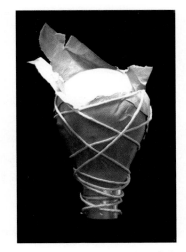

© Kelly Young—Fotolia

Freewriting. When you *freewrite,* you jot down whatever comes to mind without censoring ideas or worrying about grammar, spelling, punctuation, and organization. Freewriting helps you think creatively

KEY 10.1   Brainstorming leads to topic ideas and sets the stage for organizing your thoughts.

Topic: <u>Business Ethics</u>

— What are business ethics?
— Recent scandals that raised ethical issues:
  — Enron
  — WorldCom
— Who is responsible—the individual or the corporation?
— How do companies encourage ethical business practices?
  — Some companies have written codes of ethics.
  — Codes are based on core ethical values that remain constant even as the environment changes.
  — Codes of ethics only work if they are part of the corporate culture.
— Why do people act unethically in business?
  — The bottom-line culture puts pressure on managers to show increasing profits every quarter.
  — Corporate cultures stress workers out to the point that they no longer ask whether actions are right or wrong.
  — People have such expensive lifestyles that they are willing to cut ethical corners to keep their jobs and earn large bonuses.

and gives you an opportunity to piece together what you know about a sub-idea to see if you want to pursue it. A sample of freewriting for the business ethics paper follows:

Top executives at Tyco, Enron, and so many other companies give the impression that business is filled with greedy people willing to cheat and steal to get rich. It's hard to trust businesses when there are so many executives going to jail and so many companies engaged in outright fraud. But all companies aren't bad. Many who are trying to do a good job use a code of ethics, based on core values. They help employees decide how to handle difficult situations. Examples: Texas Instruments and Johnson & Johnson. Both companies have had codes for decades and use them to respond to crises.

Asking journalists' questions. When journalists start working on a story, they ask themselves: Who? What? Where? When? Why? How? (See the example at the bottom of this page.) Asking these questions about sub-ideas will help you choose a writing topic.

Prewriting helps you develop a topic that is broad enough for investigation but narrow enough to be manageable. Prewriting also helps you see what you know and what you don't know. If your assignment requires more than you already know, you need to do research.

Conduct Research and Make Notes

Your research will develop in stages as you narrow and refine your ideas. In the first brainstorming-for-ideas stage, look for an overview that can lead to a thesis statement. Use what you learn to answer your critical-thinking questions and to help you choose a thesis.

In the second stage, go into more depth, tracking down information that fills in gaps. Investigate using the Internet as well as books, journals, and other library sources. Ultimately, you will have a body of information that you can evaluate to develop and implement a thesis. (See the end-of-text appendix for helpful library and Internet research guidelines.)

Write a Thesis Statement

Your next task is to organize your research and formulate a *thesis statement*, which declares your specific subject and point of view, reflects your writing purpose and audience, and acts as the organizing principle of your paper. In one

Who?	To whom do companies have an ethical responsibility? Who maintains ethical standards within corporations?	
What?	What are business ethics? What is the difference between acting unethically and acting illegally, or are they the same? What is the impact of business codes of ethics on behavior? What companies have these codes, and what impact have they had on behavior? What role do core values play in business ethics?	
When?	When is the best time for companies to address ethics problems—before or after they occur?	
Where?	Do companies all over the country have ethics problems, or is the problem centered in certain geographic areas or industries?	
Why?	Why do ethics problems surface? Why do companies make so many mistakes in handling ethics problems?	
How?	How do companies train employees to act ethically? How do companies maintain their ethical standards in an ever-changing business environment?	

TAKE ACTION

Use Prewriting Strategies to Narrow a Topic

Start here to apply prewriting strategies to a writing assignment from this course or one of your other courses.

Define the assignment's general topic, the paper's purpose, and audience (continue on a separate page, if necessary):

_____

_____

Brainstorm to narrow your topic. (Remember that you may have to do some preliminary research.) Write down the results of your brainstorming session:

_____

_____

Freewrite what you know and look for threads of an idea (continue on a separate page, if necessary):

_____

_____

_____

Ask the six journalists' questions to focus on possible writing topics:

Who? _____

What? _____

When? _____

Where? _____

Why? _____

How? _____

Finally, describe your progress in choosing a topic for your paper. List one or two possibilities:

Idea #1 _____

Idea #2 _____

or two sentences, it tells readers what to expect. If you are unsure whether your thesis meets the assignment's requirements, get your instructor's approval before you begin writing. An example from the paper on business ethics appears at the top of the following page.

Topic	Business ethics
Purpose	To inform
Audience	Instructor who assumes the position of an uninformed reader

Thesis statement: In an environment where so many executives are behaving badly and where corporate reputations are being tarnished, companies are struggling with how to set expectations of ethical behavior. Most major corporations, including Texas Instruments and Johnson & Johnson, now believe that creating a corporate code of ethics is a critical first step in the process of sensitizing employees to how they should act under normal circumstances and during crises.

Although the thesis statement typically comes at the conclusion of an introductory paragraph, there is no hard and fast placement rule. Make your decision based on how your paper is organized and on instructor guidelines. Use your thesis statement to guide your writing, knowing that it may shift as ideas develop.

TAKE ACTION

GET PREPARED

Write a Thesis Statement

Continue your work on your paper by crafting a thesis statement that informs readers what the paper will accomplish. Link your thesis to your purpose, audience, and topic:

_____

_____

_____

_____

How do you think writing a clear thesis statement for every paper will help you develop the habit of mind of *thinking and communicating with clarity and precision?*

_____

_____

_____

<u>Introduction</u>
  —Corporate executives have abused the public trust at Enron, WorldCom, Tyco, Computer Associates, and other companies.
  —At the same time many companies are defining themselves in ethical terms through a corporate code of ethics.
  —Thesis: Companies like Texas Instruments and Johnson & Johnson use a code of ethics to sensitize employees to how to behave under normal circumstances and during crises.

<u>Body of Paper</u>
  —Business ethics are based on values that define actions as right or wrong.
  —When choices are ambiguous, companies look to core values. The Josephson Institute of Ethics defines "six pillars of character" to help managers evaluate competing choices.
  —Texas Instruments' code of ethics and "ethics test"
  —Johnson & Johnson's credo and how it helped managers respond to the Tylenol crisis of 1982

<u>Conclusion</u>
  —Ethics codes are effective only if they are followed. Companies like TI and J & J show that it is possible to establish a corporate ethical climate that guides daily decisions and actions.

Write a Working Outline or Think Link

The final planning step is creating a working outline or think link to use as a loose structural guide. As you draft, your ideas and direction may change, so be open to shifts that reflect new material and thoughts. As a way of organizing your research, consider keying your research to the outline so you know what sources to use at different points. A sample outline appears above.

Drafting

As its name implies, a *first draft* is the first of many versions of your paper. Each version moves you closer to mastering this chapter's habit of mind—***thinking and communicating with clarity and precision***. The main challenges you face at this stage are the following:

- Defining an organizational structure
- Integrating source material into the body of your paper to fit your structure
- Finding additional sources to strengthen your presentation

- Choosing the right words, phrases, and tone
- Connecting ideas with logical transitions
- Creating an effective introduction and conclusion
- Checking for plagiarism
- Creating a list of works cited

Some people aim for perfection when they write a first draft. They want to get every detail right. Do everything you can to resist this tendency because it may shut the door on ideas before you even know they are there.

Freewriting Your Rough Draft

Use everything that you developed in the planning stage as the raw material for freewriting a rough draft. For now, don't consciously think about your introduction, conclusion, or the structure within the paper's body. Simply focus on getting your ideas on paper. You can then start to shape it into something with a more definite form. Many people start with the introduction because it is the beginning of the paper, while others save the introduction until last to make sure it reflects the final product.

Writing an Introduction

The introduction tells readers what the paper contains and includes a thesis statement. Look at the introduction for the paper on business ethics, at the bottom of this page. The thesis statement is underlined at the end of the paragraph.

Open to the business section of any newspaper and you are likely to find at least one story of a corporate executive on trial and facing jail or a company paying huge fines or court settlements to the government, consumers, or investors. In the last few years, stories of alleged wrongdoing at Enron, WorldCom, Tyco International, Computer Associates, Sotheby's, and Adelphi Communications, to name just a few, have been front-page news. In an environment where so many executives are behaving badly and where corporate reputations are being tarnished, companies are struggling with how to set expectations of ethical behavior. Most major corporations, including Texas Instruments and Johnson & Johnson, now believe that creating a corporate code of ethics is a critical first step in the process of sensitizing employees to how they should act under normal circumstances and during crises.

Chang W. Lee/ *The New York Times*

Working at the college computer center gives you a chance to use software as well as consult with peers who may be nearby. This group of students is working at Shanghai Normal University.

Creating the Body of a Paper

The body of the paper contains your central ideas and supporting *evidence,* which supports your position with facts, statistics, examples, and expert opinions. Try to find a structure that helps you organize your ideas and evidence into a clear pattern. Several organizational options are presented in Key 10.2.

Writing the Conclusion

A conclusion brings your paper to a natural ending by summarizing your main points (if material is longer than three pages), showing the significance of your thesis and how it relates to larger issues, calling the reader to action, or looking to the future. Let the ideas in the body of the paper speak for themselves as you wrap up.

KEY   10.2   Find the best way to organize the body of the paper.

Organizational Structure	What to Do
Arrange ideas by time.	Describe events in order or in reverse order.
Arrange ideas according to importance.	Start with the idea that carries the most weight and move to less important ideas. Or move from the least to the most important ideas.
Arrange ideas by problem and solution.	Start with a problem and then discuss solutions.
Arrange ideas to present an argument.	Present one or both sides of an issue.
Arrange ideas in list form.	Group a series of items.
Arrange ideas according to cause and effect.	Show how events, situations, or ideas cause subsequent events, situations, or ideas.
Arrange ideas through the use of comparisons.	Compare and contrast the characteristics of events, people, situations, or ideas.
Arrange by process.	Go through the steps in a process: a "how-to" approach.
Arrange by category.	Divide topics into categories and analyze each in order.

Citing Sources and Avoiding Plagiarism

The bibliography cards you wrote while researching your topic should contain every source you used while writing (see chapter 7 for a discussion of research notes). Your instructor may ask you to use this information to create different source lists:

- A *references* list, also called a list of *works cited,* includes only the sources you actually cited in your paper.
- A *bibliography* includes all the sources you consulted, whether or not they were cited in the paper.
- An *annotated bibliography* includes all the sources you consulted as well as an explanation or critique of each source.

Besides being the ethical thing to do, citing your sources according to the directions your instructor provides adds credibility to your work. When instructors scan your list of works cited, they will know that you did research to uncover information.

Your instructor will tell you what style to use to document your sources and whether to position footnotes at the end of the paper or at the bottom of the page. The general styles of documentation are discipline specific:

- The Modern Language Association (MLA) format is generally used in the humanities, including history, literature, the arts, and philosophy. To learn more about MLA style, consult the official MLA handbook (*The MLA Handbook for Writers of Research Papers,* 6th edition, by Joseph Gibaldi) or go to the MLA Web site (**www.mla.org/style**).
- The American Psychological Association (APA) style is the appropriate format in psychology, sociology, business, economics, nursing, criminology, and social work. For information on APA style, see the official APA handbook (*Publication Manual of the American Psychological Association,* 5th edition) or visit the APA Web site (**www.apastyle.org/ previoustips.html**).
- An alternate documentation style is found in the 15th edition of *The Chicago Manual of Style,* published by the University of Chicago Press. To learn more, go to the Web site (**www.press.uchicago.edu/Misc/Chicago/ cmosfaq/cmosfaq.html**).
- The Council of Science Editors (CSE)—formerly known as the Council of Biology Editors (CBE)—has defined the style used to cite scientific sources. For information on this style, see the official CSE style manual (*Scientific Style and Format*) or go to the organization's Web site (**www.councilscienceeditors.org/ publications/style.cfm**).
- The Columbia Online Style (COS) is often used to cite online sources. For information, see the official COS manual (*The Columbia Guide to Online Style,* by Janice R. Walker and Todd Taylor) or visit the Columbia University Web site (**www.columbia.edu/cu/cup/cgos/index.html**).

Consult a college-level writers' handbook for an overview of these documentation styles.

Finally, academic integrity requires that you follow the guidelines you learned in chapter 1 to avoid *plagiarism*—claiming that another writer's words, content, unique approach, or illustrations are your own.

TAKE ACTION

Avoid Plagiarism

Think about plagiarism and explore your views on this growing problem.

Complete the following:

Why is plagiarism considered an offense that involves both stealing and lying? Describe how you look at it.

_____

_____

_____

Citing sources indicates that you respect the ideas of others. List two additional ways that accurate source citation strengthens your writing and makes you a better student:

1. _____

2. _____

What specific penalties for plagiarism are described in your college handbook? Explain whether you feel that these penalties are reasonable or excessive and whether they will keep students from plagiarizing.

_____

_____

_____

Many experts believe that researching on the Internet is behind many acts of plagiarism. Do you agree? Why or why not?

_____

_____

Soliciting Feedback

Because it is difficult to be objective about your own work, asking for someone else's perspective can be very helpful. Talk with your instructor about your draft, or ask a study partner to read it and answer specific questions:

- Is my thesis clear and did my evidence back it up?
- Are the ideas logically connected?
- Are there places where my writing style, choice of words, paragraph structure, or transitions detract from what I am trying to say?
- Am I missing anything?

Be open-minded about the comments you receive. Consider each carefully, and then make a decision about what to change.

Revising

When you *revise,* you critically evaluate the content, organization, word choice, paragraph structure, and style of your first draft as you move toward the goal of *thinking and communicating with clarity and precision.* You evaluate the strength of your evidence and whether there are logical holes. You can do anything you want with your draft at this point to strengthen your work. You can turn things around, presenting information from the end of your paper up front, or even choose a totally different organizational structure.

If your instructor evaluates an early draft, be sure to incorporate his ideas into the final product. If you disagree with a point or don't understand the revision directions, schedule a conference to talk it over.

Key 10.3 shows an excerpt from the first draft of the business ethics paper, with revision comments added.

Incorporate revision comments to strengthen your paper.   **KEY 10.3**

Like Texas Instruments, Johnson & Johnson developed a code of ethics that *written in plain English,*

is a cornerstone of its corporate culture
~~employees rely on to make decisions.~~ A simple one-page document that has

add more detail here

been in place for more than 60 years, "Our Credo," as the code is called, states

customers, employees, communities, stockholders
J & J's ethical responsibilities to ~~everyone it does business with.~~ It has been

translated into 36 languages for employees, customers, suppliers, governments,

to consult
and shareholders in every market in which it operates, from North America

the
to the far reaches of Africa, Europe, Latin America, the Middle East, and

Asia/Pacific *region (add footnote—Johnson & Johnson: Our Credo).*

When Johnson & Johnson updated its credo in the mid-1970s, executives

it continued to represent company values.
examined every word and phrase to make sure ~~they still applied~~ "These meetings

infused the values in the minds of all of us managers," explained Bob Kniffin,

who was   *at the time*
Vice President of External Affairs. J & J's managers had no way of knowing that

prepare them   *one of the most*
the exercise they were engaged in would give ~~them the skills~~ to handle a difficult

ever faced by an American company.   *scrutinized*
challenge. Only a few years later, many of the same executives who ~~examined~~ the

company's credo struggled with how to protect consumers, company employees

and shareholders when bottles of Tylenol were poisoned on store shelves and

innocent people died.

MULTIPLE PATHWAYS
TO LEARNING

The techniques below can help you uncover valuable research sources and clearly communicate what you want to say.

INTELLIGENCE	SUGGESTED STRATEGIES	WHAT WORKS FOR YOU? WRITE NEW IDEAS HERE
Verbal-Linguistic	■ Read many resources and take comprehensive notes on them. Summarize the main points from your resources. ■ Interview someone about the topic and take notes.	
Logical-Mathematical	■ Take notes on 3-by-5 cards and organize them according to topics and subtopics. ■ Create a detailed, sequential outline of your writing project. If your assignment requires persuasive writing, make sure that your argument is logical.	
Bodily-Kinesthetic	■ Visit places/sites that hold resources you need or that are related to your topic—businesses, libraries, etc. ■ After brainstorming ideas for an assignment, take a break involving physical activity. During the break, think about your top three ideas and see what insight occurs to you.	
Visual-Spatial	■ Create full-color charts as you read each resource or interview someone. ■ Use think link format or another visual organizer to map out your main topic, subtopics, and related ideas and examples. Use different colors for different subtopics.	
Interpersonal	■ As you gather resource material, discuss it with a fellow student. ■ Pair up with a classmate and become each other's peer editors. Read each other's first drafts and next-to-final drafts, offering constructive feedback.	
Intrapersonal	■ Take time to mull over any assigned paper topic. Think about what emotions it raises in you, and why. Let your inner instincts guide you as you begin to write. ■ Schedule as much research time as possible.	
Musical	■ Play your favorite relaxing music while you brainstorm topics for a writing assignment.	
Naturalistic	■ Pick a research topic that relates to nature. ■ Build confidence by envisioning your writing process as a successful climb to the top of a mountain.	

Use Critical Thinking Abilities as You Revise

Engage your critical-thinking skills to evaluate the content and form of your paper. Ask yourself these questions as you revise:

- Does the paper fulfill the requirements of the assignment?
- Will my audience understand my thesis and how I've supported it?
- Does the introduction prepare the reader and capture attention?
- Is the body of the paper organized effectively?
- Does each paragraph have a *topic sentence* that is supported by the rest of the paragraph? (See chapter 5 for an analysis of where to look for a topic sentence.)
- Is each idea and argument developed, explained, and supported by examples?
- Are my ideas connected to one another through logical transitions?
- Do I have a clear, concise, simple writing style?
- Does the conclusion provide a natural ending without introducing new ideas?

REFLECT

The great boxing champion Muhammad Ali once said, "Inside of a ring or out, ain't nothing wrong with going down. It's staying down that's wrong." Apply Ali's sentiments to the process of developing the habit of mind of *thinking and communicating with clarity and precision.* When you work hard on a draft and an instructor tells you that your paper requires major revisions, how do you feel? Do you give up or try even harder to succeed? What steps will you take to work with your instructor's feedback so that you never "stay down"?

RESPOND

Check for Clarity and Conciseness

Now check for sense, continuity, and clarity. Focus also on tightening your prose and eliminating wordy phrases. Examine once again how paragraphs flow into one another by evaluating the effectiveness of your *transitions*—the words, phrases, or sentences that connect ideas. Make sure your transitions signal what comes next.

Choose a Title

You can choose a title as you revise your paper, or earlier after you develop the thesis. Your goal is to be sure that the title reflects what the paper *actually* says rather than what you planned to write.

Editing

Editing involves correcting technical mistakes in spelling, grammar, and punctuation, as well as checking for consistency in such elements as abbreviations and capitalizations. Editing comes last, after you are satisfied with your ideas, organization, and writing style. If you use a computer, start with the grammar-check and spell-check to find errors, realizing that you still need to check your work manually. Look also for *sexist language,* which characterizes people according to gender stereotypes and often involves the male pronouns *he* or *his* or *him.* If you have a number of general examples that use gender references, you might choose to alternate between male and female, following the example of this text.

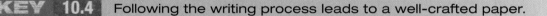

© Oleg Ivanov—Fotolia

Proofreading is the last editing stage and happens after your paper is in its final form. Proofreading means reading every word and sentence for accuracy. Look for technical mistakes, run-on sentences, and sentence fragments. Look for incorrect word usage and unclear references. A great way to check your work is to read it out loud. Consider teaming up with a classmate to proofread each other's work, since you may be too close to the material to catch even obvious errors.

Your final paper reflects all the hard work you put in during the writing process. It also reflects your progress in developing the habit of mind of ***thinking and communicating with clarity and precision***. Ideally, when you are finished, you have a piece of work that shows your writing ability and clearly communicates and proves your thesis. Key 10.4, the final version of the business ethics paper, is a product of this writing process.

As you complete this review of the writing process, keep in mind that the writing skills you develop in college will be reflected in the documents you give prospective employers, and these, in turn, will impact the success of your job search. June Brown, of Olive Harvey College, explains how good writing is at the center of your efforts:

> The written documents you leave with a company may be your most lasting calling card. If your documents are incorrect, messy, or poorly organized, they will leave a negative impression. No matter how well you do in a face-to-face meeting, your cover letter, résumé, and other work-related documents are a record that memorializes who you are. Make sure it is your best work.[2]

You can also use your improved writing and research skills to craft effective speeches and oral presentations. Being an effective speaker will work to your advantage in school, your community, and your career.

KEY 10.4   Following the writing process leads to a well-crafted paper.

CODES OF ETHICS ENCOURAGE COMPANIES TO DO WHAT IS RIGHT

Open to the business section of any newspaper and you are likely to find at least one story of a corporate executive on trial and facing jail or a company paying huge fines or court settlements to the government, consumers, or investors. In the last few years, stories of alleged wrongdoing at Enron, WorldCom, Tyco International, Computer Associates, Sotheby's, and Adelphi Communications, to name just a few, have been front-page news. In an environment where so many executives are behaving badly and where corporate reputations are being tarnished, companies are struggling with how to set expectations of ethical behavior. Most major corporations, including Texas Instruments and Johnson & Johnson, now believe that creating a corporate code of ethics is a critical first step in the process of sensitizing employees to how they should act under normal circumstances and during crises.

Business ethics, like personal ethics, are based on values that define actions as right or wrong, good or bad, proper or improper. Sometimes ethical decisions are clear—for example, almost no one would argue that it is acceptable for an automaker to hide a major safety defect in order to avoid the cost of recalling thousands of vehicles—but often they are not. (Should the same manufacturer issue the recall if the defect is likely to affect only 1 in 10,000 cars?) Business decisions in today's complex, competitive marketplace often involve choices that put a company's morals to the test.

The Josephson Institute of Ethics defines six key concepts to help managers evaluate competing choices (Josephson Institute of Ethics, "Six Pillars of Character," 2002). These are trustworthiness (honesty, integrity, promise-keeping, loyalty), respect (civility, courtesy and decency, dignity and autonomy, tolerance and acceptance), responsibility (accountability, pursuit of excellence, self-restraint), fairness (procedural fairness, impartiality, equity), caring (compassion, consideration, giving, sharing, kindness), and citizenship (law abiding, community service, protection of environment). These pillars are among the factors that underlie the ethics codes at Texas Instruments and Johnson & Johnson.

Texas Instruments places ethics at the core of its corporate culture. First published 45 years ago, TI's code sets ethical expectations, based on principles and values, for employees to consider every time they make a decision or take action. To encourage adherence to the highest ethical standards, TI gives each employee a business-card-sized "Ethics Test" to carry at all times (Texas Instruments, "The TI Ethics Quick Test," 1988). The test—with seven clear bullet points—is based on TI's core principles and on legal and societal values:

- Is the action legal?
- Does it comply with our values?
- If you do it, will you feel bad?
- How will it look in the newspaper?
- If you know it's wrong, don't do it!
- If you're not sure, ask.
- Keep asking until you get an answer.

To support employees who face ethics-related challenges in an ever-changing and increasingly competitive business environment, TI established an ethics office in the late 1980s. The function of the office is to make sure business practices continue to reflect company values, to communicate and reinforce ethical expectations to every employee, and to give employees feedback on ethics-related problems (Texas Instruments, 1988).

Like Texas Instruments, Johnson & Johnson developed a code of ethics, written in plain English, that is a cornerstone of its corporate culture. A simple one-page document that has been in place for more than 60 years, "Our Credo," as the code is called, states J & J's ethical responsibilities to its customers, its employees, the communities in which it operates, and its stockholders. It has been translated into 36 languages for employees, customers, suppliers, governments, and shareholders to consult in every market in which it operates, from North America to the far reaches of Africa, Europe, Latin America, the Middle East, and the Asia/Pacific region (Johnson & Johnson, "Our Credo," 2004).

(*continued*)

KEY 10.4   Continued

McNamara (1999) describes Johnson & Johnson's updating of its credo in the mid-1970s along with subsequent events. Executives examined every word and phrase to make sure it continued to represent company values. "These meetings infused the values in the minds of all of us managers," explained Bob Kniffin, who was Vice President of External Affairs at the time. J & J's managers had no way of knowing that the exercise they were engaged in would prepare them to handle one of the most difficult challenges ever faced by an American company: Only a few years later, many of the same executives who scrutinized the company's credo struggled with how to protect consumers, company employees, and shareholders when bottles of Tylenol were poisoned on store shelves and innocent people died.

Experts inside and outside the company believed that the examination of the company's credo that had taken place in these meetings guided J & J's decision to recall every bottle of Tylenol and repackage the product at a cost of $100 million. According to Kniffin, who was a key player in the crisis, the ethical road was set before the crisis began. "In a crisis, there's no time for moral conclusions," he said. Those must be made beforehand (*Ethics Tools: Codes of Ethics, "About Codes of Ethics"*).

Corporate codes of ethics are effective only if they are followed. (Even Enron had a code of ethics that was set aside by the board of directors to allow the company to complete unscrupulous deals.) While products and marketing strategies change frequently to meet competitive pressures, core values never change, nor does the expectation (in companies like TI and J & J) that managers will weigh business decisions and actions against these values. The old joke about "business ethics" being a contradiction in terms does not apply at these companies—not only because they have taken the time to institutionalize a code of ethics and to use it to evaluate job candidates, but also because employees are expected to follow its guidelines, even when it hurts the bottom line. Taking the idea of a written ethics code to another dimension, financial services companies are considering adopting an industry-wide code to set uniform standards of right and wrong for every company (Berman, 2005). That would mean that even in the toughest competitive situations—where millions of dollars in commissions were up for grabs—everyone would be playing by the same ethical rules.

References

Berman, Dennis K. (2005, March 10). "Does Wall Street finally need an ethics code?" *Wall Street Journal,* p. C1.

Johnson & Johnson (2004). Our Credo (last updated August 18, 2004). Retrieved February 16, 2005, from www.jnj.com/our_company/our_credo/index.htm

Josephson Institute of Ethics (2002). *Making Ethical Decisions: Introduction and Table of Contents* [Electronic version]. Retrieved February 22, 2005, from www.josephsoninstitute.org/MED/MED-intro+toc.htm

McNamara, Carter. (1999). *Complete Guide to Ethics Management: An Ethics Toolkit for Managers* [Electronic version]. Retrieved February 16, 2005, from www.mapnp.org/library/ethics/ethxgde.htm

Texas Instruments (1988). Ethics at TI. Retrieved March 4, 2005, from www.ti.com/corp/docs/company/citizen/ethics/quicktest.shtml

How can you deliver an effective oral presentation?

In school, you may be asked to deliver a speech, take an oral exam, or present a team project. Even when you ask a question or make a comment in class, you are using public speaking skills.

The public speaking skills that you learn for *formal* presentations help you make a favorable impression in *informal* settings, such as when you meet with an instructor, summarize a reading for your study group, or participate in a planning session at work. When you are articulate, others take notice.

Suzanne DeChillo/ *The New York Times*

When preparing for an oral presentation, be sure you understand how to use the technology available to you. At presentation time, focus on maintaining a positive, confident attitude.

Prepare as for a Writing Assignment

Speaking in front of others involves preparation, strategy, and confidence. Planning a speech is similar to planning a piece of writing: You must know your topic and audience and think about presentation strategy, organization, and word choice. Specifically, you should:

- *Think through what you want to say and why.* What is your purpose—to make or refute an argument, present information, entertain? Have a goal for your speech.
- *Plan.* Take time to think about who your listeners are and how they are likely to respond. Then, get organized. Brainstorm your topic—narrow it with prewriting strategies, determine your thesis, write an outline, and do research.
- *Draft your thoughts.* Draft your speech. Illustrate ideas with examples, and show how examples lead to ideas. As in writing, have a clear beginning and end. Start with an attention-getter and conclude with a wrap-up that summarizes your thoughts and leaves your audience with something to remember.
- *Integrate visual aids.* Think about building your speech around visual aids including charts, maps, slides and photographs, and props. Learn software programs such as PowerPoint to create presentation graphics.

With computer-generated presentations, your motto should be "Less is more." Although it's tempting to use all the options available for adding sound, animation, and fancy backgrounds, too many effects can distract your audience from the message you want to convey.

Finally, keep in mind that the rules governing plagiarism of written information also apply to graphic images. If you import graphics from Web sites into your own presentation, you must cite your source, either directly on the slide or on a reference sheet accompanying the presentation.

Be obscure clearly! Be wild of tongue in a way we can understand!

WILLIAM STRUNK JR. AND E. B. WHITE, AUTHORS OF *THE ELEMENTS OF STYLE*

© Roxana Gonzalez—Fotolia

Practice Your Performance

The element of performance distinguishes speaking from writing. Here are some tips to keep in mind:

- *Know the parameters.* How long do you have? Where will you be speaking? Be aware of the setting—where your audience will be and available props (for example, a podium, table, blackboard). If you plan to use electronic equipment such as a microphone or an overhead projector, run a test before the presentation to make sure these tools work.

- *Use index cards or notes.* Reduce your final draft to "trigger" words or phrases that remind you of what you want to say. Refer to the cards and to your visual aids during your speech.

- *Pay attention to the physical.* Your body position, voice, and clothing contribute to the impression you make. Your goal is to look and sound good and to appear relaxed. Try to make eye contact with your audience, and walk around if you are comfortable.

- *Practice ahead of time.* Do a test run with friends or alone. If possible, practice in the room where you will speak. Make an audiotape or videotape of your practice sessions and evaluate your performance.

- *Be yourself.* When you speak, you express your personality through your words and presence. Don't be afraid to add your own style to the presentation. Take deep breaths. Smile. Know that you can speak well and that your audience wants to see you succeed. Finally, envision your own success.

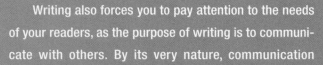

I think and communicate with clarity and precision.

Not only will clear writing make a strong impression on your instructors—and increase the likelihood of a good grade—it will also change the way you think. Clear writing forces you to test the connections among your ideas as you ask, "Does this make sense?" "Am I proving my case?" "Have I given evidence to support my conclusions?" "Have I backed up my opinion with a solid argument?" "Is there more to add?"

Writing also forces you to pay attention to the needs of your readers, as the purpose of writing is to communicate with others. By its very nature, communication involves a sender and a receiver, and successful communication occurs only when the reader understands exactly what the writer is trying to say.

The writing process you learned in this chapter requires a disciplined approach—the discipline to plan, to draft, and to revise and edit your words. The result you can expect is a clearer, more precise paper that shows the time and care you took to get it right. The result you might not expect is a sharper mind that has been enriched by clear logic and by your striving for words that say exactly what you mean.

REMEMBER

THE IMPORTANT POINTS

1 *What are the elements of effective writing?*

- Know your writing purpose.

  - In an expository paper, your purpose is to present information without arguing a viewpoint.

  - In a persuasive paper, your purpose is to present and argue a point of view to prove a thesis.

- Know your audience: Clarify whether you are writing for informed or uninformed readers.

- Know your topic: Your instructor may assign a specific, general, or broad topic.

2 *What is the writing process?*

- During the planning stage, prepare to write.

  - Pay attention to logistics, brainstorm topic ideas, use prewriting strategies to narrow your topic, conduct research, and write a thesis statement.

- During the drafting stage, put ideas on paper and create an organizational structure.

  - Drafting involves freewriting a rough draft, writing an introduction, creating the body of the paper with ideas and supporting evidence within an effective organization, writing the conclusion, crediting sources, and soliciting feedback.

- During the revision stage, critically evaluate your draft.

  - Focus on content, organization, word choice, paragraph structure, strength of the evidence, logic, clarity, and conciseness.

- During the editing phase, correct technical mistakes in spelling, grammar, and punctuation.

3 *How can you deliver an effective oral presentation?*

- Public speaking requires careful preparation.

  - To be an effective speaker, you should know your audience, draft your remarks, and prepare props or visual aids.

  - Preparation also involves practicing your performance in order to make the audience care about and be interested in what you are saying.

CRITICAL THINKING
APPLYING LEARNING TO LIFE

Audience Analysis

As a reporter for your college newspaper, you have been assigned the job of writing a story about some part of campus life. You submit the following suggestions to your editor-in-chief:

- The campus parking lot squeeze: Too many cars and too few spaces
- Drinking on campus: Is the problem getting better or worse?
- Diversity: How students accept differences and live and work together

Your editor-in-chief asks you the following questions about how readers are likely to respond (consider that your different "audiences" include students, faculty and administrators, and community members):

1. Which subject would likely appeal to all audiences at your school and why?

_____

_____

_____

2. How would you adjust your writing according to how much readers know about the subject?

_____

_____

_____

3. For each topic, name the audience (or audiences) that you think would be most interested. If you think one audience would be equally interested in more than one topic, you can name an audience more than once.

Campus parking lot _____

Drinking on campus _____

Student diversity _____

4. How can you make a specific article interesting to a general audience?

_____

_____

_____

Prewriting

Choose a topic you are interested in and know something about—for example, college sports or handling stress. Narrow your topic; then, use the following prewriting strategies to discover what you already know about the topic and what you would need to learn if you had to write an essay about the subject for one of your classes (if necessary, continue this prewriting exercise on a separate sheet of paper):

1. Brainstorm your ideas:

_____

_____

_____

_____

_____

_____

2. Freewrite:

_____

_____

_____

_____

_____

3. Ask journalists' questions:

_____

_____

_____

_____

_____

_____

Writing a Thesis Statement

Write two thesis statements for each of the following topics. The first statement should inform the reader, and the second should persuade. In each case, use the thesis statement to narrow the topic.

1. The rising cost of a college education

    A. Thesis with an informative purpose:

    _____

    _____

    B. Thesis with a persuasive purpose:

    _____

    _____

2. Handling test anxiety

    A. Thesis with an informative purpose:

    _____

    _____

    B. Thesis with a persuasive purpose:

    _____

    _____

TEAM BUILDING
COLLABORATIVE SOLUTIONS

Team Research

Join with three other classmates and decide on two relatively narrow research topics that interest all of you and that you can investigate by spending no more than an hour in the library. The first topic should be current and in the news—for example, safety problems in sport utility vehicles (SUVs), body piercing, or the changing U.S. family. The second topic should be more academic and historical—for example, the polio epidemic in the 1950s, the Irish potato famine, or South African apartheid.

　　Working alone, team members should use the college library and the Internet to research both topics (see the appendix at the end of this text for helpful guidelines). Set a research time limit of no more than one hour per topic.

The goal should be to collect a list of sources for later investigation. When everyone is finished, the group should come together to discuss the research process. Among the questions group members should ask each other are these:

- How did you "attack" and organize your research for each topic?
- What research tools did you use to investigate each topic?
- How did the nature of your research differ from topic to topic? Why do you think this was the case?
- How did your use of library and Internet resources differ from topic to topic?
- Which research techniques yielded the best results? Which techniques led to dead ends?

Next, compare the specific results of everyone's research. Analyze each source for what it is likely to yield in the form of useful information. Finally, come together as a group and discuss what you learned that might improve your approach to library and Internet research.

*I recognize that my ability to **think and communicate with clarity and precision** is essential to my academic and career success. With this in mind, I have studied this chapter and identified three specific actions I will take to improve my writing:*

Action #1

_____

_____

Action #2

_____

_____

Action #3

_____

I will choose the action that is likely to yield the greatest improvement in my writing and describe a plan for using it to complete all my papers this term. My plan is:

_____

_____

_____

_____

Here is what actually happened to the quality of my writing when I implemented what I consider to be my most important action step:

_____

_____

_____

_____

*I am certain that **thinking and communicating with clarity and precision** will help me get a job and succeed in my career after I graduate. If I had to explain to a friend why I am so certain, I would say:*

_____

_____

_____

*How am I doing? **Later in the term, be accountable for your progress on page 377.***

SUGGESTED READINGS

Becker, Howard S. *Tricks of the Trade: How to Think About Your Research While You're Doing It.* Chicago: University of Chicago Press, 1998.

Booth, Wayne C., Gregory G. Colomb, and Joseph M. Williams. *The Craft of Research.* Chicago: University of Chicago Press, 1995.

Cameron, Julia. *The Right to Write: An Invitation into the Writing Life.* New York: Putnam, 1999.

Gibaldi, Joseph, and Phyllis Franklin. *MLA Handbook for Writers of Research Papers,* 5th ed. New York: Modern Language Association of America, 1999.

LaRocque, Paula. *Championship Writing: 50 Ways to Improve Your Writing.* Oak Park, IL: Marion Street Press, 2000.

Markman, Peter T., and Roberta H. Markman. *10 Steps in Writing the Research Paper,* 5th ed. New York: Barron's Educational Series, 1994.

Strunk, William, Jr., and E. B. White. *The Elements of Style,* 4th ed. New York: Allyn & Bacon, 2000.

Troyka, Lynn Quitman. *Simon & Schuster Handbook for Writers,* 7th ed. Upper Saddle River, NJ: Prentice Hall, 2005.

Walsch, Bill. *Lapsing into a Comma: A Curmudgeon's Guide to the Many Things That Can Go Wrong in Print—And How to Avoid Them.* New York: Contemporary Books, 2000.

Williams, Joseph M. *Style: Ten Lessons in Clarity and Grace.* Chicago: University of Chicago Press, 2003.

INTERNET RESOURCES

Prentice Hall's Student Success Supersite: Academic Skills—Valuable information on writing and research (**www.prenhall.com/success/Study Skl/index.html**)

Online Writing Lab: The OWL at Purdue (**http://owl.english.purdue.edu/owl**)

How to Organize a Research Paper and Document It with MLA Citations—Specific citation rules from the Modern Language Association (**www.geocities.com/Athens/Oracle/4184**)

Plagiarism.org—An online resource concerned with the growing problem of Internet plagiarism (**www.plagiarism.org/**)

A Student's Guide to Research with the WWW—A comprehensive site developed at St. Louis University (**www.slu.edu/departments/english/research**)

ENDNOTES

1. Analysis based on Lynn Quitman Troyka, *Simon & Schuster Handbook for Writers,* Upper Saddle River, NJ: Prentice Hall, 1996, pp. 22–23.

2. Quoted in *Keys to Lifelong Learning Telecourse* (videocassette), directed by Mary Jane Bradbury, Intrepid Films, 2000.

CREATING YOUR LIFE

BUILDING A SUCCESSFUL FUTURE

*Stay open to
continuous learning*

HABITS OF MIND

"Intelligent people are in a continuous learning mode. Their confidence, in combination with their inquisitiveness, allows them to constantly search for new and better ways. . . . They seize problems, situations, tensions, conflicts, and circumstances as valuable opportunities to learn."

ART COSTA

STAY OPEN TO CONTINUOUS LEARNING

Your wellness, your career, your finances, and your overarching life goals are all subject to constant change. If you continue to learn and to seek improvement, you will be better able to manage the rapid change that characterizes the modern global world and craft the life you dream of.

U p to this point in the course, you have accumulated knowledge that will help you succeed academically. However, college and life success also involves developing competencies in personal skills—maintaining your health, handling your finances, and building a career—and putting those skills to use as you continue to learn throughout your life. At 85, working on her B.A. in American Studies, Ann Martindell shows that staying open to continuous learning can bring growth and success at any age.

Use the habits of mind that you have acquired in this text to guide you as you move forward into the world. They will help you choose a direction when you are at a fork in the road and will give you tools with which to overcome the myriad challenges you will face. The more you use them, the more you will realize how essential they are to your future success and your ability to make a difference in the world.

In this chapter, you explore answers to the following questions:

- How can you maintain a healthy body and mind?
- How can you make intelligent decisions about substances and sex?
- How can you manage your finances in school and beyond?
- How can you prepare for workplace success?
- How can the habits of mind help you aim for your personal best?

Photo: Joyce Dopkeen/The New York Times

Of all alcohol consumption, *binge drinking* (having five or more drinks at one sitting) is associated with the greatest problems. Here are statistics from a recent survey:[5]

- Forty-three percent of the students surveyed labeled themselves as binge drinkers, and 21% said that they binge-drink frequently.
- Eight out of ten students who do not binge-drink reported experiencing such "secondhand" effects as vandalism, sexual assault or unwanted sexual advances, or interrupted sleep or study.[6]
- Students who binge-drink are more likely to miss classes, be less able to work, have hangovers, become depressed, and engage in unplanned or unsafe sexual activity.[7]

The bottom line is that it is very difficult, if not impossible, to be a successful student if you drink too much. If you drink at all, think carefully about the effects on your health, safety, and academic performance.

Tobacco

The National Institute on Drug Abuse (NIDA) found that nearly 40% of college students reported smoking at least once in the year before they were surveyed, and 25% had smoked once within the previous month.[8]

© Sascha Burkard—Fotolia

When people smoke they inhale nicotine, a highly addictive drug found in all tobacco products. Nicotine's immediate effects may include an increase in blood pressure and heart rate, sweating, and throat irritation. Long-term effects may include high blood pressure, bronchitis, emphysema, stomach ulcers, and heart disease. Pregnant women who smoke increase their risk of having infants with low birth weight, premature births, or stillbirths. Furthermore, inhaling tobacco smoke damages the cells that line the air sacs of the lungs and can cause lung cancer. Lung cancer causes more deaths in the United States than any other type of cancer.[9]

Quitting smoking is difficult and should be attempted gradually, ideally with the support of friends and family. The positive effects of quitting—increased life expectancy, greater lung capacity, and more energy—may inspire any smoker to consider making a lifestyle change. Weigh your options and make a responsible choice.

Illegal Drugs

The NIDA reports that nearly 32% of college students have used illicit drugs at least once in the year prior to being surveyed, and 16% in the month before.[10] College students may use drugs to relieve stress, to be accepted by peers, or just to try something new.

In most cases, the negative consequences of drug use outweigh any temporary high. Drug use violates federal, state, and local laws, and you may be arrested, tried, and imprisoned for possessing even a small amount of drugs. You can jeopardize your reputation, your student status, and your ability to get a job if you are caught using drugs or if drug use impairs your performance. Finally, long-term drug use can damage your body and mind. Key 11.1 shows commonly used drugs and their potential effects.

The ways in which drugs affect body and mind.   KEY 11.1

Drug Category	Drug Types	How They Make You Feel	Physical Effects	Danger of Physical Dependence	Danger of Psychological Dependence
Stimulants	Cocaine, amphetamines	Alert, stimulated, excited	Nervousness, mood swings, stroke or convulsions, psychoses, paranoia, coma at large doses	Relatively strong	Strong
Depressants	Alcohol, Valium, Xanax, Rohypnol	Sedated, tired, high	Cirrhosis; impaired blood production; greater risk of cancer, heart attack, and stroke; impaired brain function	Strong	Strong
Opiates	Heroin, codeine, other pain pills	Drowsy, floating, without pain	Infection of organs, inflammation of the heart, hepatitis	Yes, with high dosage	Yes, with high dosage
Cannabinols	Marijuana, hashish	Euphoria, mellowness, little sensation of time	Impairment of judgment and coordination, bronchitis and asthma, lung and throat cancers, anxiety, lack of energy and motivation, reduced ability to produce hormones	Moderate	Relatively strong
Hallucinogens	LSD (acid), mushrooms	Heightened sensual perception, hallucinations, confusion	Impairment of brain function, circulatory problems, agitation and confusion, flashbacks	Insubstantial	Insubstantial
Inhalants	Glue, aerosols	Giddiness, lightheadedness	Damage to brain, heart, liver, and kidneys	Insubstantial	Insubstantial

Source: Adapted from Marc Alan Schuckit, M.D., *Educating Yourself About Alcohol and Drugs: A People's Primer*, New York: HarperCollins, 1998.

One drug that doesn't fit cleanly into a particular category is methylene-dioxymethamphetamine (MDMA), better known as Ecstasy. The use of this drug, a combination stimulant and hallucinogen, is on the rise at college parties, raves, and concerts. Its immediate effects include diminished anxiety and relaxation. When the drug wears off, nausea, hallucinations, shaking, vision problems, anxiety, and depression replace these highs. Long-term users risk permanent brain damage in the form of memory loss, chronic depression, and other disorders.[11]

You are responsible for analyzing the potential consequences of what you introduce into your body. Ask yourself questions like the following: "Why do I want to do this?" "Am I taking drugs to escape from other problems?" "What positive and negative effects might my behavior have?" "Why do others want me to take drugs?" "What do I really think of these people?" "How would my drug use affect the people in my life?"

The more carefully you analyze your situation, the more likely you will be to make choices that are in your own best interest.

Facing Addiction

People with addictions have lost control. If you think you may be addicted, take the initiative to seek help. (The self-assessment on the following page can help you evaluate your level of substance use.) Because substances often cause physical and chemical changes and psychological dependence, habits are tough to break and quitting may involve a painful withdrawal. Asking for help isn't an admission of failure but a courageous move to reclaim your life. The following resources can help you generate options and plans for recovery.

Counseling and medical care. You can find help from school-based, private, government-sponsored, or workplace-sponsored resources. Ask your school's counseling or health center, your personal physician, or a local hospital for a referral.

Detoxification ("detox") centers. If you have a severe addiction, you may need a controlled environment where you can separate yourself completely from drugs or alcohol.

Support groups. Alcoholics Anonymous (AA) is the premier support group for alcoholics. AA has led to other support groups for addicts such as Overeaters Anonymous (OA) and Narcotics Anonymous (NA). Many schools have AA, NA, or other group sessions on campus.

Another important aspect of physical and mental health involves being comfortable with your sexuality and making wise sexual decisions. Choosing birth control and knowing how to avoid sexually transmitted diseases have short- and long-term consequences for the rest of your life.

Sexual Decision Making

What sexuality means to you and the role it plays in your life are your own business. However, the physical act of sex goes beyond the private realm. Individual sexual conduct can result in an unexpected pregnancy and in contracting or passing a *sexually transmitted infection (STI)*. These consequences affect everyone involved in the sexual act and, often, their families.

Evaluate Your Substance Use

Even one "yes" answer may indicate a need to evaluate your substance use. Answering "yes" to three or more questions indicates that you may benefit from discussing your use with a counselor.

WITHIN THE LAST YEAR:

Y N   1. Have you tried to stop drinking or taking drugs but couldn't do so for long?

Y N   2. Do you get tired of people saying they're concerned about your drinking or drug use?

Y N   3. Have you felt guilty about your drinking or drug use?

Y N   4. Have you felt that you needed a drink or drugs in the morning—as an "eye-opener"—in order to improve a hangover?

Y N   5. Do you drink or use drugs alone?

Y N   6. Do you drink or use drugs every day?

Y N   7. Do you regularly think or say "I need" a drink or any type of drug?

Y N   8. Have you lied about or concealed your drinking or drug use?

Y N   9. Do you drink or use drugs to escape worries, problems, mistakes, or shyness?

Y N 10. Do you find you need increasingly larger amounts of drugs or alcohol in order to achieve a desired effect?

Y N 11. Have you forgotten what happened while drinking or using drugs (had a blackout)?

Y N 12. Have you been surprised by how much you were using alcohol or drugs?

Y N 13. Have you spent a lot of time, energy, or money getting alcohol or drugs?

Y N 14. Has your drinking or drug use caused you to neglect friends, your partner, your children, or other family members, or caused other problems at home?

Y N 15. Have you gotten into an argument or a fight that was alcohol- or drug-related?

Y N 16. Has your drinking or drug use caused you to miss class, fail a test, or ignore schoolwork?

Y N 17. Have you rejected planned social events in favor of drinking or using drugs?

Y N 18. Have you been choosing to drink or use drugs instead of performing other activities or hobbies you used to enjoy?

Y N 19. Has your drinking or drug use affected your efficiency on the job or caused you to fail to show up at work?

Y N 20. Have you continued to drink or use drugs despite any physical problems or health risks that your use has caused or made worse?

Y N 21. Have you driven a car or performed any other potentially dangerous tasks while under the influence of alcohol or drugs?

Y N 22. Have you had a drug- or alcohol-related legal problem or arrest (possession, use, disorderly conduct, driving while intoxicated, etc.)?

Sources: Compiled and adapted from the Criteria for Substance Dependence and Criteria for Substance Abuse in the *Diagnostic and Statistical Manual of Mental Disorders,* 4th ed., published by the American Psychiatric Association, Washington, DC, and from materials titled "Are You an Alcoholic?" developed by Johns Hopkins University.

Your self-respect depends on making choices that maintain health and safety—yours as well as those of the person with whom you are involved. Analyze sexual issues carefully, weighing the positive and negative effects of your choices.

Birth Control

If you choose to be sexually active, evaluate the pros and cons of each available birth control option for yourself and your partner. Consider cost, ease of use, reliability, comfort, and protection against STIs. Communicate with your partner, and together make a choice that is comfortable for both of you.

For more information, check your library, the Internet, or a bookstore; talk to your doctor; or ask a counselor at the student health center. Key 11.2 describes established methods, with effectiveness percentages and STI prevention based on proper and regular use.

Sexually Transmitted Infections

STIs are spread through sexual contact (intercourse or other sexual activity that involves contact with the genitals). All are highly contagious. The only birth control methods that offer protection are the male and female condoms (latex or polyurethane only), which prevent skin-to-skin contact. Most STIs can also spread to infants of infected mothers during birth. Have a doctor examine any irregularity or discomfort as soon as you detect it. Key 11.3 describes common STIs.

The most serious STI is AIDS (acquired immunodeficiency syndrome), which is caused by the human immunodeficiency virus (HIV). Not everyone who tests positive for HIV will develop AIDS, but AIDS has no cure and results in eventual death. Medical science continues to develop drugs to combat AIDS and its related illnesses. The drugs can cause severe side effects, however, and none are cures.

HIV is transmitted through two types of bodily fluids: fluids associated with sex (semen and vaginal fluids) and blood. People have acquired HIV through sexual relations, by sharing hypodermic needles for drug use, and by receiving infected blood transfusions. You cannot become infected unless one of those fluids is involved. Therefore, it is unlikely you can contract HIV from toilet seats, hugging, kissing, or sharing a glass. Other than not having sex at all, a latex condom is the best defense against AIDS. Although some people dislike using condoms, it's a small price to pay for preserving your life.

To be safe, have an HIV test done at your doctor's office or at a government-sponsored clinic. Your school's health department may also administer HIV tests, and home HIV tests are available over the counter. If you are infected, first inform all sexual partners and seek medical assistance. Then, contact support organizations in your area or call the National AIDS Hotline at 1-800-342-AIDS.

Sexual Abuse

The more informed you are, the less likely you are to become a victim of sexual harassment, relationship violence, or rape.

Method	Approximate Effectiveness	Prevents STIs?	Description
Abstinence	100%	Only if no sexual activity occurs	Just saying no. No intercourse means no risk of pregnancy. However, alternative modes of sexual activity can still spread STIs.
Condom (male)	94%	Yes, if made of latex	A sheath that fits over the penis and prevents sperm from entering the vagina.
Condom (female)	90%	Yes	A sheath that fits inside the vagina, held in place by two rings, one of which hangs outside. Made of polyurethane.
Diaphragm or cervical cap	85%	No	A bendable rubber cap that fits over the cervix and pelvic bone inside the vagina (the cervical cap is smaller and fits over the cervix only). Both must be fitted initially by a gynecologist and used with a spermicide.
Oral contraceptives (the pill)	97%	No	A dosage of hormones taken daily by a woman, preventing the ovaries from releasing eggs. Side effects can include headaches, weight gain, and increased chances of blood clotting. Various brands and dosages; must be prescribed by a gynecologist.
Spermicidal foams, jellies, inserts	84% if used alone	No	Usually used with diaphragms or condoms to enhance effectiveness, they have an ingredient that kills sperm cells (but not STIs). They stay effective for a limited period of time after insertion.
Intrauterine device (IUD)	94%	No	A small coil of wire inserted into the uterus by a gynecologist (who must also remove it). Prevents fertilized eggs from implanting in the uterine wall. Possible side effects include bleeding.
Depo-Provera (the shot)	Nearly 100%	No	An injection that a woman must receive from a doctor every few months. Possible side effects may resemble those of oral contraceptives.
Tubal ligation	Nearly 100%	No	Surgery for women that cuts and ties the fallopian tubes, preventing eggs from traveling to the uterus. Difficult and expensive to reverse. Recommended for those who do not want any, or any more, children.
Vasectomy	Nearly 100%	No	Surgery for men that blocks the tube that delivers sperm to the penis. Like tubal ligation, difficult to reverse and recommended only for those who don't want any, or any more, children.
Rhythm method	Variable	No	Abstaining from intercourse during the ovulation segment of the woman's menstrual cycle. Can be difficult to time and may not account for cycle irregularities.
Withdrawal	Variable	No	Pulling the penis out of the vagina before ejaculation. Unreliable, because some sperm can escape in the fluid released prior to ejaculation. Dependent on a controlled partner.

KEY 11.3   To stay safe, know these facts about sexually transmitted diseases.

Disease	Symptoms	Health Problems if Untreated	Treatments
Chlamydia	Discharge, painful urination, swollen or painful joints, change in menstrual periods for women	Can cause pelvic inflammatory disease (PID) in women, which can lead to sterility or ectopic pregnancies, infection, miscarriage, or premature birth.	Curable with full course of antibiotics; avoid sex until treatment is complete.
Gonorrhea	Discharge, burning while urinating	Can cause PID, swelling of testicles and penis, arthritis, skin problems, infections.	Usually curable with antibiotics; however, certain strains are becoming resistant to medication.
Genital herpes	Blisterlike itchy sores in the genital area, headache, fever, chills	Symptoms may subside and then reoccur, often in response to high stress levels; carriers can transmit the virus even when it is dormant.	No cure; some medications, such as Acyclovir, reduce and help heal the sores and may shorten recurring outbreaks.
Syphilis	A genital sore lasting one to five weeks, followed by a rash, fatigue, fever, sore throat, headaches, swollen glands	If it lasts over four years, it can cause blindness, destruction of bone, insanity, or heart failure; can cause death or deformity of a child born to an infected woman.	Curable with full course of antibiotics.
Human papilloma virus (HPV, or genital warts)	Genital itching and irritation, small clusters of warts	Can increase risk of cervical cancer in women; virus may remain in body and cause recurrences even when warts are removed.	Treatable with drugs applied to warts or various kinds of wart removal surgery.
Hepatitis B	Fatigue, poor appetite, vomiting, jaundice, hives	Some carriers will have few symptoms; others may develop chronic liver disease that may lead to other diseases of the liver.	No cure; some will recover, some will not. Bed rest may help ease symptoms. Vaccine is available.

Sexual Harassment

Sexual harassment can be *quid pro quo harassment* (a request for a sexual favor or activity in exchange for something else) or *hostile environment harassment* (any situation where sexually charged remarks, behavior, or items cause discomfort). If you feel degraded by anything that goes on at school or work, address the person you believe is harassing you, or speak to a dean or supervisor. Both men and women can be victims of sexual harassment, although the most common targets are women.

Violence in Relationships

Statistics indicate that violent relationships among students are increasing. One in five college students has experienced and reported at least one violent incident while dating; in 60% of these cases, drinking and drugs are associated with the violence.[12] If you see warning signs such as controlling behavior, angry outbursts, or personality changes associated with alcohol and drugs, consider ending the relationship. If you are being abused, call a shelter or abuse hotline or seek counseling. If you need medical attention, go to a clinic or hospital emergency room. If you believe that your life is in danger, obtain a restraining order that requires your abuser to stay away from you.

Rape and Date Rape

Rape—intercourse or anal or oral penetration against another person's will—is primarily an act of rage and control, not sexual desire. Acquaintance rape or *date rape* refers to sexual activity occurring during an arranged social encounter that is against one partner's will (including situations where one partner is too drunk or drugged to give consent). Date rapists sometimes use a difficult-to-detect drug called Rohypnol, or *roofies,* to sedate victims.

Protect yourself by communicating—clearly and early—what you want and don't want to do. When on a date with someone who seems unstable or angry, stick to safe, public places. Keep a cell phone handy. Avoid alcohol or drugs that might make it difficult for you to stay in control. If you are raped, whether by an acquaintance or a stranger, seek medical attention immediately. Next, talk to a close friend or counselor. Consider reporting the incident to the police or to campus officials. Whether or not you take legal action, continue to get help through counseling, a rape survivor group, or a hotline.

Even the most academically committed, physically and mentally healthy student needs to be a good money manager in order to pay tuition and living expenses. The next section will show you ways to maintain financial well-being.

How can you manage your finances in school and beyond?

At the core of personal financial management is effective budgeting and credit card use. While you are in school, it also involves learning the ins and outs of financial aid.

Effective Budgeting

For the vast majority of college students, money is tight. Effective budgeting helps relieve money-related stress so that you feel more in control. *Budgeting* involves making a plan that coordinates resources and expenditures and setting financial goals and priorities.

Your biggest expense right now is probably the cost of your education, including tuition and room and board. However, that expense may not hit you fully until after you graduate and begin to repay your student loans. For now, include in your budget only the part of the cost of your education you are paying while you are in school.

Budgeting demands creative and critical thinking. Most people budget on a month-by-month basis. You gather information about your resources (money flowing in) and expenditures (money flowing out) and analyze the difference. Next, you come up with ideas about how you can make changes. Finally, you adjust spending or earning so that you come out even or ahead. No two months will be the same; being in a *continuous learning* mode will help you make new and effective choices when changes occur in your cash flow.

Stephen Crowley/ *The New York Times*

Many students work part-time or even full-time in order to support their tuition and other costs. Some jobs enhance classroom learning—this student is working for a political candidate while taking a political science course.

Figure Out What You Earn

Add up all of the money you receive during the year—the actual after-tax money you have to pay your bills. Common sources of income include the following:

- Take-home pay from a regular full-time or part-time job during the school year
- Take-home pay from summer and holiday employment
- Money you earn as part of a work-study program
- Money you receive from your parents or other relatives for your college expenses
- Scholarships or grants that provide spending money

If you have savings specifically earmarked for your education, decide how much you will withdraw every month for your school-related expenses.

Figure Out What You Spend

Start by recording every check you write for fixed expenses like rent and telephone. Then, over the next month, record personal expenditures in a small notebook. Indicate any expenditure over five dollars, making sure to count smaller expenditures if they are frequent (for example, a bus pass for a month, soda or newspaper purchases per week).

Some expenses, like automobile and health insurance, may be billed only a few times a year. In these cases, convert the expense to monthly by dividing the yearly cost by 12. Be sure to count only current expenses, not expenses that you will pay after you graduate. Among these are the following:

- Rent or mortgage
- Tuition that you are paying right now (the portion remaining after all forms of financial aid, including loans, scholarships, and grants, are taken into account)

- Books, lab fees, and other educational expenses
- Regular bills (electric, gas, phone, water)
- Food, clothing, toiletries, and household supplies
- Child care
- Transportation and auto expenses (gas, maintenance)
- Credit cards and other payments on credit (car payments)
- Insurance (health, auto, homeowner's or renter's, life)
- Entertainment and related items (cable TV, movies, eating out, books and magazines)
- Computer-related expenses, including the cost of your online service
- Miscellaneous unplanned expenses

Use the total of all your monthly expenses as a baseline for other months, realizing that your expenditures will vary depending on what is happening in your life.

Evaluate the Difference

Focusing again on your current situation, subtract your monthly expenses from your monthly income. Ideally, you have money left over—to save or to spend. However, if you are spending more than you take in, you need to analyze the problem by looking at your budget, spending patterns, and priorities. Use your critical-thinking skills to ask some focused questions:

- *Question your budget.* Did you forget to budget for recurring expenses, or were you derailed by an emergency expense that you did not foresee? Is your income sufficient for your needs?
- *Question your spending patterns and priorities.* Did you spend money wisely or did you overspend on luxuries? Are you putting too many purchases on your credit card and being hit by high interest payments?

Adjust Spending or Earning

Look carefully at what may cause you to overspend, and brainstorm possible solutions that address those causes. Solutions can involve either increasing resources or decreasing spending. To deal with spending, prioritize your expenditures and trim the ones you really don't need to make. As for resources, investigate ways to take in more money, such as taking a part-time job or hunting down scholarships or grants.

In addition, think analytically about the big picture of where your money goes. Every budgetary decision you make has particular effects, often involving a trade-off among options. When you spend $80 for that new pair of sneakers, for example, you may not have enough for movie tickets and dinner with friends that weekend. Often, making some short-term sacrifices in order to save money can help you tremendously in the long run. If you do what you can to spend less than you make and to "pay yourself"—put some money away in your savings, each month if possible—you'll have a better chance of providing for your future wants and needs.

MULTIPLE INTELLIGENCE STRATEGIES FOR BUDGETING

Looking into the strategies associated with your strongest intelligences helps you identify effective ways to manage your money.

INTELLIGENCE	SUGGESTED STRATEGIES	WHAT WORKS FOR YOU? WRITE NEW IDEAS HERE
Verbal-Linguistic	▪ Talk over your budget with someone you trust. ▪ Write out a detailed budget outline. If you can, keep it on a computer where you can change and update it regularly.	
Logical-Mathematical	▪ Focus on the numbers; using a calculator and amounts as exact as possible, determine your income and spending. ▪ Calculate how much money you'll have in 10 years if you start now to put $2,000 in an IRA account each year.	
Bodily-Kinesthetic	▪ Consider putting money, or a slip with a dollar amount, each month in different envelopes for various budget items—rent, dining out, etc. When the envelope is empty or the number is reduced to zero, your spending stops.	
Visual-Spatial	▪ Set up a budgeting system that includes color-coded folders and colored charts. ▪ Create color-coded folders for papers related to financial and retirement goals—investments, accounts, etc.	
Interpersonal	▪ Whenever budgeting problems come up, discuss them right away. ▪ Brainstorm a five-year financial plan with a financial planner or a money-savvy friend or family member.	
Intrapersonal	▪ Schedule quiet time and think about how you want to develop, follow, and update your budget. Consider financial management software, such as Quicken. ▪ Think through the most balanced allocation of your assets— where you think your money should go.	
Musical	▪ Include a category of music-related purchases in your budget—going to concerts, buying CDs—but keep an eye on it to make sure you don't go overboard.	
Naturalistic	▪ Remember to include time and money in your budget to enjoy nature. ▪ Sit in a spot you like. Brainstorm how you will achieve your short- and long-term financial goals.	

Credit Card Management

College students often receive dozens of credit card offers. These offers— and the cards that go along with them—are a double-edged sword: They are a handy alternative to cash and can help you build a strong credit history if used appropriately, but they also can plunge you into a hole of debt that may take you years to dig out of. Some recent statistics from a Nellie Mae survey of undergraduates illustrate the challenging situation:[13]

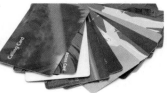

© Graça Victoria—Fotolia

- Average number of credit cards per student—3.2
- Average credit card debt per student—$1,843
- Average available credit card limit—$3,683
- Percentage of students with debt between $3,000 and $7,000—9%
- Percentage of students with more than $7,000 in credit card debt—5%

Often cash-poor, college students can be susceptible to credit overuse. They may charge books and tuition on cards as well as expenses like car repair, food, and clothes. Before they know it, the debt has become unmanageable. Although the majority of American citizens carry some level of debt, falling behind on payments could result in a poor credit rating that makes it difficult for you to make large purchases or take out loans. Particular resources can help you solve credit problems—for instance, the National Foundation for Credit Counseling has a Website (**www.nfcc.org**) and can also be reached by telephone, toll-free (1-800-388-2227; for Spanish, 1-800-682-9832).

To avoid unmanageable debt that can lead to a personal financial crisis, learn as much as you can about credit cards, starting with the important concepts in Key 11.4. Remember, too, that the most basic way to stay in control is to pay your bills regularly and on time. If you get into trouble, call the *creditor* (the person or company to whom you owe a debt) and see if you can pay your debt gradually using a payment plan. Finally, examine what got you into trouble and avoid it in the future if you can. Cut up a credit card or two if you have too many.

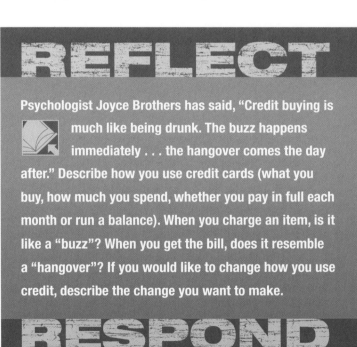

REFLECT

Psychologist Joyce Brothers has said, "Credit buying is much like being drunk. The buzz happens immediately . . . the hangover comes the day after." Describe how you use credit cards (what you buy, how much you spend, whether you pay in full each month or run a balance). When you charge an item, is it like a "buzz"? When you get the bill, does it resemble a "hangover"? If you would like to change how you use credit, describe the change you want to make.

RESPOND

Effective Use of Financial Aid

Financing your education—alone or with the help of your family—involves gathering financial knowledge and making financial decisions. Visit your school's financial aid office in person or on the Internet, research the available

What to Know About . . .	. . . And How to Use What You Know
Account balance—a dollar amount that includes any unpaid balance, new purchases and cash advances, finance charges, and fees. Updated monthly.	Charge only what you can afford to pay at the end of the month. Keep track of your balance. Hold on to receipts and call customer service if you have questions.
Annual fee—the yearly cost some companies charge for owning a card.	Look for cards without an annual fee or, if you've paid your bills on time, ask your current company to waive the fee.
Annual percentage rate (APR)—the amount of interest charged on your unpaid balance, meaning the cost of credit if you carry a balance in any given month. The higher the APR, the more you pay in finance charges.	Shop around (check **www.studentcredit.com**). Also, watch out for low, but temporary, introductory rates that skyrocket to over 20% after a few months. Look for *fixed* rates (guaranteed not to change).
Available credit—the unused portion of your credit line, updated monthly on your bill.	It is important to have credit available for emergencies, so avoid charging to the limit.
Cash advance—an immediate loan, in the form of cash, from the credit card company. You are charged interest immediately and may also pay a separate transaction fee.	Use a cash advance only in emergencies because the finance charges start as soon as you complete the transaction. It is a very expensive way to borrow money.
Credit limit—the debt ceiling the card company places on your account (e.g., $1, 500). The total owed, including purchases, cash advances, finance charges, and fees, cannot exceed this limit.	Credit card companies generally set low credit limits for college students. Many students get around this limit by owning more than one card, which increases the credit available but most likely increases problems as well.
Delinquent account—an account that is not paid on time or for which the minimum payment has not been met.	Avoid having a delinquent account at all costs. Not only will you be charged substantial late fees, but you also risk losing your good credit rating, affecting your ability to borrow in the future. Delinquent accounts remain part of your credit record for many years.
Due date—the date your payment must be received and after which you will be charged a late fee.	Avoid late fees and finance charges by mailing your payment a week in advance.
Finance charges—the total cost of credit, including interest and service and transaction fees.	The only way to avoid finance charges is to pay your balance in full by the due date.
Minimum payment—the smallest amount you can pay by the statement due date. The amount is set by the credit card company.	Making only the minimum payment each month can result in disaster if you charge more than you can afford. When you make a purchase, think in terms of total cost.
Outstanding balance—the total amount you owe on your card.	If you carry a balance over several months, additional purchases are hit with finance charges. Pay cash instead.
Past due—your account is considered "past due" when you fail to pay the minimum required payment on schedule.	Three credit bureaus note past due accounts on your credit history: Experian, Trans Union, and Equifax. You can contact each bureau for a copy of your credit report to make sure there are no errors.

options and decide what works best, and then apply early. Never assume you are not eligible for aid. The types of aid available are student loans, grants, and scholarships.

- *Student loans.* As the recipient of a student loan, you are responsible for paying back the amount you borrow, plus interest, according to a predetermined payment schedule that may stretch over a number of years. The federal government administers or oversees most student loans. To receive aid from any federal program, you must be a citizen or eligible noncitizen and be enrolled in a program that meets government requirements. Federal loan programs include Perkins (for those with exceptional financial need), Stafford (available to students enrolled at least half-time, exceptional need not required), and PLUS (available to students enrolled at least half-time and who are claimed as dependents by their parents).

- *Grants.* Unlike student loans, grants do not require repayment. Grants, funded by federal, state, or local governments as well as private organizations, are awarded to students who show financial need. Federal grant programs include Pell (need-based, available to undergraduates) and FSEOG (need-based, encouraging community service work or work related to your course of study).

- *Scholarships.* Scholarships are awarded to students who show talent or ability in specific areas (academic achievement, sports, the arts, citizenship, or leadership). They may be financed by government or private organizations, schools, or individuals.

It can take work to locate financial aid opportunities; many aren't widely advertised. Start digging at your financial aid office and visit your library, bookstore, and the Internet. Guides to funding sources catalog thousands of financial aid offers, and the Internet features online scholarship search services. Additional information about federal grants and loans is available from the Department of Education in the current version (updated yearly) of *The Guide to Federal Student Aid.* This publication can be found at your school's financial aid office, or you can request it by mail or phone (1-800-433-3243), or online (**http://studentaid.ed.gov/students/publications/student_guide/index.html**).

When you are applying for aid, fill out applications as neatly as possible and submit them on time. You can find the Free Application for Federal Student Aid (FAFSA) form at your library, at the Federal Student Aid Information Center, through your college's financial aid office or Web site, or via the U.S. Department of Education's Web site at **www.ed.gov/finaid.html.**

Finally, if you are receiving aid from your college, follow all the rules and regulations, including meeting application deadlines and remaining in academic good standing. In most cases, you will have to reapply yearly for aid. Take a new look at what's available to you each year; you may be eligible for different grants or scholarships at various points in your college career.

No matter where your money comes from—job paychecks or financial aid—learning to manage your money well while you are in college will prepare you for successful money management after you graduate and enter, or reenter, the workplace. The best jobs are those that bring both financial reward and satisfaction. Following are some important points to keep in mind as you set yourself up to succeed on the job.

How can you prepare for workplace success?

You are already preparing for career success with your work in this course, because the skills in this book—thinking, teamwork, writing skills, and goal setting, among others—are tools you will need in the workplace. Your student success experience reinforces the habit of *continuous learning* that will prove useful on the job. Use the following strategies to get more specific in your preparation.

Investigate Career Paths

The working world changes all the time. You can get an idea of what's out there—and what you think of it all—by exploring potential careers and building knowledge and experience.

Explore potential careers. Career possibilities extend far beyond what you can imagine. Ask instructors, relatives, mentors, and fellow students about careers they are familiar with. Explore your school's career center. Check your library for books on careers or biographies of people who worked in fields that interest you. Look at Key 11.5 for the kinds of questions that will aid your search. You may discover that a wide array of job possibilities exists for most career fields, and that within each job lies a variety of tasks and skills.

KEY 11.5 Ask questions like these to analyze how a career area or job may fit you.

What can I do in this area that I like and do well?	Do I respect the company or the industry? The product or service?
What are the educational requirements (certificates or degrees, courses)?	Does this company or industry accommodate special needs (child care, sick days, flex time)?
What skills are necessary?	Do I need to belong to a union? What does union membership involve?
What wage or salary and benefits can I expect?	Are there opportunities near where I live (or want to live)?
What personality types are best suited to this kind of work?	What other expectations exist (travel, overtime, etc.)?
What are the prospects for moving up to higher-level positions?	Do I prefer the service or production end of this industry?

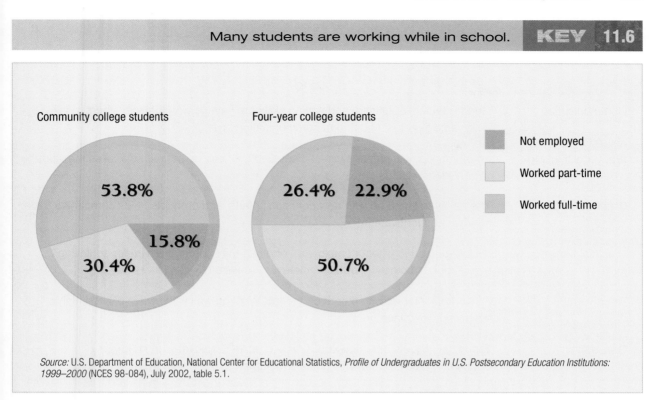

Many students are working while in school.   KEY 11.6

Community college students

53.8%

15.8%

30.4%

Four-year college students

26.4%   22.9%

50.7%

■ Not employed

□ Worked part-time

□ Worked full-time

Source: U.S. Department of Education, National Center for Educational Statistics, *Profile of Undergraduates in U.S. Postsecondary Education Institutions: 1999–2000* (NCES 98-084), July 2002, table 5.1.

Build knowledge and experience. Having knowledge and experience specific to the career you wish to pursue is valuable on the job hunt. Courses, internships, jobs, and volunteering are four great ways to build both:

- *Courses.* Take a course or two in your areas of interest to determine if you like the material. Find out what courses are required for a major in those areas.
- *Internships.* A temporary work program, called an *internship,* in which you can gain supervised practical experience in a particular professional field is a great way to gain real-world experience. Your career center may list summer or year-round internship opportunities.
- *Jobs.* Many students need or want to work while in school (Key 11.6 shows more about who works while enrolled in college). You may discover career opportunities while working a full- or part-time job. Someone who answers phones for a newspaper company, for example, might be drawn into journalism.
- *Volunteering.* Helping others in need can introduce you to careers and increase your experience. Many employers look favorably on volunteering.

Know What Employers Want

In the jobs you seek after you graduate, employers will look for specific technical skills, work experience, and academic credentials. They will also look for other skills and qualities that indicate that you are a promising candidate.

Key 11.7 describes the particular skills and qualities that tell an employer that you are likely to be an efficient and effective employee. These skills, which you

KEY 11.7 Employers look for candidates with these important skills.

Skill	Why is it useful?
Communication	Good listening, speaking, and writing skills are keys to working with others, as is being able to adjust to different communication styles.
Analytical thinking	An employee who can analyze choices and challenges, as well as assess the value of new ideas, stands out.
Creativity	The ability to come up with new concepts, plans, and products helps companies improve and innovate.
Practical thinking	No job gets done without employees who can think through a plan for achieving a goal, put it into action, and complete it successfully.
Teamwork	All workers interact with others on the job. Working well with others is essential for achieving workplace goals.
Goal setting	Teams fail if goals are unclear or unreasonable. Employees and company benefit from setting realistic, specific goals and achieving them reliably.
Cultural competence	The workplace is increasingly diverse. An employee who can work with, adjust to, and respect people from different backgrounds and cultures is valuable.
Leadership	The ability to influence and motivate others in a positive way earns respect and career advancement.
Positive attitude	Other employees will gladly work with, and often advance, someone who completes tasks with positive, upbeat energy.
Integrity	Acting with integrity at work—communicating promptly, being truthful and honest, following rules, giving proper notice—enhances value.
Flexibility	The most valuable employees understand the constancy of change and have developed the skills to adapt to its challenge.
Continual learning	The most valuable employees take personal responsibility to stay current in their fields.

have built throughout this book, are as much a part of your school success as they are of your work success. The more you develop them now, the more employable and promotable you will be.

Consider Learning Style

What you know about your learning style from chapter 3 will give you important clues in the search for the right career. The multiple intelligences assessment in that chapter points to information about your innate learning strengths and

TAKE ACTION

Match Curriculum to Career

Put your listening and note-taking skills to work as you investigate career options. Interview two people in an area that interests you—one from an academic setting (such as an instructor or an academic advisor) and one from the working world (such as a person working in that career or a career planning and placement office counselor). Choose a setting where you can listen well and take effective notes, then ask your interviewees questions in three categories:

- *Curriculum:* What courses are required for this area, and what courses are beneficial but not required?

- *Nontraditional ways to explore this career area:* Ask about extracurricular activities, internships, leadership roles, part-time work, and any other helpful pursuits.

- *Requirements for learning throughout the career:* Ask how the habit of mind of *continual learning* plays a role in success in this career area, such as through training, additional courses or degrees, or periodic testing.

When you have completed your interviews, create two lists—one of recommended courses, marking the required ones with a star, and one of activities, internships, and any other recommendations.

challenges, which, in turn, can lead you to careers that involve these strengths. Your Personality Spectrum assessment is equally significant, as it focuses on how you work best with others. Career success depends, in large part, on your ability to function in a team.

Key 11.8 focuses the eight multiple intelligences and the four dimensions of the Personality Spectrum on career ideas and strategies. Look for your strengths and decide what you may want to keep in mind as you search. Look also at areas of challenge because even the most ideal job involves some tasks that may not be in your area of comfort. Identifying ways to boost your abilities in those areas will help you succeed. And remember that these lists are by no means complete. Rather, they represent only a fraction of the available opportunities. Use what you see here to inspire thought and spur investigation.

Use Available Resources

Use your school's career planning and placement office, your networking skills, and online services to help you explore career opportunities.

Your school's career planning and placement office. Generally, the career planning and placement office deals with post-graduation job opportunities, whereas the student employment office and the financial aid office have information about working during school. At either location you might find general workplace information, listings of job opportunities, interview sign-up sheets, and company contact information. The career office may hold frequent informational

KEY 11.8   Multiple intelligences may open doors to majors, internships, and careers.

Multiple Intelligence	Think About Majoring In . . .	Consider an Internship At . . .	Look into a Career As . . .
Bodily-Kinesthetic	Kinesiology Construction engineering Chiropractics Sports medicine Dance or theater	Sports physician's office Physical therapy center Chiropractor's office Construction company Dance studio or theater	Carpenter or draftsman Physical therapist Mechanical engineer Dancer or actor Exercise physiologist
Intrapersonal	Psychology Finance Liberal arts Computer science Engineering	Accounting firm Computer company Publishing house Pharmaceutical company Engineering firm	Research scientist Computer engineer Psychologist Economist Author
Interpersonal	Sociology Education Nursing Business Rhetoric/communications	Social services agency Public relations firm Human resources Teaching assistant Marketing/sales	Social worker PR rep or HR employee Sociologist Teacher Nurse
Naturalistic	Forestry Biology Geology Agriculture Environmental law	Museum National park Environmental law firm Outward Bound Biological research firm	Forest ranger Geologist Ecologist Farm management Landscape architect
Musical	Music Musical theory Performing arts Composition Voice	Radio station Record label Recording studio Children's music camp Orchestra or opera company	Singer or voice coach Music teacher Record executive Musician or conductor Radio DJ or sound engineer
Logical-Mathematical	Math Accounting Economics Sciences Law	Law firm Accounting firm Science lab Pharmaceutical firm Bank	Doctor or dentist Accountant Attorney Chemist Investment banker
Verbal-Linguistic	Communications English/literature Journalism Foreign languages Political science	Newspaper/magazine Network TV affiliates Publishing house PR/marketing firm Ad agency	Author or journalist TV/radio producer Literature teacher Business executive Copywriter or editor
Visual-Spatial	Visual arts Architecture Multimedia design Photography Art history	Gallery or museum Photography or film studio Design firm Multimedia firm Architecture firm	Graphic artist or illustrator Photographer Architect Art museum curator Art teacher

Personality Spectrum dimensions indicate strengths and challenges.   **KEY   11.8**

Dimension	Strengths on the Job	Challenges on the Job	Look for Jobs/Careers That Feature . . .
Thinker	Problem solving Development of ideas Keen analysis of situations Fairness to others Efficiency in working through tasks Innovation of plans and systems Ability to look strategically at the future	A need for private time to think and work A need, at times, to move away from established rules A dislike of sameness—systems that don't change, repetitive tasks Not always being open to expressing thoughts and feelings to others	Some level of solo work/think time Problem solving Opportunity for innovation Freedom to think creatively and to bend the rules Technical work Big-picture strategic planning
Organizer	High level of responsibility Enthusiastic support of social structures Order and reliability Loyalty Ability to follow through on tasks according to requirements Detailed planning skills with competent follow-through Neatness and efficiency	A need for tasks to be clearly, concretely defined A need for structure and stability A preference for less rapid change A need for frequent feedback A need for tangible appreciation Low tolerance for people who don't conform to rules and regulations	Clear, well-laid-out tasks and plans Stable environment with consistent, repeated tasks Organized supervisors Clear structure of how employees interact and report to one another Value of, and reward for, loyalty
Giver	Honesty and integrity Commitment to putting energy toward close relationships with others Finding ways to bring out the best in self and others Peacemaker and mediator Ability to listen well, respect opinions, and prioritize the needs of coworkers	Difficulty in handling conflict, either personal or between others in the work environment Strong need for appreciation and praise Low tolerance for perceived dishonesty or deception Avoidance of people perceived as hostile, cold, or indifferent	Emphasis on teamwork and relationship building Indications of strong and open lines of communication among workers Encouragement of personal expression in the workplace (arrangement of personal space, tolerance of personal celebrations, and so on)
Adventurer	Skillfulness in many different areas Willingness to try new things Ability to take action Hands-on problem-solving skills Initiative and energy Ability to negotiate Spontaneity and creativity	Intolerance of being kept waiting Lack of detail focus Impulsiveness Dislike of sameness and authority Need for freedom, constant change, and constant action Tendency not to consider consequences of actions	A spontaneous atmosphere Less structure, more freedom Adventuresome tasks Situations involving change Encouragement of hands-on problem solving Travel and physical activity Support of creative ideas and endeavors

Angel Franco/*The New York Times*

Career centers offer opportunities to connect with potential employers. You may meet with company representatives at a career fair or even have a job interview arranged through your career center.

sessions on different topics. Your school may also sponsor job or career fairs that give you a chance to explore job opportunities. Start exploring your school's career office early in your college life.

Networking. *Networking*—talking to people about fields and jobs that interest you—is one of the most important job-hunting strategies. Networking *contacts* (people who serve as carriers or sources of information) can answer questions regarding job hunting, job responsibilities and challenges, and salary expectations. You can network with friends and family members, instructors, administrators, counselors, alumni, employers, coworkers, and others.

Online services. The Internet has exploded into one of the most fruitful sources of job listings. There are many different ways to hunt for a job on the Web, including these:

- Look up career-focused and job listing Web sites such as CareerBuilder.com, Monster.com, Yahoo! HotJobs, or Futurestep.com.
- Access job search databases such as the Career Placement Registry and U.S. Employment Opportunities.
- Check the Web pages of individual associations and companies, which may post job listings and descriptions.

If nothing happens right away, keep at it. New job postings appear; new people sign on to look at your résumé. Plus, sites change all the time. Do a general search using the keywords "hot job sites" or "job search sites" to stay current on what sites are up and running.

Remember Your Values and Your Passions

As you work through all of the other career exploration strategies, keep what is important to you in the forefront. Think about:

- *What you value.* Focus on the principles that guide your life—service to others, financial security, a broad-based education, time for family, and so on—and look carefully at what careers support these principles.
- *What you are passionate about.* Notice what you truly love to see, hear, feel, and do. Find something you love doing more than anything else in the world, and then find a way to make money doing it. If you are sure of what you love to do but cannot pinpoint a career niche, open yourself to your instructors' advice.

As you complete your work in this course, know that you are only beginning your career as a learner. You will continue to discover the best ways to harness the habits of mind you learned about in this book to solve problems and achieve goals.

How can the habits of mind help you aim for your personal best?

Now that you have mastered the basics of learning and studying, you are poised to be an invaluable asset to the companies that hire you once you graduate. If you put the habits of mind to work in all areas of your life and break out of the college gate strong, prepared to be disciplined and driven in your work, you can achieve your personal best in any challenge or situation you face.

Your *personal best* is simply the best that you can do. It may not be the best you have ever done. It may include mistakes, for nothing significant is ever accomplished without making mistakes and taking risks. It may shift from situation to situation. As long as you aim to do your best, though, you are inviting growth and success. The habits of mind that you have acquired as you worked through this book—see Key 11.9 for the list—will help you move toward success.

Habits of Mind Help You Solve Problems in School and Out

Remember that the habits of mind are, in essence, problem-solving tools, ready for you to apply to the problems that inevitably arise in school, work, and personal situations. Professor Art Costa reminds problem solvers of two steps in applying the habits of mind to any situation:

1. First, work to choose the habit or habits that will be most effective in the particular situation.
2. Then, ask questions that help you decide how specifically to apply the habit or habits you have chosen.

With these two steps, you will be able to put the habits to continual use as you strive for your personal best in your ability to solve problems.

Your work has earned you these 11 habits of mind.	KEY 11.9

Persisting (chapter 1)

Managing impulsivity (chapter 2)

Gathering data through all senses (chapter 3)

Questioning and posing problems (chapter 4)

Applying past knowledge to new situations (chapter 5)

Listening with understanding and empathy (chapter 6)

Thinking flexibly (chapter 7)

Taking responsible risks (chapter 8)

Striving for accuracy and precision (chapter 9)

Communicating with clarity and precision (chapter 10)

Staying open to continuous learning (chapter 11)

Habits of Mind Build Characteristics That Promote Success

The habits of mind encourage you to perform at your best by acting intelligently and appropriately in any situation. "As Aristotle said, 'We are what we repeatedly do. Excellence, then, is not an act but a habit,'" says Professor Costa. "Only by routinely practicing these habits of mind can we assure ourselves that we are thinking clearly, confronting problems intelligently, and making wise decisions."[14]

Through his research, Costa has found that people who have made habits of the habits of mind tend to demonstrate five particular characteristics:

1. *Inclination:* They tend to use behavior patterns that work.
2. *Value:* They value the behaviors that work rather than other, less useful ones.
3. *Sensitivity:* They notice when it is possible, and appropriate, to use certain behaviors.
4. *Capability:* They have the basic skills and ability to carry out the behaviors.
5. *Commitment:* They make a continual effort to evaluate how they did and to improve upon their performance.[15]

These characteristics all have *action* in common. People who use the habits of mind take action when they confront problems. They look for opportunities to use a behavior, choose and employ the most effective one, and strive to improve upon their performance. They use the habits to stay in continual motion toward improvement and solutions.

Make these characteristics your personal motivational tools. Return to them when you need reactivation. Use them to make sure that you move ahead toward your personal best, and toward achievement of the goals that mean the most to you.

Habits of Mind Help You Live with Integrity

Having integrity puts your sense of what is right into day-to-day action. When you act with integrity, both in academic settings and elsewhere, you earn trust and respect. If people can trust you to be honest, to be sincere in what you say and do, and to consider the needs of others, they will be more likely to encourage you, support your goals, and reward your work.

When you leave college, there are thousands of people out there with the same degree you have; when you get a job, there will be thousands of people doing what you want to do for a living. But you are the only person alive who has sole custody of your life.

ANNA QUINDLEN, AUTHOR AND COLUMNIST

As you use habits of mind in your day-to-day life, you build qualities characteristic of a person of integrity. Persisting develops your focus and commitment, for example; listening with empathy develops your respect for others; managing impulsivity develops your ability to follow through on promises; striving for accuracy and precision develops your responsibility as a student. The more you make the habits your own, the more capable you will be of living according to your values and principles, continually striving to learn from mistakes and to improve.

Aim for your personal best in everything you do. As you continue to learn, take classes, and do your highest quality work, you will strengthen your skills and set yourself up for success with people from all backgrounds, cultures, ages, and stages. As you use your habits of mind to find intelligent approaches to problems, you will join people everywhere who aspire to be their best, do their best, and create the best for the world in which they live.

The opportunity to make a difference for yourself and those around you has never been greater. As you achieve your most valued goals, you will have a positive effect on the future of the world and its people.

REFLECT

Look at the list of habits of mind in Key 11.9. Write down the five that you feel most closely support your values and goals. Now envision your retirement dinner: A close friend steps up to the podium to talk about how your values and hard work brought you success. Freewrite what you would want to hear this friend say about how you put your five most important habits to work. Finally, discuss how the habit of mind of *continuous learning* will enable you to use those habits to reach that retirement dinner someday.

RESPOND

I stay open to continuous learning.

Think for a moment: Do you feel more secure when you know something solidly, or when you are learning it for the first time? Most people feel more comfortable when they already know something. New learning experiences often provoke fear and avoidance in people, resulting in a retreat from the new and a settling back inside the fortress of what is known and seemingly certain. As comfortable as it seems, the spot inside the fortress can shut you off from growth and knowledge.

Staying open to continuous learning means letting yourself out of the fortress and embracing the unsure, the unanswered, and the new. Even beyond seeking new knowledge, continuous learners welcome problems and situations of conflict because they see the underlying opportunity to learn and grow. Such people are comfortable with *not* knowing—because they realize that the path of resolving what they do not know will lead them to ever-increasing knowledge. Be a continuous learner and you will spend your life improving, growing, learning, and moving ever closer to the person you know you can be.

REMEMBER
THE IMPORTANT POINTS

1 **How can you maintain a healthy body and mind?**

- Eat right, exercise, and get enough sleep.
- Recognize and manage mental health problems.

2 **How can you make intelligent decisions about substances and sex?**

- Understand effects of alcohol consumption, especially binge drinking.
- Know the risks of tobacco use.
- Explore the negative consequences of using illegal drugs.
- Be responsible for analyzing the potential consequences of anything you introduce into your body, and understand how to face and overcome addiction.
- Make sexual decisions that are right for you.
- Take steps to avoid sexual abuse.

3 **How can you manage your finances in school and beyond?**

- Use an effective budgeting strategy.
- Manage credit card use.
- Solicit financial aid (grants, loans, and scholarships).

4 **How can you prepare for workplace success?**

- Investigate career paths through discussions, internships, courses, and volunteering.
- Know what skills and qualities employers seek.
- Consider what careers suit your learning style.
- Use your school's career offices, networking, and online services.
- Keep your values and passions in mind as you look for the right career.

5 **How can the habits of mind help you aim for your personal best?**

- Habits of mind are tools for problem solving that you can apply to any situation. First, choose the most effective habits. Then, ask questions that help you decide how to apply the habits you have chosen.
- Using the habits builds five active characteristics that promote success.
- Habits of mind encourage you to act with integrity and responsibility.

CRITICAL THINKING

APPLYING LEARNING TO LIFE

Map Out Your Budget

Step 1: Estimate your current expenses in dollars per month, using the following table. This may require tracking expenses for a month, if you don't already keep a record of your spending. The grand total is your total monthly expenses.

EXPENSE	AMOUNT SPENT
Rent/mortgage or room and board payment	$
Utilities (electric, heat, gas, water)	$
Food (shopping, eating out, meal plan)	$
Telephone (land line and mobile phone)	$
Books, lab fees, other educational expenses	$
Loan payments (educational or bank loans)	$
Car (repairs, insurance, payments, gas)	$
Public transportation	$
Clothing/personal items	$
Entertainment	$
Child care (caregivers, clothing/supplies, etc.)	$
Medical care/insurance	$
Other	$
TOTAL	$

Step 2: Calculate your average monthly income. If it's easiest to come up with a yearly figure, divide by 12 to derive the monthly figure. For example, if you have a $6,000 scholarship for the year, your monthly income would be $500 ($6,000 divided by 12).

INCOME SOURCE	AMOUNT RECEIVED
Regular work salary/wages (full-time or part-time)	$
Grants or work-study programs	$
Scholarships	$
Assistance from family members	$
Other	$
TOTAL	**$**

Step 3: Subtract the grand total of your monthly expenses from the grand total of your monthly income.

Income per month	$
Expenses per month	−$
CASH FLOW	**$**

Step 4: If you have a negative cash flow, you can increase your income, decrease your spending, or both. Think about what's possible for you to accomplish. List here four workable ideas about how you can get your cash flow back in the black—two that increase income, and two that decrease spending.

To increase income, I can:

1. _____

2. _____

To decrease spending, I can:

1. _____

2. _____

TEAM BUILDING

COLLABORATIVE SOLUTIONS

Building Interview Skills

Divide into pairs—students will take turns interviewing each other about themselves and their career aspirations. Follow these steps:

1. Independently, take three minutes to brainstorm questions you'll ask the other person. Focus on learning style, interests, and initial career ideas. You might ask questions like these:

   ■ If you could have any job in the world, what would it be?
   ■ What do you think would be the toughest part of achieving success in that profession?
   ■ Who are you as a learner and worker—what is your learning style?
   ■ What sacrifices are you willing to make to realize your dreams?
   ■ What is your greatest failure, and what have you learned from it?
   ■ Who is a role model to you in terms of career success?

2. Person A interviews Person B for 5 to 10 minutes and takes notes.

3. Switch roles: Person B interviews Person A and takes notes. Remember that each person uses his or her own questions, developed in step 1.

4. Share with each other what interesting ideas stand out to you from the interviews. If you have any, offer constructive criticism to your interviewee about his or her interview skills.

5. Finally, submit your notes to your instructor for feedback.

This exercise will build your ability to glean information from others and to answer questions during an interview. You will use this skill throughout your professional life. Probe deeply when interviewing others so that you develop the ability to draw out the best in someone. Be as interested—and interesting—as you can.

*I recognize that my ability to **learn continuously** is essential for problem solving. With this in mind, I will explore two problems (academic, personal, or work-related) that I faced during the term and identify how I handled them and what I learned.*

Problem #1 description:

How did I handle it?

What did I learn as a result?

Problem #2 description:

How did I handle it?

What did I learn as a result?

How am I doing? **Later in the term, be accountable for your progress on page 377.**

SUGGESTED READINGS

Adams, Robert Lang, and Laura Morin. *The Complete Résumé and Job Search Book for College Students.* Holbrook, MA: Adams, 1999.

Beatty, Richard H. *The Resume Kit,* 5th ed. New York: Wiley, 2003.

Bolles, Richard Nelson. *What Color Is Your Parachute? 2006: A Practical Manual for Job Hunters and Career Changers.* Berkeley, CA: Ten Speed Press, 2005.

Detweiler, Gerri. *The Ultimate Credit Handbook,* 3rd ed. New York: Plume, 2003.

Duyff, Roberta Larson. *The American Dietetic Association's Complete Food and Nutrition Guide.* Hoboken, NJ: Wiley, 2003.

Kadison, Richard D., and Theresa Foy DiGeronimo. *College of the Overwhelmed: The Campus Mental Health Crisis and What to Do About It.* San Francisco: Jossey-Bass, 2004.

Kuhn, Cynthia, Scott Swartzwelder, and Wilkie Wilson. *Buzzed: The Straight Facts About the Most Used and Abused Drugs from Alcohol to Ecstasy,* 2nd ed. New York: Norton, 2003.

Selkowitz, Ann. *The College Student's Guide to Eating Well on Campus.* Bethesda, MD: Tulip Hill Press, 2000.

Tyson, Eric. *Personal Finance for Dummies.* Foster City, CA: IDG Books Worldwide, 2000.

Ward, Darrell. *The AmFAR AIDS Handbook: The Complete Guide to Understanding HIV and AIDS.* New York: Norton, 1998.

INTERNET RESOURCES

Prentice Hall's Student Success Supersite: Fitness & Well-Being (**www.prenhall.com/success/Fitness/index.html**)

Federal Centers for Disease Control and Prevention, Department of Health and Human Services (**www.cdc.gov**)

The Sexual Health Network (**www.sexualhealth.com/**)

MayoClinic.com—Medical information from this world-renowned medical center (**www.mayohealth.org**)

The Body: The Complete HIV/AIDS Resource (**www.thebody.com/safesex.html**)

U.S. Department of Labor, Bureau of Labor Statistics: *Occupational Outlook Handbook* (**www.bls.gov/oco/**)

The Motley Fool—Money and investment advice (**www.fool.com/**)

1st Steps in the Hunt—Daily news for online job hunters (**www.interbiznet.com/hunt/**)

College Grad Job Hunter—Advice on résumés, interviews, and a database of entry-level jobs (**www.collegegrad.com**)

JobWeb—Career development and job-search advice for new college graduates (**www.jobweb.com/**)

Prentice Hall's Student Success Supersite: Money Matters (**www.prenhall.com/success/MoneyMat/index.html**)

Prentice Hall's Student Success Supersite: Career Path (**www.prenhall.com/success/CareerPath/index.html**)

ENDNOTES

1. CBS News/Associated Press, "Help for Sleep-Deprived Students," April 19, 2004, accessed May 2004 (**www.cbsnews. com/stories/2004/04/19/health/ main612476.shtml**).

2. Herbert Benson, Eileen M. Stuart, et al., *The Wellness Book*, New York: Simon & Schuster, 1992, p. 292; and Gregg Jacobs, "Insomnia Corner," Talk About Sleep, accessed May 2004 (**www.talkaboutsleep.com/sleepdisorders/ insomnia_corner.htm**).

3. Kim Hubbard, Anne-Marie O'Neill, and Christina Cheakalos, "Out of Control," *People,* April 12, 1999, p. 54.

4. J. McGinnis and W. Foege, "Actual Causes of Death in the United States," *Journal of the American Medical Association (JAMA), 270* (18), November 10, 1993, p. 2208.

5. H. Wechsler, G. W. Dowdall, G. Maenner, J. Gledhill-Hoyt, and H. Lee, "Changes in Binge Drinking and Related Problems Among American College Students Between 1993 and 1997," *Journal of American College Health, 47* (September 1998), p. 57.

6. Ibid., pp. 63–64.

7. National Institute on Alcohol Abuse and Alcoholism, "Alcohol Alert," No. 29 PH 357, July 1995.

8. National Institute on Drug Abuse, Capsule Series C-83-08, "Cigarette Smoking," Bethesda, MD: National Institutes of Health, 1994.

9. David Stout, "Direct Link Found Between Smoking and Lung Cancer," *New York Times,* October 18, 1996, pp. A1, A19.

10. National Institute on Drug Abuse, "National Survey Results on Drug Abuse from Monitoring the Future Study," Bethesda, MD: National Institutes of Health, 1994.

11. Drug Enforcement Administration, U.S. Department of Justice, "MDMA: Ecstasy," accessed August 2006, (**www.usdoj.gov/dea/ concern/mdma/mdma_factsheet.html**).

12. Tina Kelley, "On Campuses, Warnings About Violence in Relationships," *New York Times,* February 13, 2000, p. 40.

13. Laura A. Bruce, "College Student Credit Card Use Can Leave Them Drowning in Debt," March 6, 2001, accessed March 2001 from Bankrate.com (**www.bankrate.com/brm/news/cc/ 20000815.asp**).

14. Arthur L. Costa, "Habits of Mind," in *Developing Minds: A Resource Book for Teaching Thinking,* Arthur L. Costa, ed., Alexandria, VA: Association for Supervision and Curriculum Development, 2001, p. 85.

15. Costa, "Habits of Mind," p. 80.

■ **MULTIPLE CHOICE**

Circle or highlight the answer that seems to fit best.

1. Being able to recognize the meaning of prefixes, roots, and suffixes will help you
   A. do well when you study a foreign language.
   B. figure out the meaning of many new vocabulary words and remember information.
   C. create visual aids.
   D. identify your purpose for reading.

2. Skills employed by effective note takers include all of the following *except*:
   A. arriving on time and with the necessary supplies ready.
   B. using the same note-taking system in every situation.
   C. reviewing notes as soon as possible after a lecture.
   D. taking notes on relevant comments made during discussions.

3. Careful reading is essential to solving word problems because
   A. word problems make up over half of the math problems you will encounter.
   B. you must understand exactly what the question is asking in order to translate it into an equation.
   C. word problems are written out and therefore depend more on reading skills than on math skills.
   D. you must translate numbers back into words when you answer the question.

4. Stress reduction prior to a test is important for all of the following reasons *except*:
   A. It reduces memory interference when you study.
   B. It enables you to effectively organize your study time.
   C. It gives you time to go to a movie or see friends.
   D. It clears your mind so you are receptive to the input from study group members.

5. Actively reviewing your combined class and text notes helps you prepare for exams for *all but one* of the following reasons:
   A. The critical thinking you do during your review encourages active involvement with the material.
   B. Because your key term combined outline is short, you will have time to study other topics.
   C. You maximize your study time because you have all your notes in one place.
   D. Your key term summary will give you cues to recite what you know about the material.

6. Of these aspects of the planning process for writing, which involves the least amount of critical thinking?

A. researching

B. asking journalists' questions

C. proofreading

D. writing a thesis statement

▥ TRUE/FALSE

Place a T or an F beside each statement to indicate whether you think it is true or false.

1. _____ When you highlight your text, it is important to start marking the first time you read the page.

2. _____ The main advantage of receiving guided notes from your instructor is that you do not have to take your own class notes.

3. _____ Students who binge-drink are more likely to do poorly in school, to have emotional problems, and to engage in risky behaviors than students who do not binge-drink.

4. _____ Students should devote as much time studying for a quiz as they do a final exam.

5. _____ Marking up test questions will help you focus on directions and key terms.

6. _____ How you present your ideas in writing may have a major influence on your ability to win and keep a job.

▥ FILL-IN-THE-BLANK

Complete the following sentences with the appropriate word(s) or phrase(s) that best reflect what you learned in part II. Choose from the items that follow each sentence or blank.

1. The Q stage of SQ3R is a two-step process in which you _____ and _____. (write questions as they occur to you/question your instructor about what the material means, ask yourself what you know about a topic/write questions linked to chapter headings, write questions linked to underlined words and bolded type in the text/write questions linked to chapter headings)

2. The most important way to prepare for taking notes successfully during a class period is to _____ that day's assigned course materials. (check out, read, gather)

3. Investigate different careers while you are in college by working with your school's _____ (career planning and placement, admissions, financial aid) office, developing _____ (business, friendly, networking) contacts, and exploring _____ (dating, cleaning, online) services.

4. When dealing with matching questions, working from the column with the _____ entries will save _____. (shortest/time, longest/time, shortest/mistakes)

5. It is important to be sensitive to _____ verbs on essay tests. (action, passive, static)

6. Writing without an understanding of your _____ will almost always lead to _____. (topic/writing success, audience/poor communication, research/a disorganized presentation)

■ ESSAY QUESTION

The following essay question will help you learn to organize and communicate your ideas in writing, just as you must do on an essay test. Before you begin answering a question, spend a few minutes planning (brainstorm possible approaches, write a thesis statement, jot down main thoughts in outline or think link form). To prepare yourself for actual test conditions, limit your writing time to no more than 20 minutes.

> Write an essay that supports or rejects all or part of the following statement: *"The tests you take in college not only help ensure that you acquire important skills and knowledge, but also help prepare you for the day-to-day learning demands that are associated with 21st century careers."* If possible, support your position with references to career areas that interest you.

BE ACCOUNTABLE FOR YOUR HABITS OF MIND FROM PART II

Look back at the "Activate the Habit of Mind" exercises in chapters 5 through 11 (pages 175–176, 208, 239–240, 274, 306, 336, and 372), and specifically at your plans for incorporating each habit into your study routine. On a separate sheet of paper, write a short journal entry that assesses the progress you've made on each habit. Consider questions such as the following:

- ■ Have I put into action the strategies I planned to use?
- ■ How have the strategies helped or changed how I work?
- ■ Do I feel that I now "own" each habit of mind? In what way?
- ■ What is my plan going forward to further develop and use these habits of mind?

Appendix

A Guide to Library and Internet Research

The following material will help you improve your skill in finding information at your college library and on the Internet. In school and in your career, researching is essential to success.

How Can You Make the Most of Your College Library?

Consider the library to be the "brain" of your college. The library is and will continue to be your most reliable information source—so much so that instructors expect to see library research citations in your work.

Start with a Road Map. The better you know the "road map" of your library, the less time you'll spend searching for elusive resources. Here are some key resources:

- *Circulation desk.* All publications are checked out at the circulation desk, which is usually near the library entrance.
- *Reference area.* Here you'll find reference books, including encyclopedias, directories, dictionaries, almanacs, and atlases. You'll also find library employees who can direct you to information. Computer terminals, containing the library's catalog of holdings, as well as online bibliographic and full-text databases, are usually part of the reference area.
- *Book area.* Books—and in many libraries, magazines and journals in bound or boxed volumes—are stored in the *stacks*. A library with *open stacks* allows you to search for materials. In a *closed-stack* system, a staff member retrieves materials for you.
- *Periodicals area.* Here you'll find recent issues of popular and scholarly magazines, journals, and newspapers.
- *Audiovisual materials areas.* Many libraries have special locations where you can study nonprint materials including video, art and photography, and recorded music collections.
- *Electronic library resources.* Computer terminals, linked to college databases and the Internet, may be scattered throughout the library or clustered in specific areas. Most schools have network systems or library Web sites that allow access to online library materials via personal computer.

Almost all college libraries offer orientation sessions on how to find what you need. To learn what your library offers, take a real or virtual tour and sign up for training.

Learn How to Conduct an Information Search. The most successful and time-saving search for information involves a practical, step-by-step method that takes you from general to specific sources. At any point in your search, you can conduct a *keyword search*—a method for locating sources through the use of topic-related words and phrases. A keyword is any natural-language word or phrase that is used as a point of reference to locate other information. To narrow your topic and reduce the number of "hits" (resources pulled up by your search), add more keywords. For example, instead of searching through the broad category *art*, focus on *French art* or, more specifically, *19th century French art*.

Key A.1 provides tips for using the keyword system. The last three entries describe how to use "OR," "AND," and "NOT" to narrow searches with what is called *Boolean logic*.

Perform an effective keyword search.		KEY A.1
If you are searching for . . .	**Do this**	**Example**
A word	Type the word normally.	aid
A phrase	Type the phrase in its normal word order (use regular word spacing) or surround the phrase with quotation marks.	financial aid, or "financial aid"
Two or more keywords without regard to word order	Type the words in any order, surrounding the words with quotation marks. Use *AND* to separate the words.	"financial aid" AND "scholarships"
Topic A or topic B	Type the words in any order, surrounding the words with quotation marks. Use *OR* to separate the words.	"financial aid" OR "scholarships"
Topic A but not topic B	Type topic A first within quotation marks, and then topic B within quotation marks. Use *NOT* to separate the words.	"financial aid" NOT "scholarships"

Start with General Reference Works. These works cover topics in a broad, nondetailed way and are often available in print, online, or on CD-ROM. Examples of general reference works include encyclopedias, almanacs, dictionaries, biographical references (such as *Webster's Biographical Dictionary*), and bibliographies (such as *Books in Print*). Scan these sources for a topic overview and more specialized sources.

Search Specialized Reference Works. Turn next to *specialized reference works* for more specific facts. Specialized reference works include encyclopedias and dictionaries that focus on a narrow field (such as the *Encyclopedia of American History*). Although the entries in these volumes are short summaries, they focus on critical ideas and introduce keywords you can use to conduct additional research. Bibliographies that accompany the articles point to the works of recognized experts.

Browse Through Books and Articles on Your Subject. Use the computerized library catalog to find books and other materials on your topic. The catalog, searchable by author, title, and subject, tells you which publications the library owns. Each catalog listing refers to the library's classification system, which in turn tells you exactly where to find the publication.

Periodicals include journals, magazines, and newspapers. *Journals* are written for readers with specialized knowledge (while *Newsweek* magazine may run a general-interest article on AIDS research, for example, the *Journal of the American Medical Association* may print the original scientific study for a medical audience). Many libraries display recent periodicals and convert older copies to microfilm or microfiche. Many full-text articles are also available online.

Periodical indexes such as *The Reader's Guide to Periodical Literature* lead you to specific articles and are generally available in print and on CD-ROM. Because there is no all-inclusive index for technical, medical, and scholarly journal articles, you'll have to search indexes that specialize in narrow subject areas.

Ask the Librarian. Librarians can assist you in solving research problems, usually more quickly than you can on your own. They can help you locate unfamiliar or hard-to-find sources, navigate catalogs and databases, and uncover research shortcuts. To obtain the best guidance, focus on your specific topic. For instance, if you are researching how President

Franklin D. Roosevelt's physical disability may have affected his leadership during World War II, let the librarian know instead of simply asking for information about Roosevelt. Librarians can give you guidelines about the most useful sources for specific disciplines. They can also lead you to a variety of online reference sources, such as those listed in Key A.2.

KEY A.2 Become familiar with online reference sources to improve your research efficiency.

If you want to search . . .	Visit this Internet address
Copyrighted books in print	Amazon.com: **www.amazon.com** Barnes and Noble: **www.barnesandnoble.com** Google Book Search: **http://books.google.com** (access to thousands of scanned books)
Encyclopedia entries	Wikipedia: **www.wikipedia.org/** Encarta: **http://encarta.msn.com**
Magazine and newspaper articles	AJR Newslink: **http://newslink.org**
Academic publications	Google Scholar: **http://scholar.google.com** (search engine with access to academic journals and other sources)
Library of Congress	**www.loc.gov** (primary sources in U.S. history, culture, politics, including scanned maps, photos and recordings) Library of Congress American Memory: **http://memory.loc.gov/ammem/**
Federal legislation	Thomas: **http://thomas.loc.gov** (in the spirit of Thomas Jefferson, legislative information from the Library of Congress)
Biographies	Biographical Dictionary: **www.s9.com/biography** Biography.com, Search Bios: **www.biography.com/search** Biography-Center: **www.biography-center.com**
Maps	Google Earth: **http://earth.google.com/** Perry-Castañeda Library Map Collection, University of Texas Libraries: **www.lib.utexas.edu/maps/** Maptech MapServer: **http://mapserver.maptech.com**
Country profiles	Atlapedia Online: **www.atlapedia.com/online/country_index.htm**
U.S. population and economic data	U.S. Census Bureau, U.S. Department of Commerce: **www.census.gov/**
U.S. historical documents	The Avalon Project at Yale Law School: **http://yale.edu/lawweb/avalon/avalon.htm** (documents from colonial period to today)
Company information	ThomasNet, powered by Thomas Register: **www.thomasnet.com**
European primary sources	EuroDocs: **http://eudocs.lib.byu.edu/index.php/Main_Page** (historical sources from two dozen European countries)

How Can You Conduct Internet Research?

The *Internet,* a computer network that links organizations and people around the world, can connect you to billions of information sources. Because of its widespread reach, the Internet is an essential research tool—if used wisely. Unlike your college library collection, which is evaluated and selected for usefulness and reliability by educated librarians, Web sites and Internet resources are not necessarily evaluated or overseen by anyone. As a result, Internet research depends on your critical judgment.

Most Internet information is displayed on *Web sites,* cyberspace locations developed by companies, government agencies, organizations, and individuals. Together, these sites make up the World Wide Web. Information can also be found on other types of sites including *blogs.* Also known as *weblogs,* these increasingly popular and influential Web sites focus on particular topics and may combine text, images, and links to other Web sites and blogs.

Start with Search Engines. *Search engines* are tools for finding information on the Internet. Using a keyword search, you gain access to Web sites, blogs, and other resources. With the power of the search engine to access the Internet comes the potential for an enormous list of "hits" unless you carefully limit your keyword search. Among the most popular and effective search engines are these:

- Google (www.google.com)
- Yahoo! (www.yahoo.com)
- AltaVista (http://www.altavista.com/)
- HotBot (www.hotbot.com)
- Ask (www.ask.com)
- Excite (www.excite.com)
- Go (www.go.com)
- Lycos (www.lycos.com/)

Search engines aimed at academic audiences are the Librarian's Internet Index (www.lii.org), InfoMine Mining Intelligence and Technology (www.infomine.com), and Academic Info (www.academicinfo.net). The advantage of using academic directories is that you know someone has screened the sites and listed only those that have been determined to be reliable, regularly updated and reputable.

Meta-search engines, which compare results across different search engines, include Dogpile.com, Search.com, Mamma.com, Webmetasearch.com, and Kartoo.com.

Use a Search Strategy. The World Wide Web has been called "the world's greatest library, with all its books on the floor." With no librarian in sight, you need to master a basic search strategy that will help you avoid becoming overwhelmed while researching online.

1. *Think carefully about what you want to locate.* University of Michigan professor Eliot Soloway recommends phrasing your search in the form of a question—for example, "What vaccines are given to children before age 5?" Then he advises identifying the important words in the question (vaccines, children, before age 5) as well as other related words (polio, shot, pediatrics, and so on). This will give you a collection of terms to use in different combinations as you search.[1]

2. *Use a search engine to isolate sites under your desired topic or category.* Save the sites that look useful. Most Internet software programs have a "bookmark" or "favorites" feature for recording sites you want to visit again.

3. *Explore these sites to get a general idea of what's out there.* Usually, in academic research, you will need to go beyond the search engine's listings. Use what you find there to notice useful keywords and information locations.

4. *Use your keywords in a variety of ways to uncover more possibilities:*
- Vary word order if you are using more than one keyword (for example, search under *education, college, statistics* and *statistics, education, college*).
- Limit your search through Boolean operators, such as "AND," "NOT," and "OR."

5. *Evaluate the number of links that appear.* If there are too many, narrow your search by using more, or more specific, keywords (*Broadway* could become *Broadway* AND "*fall season*" AND *2004*). If there are too few, broaden your search by using fewer or different keywords.

6. *When you think you are done, start over.* Choose another search engine and search again. Different systems access different sites.

Use Critical Thinking to Evaluate Every Source. Getting the most value from your time on the Internet requires you to carefully evaluate every source. Your research will only be as strong as your critical thinking.

Robert Harris, professor and author of *WebQuester: A Guidebook to the Web*, has developed an easy-to-remember system for evaluating Internet information, called the CARS test for information quality (Credibility, Accuracy, Reasonableness, Support).[2] Use the information in Key A.3 to question any source you find as you conduct research.

Educational and government sites are generally more likely to have been screened and selected by educated professionals than other sites. You can identify these sites by looking at the *URL* (uniform resouce locator)—the string of text and numbers that identifies an

KEY A.3   Use the CARS test to determine information quality on the Internet.

Credibility	Accuracy	Reasonableness	Support
Examine whether a source is believable and trustworthy.	Examine whether information is correct—factual, comprehensive, detailed, and up-to-date (if necessary).	Examine whether material is fair, objective, moderate, and consistent.	Examine whether a source is adequately supported with citations.
What are the author's credentials?	*Is it up-to-date, and is that important?*	*Does the source seem fair?*	*Where does the information come from?*
Look for education and experience; title or position of employment; membership in any known and respected organization; reliable contact information; biographical information; and reputation.	If you are searching for a work of literature, such as Shakespeare's play *Macbeth*, there is no "updated" version. However, if you want reviews of its latest productions in major theaters, you will need to note when material was created. For most scientific research, you will need to rely on the most updated information you can find.	Look for a balanced argument, accurate claims, and a reasoned tone that does not appeal primarily to your emotions.	Look at the site, the sources used by the person or group who complied the information, and the contact information. Make sure that the cited sources seem reliable and that statistics are documented.

Credibility	Accuracy	Reasonableness	Support
Is there quality control? Look for ways in which the source may have been screened. For example, materials on an organization's Web site have most likely been reviewed and approved by several members; information coming from an academic journal has to be screened by several people before it is published.	*Is it comprehensive?* Does the material leave out any important facts or information? Does it neglect to consider alternative views or crucial consequences? Although no one source can contain all of the available information on a topic, it should still be as comprehensive as is possible within its scope.	*Does the source seem objective?* While there is a range of objectivity in writing, you want to favor authors and organizations who can control their bias. An author with a strong political or religious agenda or an intent to sell a product may not be a source of the most truthful material.	*Is the information corroborated?* Test information by looking for other sources that confirm the facts in this information—or, if the information is opinion, that share that opinion and back it up with their own citations. One good strategy is to find at least three sources that corroborate each other.
Is there any posted summary or evaluation of the source? You may find abstracts of sources (summary), or a recommendation, rating, or review from a person or organization (evaluation). Either of these—or ideally, both—an give you an idea of credibility before you decide to examine a source in depth.	*For whom is the source written, and for what purpose?* Looking at what the author wants to accomplish will help you assess whether it has a bias. Sometimes biased information will not be useful for your purpose; sometimes your research will require that you note and evaluate bias (such as if you were to compare Civil War diaries from Union soldiers with these from Conferterate soldiers).	*Does the source seem moderate?* Do claims seem possible, or does the information seem hard to believe? Does what you read make sense when compared to what you already know? While wild claims may turn out to be truthful, you are safest to check everything out.	*Is the source externally consistent?* Most material is a mix of both current and old information. External consistency refers to whether the old information agrees with what you already know. If a source contradicts something you know to be true, chances are higher that the information new to you may be inconsistent as well.
Signals of a potential lack of credibility: Anonymous materials, negative evaluations, little or no evidence of quality control, bad grammar or misspelled words	*Signals of a potential lack of accuracy:* Lack of date or old date, generalizations, one-sided views that do not acknowledge opposing arguments	*Signals of a potential lack of reasonableness:* Extreme or emotional language, sweeping statements, conflict of interest, inconsistencies or contradictions	*Signals of a potential lack of support:* Statistics without sources, lack of documentation, lack of corroboration using other reliable sources

Source: Robert Harris, "Evaluating internet Research Sources," November 17, 1997, accessed April 8, 2005, from VirtualSalt (www.virtualsalt.com/evalu8it.htm).

Internet site. Look for URLs ending in *.edu* (these sites originate at educational institutions) and *.gov* (these sites originate at government agencies). If you are unsure of the credibility of a source, ask your instructor about it.

Be Prepared for Internet-Specific Problems. The nature of the Internet causes particular problems for researchers. Stay aware of the possibility of the following:

■ *Information that may or may not be current.* If your particular research depends on having the most updated information available, pay attention to how (or whether) material is dated and use the latest material you can find.

■ *Technology problems.* Web sites may move, be deleted, or have technical problems that deny access, so it's smart to budget extra time for unforeseen problems. Write out full citations for Web sites while they're on your screen, and consider printing a hard copy of each site for reference.

How Do You Know When to Use the Library and When to Use the Internet?

The ease of Internet searches has led many students to shift their focus from the library stacks to the computer terminal. This may create research problems, however, because of the limitations of the Internet. As a result, an increasing number of savvy researchers are combining Internet research with more reliable library research.

Some Limitations of the Internet. Focusing on Internet searches at the exclusion of traditional library searches may affect the quality of your research, because of several factors, including the following:

■ *Search engines can't find everything.* As wide-reaching as they are in scanning the Internet, Google and other search engines do not index numerous academic publications cataloged in some library Web databases.

■ *The Internet prioritizes current information.* Because the vast majority of Web pages have been created during the last decade and because many focus on current information, researchers looking for historical information are at a disadvantage.

■ *Not all sources are in digital format.* There is always the chance that something you are looking for will be available only to researchers willing to comb through library stacks.

■ *Some digital sources cost money.* As a student, you have free access to all of the valuable materials collected for your library. However, as an independent Internet researcher, you may have to be a paid subscriber to read any number of publications, including many respected academic journals, online.

When to Prioritize the Library. For certain situations the library is a better, or first, choice. Head to the library when:

■ You are conducting in-depth research, requiring an historical perspective. Older information is more likely to available at the library than on the Web.

■ You want to verify the authenticity of what you discover on the Internet.

■ You need personal, face-to-face help from a librarian.

■ You feel more comfortable navigating the established library system than the tangle of Internet sites.

One of the clear advantages of using a library is access to librarians. Researchers work in tandem with librarians and others who know where and how to find valuable resources. The Internet has no comparable component.

Combining Library and Internet Searches—The Best Research Strategy. The Internet is a modern reality—but it has not, as some predicted, replaced the printed word. Both sides are slowly learning to work together, ultimately to the benefit of researchers using materials from both sources.

Libraries are responding to the Internet boom in two ways: (1) They are working to make scholarly material more available online, and (2) they are overhauling physical layouts to combine electronic search stations with traditional print holdings. Companies that run search engines are responding as well. For example, Google plans to digitize, through scanning, some of the holdings at a few of the world's major libraries—Stanford, Oxford, the University of Michigan, and the New York Public Library.

Your research and critical-thinking skills give you the ability to collect information, weigh alternatives, and make decisions. Your need to use these skills doesn't stop at graduation—especially in a workplace dominated by information and media. Says Victor Yipp of Commonwealth Edison:

> Work projects may involve interviewing people, researching on the Web, library research, taking a look at costs, providing input on support levels, and more. . . . These basic skills—being inquisitive and using the library, the Internet, and other people to uncover information—will do well for you in school and later on in life.[3]

ENDNOTES

1. In Lori Leibovich, "Choosing Quick Hits over the Card Catalog," *New York Times,* August 10, 2001, p. 1.

2. Robert Harris, "Evaluating Internet Research Sources," November 17, 1997, accessed April 8, 2005, from VirtualSalt (**www.virtualsalt.com/evalu8it.htm**).

3. Quoted in *Keys to Lifelong Learning Telecourse* (videocassette), directed by Mary Jane Bradbury, Intrepid Films, 2000.

Part I: Getting Ready to Learn

Multiple Choice

1. C
2. A
3. A
4. D
5. D
6. B

True/False

1. F
2. T
3. T
4. F
5. F
6. T

Fill-in-the-Blank

1. academic integrity/respect/responsibility
2. priorities
3. learning preferences/personality traits
4. cultural competence
5. creativity
6. brainstorm

Part II: Targeting Success in School and Life

Multiple Choice

1. B
2. B
3. B
4. C
5. B
6. C

True/False

1. F
2. F
3. T
4. F
5. T
6. T

Fill-in-the-Blank

1. ask yourself what you know about a topic/write questions linked to chapter headings
2. read
3. career planning and placement/networking/online
4. longest/time
5. action
6. audience/poor communication

Index